1985

Public speaking as a liberal art

Public speaking as a liberal art

FIFTH EDITION

John F. Wilson
HERBERT H. LEHMAN COLLEGE
OF THE CITY UNIVERSITY
OF NEW YORK

Carroll C. Arnold
THE PENNSYLVANIA
STATE UNIVERSITY

ALLYN AND BACON, INC.
Boston London Sydney Toronto

Chapter opening photographic credits: p. 2, U.P.I.; p. 20, Frank Siteman/Stock Boston; p. 42, Helen D. Kerrick/St. Mark's School; p. 72, Elliott J. Echelman; p. 106, Ellis Herwig/Stock Boston; p. 150, Camerique/E.P. Jones; p. 174, © Ken Robert Buck/THE PICTURE CUBE; p. 202, © Eric Roth/THE PICTURE CUBE; p. 224, Peter Southwick/Stock Boston; p. 254, Owen Franken/Stock Boston; p. 284, Jerry Berndt/Stock Boston.

Library of Congress Cataloging in Publication Data

Wilson, John Fletcher, 1923–
   Public speaking as a liberal art.

   Bibliography: p.
   Includes indexes.
   1. Public speaking. I. Arnold, Carroll C. II. Title.
PN4121.W46 1983   808.5′1   82–22685
ISBN 0–205–07971–7

Printed in the United States of America

10 9 8 7 6 5 4 3 2 1   88 87 86 85 84 83

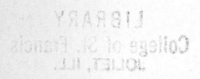

Contents

Preface

It has been twenty years since the first words of the first edition of *Public Speaking as a Liberal Art* were written. The book was first published in 1964 and subsequently revised in 1968, 1974, and 1978. These and the present edition have reflected the shifts in ideas about public communication brought about by fresh thinking and research in public and interpersonal communication. Nonverbal communication was scarcely a topic of discussion and scholarship in 1961; Jurgen Ruesch and Weldon Kees had broached the subject formally only in 1956. Chaim Perelman and L. Olbrecht-Tyteca's *New Rhetoric,* with its fresh conceptions of argumentation, existed in French but appeared in English only in 1969. Lloyd Bitzer's distinguished essay on rhetorical situations appeared in 1968 and was expanded in 1980. Vigorous experimentation on such subjects as *ethos, dispositio,* topical *invention,* and intensity in language has enhanced our understanding across two decades. And from the late 1960s to the present, the study of rhetorical communication has been especially enriched by attention given it by a growing number of philosophers and literary critics around the world. We have been constantly influenced by all of these changes and more.

Our focus on "public speech," present since our third edition, reflects conceptual shifts that have occurred in social and philosophical thinking. The notion that "a speech" is necessarily a predictable verbal form has disappeared, except as a concept of tradition, from our two most recent editions. With that change has come our growing conviction that public speech is best and most liberally taught in conjunction with problem solving and speech criticism. In matters of detail we believe we have again drawn abreast of the firmest and most pragmatically useful conclusions from recent speculative and experimental research. And the general applicability of principles of public speaking we have sought to highlight with special objectives at the opening of each chapter.

On the other hand, we continue to affirm that public speaking *is* an *art,* not an amalgam of techniques, or a science, or an illegitimate offshoot from dialectic or other analytic discourse. We continue to hold that the kinds of reflection and understanding that must precede informed practice of public speech are the kinds of reflection and understanding that undergird all liberal education. Inculcating intelligent behavioral, social, and verbal choices in the exercise of personal freedom is, we think, among the noblest ends of a liberal education. We hope to have provided a program of inquiry and practice that contributes directly to that end.

Our book proposes that a spirit of inquiry ought to prevail in the study of speech and that prescriptions should be minimally used in considering the general problems of rhetorical invention, disposition, style, delivery, and *memoria.* These are problems confronted in creating and maintaining human relations behaviorally, socially, and verbally everywhere. Inquiringly directed, study of public speech becomes laboratory study of social relations.

Suggestions from users of our fourth edition have prompted us to revise our treatments of standard topics extensively. Chapters 3, 5, 9, 10, and 11 have undergone greatest change, substantively, organizationally, or both. All chapters have been reworked, but the appendices are as they appeared in the fourth edition. Throughout we have sought to make learning and teaching easier wherever possible.

In preparing this edition we have incurred special debts to the numerous students who have allowed us to use their classroom work, and to Bie Arnold, Marjorie Griffiths, and Winifred Hodges of Bywater Production Services.

J.F.W.
C.C.A.

Public speaking
as a liberal art

CHAPTER 1

We ought, therefore, to think of the art of discourse just as we think of the other arts, and not to form opposite judgments about similar things, nor show ourselves intolerant toward that power, which, of all the faculties which belong to the nature of man, is the source of most of our blessings. For in the other powers which we possess . . . we are in no respect superior to other living creatures; nay, we are inferior to many in swiftness and in strength and in other resources; but, because there has been implanted in us the power to persuade each other and to make clear to each other whatever we desire, not only have we escaped the life of the wild beasts, but we have come together and founded cities and made laws and invented arts; and generally speaking, there is no institution devised by man which the power of speech has not helped us to establish.
—Isocrates, "Antidosis" [1]

The art of public speaking

Where can you apply the principles of this chapter in everyday life?

1. Wherever it is necessary to decide whether you dare just express yourself or whether you must *adjust* yourself and your ideas to other people's expectations and needs.
2. Wherever it is necessary to decide whether talk can accomplish anything in a situation.
3. When you need to estimate what *your* possibilities for influence are in:
   - classrooms
   - employment or other business interviews
   - making proposals or reports to colleagues, superiors, committees, or larger audiences
   - composing instructions, editorials, advertisements
   - formal speeches to specific, face-to-face audiences
4. Where you must decide whether to memorize, read, or speak extemporaneously in presenting oral messages to someone else.

This is a textbook intended to help you become more effective when you speak in public. Most of you who have opened the book have done so because you are required to take a course in speaking or because you have elected such a course. Whatever your reason for reading this page, we want to be clear about what we are and are not going to try to help you accomplish.

We are going to focus on a kind of speaking that is commonplace for educated, professional people. They speak *in public* when they report, give instructions, talk to committees, support ideas in small or large groups, or talk to entertain others. This is all "public speaking," as we will be using that phrase. We are not going to focus on "oratory," or public address to massive audiences. Neither are we going to focus on "manners" in pronunciation and general delivery, though how to think about and manage yourself when speaking in different circumstances will come up in our study. Our concern in this book is with how you or anyone else can build up an effective, influential talking relationship with other people when the responsibility for exercising influence falls on you. We call this book *Public Speaking as a Liberal Art* because we think (1) building sound talking relationships "liberates" or "frees" a person from social inadequacy and (2) that building productive talking relationships is an art rather than something that can be accomplished "by the numbers" or by following recipes.

We mean nothing obscure or remote by saying that speaking effectively is an *art*. We mean what a stock market analyst meant when he called stock market analysis an art. He said:

> If calling the market merely consisted of programming history into a computer, we would all be rich, but art is involved here. The artist doesn't just accumulate all of the evidence and weight it, he determines which rule is applicable at a given time.[2]

Mr. Gintel's art is the art of choosing and interrelating economic and psychological rules to fit a particular business situation. Artistic speaking depends on determining which logical, linguistic, psychological, and physical rules you should apply in a given communicative situation. A famous French writer said, "By 'art' I mean . . . the expression of *significant* relations between human beings, or between minds and things."[3] And a British author wrote that the art of speaking is "a development of the relation between [a speaker] . . . and his hearers."[4] We are saying that effectively using speech as a means of developing relations between yourself and others is a matter of knowing how to *choose* which rules or guidelines need to be applied in a given situation if significant, purposeful relations are to be created between your own mind and the minds of others. For this choosing you have to get beyond sheer technique or skill. You have to be able to *think out* how meanings, surroundings, and human relationships can be combined for an immediate purpose in a particular setting.

Public speaking is also an art in the sense that there is a great difference between "getting by" in talking relationships and understanding how to make the most of them. We make the same distinction about the capacities of writers, basketball players, chefs, engineers, journalists, parents, and virtually every other kind of skilled person. Some people are workerlike: they have learned some techniques or have a "knack." But others—the ones who are first-rate—*know the possibilities* and apply skills and rules *thinkingly*. They think out how to make the most of the circumstances in which they play, cook, design, write, or relate to their children. To achieve this kind of command of speaking in public, you will have to learn sophisticated ways of thinking about yourself, about the kinds of communicative situations you are likely to enter, and about the possibilities of language, speech, action, and people who will become your audiences. Acquiring that kind of thinking and speaking is a *liberal study*.

SPEECH AS A LIBERAL STUDY

When a subject has uses that reach well beyond the subject itself, it is common to call that subject liberal or general. The study is useful in more vocations than one. To command a liberal study helps a person to get more out of other studies while providing useful skills of its own. The special value of a liberal study is that it introduces you to additional ways you can think about and understand general facts of life. A study deserving to be called liberal gives you background into which to fit your specialized concerns. Consider a simple case.

You want to plan a house. If you know house planning as, say, a carpenter might know it, you could plan a solid, roomy house, and that would be all. But with broader knowledge of people and society you could plan a solid, roomy house that would suit the real estate market (economics), would conform to the ordinances of the community in which the house is to be built (politics and sociology), would be attractive on the lot on which it is to stand (aesthetics), and would have features that are readily and attractively described so as to make the house salable (communication).

There are many ways in which a knowledge of speaking in public is applicable beyond itself, but we draw your attention to two that are especially important to students and professionals. Because public speaking is an art in the sense of demanding that methods be thought out for each special application, study and practice of public speaking is study and practice of general decision making. Secondly, because you will be developing your command of informative and persuasive skills as you develop as a speaker, you will find that what you learn here has application wherever you need to explain and defend decisions.

Speaking as decision making

In all decision making, no matter what the subject, we need to assemble the knowledge that is pertinent, sort out the more important from the less important, identify what options the sorting leaves us, calculate the consequences of each of our choices, and finally choose the course of action or belief to which we are willing to commit ourselves. Skill and discipline in carrying out these steps are expected of all professionals such as physicists and engineers, administrators, social workers, psychiatrists, and wildlife managers. So it is no small benefit of the study of public speaking that every time you prepare a public communication you practice the general art of decision making. You will collect and sort socially pertinent information, identify what you *could* do with the information in a social situation, make your decisions, and, most importantly perhaps, *test* the wisdom of your decision making in an actual speaking situation. This is one respect in which the study you are now beginning has applications and uses beyond itself.

Promoting and defending ideas

Your study of speaking in public is direct exercise in promoting and defending ideas—whether to yourself, informally to someone else, or publicly. If you can explain and argue efficiently and attractively in public, you will have resources and methods that work in the home, in research, in general social life, as well as when talking to an audience of a few or of many people. Once more, it is a matter of being able to choose what will work in a particular situation. Dean Everett Lee Hunt of Swarthmore College said in this connection:

> An enlightened choice is a choice based upon a wide knowledge of all the alternatives, but knowledge about the alternatives is not enough. There must be imagination to envisage all the possibilities, and sympathy to make some of the options appeal to the emotions and powers of the will. Such dignity as man may have is achieved by the exercise of free choice through the qualities of learning, imagination, and sympathy; and we should add to these qualities as a fitting accompaniment, what may be called civility.[5]

Hunt's phrases "imagination to envisage all the possibilities," "sympathy to make some of the options appeal," and "exercise of free choice through the qualities of learning" tell why artistic communicating is not the product of routine learning. To speak well requires that you consider the *possibilities* of a situation and of your resources in order to "develop creative, never-before-tried methods of dealing with others" as a "human-in-control-of-self." [6] When you can make an argument or an explanation that precisely fits a situation, you will have joined your thoughts and feelings to someone else's thoughts and feelings in a new, never-before-tried way. You will not only have created a unique human relationship by means of *your* thought and design; you will have disciplined and tested your general ability to make knowledge interesting and appealing. The values of this kind of learning most certainly do not cease when you have completed your course in public speaking.

If you study and practice public speaking in the ways we suggest, you will also learn some specific principles of oral communication, many of which have proved effective across more than two thousand years. You will choose subjects to talk about. To talk about them influentially you will need additional ideas and evidence with which to develop them. The methods of discovery and selection that must guide you here are those we shall treat under the traditional heading of *invention*. We shall also show you various ways of organizing ideas and how to choose among them. These principles and methods we shall treat as considerations of *disposition*. If you are to talk about ideas, there arise problems of what language to use. These we shall deal with under the heading of *style,* suggesting guidelines for finding the most useful grammatical forms and the best images. Since you must make decisions about what bodily actions and vocal patterns are appropriate in various situations, we shall offer you some principles of *delivery*. Finally, because we focus on communication that is oral, there will be special problems of managing yourself and your plans during talk, and we shall discuss those problems as problems of *memoria,* a Latin term having the special sense of "command of the total speech." As we shall show, commanding a total speech depends to a large extent on observing sound principles of disposition and delivery.

    The study to which we invite you, then, is a sophisticated exploration of how you and your ideas can be related to the lives of other people in influential ways. The exploration is significant beyond concerns of "making a speech." You will free yourself from private isolation by learning to transform private feelings and ideas into public feelings and ideas. You will discover how to liberate yourself socially through decision making and imaginative expository, argumentative, and entertaining talk.

WHEN SPEECH IS PUBLIC

We have repeatedly used such terms as *speaking in public* and *public speaking*. What do we mean by *public?* We mean any speech where someone is given responsibility for maintaining communication over a certain period, while someone else or some group assumes the role of a relatively quiet listener. That is a loose definition, and it may at first seem strange to you. But what is it that the term *public* really means? It means "open to the view of all." We talk of public business and private business, of the public papers of a president and his or her private correspondence, of public showings and private showings. Using *public* in that sense, we want in this book to discuss all speech that is open to and addressed to those present, whether one or many. "Open to all" implies that as speech occurs someone has assumed a responsibility to others. Someone is in charge of maintaining communicative relationships with those present. There is a speaker, and there is a public to whom the speaker's behavior is open and to whom the speaker ought to direct attention. What would *private speech* be by contrast? It would be talk to and for one's self or talk with others in circumstances where there is no particular public and where responsibility for maintaining communicative relations has not become fixed on anyone in particular. This seems to us to be the only reasonable way to distinguish public speech from speech that is not public.

    No one would say, "Speech is public if seven people hear it but private when six or fewer hear." So, it is not the *numbers* of people involved that make us all feel some of our speaking is public and some is not. Yet no one would deny that he or she believes that conversation is different from public speaking. Then, where is the difference, if not in numbers? We think it is in the key fact that in conversational settings *no one in particular bears responsibility* for creating and maintaining interpersonal relations through speech. In conversation, in private speech, the location of responsibility is unpredictable, and assumption of it is, on the whole, voluntary. Also, the questions of who shall be talked with and whether there shall be any talk at all are unpredictable in some settings. In other settings a tacit understanding has somehow evolved that Mr. X or Ms. Y *will* talk. Such a situation could even occur during an interview. It is in that moment of obligation that Mr. X or Ms. Y feels differently. He or she is "on" now. The situation has become public. It is on speaking in all such moments of responsibility or obligation that we choose to focus as we treat public speaking. The audience may be one or many persons. The public is simply those people who are in a position to listen. The public speaker is the person who is assigned or who assumes responsibility for addressing them.

Is there much of this kind of public speaking? It goes on all about us. We all participate in it, sometimes well and sometimes not so well. One study of clerks, secretaries, technicians, and engineers in a large research and development laboratory found the staff spending 35 percent of all working time in face-to-face talk. The observers did not examine whether the face-to-face talk was public or private in the senses we are using these terms, but in a working place much of it must have been reporting or otherwise functioning in a public way.[7] A secretary tells a supervisor what supplies are in the office inventory and what must be bought. A lab assistant reports data to the supervising chemist, or the chemist gives directions to his assistants. Thousands of small public speeches take place in every business organization—and not only there. An athletic scout returns from scouting a future opponent and tells its game strategies to the head coach, or to two or three coaches, or to the coaches and the entire team. A committee member tells the committee the facts he was asked to collect. You summarize a research report for your professor or for your classmates. A teacher talks briefly or at length to a class. It is all public speaking, for someone has responsibility for maintaining mutually rewarding communication.

To do its work well, all of this speaking needs rightly chosen information, cogent organization, clear and evocative language, and direct, expressive delivery. Therefore, this book is about minispeeches as well as about extended speaking.

MISCONCEPTIONS ABOUT SPEAKING

Just as there are misconceptions about how speech becomes public, there are misconceptions of what speaking and developing skill in speaking involve. Some of the misconceptions are understandable because the very ways we learn speech discourage us from thinking systematically about it. This unique ability, which only human beings seem to have, is learned from those around us: parents, friends, teachers, social and religious leaders, and movie and television personalities. The learning is largely unself-conscious. So naturally enough, we take our speech habits for granted. This is the source of the first serious misconception about speaking: that effectiveness isn't learned, that it is inherited or just rubs off on you, or fails to. Unquestionably, a good environment and good models encourage good speech. But it is equally true that few people who study and practice speech as an art fail to improve the skills and understanding they begin with. Educators and corporation managers have tested for the effects of speech training as rigorously as they know how and have concluded that able people become abler communicators after studying speaking in systematic ways.[8] The testimony of those who have studied speech seriously and the improvement students show in speech classes also confirm that whatever may have been inherited or have rubbed off can be refined by thoughtful study and practice.

A second and long-held misconception is that if you have something to say, you need not worry about how to say it. Good content assures its effective presentation. This idea dies hard, yet everyone knows from experience that good subject matter does not guarantee interesting communication. You have probably had a teacher or friend who knew his or her stuff, yet was constantly unclear or boring. You have heard and watched well-qualified speakers talk to their shoes rather than their listeners. Such experiences amply refute the content-is-enough notion. Being fully informed about, say, the public welfare system in your state does not at all guarantee you will explain the system clearly and effectively to a welfare client or an audience of your classmates. You must also know how to adapt ideas to different kinds of people.

Equally unfounded is a third misconception that content is *not important*. The folk saying, "It's not what you say, it's how you say it," contains a grain of truth in a bushel of falsehood. Experiments have shown clearly that so-called dynamic speakers are greeted with suspicion rather than conviction. You probably know someone you have considered a windbag or too smooth because he or she talked glibly but did not know very much. You can sense the difference between performers and real teachers. The playwright Arthur Miller wrote *Death of a Salesman,* often called an American tragedy, in part to dramatize the sad insufficiency of the doctrine that a good shoe shine and a smile can sustain either a reputation or a life. "How you say it" is important, but manner alone does not protect the absence of matter in talk.

Closely related to this third misconception is a fourth. Some hold that instruction in public speaking is instruction in sophistry, in dishonesty. They find it distasteful or dishonest to tamper with what comes naturally in talk; they view the adaptation of thoughts for different situations as somehow hypocritical. They say, in effect, "Let my speech alone. Let me be me. I won't be myself if I change my spontaneous impulses, even though I might be a better speaker in other people's eyes." But there is nothing dishonest about improving the likelihood that other people will understand you as you wish to be understood. That is what working to improve your public speech is, as we mean to teach it. Listeners have rights as well as speakers. Listeners have the right not to be bored unnecessarily. They have the right to learn from you as easily and interestingly as possible. They have the right to have their feelings and knowledge taken into account whenever you occupy their time and attention. Principles of fitting your best thoughts to listeners' best understanding are not principles of trickery or self-sacrifice; they are principles of respectful, decent, human relationship. They are principles that allow you to reveal your best, humanly sympathetic self. This book is about ways to become a fuller, more regardful human being in public situations. It is about how you can be *you* more fully.

A fifth misconception has to do with what courses in public speaking ought to be like. Many students who register for a speech course suppose it will be primarily concerned with management of body and voice, and with how to move about a lectern and speak compellingly. Others think it will be, or ought to be, a practice-only course—that ideas *about* speaking are not important. Both views are necessarily mistaken. Vocal and physical behaviors are significant aspects of speaking effectively, but they are by no means the *whole* of what is involved in personal communication. Think of any talker you consider too glib, and you will see that smooth utterance and action are not the whole story. You call that speaker too glib because you sense that he or she does not think about you, does not relate to you in a thoughtful, caring way. You sense that that speaker has thought about his or her own ideas and feelings in ways that leave you and your interests out or in ways that treat you slightingly. The very fact that we have phrases like "too smooth" and "off the wall," and say of some speakers that they are "too wrapped up in themselves" shows that how speakers *think about* their ideas and the people they talk to makes a great difference in their effectiveness. By these phrases we acknowledge that before there can be appropriate physical action in communication there must be appropriate mental preparation of ideas in order to adjust them and the manner of their expression to us as listeners. To be fully helpful a course in public speaking must help you understand how speaking and listening work, so that you will have facts with which to *think* more wisely and informedly about adjusting ideas and feelings to particular listeners. That is why you will find us emphasizing how communicable ideas are discovered, how they can be adjusted to varying public situations, and, only then, how practice and delivery can strengthen those ideas.

A sixth misconception is that speaking to an audience is something like acting. A number of students enter public speaking courses thinking that public speakers learn to play roles, learn how to become someone other than themselves. Actually speakers rarely dare project personalities other than their own. Why? Because listeners in our culture expect their speakers to talk as themselves and for themselves. Tomorrow an audience will hold a speaker responsible for what he or she said yesterday. That speaker had better be himself or herself on both days. Just how we are attracted or repelled by one another still perplexes social psychologists, but that sincerity is a positive quality is not disputed, and the speaker perceived as acting has just lost that positive value in the eye of the perceiver. We shall develop this topic more fully in Chapter 5 when we consider how speakers make themselves proofs of what they say.

Seventh, there is a widespread notion that reading aloud and speaking extemporaneously require and communicate substantially the same kind of attitude toward what one is doing. *By extemporaneous speaking we mean speaking with preparation but without memorizing or using a text.* In fact, extemporaneous speaking and reading aloud (1) each put *you* into different relationships with what you say and (2) each put your *listeners* into different relationships with you. When you read, you are always in some degree a transmitter of ideas formed at an earlier time. When you speak extemporaneously, you are creating anew and *for this moment* ideas you worked over in planning. If you read, you are committed to preexisting ideas and forms; if you speak extemporaneously, you are prepared to adjust and readjust ideas and forms to fit the moment of communication. Your listener's relationship to you differs also.

If your listener sees that you are reading, he or she knows that however well and directly you communicate the material, you are *bound* to that material in the form it was given at some other time. You cannot, then, be wholly concerned with the listener's immediate needs and interests. You can't have a completely communicative tie with that listener, however hard you try. Your listener knows that something—the preexisting document—stands between you as person and the listener as person. You are now deliverer of a message, and the listener feels himself or herself to be a receiver or a spectator.

The great advantage of extemporaneous speaking over reading speeches is that if you are extemporaneous you can participate directly with your listener in thinking and feeling about freshly created notions; and your listener can participate actively, feelingly in their adaptation to *now*. The nub of it is that reading your speeches is usually a second-best choice. If you read, you cannot quite be your total, believable self. You can get closest to an audience by speaking extemporaneously. Whenever you read, you draw away from the audience in some degree.

The final misconception we want to deal with is the idea that a classroom is such an artificial place that meaningful public communication can't take place there. Those who hold this view say such things as, "An instructor is always there. The audience is a captive one. Time limits are arbitrary. The audience can't *do* anything anyway. Purposes and sometimes subjects are assigned. So the atmosphere is unreal!" We have two answers.

First, all these things are true, at least to a degree. But despite this, any speech classroom can be and ought to be a communication laboratory where experiments are made under conditions that *represent* the real world. A football team scrimmaging on its practice field works and learns in a comparable laboratory. But nobody would say that all that goes on on the practice field is unreal. *Real* plays are developed. Part of the squad *really* represents Saturday's opponent. The blocking and tackling and passing assignments practiced are the same ones that will be used on Saturday. True, the *real* game will not take place until Saturday, but practice is *realistic* because everyone's eye is focused on how things work "in reality." A speech classroom can be turned into just this kind of realistic *representation* of the world of human communication.

Second, despite its constraints and sometimes because of them, *real* communication occurs in classrooms. In our own classrooms we constantly hear real speeches that are made because other real things have happened. We have heard other speeches that produce real results: a petition signed and sent, a canister passed for contributions to research on leukemia, pledge cards signed promising donations of blood and of organs after death. In some instances there have been conversations that showed real learning had taken place or that some real decisions had been made on the basis of what had been said by classroom speakers.

In one of our classes a group of students invited a university administrator to visit the class to hear and respond to their carefully worked-out critique of a speech he had given. He came, listened to the series of speeches about his speech, and responded—happily confessing that the students had rightly divined his original purposes. Here was reality, and *in a classroom!* (See Appendix B. Since we will refer to Dr. Upcraft's speech often in the pages that follow, we suggest you take a few minutes to read it now.)

Only students and teachers can drive reality from classrooms!

RHETORICAL SITUATIONS

Whenever we talk seriously to one another, we have to make adjustments. We have to build a new and special relationship, not quite like any other, between ourselves and whoever is listening. This is the most important fact about speaking as a way of communicating. *To speak effectively is to present particular ideas to particular people in a particular place at a particular time.* Speaking is special in this respect. Not all communication is of this sort. If someone writes a bit of music, a poem, or makes some class notes in a notebook, there is no need to worry about who is listening, in what way, and under what circumstances. But talk is different. Even if you talk to yourself, you do it for the sake of helping yourself, or pleasing yourself, or interesting yourself *now,* in the moments of talk.

In especially important ways the success of any public speech depends on how closely it fits the wide-ranging requirements of the "rhetorical situation" into which it is introduced. The phrase "rhetorical situation" refers to any set of circumstances in which people can be influenced or changed by communication. The peculiarity of speaking is that you always *bring* your message *to* an audience in a specific kind of situation, and you invite them to attend to the message *now,* in that place and time. Speaking is never even remotely like attaching a message to a helium-filled balloon and sending it aloft to come down in some place you can't predict or describe. To speak is to direct a message to particular listeners in specific, intelligible circumstances. A contemporary thinker who has helpfully clarified this fact is Lloyd F. Bitzer.[9]

Bitzer depicts events in which speakers face audiences. But, he points out, not all situations with a speaker and an audience are rhetorical. For a situation to be *rhetorical* there must be a potential, a possibility, for change as a result of the speaker's communication. The event must be ripe for action, at least of mind, and perhaps of body. Some set of forces in the setting and in the relationship of speaker to listeners must have created a possibility of change. If there is no possibility of change, of action within the situation, you have a situation that is *nonrhetorical.* Consider a pair of examples.

Imagine yourself having something of some importance to say to a friend or several friends. The question that ought to come before everything else is: will they listen to you seriously enough to act at least to the extent of taking your idea as something worth considering? If your friend or friends are engrossed in watching a favorite television program, the situation may be nonrhetorical. This may *not* be a time or place in which you can reasonably hope to influence your friends through speaking of the idea you have in mind. But it is also possible that you could change this situation into a rhetorical one by urging your friends to attend to you, right now, rather than to the television program. If you succeed, the situation becomes rhetorical. Or you might choose to wait until the program is finished and the situation becomes a rhetorical one for you in a natural way.

Professor Bitzer says that a *rhetorical situation* is "a complex of persons, events, objects, and relations presenting an actual or potential exigence" that can be modified by "creation of discourse which changes reality through the mediation of thought and action." [10] As synonyms for *exigence* you could use *need* or *readiness*. For *mediation of thought and action* you could substitute *creating social change* or *change in perceptions*. Another way of putting this might be: a rhetorical situation is made up of people, conditions, physical features, and human relations within which there exists some need that practical communication can change in some degree. In any situation, then, anyone who wants to make practical talk needs, first, to ask what possibilities there *are* for change, given the people (audience), the conditions and physical features (the occasion), the speaker, and his or her subject matter.

Consider another example: your speech class. Is it a rhetorical situation? Yes. The people, the fact that it is a class, and the meeting place with all of its physical features make it so. In addition, previous relations with your classmates and theirs with you and each other create a situation in which changes are possible. Talk can make those changes. Things said during a class period, speeches made there, can generate new ideas and actions or modify existing ideas or ways of acting. But, of course, there will be times when the content of what is said, its organization, its style, or the way it is said (delivered) will turn off the audience because in one way or another the speaking is not what Bitzer calls a "fitting response" to the exigences or readinesses the classroom provided. If this happens, it does not prove that the class was not a rhetorical situation; most speech classes are rhetorical situations all of the time. The turn-off probably means simply that even though possibilities for change existed, the communication failed in some way to touch those possibilities.

The notion that there are rhetorical situations that invite influential talk implies that in order to make a difference in a situation we need to analyze it to find out whether there really are possibilities for change, where they lie, and why they are there. We must identify the exigences or readinesses in each situation we expect to enter and aim our ideas toward *real* possibilities instead of attempting changes that simply aren't possible. And there is a fairly uncomplicated way of taking this kind of "sighting" on a situation.

Figure 1–1 is a diagram that suggests the kinds of questions we ought to ask about any situation in which we expect to speak. The *audience* side of the square represents everyone who will be a part of the public you intend to address. The *occasion* side stands for the psychological and physical facts about the setting within which you and the audience will meet. *Material* is whatever you know about your subject, yourself, and ways of communicating. And the *speaker* is, of course, yourself as a person appearing in this situation. When you enter a situation as a speaker, all of the relationships suggested by the double-headed arrows in the diagram have at least possible influences on what can transpire between you and your listeners. Here are the kinds of questions you ought to review in your mind as a preliminary to

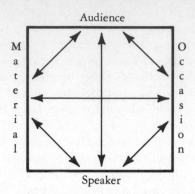

FIGURE 1-1   *A model of public speaking*

shaping a message for the situation. In each case the first question is the general one to be asked; the examples that follow illustrate special versions of the question that a particular speaker might want to raise.

1. Does my relationship to the audience make any particular kind of talk especially appropriate or inappropriate for me? (For example, will I come in as a specially qualified person or just as an equal among equals?)
2. Will the audience see itself as having any significantly special kind of relationship with me? (For example, will they feel they are supposed to gain something special from me, or will they leave it to me to make what I choose out of our relationship?)
3. Is there anything significant in the audience's relation to the psychological and/or physical features of the occasion? (For example, did the audience create this occasion for special reasons that deserve recognition, or is the occasion equally impersonal for them and me?)
4. What significant effects do the circumstances of the occasion have on the audience? (For example, will seating, fixtures, and decorations encourage light-heartedness, learning, getting business done, or something else?)
5. What relationships already exist or could be created between the audience and the material I have or will have? (For example, do they already want my material, or will they have to be interested in it to start with?)
6. What immediate or possible relationships are there between my material and the audience? (For example, are there special aspects of what I know that will be interesting and other aspects that will be too technical or seem irrelevant to their interests?)
7. Is there anything specially significant about my relationship to my material? (For example, are there parts of the material about which I can and ought to claim

special knowledge or experience, or will the listeners and I be equals with respect to what I'll have to say?)

8. Do my materials have special effects on me as a speaker? (For example, does having the material specially qualify me to speak? Are there parts of it that excite me so I can communicate that excitement?)

9. Do I have any significant relation to the occasion? (For example, am I a natural sharer of the occasion, or will I need to earn my right to appear at this time?)

10. What is the effect of the occasion on me as a speaker? (For example, does the occasion require me to qualify myself in any particular way or to pay special attention to any features of the setting?)

11. Does the occasion have any significant relationship to what I have to say? (For example, does the occasion suggest that I should emphasize some of my available material and minimize other parts? Does the occasion make certain materials my natural starting points?)

12. Can the material I have modify this occasion? (For example, can material such as mine be developed so as to shift a convivial occasion to a serious, business-like one? Do I have material that could introduce curiosity into an occasion that encourages apathy?)

Depending on your circumstances, some answers to questions like these will prove more informative than others, and on many matters you will be able to give only educated guesses, as our example below indicates. We hope, too, that our example will illustrate that the questions we have suggested are not a checklist that *mechanically* produces an analysis of a potentially rhetorical situation. What the questions allow is a canvass, a "boxing of the compass," that will somewhere reveal the exigences or readinesses that are practical to address if the situation is a rhetorical one.

Here is a summary of the thoughts of a student who wanted to make a talk praising B. F. Skinner and George Orwell for the fact that each had illustrated the nature of a controlled society.[11] The talk would be the student's first in a speech class. She supplied her instructor with an analysis of the situation she would confront.

Considering her relationship with the audience and its relationship with her, this student concluded that nothing special needed to be taken into account. These were first speeches in the class. She had so far said little. She had no basis for special claims on the audience nor they on her. She and they would meet as relative strangers, sharing only the fact that all had to speak publicly to all others. What was required of her was only what is required of any relatively unknown speaker: that she make her ideas seem significant and interesting.

The only possible influence of the occasion that this student could perceive was that she would be one of the later speakers in the series. Would the audience be tired of hearing speeches? She thought not, since two days of speaking had already gone by and there were no signs of restlessness. She decided the occasion would demand no special adaptations.

It was when this speaker began to consider the significance of her intended material that she discovered there was, indeed, a special rhetorical exigence or readiness that she could address and thereby turn the classroom into a rhetorical situation for *her* intended speech. The exigence lay in the fact that though her listeners might not have read Skinner or Orwell, they would still feel somewhat fearful of controlled societies. She could awaken this unease and thereby gain interest in Skinner's and Orwell's pictures of social control. This attention would allow her to stress the value of such clear images of the possible future. "They already have a certain relationship to my material," she wrote. "I hope to broaden it." Thinking about question 7 led her to write: "I am concerned about . . . a controlled society and the significance of humans as individuals. . . . If I am able to communicate effectively, I can at least bring [about] a sense of concern [in the audience]." At this point the student knew a true rhetorical situation would exist for her on the day she would speak to her classmates. The possibility—and her task—was to intensify listeners' latent concerns about social controls. There lay the available exigence or readiness.

When she reflected on her own relationship to her intended material, she concluded that, having read the authors she would discuss and having thought about them until she had formed a clear attitude toward them, she was in sufficient command of the raw material for a speech. Looking at questions 7 and 8 led her to summarize her position: this reading "makes me realize how extensive a control over others people could gain." Here was her motivation for speaking on the subject she had chosen.

We should notice that in surveying the various possibilities of the rhetorical situation, this preparing speaker was able to sort out the important from the unimportant features that would influence her communication. Her analysis turned up the facts that the role of the occasion would be routine—neither very helpful nor unhelpful—but her own knowledge and feelings about her materials and the audience's general attitudes toward social controls were the factors that would make the classroom a rhetorical situation which *she* could hope to alter somewhat *if* she remembered to work from the listeners' distaste for imposed social controls. Using this readiness as a starting point, she would be able to carry the listeners to an appreciation of Skinner's and Orwell's skills in picturing a world of such controls, which was the ultimate goal she had set for herself. Thus, in a true case a speaker was able to conceptualize what Bitzer calls "a *fitting* response" to a particular speaking situation. Hers is the kind of reflective analysis of possibilities that each of us needs to carry out before speaking to any public.

This, then, is a book about *public speech* which encompasses all speaking that is relatively uninterrupted and in which a speaker recreates his or her own ideas with the aim of drawing out practical responses from listeners who have general but perhaps changeable attitudes toward the world, the specific situation, and the speaker who talks to them. Devising appropriate messages in such circumstances is a task that calls for more than isolated techniques. It requires reflective analysis of all of the resources and relationships that play a part in shaping the possibilities of a given moment; it demands knowledge of the principles according to which *fitting* rather than random responses can be constructed for such situations. Because its successful execution entails reflective analysis and creation of messages according to principles, public speaking needs to be looked on as an art rather than as routine application of a set of skills. And pursuing this art is practice in the general human tasks of making decisions, choosing among alternatives, and defending one's choices.

Speaking to publics effectively is not a product of thoughtlessly doing what comes naturally, or of being glib, or of pretending to be what you are not, or of concentrating on delivery to the neglect of fitting ideas to situations. Speaking effectively is first and foremost the fruit of thoughtful study and understanding—of human situations, of rhetorical possibilities and impossibilities, and of principles according to which communication can be *adapted* to circumstances in which we find ourselves.

We have repeatedly used the term *principles* in what we have said. A principle is a general rule on which the appropriateness of specific procedures and actions depends. A principle of American government is that people are created equal, as the Declaration of Independence asserts. An application of this principle is the legal decision that all citizens of a certain age must have the same right to vote. A principle of economics is that if other things are equal, scarcity of a commodity will be accompanied by an increase in its economic value, its price. An application of that principle occurs when government pays farmers to leave some of their lands unplanted in order to maintain a "fair" price for the products that are planted and grown. There are principles of public speech too. We have been discussing a major one: to bring about change, speech must give promise of fulfilling some need or readiness that exists within the situation in which the speech occurs. There are a good many other such principles of public speech, and this book is chiefly about them. They are principles that people have learned over generations; a good many have been confirmed by scientific research. We offer a history of those principles in Appendix A. We shall pause now to present some first considerations that will help you to begin the performance aspects of your course; then we shall continue to explain and to show how to apply the basic principles of speaking effectively in public.

EXERCISES

Written

1. Keep a diary on two or three hours of your normal activities, noting occasions on which you found people, including yourself, speaking to others in relatively uninterrupted fashion and with the aim of altering listeners' perceptions of their relationships with other people, toward ideas, or toward things.
2. Write a criticism of the definition of public speech given in this chapter on page 7. Support, expand, refute, or alter the definition but give reasons for each change you make.
3. After viewing a movie, television, or live theatre performance, list the major things you observed the actors doing that were (a) similar to and (b) different from the things you have observed in the practices of public speakers you consider superior.

4. In anticipation of your first speech in your class, choose a subject for the speech and analyze the class as a rhetorical situation for the speech, answering the twelve questions posed on pages 14–15 as far as is possible. Write a paragraph or two explaining what advantages and disadvantages you will have in speaking on your chosen subject.

Oral

1. Form a group with four or five other members of your class and, in discussion, work out a general description of the class as a rhetorical situation in which you will all speak. Report your conclusions to the rest of the class, together with the group's advice on how speakers can best adjust to the requirements of this situation. (If the entire class follows through on this exercise, compare and evaluate the groups' conclusions.)
2. Make a short talk in which you describe a specific rhetorical situation and point out aspects of it of which you might have been unaware had you not attended this class and read this chapter.
3. Report to your classmates how many public speeches (as defined in this chapter) you have given in the last twenty-four hours. Indicate where you were most and least successful and why.
4. Observe a public speaker (student, teacher, television personality, or any other) and report on his or her strengths and weaknesses in adapting to the rhetorical situation.
5. Prepare a class report in which you discuss the similarities and differences of two kinds of rhetorical situations. For example: inaugurals and commencements, funerals and personal anniversaries, situations for selling merchandise and teaching situations, occasions for welcomes and occasions for goodbyes, reporting in a classroom and reporting to a "boss," an employment interview and a news interview, the situation that exists when you read something on the editorial page and the situation that exists when you turn to the feature section (or sports or some other section).

ENDNOTES

1. From Isocrates, "Antidosis," trans. George Norlin in *Isocrates* (Cambridge, Mass.: Harvard University Press, 1956), II, p. 327.
2. Robert Gintel of Equity Advisors, quoted in *Forbes,* October 30, 1978, p. 134.
3. André Malraux, "Sketch for a Psychology of the Moving Pictures," first published in the journal *Verve* VIII (1940): 69–73, and reprinted in Susanne K. Langer, ed., *Reflections on Art* (Baltimore: The Johns Hopkins Press, 1958), p. 326.
4. J. A. K. Thomson, *The Art of Logos* (London: George Allen & Unwin, 1935), p. 180.

5. Everett Lee Hunt, "Rhetoric as a Humane Study," *Quarterly Journal of Speech* XLI (April 1955): 114. Used by permission of the author and the Speech Communication Association.

6. Julia T. Wood and Gerald M. Phillips, "Metaphysical Metaphors and Pedagogical Practice: Biological Beings, Pawns, Interchangeable Components, Puppets, and Hunting Packs," *Communication Education,* XXIX (May 1980): 154–55.

7. E. T. Klemmer and F. W. Snyder, "Measurement of Time Spent Communicating," *The Journal of Communication* XXII (June 1972): 142–58.

8. There is relatively little published research on this point, but our product has never been more rigorously tested than when we taught public speaking for industrial firms and other private organizations. One of our universities has for several years maintained a flourishing in-service training program in speech communication for school systems and their teachers, which supervisors and teachers agree enhances the work of even experienced teachers. See A. F. Dauria, D. L. Blumen, and S. C. Rhodes, "A Rhetorical Model of Teaching," *Communication Education* XXX (January 1981): 64–70.

9. Lloyd F. Bitzer, "The Rhetorical Situation," *Philosophy and Rhetoric* I (January 1968): 1–14, and "Functional Communication: A Situational Perspective," in Eugene E. White, ed., *Rhetoric in Transition* (University Park: The Pennsylvania State University Press, 1980): 21–38.

10. Bitzer, "The Rhetorical Situation," pp. 4, 6.

11. This paper was prepared by Lisa Roberts of the University of California, Santa Barbara, for a public speaking course taught by Janice E. Peterson.

CHAPTER 2

First considerations

Where can you apply the principles of this chapter in everyday life?

1. Where you want to refine your capacity to listen to instructions, explanations, and arguments from any source.
2. When you are planning, rehearsing, and presenting single-point explanatory, persuasive, or reinforcing statements in interviews, committee discussions, instructional situations, reporting, or formal speaking.
3. When you want to control undue nervousness in any situation involving speaking.

When evaluating someone else's *one-point* speech consider:

1. Is this speaker easy and interesting to listen to?
2. Has the speaker actually narrowed to a single point, or is the speaker attempting to present a full-blown speech of several points?
3. Do the materials chosen by the speaker really support the point being explained or proved, or were some of them irrelevant?
4. Does the speaker use several kinds of materials to support or amplify the main point?
5. What evidence is there that the speaker prepared and rehearsed well?

One day in your class a speech will be assigned to you. A time for the speech will be set. You will know when you are expected to appear and make a talk. When the announcement is made, questions will begin to crowd your brain. What shall I talk about? What must I do to carry off the assignment successfully? How can I avoid saying things that have been said a dozen times before? How shall I start to prepare? How can I avoid being too nervous to talk at all?

Ideally, you should know all the theoretical and practical knowledge in this book before making a speech; but to have ample opportunity to learn from experience, your experiments in speaking must begin early. There is more to be gained than lost from this. Each opportunity to speak will allow you to explore your own nature and abilities as a communicator and to study others as they listen and react to what you say. You can learn enough quickly to make useful *experiments* in public speech, as we will show in this chapter.

Your full command of public speaking will develop gradually. As your understanding and control develop, you will become able to meet increasingly high standards and to solve increasingly difficult problems in communication. But your first classroom experiences can be profitable if you proceed in an informed way. That is why we are asking you to look at some elemental observations about public speech in this chapter. We will deal with six topics you need to think about before addressing any audience. The topics are listening, basic procedures in speech preparation, preparing a first assignment, kinds of delivery, rehearsal and attitudes toward speaking, and stage fright. Even if you have never spoken in public before, you should be able to handle first assignments satisfactorily if you understand and use your options associated with these six topics.

LISTENING

The speech situation we described in Chapter 1 had an audience, made up of listeners, as one of its vital ingredients. For there to be speech there must be listeners. So some basic facts about listening are worth thinking about.

There are at least three ways in which listening directly concerns you as a student of public speaking: (1) you always need to adapt public speech—what you say and how you say it—to the basic ways people listen; (2) if you are to help your colleagues in a class to develop as public speakers, you will have to listen to them in ways that enable you to give them clear reports on the reasons for their achievements or weaknesses; (3) a speech class gives you special opportunities to refine your own listening so you can listen more effectively outside your class—in lecture halls, before television sets, and among friends.

What are the basic facts about how people listen? One of the best-informed students of human listening has said: "How well a person *can* listen and how well he does listen are not the same thing. Furthermore, how well he does listen depends on two factors: his listening habits and his willingness to listen." [1] There is also a third factor of great importance—the natural capacity to listen. The natural ability to listen correlates most highly with intelligence.

Listeners' habits, their intelligence, and their willingness to listen, then, are the basic things that determine what they take in and how. It is rather clear that you cannot change your listeners' habits or intelligence with any one public speech. What you have mainly to work with is your listeners' *willingness* to listen to you. You can do a great deal about that by using all the skill you have to make what you say worthy of their attention, interesting for them, and attractive to them.

It would be too simple to say that interesting listeners is the basis of the art of speaking. But no speaking can be artistic unless every effort has been made to make the listeners *want* to hear. In later pages of this chapter we will point out some basic ways you can do this.

Another thing we know about listening is that people listen in different ways under different circumstances. For example, they listen differently according to what they expect to *do* with what they hear, and they listen closely for what they *expect* to hear. You know that you listen differently when you expect to be tested than when you don't expect to be tested. And when you have some clue about what is likely to be said, you will be more ready to pick up that information than if you had no notice that it was coming. Our common experience and clear experimental evidence assure us that we can depend on these tendencies among listeners.[2] Since we know this much, we know that if you want listeners to hear you rightly, you ought to make clear what they can *do* with what you say. You ought to help them see what is to come—let them know what to expect. Here is the basis of what we shall say later about making goals clear; building orderly and motivating introductions, transitions, and conclusions; and building satisfying proofs. The psychological justification for those strategies is simply that listeners listen according to their practical interests and according to their anticipations.

That we all listen according to our expectations is also important to you as a listener. What will you listen *for*? If you think the arguments of a speech are likely to be most important, you will tend to notice the language less unless language begins to confuse you or is especially striking. If you think entertainment is the thing to be gotten from some talk, you'll pay minimal attention to arguments and maximum attention to language because you'll expect that amusement is likely to arise from quick turns of language. The point is that whenever you are listening you can guide yourself, shifting your focus from one thing to another to pick up what you think needs to be caught. If you recognize this possibility, you should be able to inspect your own listening. See whether you concentrate on what needs attention in order to get the most out of your relationships with speakers. Ask yourself such questions as these: Do you concentrate on *content* rather than on manner in classroom lectures? Do you listen for clues to what is more important and what is less important in informative talk? Do you relate what you are hearing to what you already know when that could make listening more interesting and profitable to you? Do you avoid making irrelevant associations? What we all have to recognize is that *we are in charge of how we listen*. We're not just telephone receivers; to an important degree we are makers of what we hear.

The notion that we are in charge of our listening brings us to some steps you can take to sharpen your skills as a listener. A speech class is an excellent place to do this. A classic program of research completed some years ago identified these necessities of effective listening:

1. building up experience with difficult material
2. having or developing interest in the topic at hand
3. being willing to adjust to various speakers' different ways of talking
4. being in good physical condition and having an adequate level of energy (No one can listen well when exhausted.)
5. being willing to adjust to the unexpected or abnormal in situations; that is, keeping one's mind on what is to be listened for despite unexpected developments
6. being willing to adjust to emotion-laden words—not letting them obscure what's more important
7. being willing to adjust to emotion-rousing points (as contrasted to words)
8. being able and willing to focus on central ideas rather than on nonessential details
9. being able and willing to take notes systematically where that can be of help in grasping and retaining what's important
10. being able and willing to supplement and reinforce what is heard as it is heard.[3]

The research on which this list is based says that you will be wise to build up your experience through disciplined listening to difficult material (especially on topics associated with your specialization), to try to avoid being carried into irrelevant thoughts by emotional or unexpected content, and to practice directing your thoughts toward *adding to* and interpreting what you are hearing. The same research suggests that we will all learn more and faster if we are tolerant of such things as speakers' eccentricities and distractions in listening situations. What it all adds up to is that listening effectively is significantly a matter of teaching ourselves to focus on ideas rather than on extraneous matters. A further implication is that concentrating on *main* ideas is better than focusing on details, whether we are "just listening" or listening intensely and preserving what we hear. In short, we have to work at listening to get what is there. Working at it improves habits, and better habits improve learning and retention of what we have learned.

Your classroom is a listening laboratory if you choose to make it so. You will hear very different kinds of public speeches, each giving you the opportunity to refocus your listening and to prepare yourself for the differing kinds of experiences. You can direct and redirect your listening along the lines suggested by the list just given. We urge you to do so. Research has shown that people do improve their abilities to gather in what they hear if they work at adjusting themselves in the ten ways we have cited.

Refining your ability to listen may or may not be a part of the formal syllabus used in your class; if it is not, you can still make the classroom your own laboratory for experimenting with ways of listening. But whether you do that or not, there is one thing that should be absolutely clear: you must exert yourself to *rouse your listeners' interests* and to *guide their expectations*. In all the public talking you do, these two strategies are essential because of the facts we have been emphasizing: we all listen selectively and according to our expectations. Coping with these facts begins in speech preparation.

BASIC PROCEDURES IN SPEECH PREPARATION

Preparing any speech is a matter of exercising judgment about the relations among you, your subject, your audience, and the occasion. More broadly put, your preparation for any public speaking needs to be guided by what you know about human thought and feeling, the conventions of communication, and the nature of listening. Later we shall consider these subjects more fully, but some steps you can take in your earliest public speeches can be pointed out now. In the first place, you must decide what you want to accomplish.

Setting your goal

Before you can plan an effective speech you must know your goal in speaking. Exactly when you decide this may depend on circumstances, but your goal must be set early in any case. It does not matter in classroom speaking whether you first decide to talk about drug abuse and then decide to try to clarify the problem or first decide that you will make some problem clear, and then choose drug abuse as the problem. But outside the classroom, setting the goal is usually your first step. Subjects for public speakers are often *assigned* in the sense that people are invited to give speeches on particular subjects. Often, too, speakers decide that they *must* speak on a specific topic because of what they know about it, or because of the occasion, or because of their relations with the particular audience. If your subject is more or less decided in advance, then setting your goal is the first task in preparing.

What is a *goal* in speaking? It is the *kind of response* you will seek from your audience. You can decide to get them (1) to understand, or (2) to inquire more deeply into a subject. You can decide that you want them (3) to feel and believe more or less strongly something they already feel or believe. You may decide (4) to change their views through persuasion, or you may choose simply (5) to entertain. Those are the five goals speakers usually have. If you know what your subject is, your next step is to decide which of these goals will be yours.

Determining the response

As we pointed out in Chapter 1 (see pages 11–12), you should think of classroom speaking as real communication rather than as just an exercise. The question is, then: what do you *want* from your listeners? Suppose you have decided to talk about the drama club to which you belong. What is it you want your listeners to know or think or feel about that club when you finish speaking? Should you put together information so that they will simply know more about the club's purposes and activities? Is "Yes,

I understand what the club is and does" the response you want to aim for? You would be seeking a similar kind of response if you decided to review and amplify some club project. That kind of focus would also tend to produce the response, "Yes, I understand." Notice, though, that if you aim for the response "I understand," you don't prepare material that encourages action. If you want to persuade listeners to attend a coming production by the club, you assign yourself additional tasks. You may still need to get them to "understand" what the club is, but you will need to go beyond that to draw their thoughts toward a particular action. Or you may have a very different intention, say, to get the listeners to think seriously about the functions of groups like the drama club. You may want the response, "We ought to think more about this topic." If that's what you want, you give yourself a still different assignment. Or, if you know your listeners are already favorable toward drama as an activity, you might decide to strengthen this already present feeling. Then you would seek a response something like, "Yes, drama *is* an important cultural influence on campus." Or you might decide to entertain the audience with satire or irony or amusing things you have experienced with the drama club. You then would seek smiles and laughter as chief responses. These are the normal aims people choose among in setting their communicative goals. As our example shows, most subjects can be treated in several ways. Your primary way depends on what kind of response you decide to make your main goal.

The word *primary* in the previous sentence is important. The five aims we have identified are not necessarily exclusive of one another. You may inform to both persuade and to reinforce. You may need to persuade an audience to inquire into something. You may need to entertain incidentally as you inform or persuade. But if you are to adapt to the ways people listen, you need to build your speech so that *one* goal clearly dominates and other, incidental goals will be clearly subordinate. The reason is as simple as it is inexorable; neither you nor your listeners can think clearly about any subject unless you plainly understand the *chief* reason for thinking about it at all.

Choosing your subject

As we have said, the typical ways public speech comes about are that someone is strongly motivated to speak about this or that, or one is invited or assigned to speak on a particular matter, or one's rhetorical situation dictates what the subject must be. But practice speaking in classrooms tends to be different. The assignment may simply say, "Talk about anything you want to but make the speech persuasive." That makes choosing a subject a bit more complicated than it is in nonclassroom experience. For this reason we want to give you some guidelines for choosing subjects when no particular subject is dictated.

1. Consult your own experience. It is certainly not wise to choose a subject about which you know absolutely nothing. But experience isn't the whole answer, if you recognize how people listen. We remember a student who was in fact something of an expert on turtles. It made sense for him to talk about turtles, so in his first classroom speech he talked about diamond-back turtles. His classmates were fascinated with his

concrete knowledge and his enthusiasm and thoroughness. His experience served him well in choosing a subject, but he overdid the matter. His second speech to the class was about snapping turtles. From his listeners' point of view he was in a rut. He was still interested in turtles, but the audience saw him as too narrow in his interests; they turned their attention away from his subject. His experience and interest no longer served as exclusive tests of a good subject.

We have also encountered students who, when advised to choose subjects involving their own experiences, talked about trivial subjects such as "my summer job waiting tables" or "my days as a lifeguard." A good many talks on such topics are not well received; the test is whether listeners can get something of special interest or significance out of your account of an experience.

The principle is: talk about things within your experience, but make aspects of that experience pertinent to your listeners' needs and interests.

2. What you already know ought to be considered when you are choosing a subject. If you are interested in a subject but don't know enough about it to make a speech, you must learn new knowledge before you can earn the right to take your listeners' time. Remember, five minutes spent before an audience of twenty people consumes one hundred minutes of the world's time. Therefore, you need to choose a subject you already know a good deal about or are sure you can learn enough about before your speaking engagement. That leads us to a third guideline.

3. Consider whether new material you will need is actually available to you. Can you get to the people you will need to talk to? Are needed books, pamphlets, magazine articles, and so forth really available? Unless you make such a preliminary check on what is available, you may find that there is just not enough material to justify your speaking on an otherwise promising subject. Find this out early. We mention some kinds of speech materials you may need on page 30 and discuss supporting material fully in Chapter 5.

4. Facts about your audience will have a bearing on your choice of a subject. Their age, sex, expectations, special interests, and knowledge all need to be considered. One or more of these factors might rule out some otherwise promising subjects. We treat these matters more fully in Chapter 3.

5. You ought also to consider limitations imposed by the situation in which you will speak. What will have gone on before? Does the time of day or the setting or the assignment make a certain kind of subject especially appropriate or inappropriate? Some subjects become inappropriate for classroom speaking because of the assignment, the time allowed for each speaker, and the expectations the classroom audience has developed for a given occasion.

6. Time, which we just mentioned, makes it important for you to consider whether a complex subject can be narrowed in a way that will let you treat it significantly but within the agreed-on time. You may also find that some subjects are too simple to justify the amount of time you are expected to use in speaking. The issue is: can you make your subject important in the time you will have?

7. Finally, any subject you choose—even for a first speech—ought to be an intellectual challenge to the audience and to you. Both ought to gain something. There

ought to be some news. What you talk about need not be world shaking, but you should be able to handle any subject you choose so as to give yourself and your listeners some new insight or new information or new attitude.

These are major things to think about as you choose subjects for first speeches. In presenting them we have several times implied that *how you treat* a subject is apt to have more to do with its final worth than does the subject itself. Almost no subject you can think of will have no aspects worth discussing with your colleagues. Perhaps the best way to put it is this: if a subject has a significant aspect you are qualified to speak about, that subject is a promising one for a first speech.

To summarize, if you have chosen the general topic of drama for your first speech, your next move is to decide what kind of response you want from your audience. Then ask yourself whether you can narrow the topic of drama to some precise subject that will allow you to secure the response you have decided on. For example, if you are especially interested in the subject "Off-Broadway theatre in the last ten years," the subject will allow you to take any of the goals of informing, generating inquiry, persuading, reinforcing, or amusing. You must then decide which of these goals shall predominate. Then questions arise as to whether you have or can secure the needed experience and knowledge to handle the subject in this way, and whether you can make the now-narrowed subject significant for the audience in the time allotted. These are the things you need to work out concerning any subject for a speech. As you shape it to manageable *and purposeful* dimensions, the crucial, defining question is: what response do you want from your listeners?

Locating your central idea

When you know your subject and your purpose, your next task is to frame a statement that expresses pointedly the encompassing thought that embraces all you will say. We call this the *central idea* of a speech; others sometimes refer to it as the *thesis* or the *main proposition* or the *subject sentence*. Whatever term is used, the point is that to build a coherent talk that lets listeners know what to expect, you need a compact way of saying what it's all about. Any of several images can help you see the function of such a central idea. Think of it as the hub statement from which everything else you will say extends outward like supporting spokes, or think of it as the apex of a pyramid of supporting blocks, or think of it as the roof of a pavilion that covers and is supported by all the pillars and beams that form the structure's framework. What you are looking for is such an idea, a sentence, that so precisely expresses what your speech is to accomplish that it verbally defines what is relevant and what is irrelevant. Once you have formed this idea as a sentence you have a guide for yourself in constructing the rest of the speech, and you have a guide for your future listeners. How is such a statement constructed?

Phrasing your central idea   To begin with, a little ingenuity in phrasing central ideas is a good thing. Listeners like it. A phrasing that is blunt and appears to work for you may suggest that you haven't kept your audience's interests in mind. There is nothing technically wrong with saying, "I shall inform you this morning. . . ." or "Let me teach you. . . ." or "My purpose tonight is to persuade you that . . ." Such statements of central ideas are bald and a bit trite; the ideas can be phrased more deftly and more interestingly. "The paper I am holding in my hand was produced by one of four ways for producing pulp" announces clearly but in an unhackneyed way that you are going to inform your listeners that there are four ways of producing pulp. Almost any central idea can be couched in a sentence that is fresh and clear without being flashy.

Such a sentence can also clarify your purpose and intended coverage by its form. Assertions are usually used in stating the central ideas of speeches to inform or amuse. Questions usually indicate that a speaker is aiming to stimulate inquiry. Propositions that suggest an "ought" or "should" are preference signals that you intend to persuade. Let us look at some examples, imagining that you have chosen to speak on televised advertising. Depending on your goal, you might frame your statement of central idea in one of these ways:

Informing: The recent history of televised advertising shows that it is a growth industry.

Persuading: The Federal Communications Commission ought to regulate televised advertising more closely than it does today.

Inquiry: To what extent, if at all, should the Federal Communications Commission regulate the content of televised advertising?

Reinforcing: Televised advertising's service in showing us new products is undervalued.

Entertaining: Televised advertising is too funny for words!

Notice that each of these sentences does three things: (1) reveals the *subject* of the speech, (2) expresses the limited *central idea* clearly, and (3) plainly implies the *kind of response* that is sought. When a statement does all three of these things, it serves you by helping you to keep the rest of your speech on target, and it serves your listeners by showing them how to listen and what to listen for.

There are some cautions about forming central ideas into sentences. The sentence should express but a *single* idea. If it doesn't, it can't guide you and your listeners clearly. Therefore, beware of compound statements—sentences that contain *and* or *but* especially. Conjunctions like these often signal that you have not yet decided what your *main* idea is. For example, the following sentence announces two major ideas: "The Scottish poets ought to be studied, and the poems of Sir Walter Scott ought to be analyzed by all students of English literature." Which will be the main thrust of the speech, study of Scottish poets or study of Sir Walter Scott? We cannot tell. Here is another statement in which the conjunction (this time *because*) shows that the aim of the speech may not be fully thought out: "The rating system for movies is unsound because the ratings express nothing about the artistic qualities of the films." If the speaker wants to make only one argument about the rating system, this statement accurately reflects the subject, limits, and goal of the speech. But if the speaker intends more than a one-point speech, then "The rating system for movies is unsound" is probably the real central idea that expresses the broader purpose. The basic point is that if conjunctions like these appear in your draft of a central idea, you ought to recheck the statement carefully. You may not have given yourself quite the aim you really intend.

Supporting your central idea   When you have before you a statement that precisely expresses your subject, central idea, and goal, your next step is to find material that will clarify, add detail to, or prove the central idea as you have formed it. What you need are things such as: (1) facts and arguments; (2) anecdotes; (3) comparisons, contrasts, and analogies; (4) definitions; (5) descriptions; (6) examples, whether long or short, real or hypothetical; (7) quotations; (8) repetitions and restatements; (9) statistics; and (10) audiovisual aids. You will hardly use all of these in a first speech, but your supporting and amplifying material will take some of these forms. When you have found what you need, you will then have to arrange these materials into a speech—a coordinated, unified whole that makes your central idea clear and believable.

In your first speeches try for clear, simple arrangements. It will be wise to select only a few pieces of support for perhaps only one or two main points. When you have prepared and given one or two of these short, simple speeches, you will begin to see that a longer speech is but a series of such simple units.

PREPARING A FIRST ASSIGNMENT

The easiest and most practical first speech is one that consists of a single point. "The rating system for movies is unsound because the ratings express nothing about the artistic qualities of the films" states the central idea for such a one-point speech. You make a speech about a point that might well be a segment of a longer speech. To prepare such a speech you ought to proceed as follows.

1. First, choose a single, simple idea from a subject area that interests you and your audience. To be sure your goal is clear and precise choose an idea that you want your listeners to understand or agree to. One way to locate such an idea is to make a rough plan of what a longer speech might say and then use one main point from it. As we have indicated above, one point of a speech on "The rating system for movies is unsound" might be, "The ratings of movies tell nothing about the artistic qualities of the films."

2. Once the single idea has been selected, phrase it accurately as the central idea for your speech. Our second statement about the rating system in the previous paragraph is such a phrasing of a single idea.

3. To keep your first speech simple it is probably wise to use just one kind of structural development. The easiest structures to handle are chronological, spatial, cause-to-effect, and problem-solution orders. They can be used either to

explain or persuade. If one of these arrangements will fit your subject, use it.

4. Get at least two or three ideas from outside your own experience to help you amplify or support your central idea. This will assure that there will be some freshness in your speech.

5. Plan even this short speech systematically. Make an outline even though it consists of only five or six items. Setting them down in outline form will give you a check on how best to relate the parts to each other.

6. As you outline, make sure that each item bears on your central idea as you have stated it. If you consciously notice how the item supports or clarifies the central idea, you can begin to compose the language that will show your audience what the connections are.

7. A final test of your plan is to ask one of these two questions: (a) Will my audience understand the subject better if I tell them these things in the order I have sketched out? (b) Will my audience tend to accept the central idea I'm proposing? The first question applies if your goal is to inform, the second applies if your goal is to persuade. If you can answer the appropriate question affirmatively as you review your plan, you are probably ready to give your talk its final fleshing out, but whether you can make the test at all depends on whether you have done a sound, simple job of outlining.

Here is a further illustration of how you might locate and outline a single-point speech. Let us imagine you want to say something about alcoholism. What might be a central idea for a full speech on this subject? It might be "Alcoholism is a problem that deserves immediate attention in public education." What would be some likely headings of such a talk? The following might occur to you:

I. Alcoholism is a serious social problem.
II. Alcoholism has become a serious problem in our public schools.
III. Early preventative action can diminish the problem.
IV. We should support educational programs attempting to deal with the problem among the young.

Any of these points could be used as a central idea for a short talk, although the fourth is least promising because its support depends partly on the other three points. If you chose the first of the four points for a one-point talk, you could then prepare a simple outline or plan that might look something like this.

Central idea:
Alcoholism is a serious social problem.

Supporting material:
    Statistics   1. More than 4,000 corporations in the United States have had to create special programs for treatment of alcoholic workers.

Example	2. A friend of mine, a teacher in high school, finds parents relieved at being told their children are heavy drinkers, not drug addicts.
Statistics	3. The National Institute on Alcohol Abuse and Alcoholism reports:
	a. About one in ten Americans who drink is either an alcoholic or a problem drinker.
	b. After heart disease and cancer, alcoholism is our biggest health problem.
	c. Half of all murders, a quarter of all suicides, and at least half of all auto deaths are alcohol related.
Definition	4. An alcoholic is one who is unable consistently to choose whether or not to drink, and who, if he drinks, is unable consistently to choose whether or not he will stop.
Fact	5. Alcoholics Anonymous is the oldest, biggest, and most successful treatment agency.
Quotation	6. An Atlanta business executive explains why Alcoholics Anonymous works: "Doctors cannot cure alcoholism because it is not simply a sickness of the body. Psychiatrists cannot do it because it is not simply a sickness of the mind. And ministers cannot do it because it is not a sickness of the spirit alone. You must treat all three areas, and that's what AA does." [4]

To show you what a complete one-point speech is, as delivered from this outline, here is the text of the actual speech.

Alcoholism is a serious problem. More than 4,000 corporations in the United States have had to create special programs for treatment of alcoholic workers. In the past few years the problem has become especially serious among teenagers and women. Alcohol consumption is presently at an all-time high.

A friend of mine, who is an instructor in high school, has had to confront parents to inform them that their children were heavy drinkers. And she's been surprised that the parents were actually relieved upon hearing this. They would usually say, "Thank God, I thought he was on drugs."

Too few people seem to realize the serious problems that can be attributed to alcohol abuse. According to the National Institute on Alcohol Abuse and Alcoholism, about one in ten of the Americans who drink is either an alcoholic or a problem drinker. After heart disease and cancer, alcoholism is the biggest health problem. It shortens the life span by ten to twelve years. In one-half of all murders in this country, either the killer or the victim, or both, had been drinking. One-fourth of all suicides show alcohol in the bloodstream. And at least one-half of each year's auto deaths and injuries can be traced to a driver or a pedestrian who is "under the influence."

An alcoholic can be defined as one who is unable consistently to choose whether he should or should not drink, and, who, if he does drink, is unable to decide whether or not he should stop.

There are many treatment centers available to the alcoholic. There is no miracle cure, but there is at least one treatment or a combination of treatments that will offer him a good chance of recovery.

Alcoholics Anonymous is the oldest, the biggest, and the most successful in treating the alcoholic. Here the treatment is nothing more than the gathering together of alcoholics. They discuss their problems with each other. But they can do so only if they will admit to one another that they are powerless to control their drinking problem. An Atlanta business executive who has been an AA member for over twenty-five years has been quoted as saying, "Doctors cannot cure alcoholism because it is not simply a sickness of the body. Psychiatrists cannot cure it because it is not simply a sickness of the mind. Ministers cannot do it because it is not a sickness of the spirit alone. You must treat all three areas, and that's what AA does."

This speech deals with a current problem. If your subject were something as familiar as an old proverb, outlining a one-point talk would be done similarly:

Central idea:
"There is nothing new under the sun" is a saying that still has meaning for us.

Supporting material:

Fact, Example	1. If we think we have new inventions, we have only to look at the ancient collections in the Egyptian Museum in Cairo where we will find such supposedly modern items as comic books, fly swatters, and jockey underwear.
Anecdote *Example, extended*	2. A friend of mine invented what he thought was a new kind of cigarette holder, but the U.S. Patent Office turned it down because they had already registered one just like it. (Tell story.)
Example, brief	3. My married sister told my mother she had found a new recipe for chocolate cake calling for coffee, but my mother said, "That's nothing new. I've been putting coffee in my chocolate cakes for years!"
Fact	4. Time and again, students have discovered that their thoughts were the same as those of others who lived long ago but whom they have never read or studied.
Restatement	5. We can put it another way by saying, "History repeats itself."
Restatement	6. Whether we are dealing with human experiences, ideas, or physical objects, we continually find that what we think is new is really "old hat."

These illustrations show how one amplifies and proves a main point. To show their variety, we have labeled the kinds of supporting material. We have also kept the outlines far simpler than the fuller speech plans we present in Chapter 8.

KINDS OF DELIVERY

There are four general ways people deliver public speeches: *impromptu, extemporaneously,* by *reading,* and from *memory.* Your first classroom talks are most likely to be presented extemporaneously. At some time in your course you are also apt to speak impromptu. You may or may not be asked to practice speaking from a printed or written text.

Impromptu and extemporaneous delivery best promote conversational quality—the quality preferred far above the others in our society. We shall therefore discuss these two methods of presentation here, returning to the general topic of delivery in Chapter 10.

How does impromptu speaking differ from extemporaneous speaking? For impromptu presentation you make no formal preparation. At most you have a few minutes to think out what to say. Impromptu speaking is spur-of-the-moment communication. You will not learn much about the art of public speech from speaking impromptu, but speaking impromptu can be a demanding test of artistic skills learned in more considered study and practice. Impromptu speaking demands that you *put quickly to use* what you already know—about pertinent information and about how to speak effectively. It is also good exercise in self-command. You will always speak better extemporaneously, but there are a good many times when you have no choice except to speak impromptu. Such situations include contributing in a committee meeting, responding to unforeseen questions, giving directions spontaneously, and so on. Impromptu public speaking is not ideal speaking, but it is frequently inevitable.

When you have ample time to think out what to say, perhaps to outline a plan and rehearse it orally, you can speak extemporaneously. Now you can be at your communicative best. A plan that guides you but does not bind you gives you freedom to adjust what you say and how you say it to specific, sometimes unforeseen, demands of your rhetorical situation. You can add or delete ideas if something like the remarks of a preceding speaker makes that seem wise. You can be spontaneous in language because you have found several ways of talking about each idea. Most importantly, you can deal with your listeners directly—in other words, converse with them.

You ought to do your planning with a sharp image of your listeners and your rhetorical situation in your mind. You should remember that everything you plan is to stimulate the particular listeners you will meet when speaking. The goal is what a famous teacher, J. A. Winans, termed "vivid realization of the idea at the moment of utterance." Achieving that goal is the essence of extemporaneity. All listeners, including you, want speakers to think and to realize their ideas anew as they talk.

If you use notes when speaking extemporaneously, keep them brief and intelligible at a glance, and use them unobtrusively but without pretending you don't have them. It is not unnatural to refer to notes to remind yourself of your plan or to help you as you present statistics or quotations that listeners would not expect you to memorize. With or without notes you need to show your listeners that you are thinking about your ideas *in relation to them.* They will not believe you are thinking in this way if your eyes are constantly on notes. It is wise, then, to bring as few notes as you can when you speak. The whole point of extemporaneous speaking is to present planned communication as conversationally and as intimately as possible.

Speaking extemporaneously allows speakers their best compromise between the cold mashed potatoes of rigidly learned talk and the haphazard mix of thoughts that impromptu speaking so often produces. For classroom speaking and for much outside speaking you will have an opportunity to prepare, rehearsing your line of thought without setting it unchangeably. This will allow you to *recreate* those thoughts vividly and spontaneously, directly realizing them for listeners.

By urging you to practice and develop skill in extemporaneous presentation we are not disparaging all use of reading and memorizing in public settings. Some people read aloud very well, and some can speak from memory so that listeners never know the material is memorized. But these abilities are not general. We are saying that a beginner is more likely to achieve conversationality if he or she speaks extemporaneously because that method allows both careful preparation for audience adaptation and spontaneous re-creation of ideas as the speech is given. To achieve these qualities most fully entails planning and rehearsal of a special kind. We will deal with that next.

REHEARSAL AND ATTITUDES TOWARD SPEAKING

The problem in preparing to speak extemporaneously is to transfer your plan to your mind and become thoroughly familiar with its sequence of ideas. It's the *order* of *ideas* you are trying to fix, not the words. The words with which you express your ideas will, and ought to, vary from one rehearsal to another. This will give you a large stock of verbal resources from which you can choose as you talk with your listeners. For this and other reasons it makes a great deal of difference *how* you rehearse for extemporaneous speaking. The following list is a method that will give you considerable reassurance, clarity of mind, and even serenity when you speak.[5]

1. Read through your written plan, fixing your mind on the succession of main points. Reread it, this time concentrating not only on the main points but on the details supporting each point.
2. Still referring to your outline, speak through the speech in whatever words happen to come. Talk out loud, not under your breath. You will find it helps to stand up and face an imaginary audience. Try out gestures as you verbalize. Get through the whole speech. If you bungle a part, go right on to the end without stopping to straighten out the troublesome section. Come back to that when you have finished running through the entire speech.
3. Without using your outline or any memoranda except those notes you will use

on the platform, stand up and speak through the speech as before. If you can find a patient listener or group of listeners, so much the better.

4. When you can get through your total speech fairly well, time yourself and adjust the speech to the time allotted for your actual presentation. Such an adjustment may call for omissions or condensations, or it may call for additions or expansions of points. It is important to acquire a sense of time on the platform and develop the habit of keeping within time limits.

5. In the moments before speaking keep the plan of your speech uppermost in your mind; review it. This is the most constructive outlet for tensions.

6. During preparation and just before speaking renew your desire to share a worthwhile message with others. Remind yourself that the experience before you is not a "performance" but an opportunity. You have earned that opportunity through the knowledge you have acquired and your position as a respected human being in a communicating society.

7. Recall that your auditors are persons not very different from yourself, that they want you to succeed.

8. Do not expect to avoid all tension. Some tension is good for you. Properly channeled, tension can serve you positively by increasing your alertness and your available supply of energy.

9. As a general rule, avoid last-minute changes in your speech, especially during your maiden efforts. Do not add to uneasiness by entertaining misgivings about choices already made. Adapt to the moment and to other speakers but do not make changes that undermine the overall plan you established in your mind by systematic rehearsal.

Systematic rehearsal of this kind is insurance. It will give you command of your thoughts and free your mind for adapting to special features of situations as you speak. From ancient times to the present even the busiest public figures who became known for effective speaking have found time to rehearse for major speeches. We know a number of superior teachers who prepare for lectures and even for presiding over discussions in essentially the way we have just outlined. They recognize what you must accept: control over self and control over content are imperative when what you say is important. Both kinds of control are established by the kind of oral rehearsal we have described, but still more importantly, this kind of rehearsal keeps you free to adjust to unforeseen features of the rhetorical situations you enter.

STAGE FRIGHT

Not everyone will admit it, but most speakers are apprehensive about facing audiences. If you are worried about how your audience will react, rest assured that your concern is normal. One of the country's leading scholars and experimenters says,

> Research has indicated that stage fright is experienced by most people at one time or another. In fact, in a nationwide survey of American adults, Bruskin Associates

(1973)[6] found that the most frequently reported fear was that of speaking in public. Thus . . . [fear] is a normal response that most people experience when confronted with oral communication in a public setting.[7]

After all, in facing even classmates anyone is taking some risk. You hope your listeners will respond favorably or at least sympathetically. Chances are that they will, but you aren't quite sure. This doubt, felt by most good speakers in some degree, results in fear and anxiety, which in turn produce a sense of conflict. How to resolve that kind of conflict, how to ease the feelings accompanying it and still adjust sensitively to an audience, becomes a special problem. It is, however, a problem that most of us can overcome by understanding the problem's nature and thinking sensibly about it.[8]

At the outset, you ought to remind yourself that the real causes of stage fright are psychological. For the most part *attitude* is at the bottom of the matter. Lack of self-confidence results in fear. Insecurity stems from the uncertainties of the situation. You become afraid if you feel you may lose control of the audience. Or you may be apprehensive about your mastery of what you are going to say. Then you are apt to experience fear because you feel unprepared or that you are not perfect. Or you may experience fear because you are anxious about how well your voice and body will function, or whether you will choose the right words. The mere fact that you are separated from the listeners in a formal situation may be responsible for feelings of insecurity and aloneness. For some people, wishes to avoid such situations, to flee from them, have caused them to make such serious excuses that they have not had to speak at all. Thus they have reinforced their fears by preserving the causes.

The fear that causes anxiety about speaking results in physiological changes. Some who undergo these changes think they are organically ill, that they may have some sort of secretion imbalance or other fundamental disorder. What actually happens is that the flow of epinephrine (adrenaline) accompanying anxiety and fear sets off additional changes. Blood pressure, rate of respiration, and nerve conductivity increase. More blood sugar, furnishing energy, enters the system. More thyroxine may be secreted, speeding the burning of blood sugar. More oxygen is taken into the blood. More poisons are removed from your system. As a result of these changes fatigue probably lessens, and you may experience the kind of increase in strength that frequently accompanies the release of tensions during anger. These bodily changes may interest you, but they are not the *causes* of fear.

How can you reduce fear and, subsequently, the tensions that afflict you? The solution to this problem can be discovered only by going back to the causes to see what can be done to remove them.

First, try to accept the fact that everyone experiences the apprehensions that you do. One of the most common myths believed by people who are chronically fearful of speaking in public is that only they are apprehensive. It simply is not so. The differences lie chiefly in how people use the tensions and the biological energy that anxiety generates. Concentrate that energy on promoting the responses you seek. Realize that you are going to talk with not so much an "audience" as some human beings like yourself. No doubt some of your calculations about how to deal with them will misfire, but if you concentrate thought on your listeners-to-be rather than on yourself, you will score more hits than misses and your worries about yourself will diminish.

We know what we have just said is sound advice. We also know that it is easier said than followed, at least for some students. Some colleges and universities have special training programs for students who are unusually fearful of speaking in public. If you cannot follow the advice we give and if such a special training program exists in your institution, you ought to seek the special help. But a most interesting finding has emerged from research on diminishing stage fright: *focusing on your goal lessens anxiety.* Your speech will give you repeated opportunities to adopt, focus on, and pursue communicative goals. It may well be that such repeated experiences are a reason that "most studies indicate that the impact [of a course in public speaking], when considering all students enrolled, is a reduction in communication apprehension." [9]

A second way to cope with stage fright is to be thoroughly prepared. If you are not well prepared and think you are not worth listening to, you will certainly be fearful of the reception you will receive. But such doubts will have no foundation if you prepare wisely. Pay close, careful attention to your pattern of organization, to your supporting and amplifying materials, to phrases of greatest importance, and to potentially troublesome spots in your plan. If fear of speaking can cause you to prepare more carefully, it has provided its own best antidote.

In the previous section we outlined a method through which you can prove to yourself that you can indeed succeed. If you will force yourself to seek repeated experiences in speaking you will gain confidence. Every public talk you make teaches you more about public situations; soon these will become so familiar to you that you can approach them as being usual rather than disturbingly special.

In addition to taking advantage of opportunities to speak, take advantage of opportunities to use bodily action. Walk about and make gestures. But do these things meaningfully, not randomly. The point is that by using bodily activity you will release tensions. Some students have found that using some sort of audiovisual aid puts them at ease because it gives them something to do with their hands and other parts of the body. This is a good idea, but be cautious in trying it (see pages 261–62). Channeling some of your excess energy, which results from your physical state, into meaningful bodily activity usually proves to be a desirable method of ridding yourself of stage fright.

Proper attitudes, preparation, practice, and movement ought to be any sensible person's response to the risks we all sense in formal communication. But the wish to communicate is a still more powerful protection against unease. If you *want* to speak, you have won half the battle. If you have more than enough to say and are determined to make the audience understand or accept your point of view, you will have come a long way toward releasing your tensions into meaningful, constructive actions that will contribute to the accomplishment of your goals.

Setting a clear goal for your talk is the first, most important step toward gaining confidence. Once you have a goal, you will have at least some desire to communicate in order to accomplish it, and your desire tends to displace worry about your hands or knees or feet and what they are doing. This is not to say that desire to accomplish something makes you forget you have a voice and body you must control. It is to say that the more you can bend your efforts toward gaining specific responses from listeners, the more your physical behaviors will serve those efforts naturally. You will be like a swimmer in a race who, having hit the water, lets nothing divert attention from swimming as skillfully as possible to the finish line. All distractions will be swept aside or ignored. Practice and strategic planning lie behind this kind of concentration; in this way speaking is not unlike participating in sports. In speaking, as in sports, practice and planning give economy of thought and action. Just so, practice with your mind focused on the response you want leads you to concentrate on *means* and to submerge unhelpful fears. The analogy goes farther. Neither in sports nor in speaking should one expect to eliminate all nervousness. Some tension is necessary to make the body and mind function at their best. What you want, however, is tension focused on *task*.

But, as we have said before, speaking is social and always creates human relationships. This will be less a source of insecurity for you if you are confident the relationship you are aiming for is one that is worthy of you, of the time spent in preparation, and of your listeners. You will have few reasons for misgivings if you choose a subject that has importance for you and your audience, set your goal clearly, and organize talk that emphasizes that goal and its significance.

AN OVERVIEW OF PREPARATION

In the foregoing pages we have emphasized the things a speaker ought to consider in preparing for a simple assignment to speak publicly. In concluding we summarize the sequence of preparatory steps serious speakers have found it important to follow. Ordinarily you will need to do the following things in getting ready to speak to an audience:

1. Considering the nature of your audience and the occasion, decide what response you seek concerning the topic you have decided or been assigned to talk about.
2. Narrow or expand your topic until you have located the specific subject that will fit your capacities, your goal, and the requirements of the situation.
3. Wed your rhetorical purpose and your central idea in a clear-cut statement expressing unambiguously the coverage of what you will say and your reason for saying it.
4. Gather the variety of materials that will most strongly and interestingly amplify or support what is expressed in your central idea.
5. Organize these materials into a structure that can be shown clearly and systematically in outline form.
6. Consider what kinds of language will best interrelate your materials to form a *whole* that interestingly asserts the basic message contained in your central idea.
7. If it is at all possible, prepare yourself to present your talk extemporaneously, so you can speak in an organized, informed way, yet spontaneously and adaptively.
8. As insurance for your plan and against stage fright, rehearse your speech orally to gain full control of the pattern of your ideas, alternative wordings, and timing.

By listing preparatory steps as we have, we do not mean you must invariably proceed in exactly the way our summary suggests. For example, a speaker asked to talk about his or her recent experiences as a member of a rehabilitation project in Peru need not pause very long over step 4 but may have more trouble than some others with the narrowing and focusing processes of steps 1 and 2. A speaker assigned to make a report on the budget has step 1 settled, as is most of the work of steps 2 and 4. The speaker who has been in Peru may find the most difficult problem to be sifting out irrelevant knowledge to accomplish step 5. The speaker giving the budget report may find that there are standard forms for budget reports that accomplish most of step 5. On the other hand, when you decide to talk to your colleagues on a topic you have only recently learned about, you will probably need to devote about the same amount of attention to each of the eight steps listed. But if a committee in your class should ask you to report on the history of the National Association for the Advancement of Colored People, you would find that most of the considerations implied by steps 1, 2, and 3 were suggested in the way the assignment was given. However, to be sure you understand the assignment clearly, it would still be useful to run through the first three steps quickly in your mind.

We have tried to summarize the normal preparatory procedures for *any* speaking in which you will bear special responsibility for creating and sustaining human interaction through speech. What needs to be done at each stage may vary from speaking assignment to speaking assignment, but *each of these speech problems must be settled somehow*. Whether some have been taken care of by an assignment or by your own experience or by your listeners' expectations is something *you* must decide. That is your freedom and burden as a communicator.

EXERCISES

Written

1. Write five simple, single ideas you think would be good ones to develop in a classroom speech of two or three minutes.
2. Identify a general subject. Frame statements of central ideas treating aspects of that subject as they might be treated in a speech to inform, a speech to persuade, a speech to generate inquiry, a speech to reinforce, and a speech to entertain.
3. Listen carefully to a speech by one of your classmates. Take notes in outline form on what he or she is saying. Following the speech, compare your outline with the one the speaker used. Check to see (a) how accurately you noted what was said and (b) how much you missed noting and why. Was the speaker obscure, or did you listen wrongly?

Oral

1. Prepare and deliver a brief speech on a proverb of your own choosing. Select at least five items to support its truth or falsity and devise a simple outline like that on page 33.

2. Deliver a three-minute speech in which you develop a single point that could be one of several main points in a longer speech. In developing your point use at least three different kinds of supporting material and prepare a simple outline like that found on pages 31–32.

3. Interview another member of your class concerning his or her life and interests; frame an *informative* central idea for a one-minute talk to the rest of the class on "Jane Doe as one of our Listeners." Present this introductory speech to the class.

===

ENDNOTES

1. Carl H. Weaver, *Human Listening: Processes and Behavior* (Indianapolis: The Bobbs-Merrill Company, 1972), p. 7.

2. For more extensive discussions of listening see Charles T. Brown, "Studies in Listening Comprehension," *Speech Monographs* XXVI (November 1959): 288–94; Charles M. Kelly, "Listening: Complex of Activities—and a Unitary Skill?" *Speech Monographs* XXXIV (November 1967): 455–66; Weaver, *Human Listening,* pp. 34–42.

3. This list is adapted from the "components of listening" as originally presented in Ralph Nichols, "Factors in Listening Comprehension," *Speech Monographs* XV, no. 2 (1948): 154–63, and later discussed at length in Ralph Nichols and Thomas Lewis, *Listening and Speaking* (Dubuque, Ia.: Wm. C. Brown Company, 1965).

4. This outline and the speech text that follows were prepared and presented by Eloise Paige, a student at Herbert H. Lehman College, City University of New York. Used by permission of Ms. Paige.

5. Adapted from H. A. Wichelns and others, *Manual for Public Speaking,* I (1932), p. 22 and from H. A. Wichelns, G. B. Muchmore, and others, *Manual for an Elementary Course,* p. 19.

6. Bruskin Associates, "What Are Americans Afraid Of?" *The Bruskin Report,* 1973, no. 53.

7. James C. McCroskey, "Oral Communication Apprehension: A Summary of Recent Theory and Research," *Human Communication Research* IV (Fall 1977): 79.

8. Otis M. Walter treats the matter of resolving anxiety-produced conflict in an excellent article entitled, "Developing Confidence," *Today's Speech* II (September 1954): 1–7. Where the problems do not yield to the kinds of attack suggested by Walter and in this chapter, the help of a specialist on "communication apprehension" or "speech reticence" ought to be sought.

9. McCroskey, "Oral Communication Apprehension," p. 90.

CHAPTER 3

When he can thus give a satisfactory account of the kind of man that is amenable to any particular kind of argument, and is further able to recognize in practice the kind of thing he was discussing when it occurs before his eyes, and can fit his speech and method of persuasion to it, when he has learned all this he must learn when to speak and when to be silent, when is the moment for brevity, when for an appeal to pity or fear and all the things he has learned. Then, and not until then, has the art of speaking been well and fully acquired. But whenever any one who falls short of this in speaking, teaching or writing boasts that he is an expert, we shall be right not to believe him.

—Plato, "Phaedrus" [1]

Understanding audiences

Where can you apply the principles of this chapter in everyday life?

1. Wherever you need to decide what kind of talk is appropriate and practical in a particular situation.
2. Wherever you need to know what motivates people regardless of their special interests.
3. Wherever you need to know what draws people's attention.
4. Wherever you need to give an idea special qualities of human interest.

When evaluating someone else's speech consider:

1. How well did the speech fit the readinesses of the immediate situation?
2. Did the speaker treat the listeners as critical thinkers?
3. How fully did the speaker use opportunities to associate ideas with listeners' general biological, age, sexual, and intellectual interests?
4. How fully did the speaker use opportunities to give ideas such features as activity, vividness, comparison and contrast, and other features discussed on pages 65–66?
5. In what ways, if at all, did the speaker display rhetorical sensitivity?

No one will achieve the knowledge Plato demands in the quotation on page 42. Plato did not attain it. No psychologist or psychiatrist has it. There are no philosopher kings of whom Plato dreamed because we all remain more than a little mysterious to ourselves and to each other. This mysteriousness in human beings makes trying to understand one another a worthy ideal. We will never know all—either about the things of which we speak or about the people to whom we speak. But that should not discourage us from being as understanding as we can be. Plato's challenge is helpful if it pushes us toward being as thoughtful as possible. That alone will encourage us to *think* our ways through the complexities of human communication. Impulse will not carry us through.

This chapter will not teach you *the nature of the soul* (human psychology, we would say, today). That is a matter of heated debate among psychologists and philosophers and theologians. We are none of these. What we hope to do here is move you a little closer toward understanding yourself and your future listeners. We will remind you of many things you already know but too seldom remember. Perhaps we will be able to bring you a few new thoughts.

SPEAKING AS RELATIONSHIP

When we speak with someone, we watch and listen for responses. We speak because we want to be heard, understood, and reacted to. So, we watch and listen in order to "read" what listeners feed back to us. Everyone knows this, but we all have some tendency to forget the importance of doing it when situations in which we speak are formal. Then college students and a good many other people tend to "talk writing" at their listeners. Have you not noticed this in televised interviews? Interviewees, especially if they are unused to being interviewed, frequently fall into the most formal kind of language they know, forgetting that beyond the microphone and camera are people who need to be reached personally through direct, conversational utterance.

If speaking is to be effective, the human relationships between speakers and listeners have to be made more intimate than those between writers and readers. Poets, novelists, composers of epigrams, writers of regulations, some scientists, and others can often afford to concentrate on the content and forms of their messages only. They may be addressing everyone or anyone or simply "making a record." But we can never afford to do only that when we speak with one another. When speech is the medium, speaker and listener are present *to* one another as persons—even if the link is merely the voice. A contemporary philosopher, thinking of face-to-face relationships, says:

> The presence of the other as face carries both the significance of pregnant silence and a call to speech and listening. The silent call of the face may give way to spoken word which then presents itself with all the surrounding, penetrating power of sound in a call which insists that I "obey" by responding.[2]

This is surely true of any setting for public speech. When someone is expected to speak and is present with others who are prepared to listen, silence is certainly "pregnant" in the sense that it declares the human relationships of the setting to be not yet fulfilled. The presence of the parties in the situation *calls* for speaking and responding.

All of these things seem obvious when attention is drawn to them, but many speakers forget that public speech is relating personally—effectively or ineffectively. A trio of scholars recently reviewed a huge array of modern research on persuasion and found a serious shortcoming: few of the investigators understood that in persuasion all parties involved are changing as they interact. Instead, the investigators thought of the process as one where persuaders *act* and targets *react*.[3] If a generation of research scholars could forget that communication, especially oral communication, is *inter*relating, we should not be surprised that anxious speakers too often think of themselves as "putting out" communications and of listeners as "taking them in."

The image of public speech you should see in your mind's eye is something like this. You are like a guest to your listeners. You seek to enter their intellectual and emotional lives. As listeners they make room for you and your ideas, welcoming you, you hope, but perhaps wondering why you have bothered to come with these ideas just now, or why you are bringing the ideas in the form you have. Your hosts have to move the furniture of their minds a bit in order to accommodate you. If you are thoughtful and gracious, you will have planned ways of helping them to make the new arrangements and to make those arrangements seem agreeable. Whether your hosts will appreciate your visit and the changes it makes depends only partly on their preconceptions of what an agreeable "household" is like. The result depends also on your considerateness of them and what they must do to entertain you at all.

We need not extend the analogy. Its points are simple: (1) a public speaker has to sustain something of a visitor-host relationship with listeners; (2) listeners are not passive receivers but active arrangers and rearrangers of their mental households; (3) if the relationship works out well, there will be respect and satisfaction on both sides during and after adjusting to one another. Speakers do not "give" and listeners "take." They stimulate one another continuously. They share in an active, ongoing relationship. The speaker's art consists in creating and directing the relationship so that the listener will want to live with an arrangement of ideas and feelings similar to the one the speaker proposed.

The image of speaking we have drawn implies that as you prepare to speak in public you need constantly to ask yourself: How will this step affect the bond between me and the listeners who will share the rhetorical situation with me? A choice of material or strategy will be practically wise only if it will help you forge a bond that will further your ultimate purpose.

The problem of egocentrism

A reason that scholars and speakers forget the relation-building that all oral communication entails is that we are all rather egocentric. Self-love tells us that listeners *ought* to attend to what we say, or that "just being myself" ought to be enough. Or we tell ourselves, "The way I *learned* it is the right way" or "They need to know it, so let them listen." Then, if they don't listen acceptingly, we complete the self-delusion by saying, "Well, that's their loss; the stuff was there." What we overlook in such moments is that for communication to work at all, listeners must be able and willing to participate in the communicative process. This is the hard fact that too much concentration on ourselves blots out.

Egocentrism is not necessarily a destroyer of communication. It is the reason we even try to communicate. We would talk to one another very little if we were not impelled by desires to express and influence. The problem is: how are we to balance egoism and concern for others in creating oral messages? The answer is to consider both ourselves and our listeners at every moment of preparing to speak and of speaking. And that is not self-sacrifice or pandering.

Adjusting to listeners' general preferences

What effective conversationalists and formal speakers seem to accomplish is to act on the premise that not even their own egos can be well served unless listeners' general preferences and expectations are accommodated. That may require adjusting one's own ideas, but it seldom requires giving up those ideas or denying them. Here is a true example of how one student worked out this problem.

A student of landscape architecture whom we will call Dick Barnes was in a basic course in speech taught by one of us. Barnes was not especially effective orally, but he recognized that in his chosen profession he had to be able to reduce abstract and often technical concepts of landscape architecture to terms and images nonspecialists could understand and think with. He, his instructor, and the class struck a bargain. Dick would talk regularly about landscape architecture, another student of architecture in the class would report on whether what Dick said was professionally sound, and the class would write down anything that confused or bored them as Dick talked. In conferences the instructor tried to help Dick think of ways to get around obscurities and causes of apathy among listeners. Twice Dick tried to explain architectural concepts; both times his colleague said he was sound, but his other listeners said things such as, "I couldn't get it," or "You told me more than I wanted to hear about that." Dick and the instructor tried to rethink his strategies, and they concluded that Dick had not translated his concepts into images his listeners could see and he had not associated his ideas with values about which they had feelings. Dick decided that next time he would concentrate on the visuals. His third try worked. His ideas were still sound, but he turned his subject, "The Values in Open Spaces," into seeable, feelable realities. Here is a bit of what he said:

> Consider the area behind the Dairy Building. It's small, but it's a pleasing area to walk through. You can walk through it and have different experiences each time because of the very different kinds of plantings—shrubbery, flowers, trees. It's an enjoyable place to be. But so is the Mall. It has a canopy. You see it walking through. Half way up, ahead of you, the trees arch together. You are "inside," yet

you're out-of-doors. And there at the center of the arch's end you see Pattee Library, with its straight columns. It completes the enclosing of the area. You feel "inside," but you know you're outside and free. These are things a landscape architect means when he says outdoor spaces have "value" or can be given "values." He's saying he tries to put things into outdoor space in such ways that you will say it's interesting to be there or that you like to be there. The value he's talking about is your good feeling; that's what he tries to create with his shapings and plantings.

There was no weakening of the architectural concepts of space and value. Barnes simply illustrated their reality by transporting his listeners to campus spots they all knew well enough to picture in their minds. Then he made them feel the values he spoke of as his words directed their eyes and movements—in imagination. In these ways the speaker's and listeners' egocentric inclinations were balanced. Barnes *willed* that listeners *should* sense what values are to an architect, but he transformed the professional concept into experienced sensations. That is what his listeners had been demanding of him. Without in any degree becoming a sycophant, he accommodated his own *and* the listeners' wishes. There was communication!

Of course, listeners do not always make it easy for speakers to adjust to their demands. They are not always as open in their demands as Dick Barnes's classmates were. We have all played the role of polite but evasive listener, signaling some kind of acceptance but actually engrossed in our private thoughts. An astute speaker will not take signs of quiet acquiescence as enough. He or she will not presume that listeners will or even can give unbroken attention to what is said. An astute speaker will plan adaptations to the ways listeners behave—to their tendencies to drift in and out, to their fascination with tangential details, to the necessity of pressing them to focus on what is important.

Here is a fair representation of how listeners listen. Notice the partly pertinent, partly irrelevant thoughts a juror recalls having had as a prosecuting attorney began to speak:

> As he faced us head-on, I noticed how weary he seemed and how arched his eyebrows were behind his glasses. His dogged determination had kept the case moving against the defendants for almost four months; this morning he suffered from laryngitis. I recalled my hostility toward him during the long days of jury selection. Now I listened intently.[4]

No doubt the juror "listened intently," but he was not thinking of the prosecutor's *ideas* in those seconds when he was reflecting on the lawyer's health, eyebrows, apparent weariness, and earlier behavior. But let every speaker take note and remember: this juror was listening as people really do listen. His attention was drifting in and out of the flow of ideas the speaker was *steadily* creating through words and action. Your experience as you listen to classmates will be the same.

So far we have said little you did not already know. We have hoped only to pull to the forefront of your mind the importance of approaching situations for speaking as the opportunities for cooperation and agreeable human relations you know most of them are in fact. How to conceptualize these situations so you can plan for them fully is a somewhat more complex matter.

SPEECHES AND RHETORICAL SITUATIONS

For a great many years it was customary to say that in formal and informal speaking a speaker sets up two-way communication with the audience. The image was of a continuous "circular response" system in which speaker responded to listener, listener to speaker, speaker readjusted to listener, and so on. Interaction was understood, but only personal forces were emphasized. The image is not mistaken, but there is a more comprehensive way of describing what goes on as people relate to one another rhetorically. As we said in Chapter 1, Lloyd F. Bitzer published in 1968 and amplified in 1980 a way of conceptualizing speakers as entering *situations* in which a variety of forces interact to create human exigences, or needs, or obstacles, or things to be corrected. If a situation is rhetorical—one that communication can do something about— Bitzer says:

> First, there must be an exigence—a problem or defect, something other than it should be. Second, there must be an audience capable of being constrained in thought or action in order to effect positive modification of the exigence. Third, there must be a set of constraints capable of influencing the rhetor and the audience.[5]

What Bitzer's conception adds to the older speaker-audience notion is the fact that for effective communication to occur both speaker and audience must come to share at least one notion of what can or needs to be done. Of course, the thing needing to be done may be trivial (for example, getting the class over with by hearing this final speaker), purely pleasure giving (for example, sharing some light entertainment), or very serious indeed (for example, working out a labor agreement or a peace treaty). And it may be up to you as a speaker to awaken your audience to facts that make it important for them, as well as you, to fulfill the need for doing something about pollution in the environment. Let us examine a fairly ordinary situation in Professor Bitzer's way to see what is revealed.

Suppose you are going to meet with a committee on intramural athletics. The committee represents your student body, and you want some financial help for a softball team from your living unit. If the committee could be of help, going before it will be an occasion for public speech, on your part at least. There will be an audience—the committee. They will not be just an aggregation of people; they will see themselves as having certain obligations for, and to, the student body and whatever agency it was that gave them power to assist intramural athletics. But that is not all. Each committee member has a different background, a different history. Those differing experiences will affect individual perceptions, just as the shared experience as a committee will affect the group's perceptions. Both sets of background factors, then, can affect what you can and cannot do through talk. Both sets of facts shape the exigences or readinesses of the committee members.

Another important factor will be how much money the committee can spend and how much they have spent so far. How your proposal stacks up beside other proposals the committee has heard will be still another factor influencing the committee's perception of what is and isn't a "fitting response" to the situation. Furthermore, outside considerations like the nature of the intramural athletic program and the size of your living unit could influence the committee's judgment of whether financing is really needed. Add to these the fact that the committee will evaluate your proposal partly by whatever they know about you, about the group you represent, about the people you and your group are associated with, and whatever any member's relation with you and your associates make him or her think. These facts about the forces that will shape your speaking situation help us see the complexity of conditions determining what the parties will perceive as calling for attention.

Summarizing these situational forces, Bitzer says we communicate within complexes "of persons, objects, events, and relations" that produce specific exigences or readinesses. Those readinesses are not invariably the kinds that talk can help. Talk about a new intramural team won't fit the needs of the committee meeting if the committee has no more money and sees no way of getting any. But in other circumstances talk seems absolutely necessary. If your committee has money to distribute and you walk into one of its meetings at a time scheduled for hearing applications, then the setting, the people assembled, the committee's function, and your appearance virtually require that you request financial support for some student activity. The complex of events *and* people *and* human relations *and* customs *and* authorizations defines what remedy-through-talk is appropriate in this place and time.

Compare the shaping of the committee situation with the shaping of a speech class on a "public speaking day." You will see how the notion of "rhetorical situation" expands your understanding of the ways limits and allowances for speaking get built up. All past experiences with public speaking days, all notions of what those days are for, and all beliefs about the course and what it is for shape the allowances and limits of classroom speaking. You can analyze a classroom situation just as we have analyzed the meeting of the finance committee, and you could do the same with a political rally, a scientific seminar, a sales meeting, or any other setting in which speakers and listeners gather. You will need to do this before addressing any audience.

Entering a rhetorical situation

Before planning what to say on any occasion for public speech you need to discover whether the forces of the situation will have already "made a place" for you. You will have to decide whether you must introduce new factors into the situation, perhaps to *reconstruct* it to make it ready for you and the subject you have in mind. There will be situations where you have been asked to say something about a particular subject. They are thus tailored for you in advance. Other situations will need some adjustment. A politician who wants to talk politics at a nonpolitical picnic will need somehow to justify raising the subject. The person making introductions might do it, or the politician might say things that would gradually shift attention from nonpolitical to political matters. Or imagine yourself in a locker room with other members of a team. It is possible to transform the setting from one where the main business is dressing and undressing to one that allows public speech about game strategy. How ready your situation will be at the outset of speaking is your first consideration.

But how do you discover what exigences exist or could be created? You do it first by reviewing questions such as those we presented in Chapter 1, pages 14–15. If from this review you decide that it is feasible to accomplish something in the situation, ask yourself: if no *strong* exigence already exists for the ideas I want to present, can I reconstruct the forces of the situation to create or intensify a readiness? Would it be better for me to readjust my goal (for example, decide to just give information rather than try to persuade) in view of the exigences that exist? Will I need to do anything special to qualify *myself* to enter this situation with the purpose I have in mind? Your answers to such questions will quickly tell you whether you have one task or two: simply to enter the situation and take advantage of its exigences, or to change the situation somehow and *then* present the talk you have in mind.

Apply these mental maneuvers to your classroom. If the class has been studying how information can best be given orally and if an assignment is made for a series of five-minute explanations, everyone will be conditioned by study, customs that have evolved in the class, and by the assignment to expect informative speaking. What will happen if in this kind of situation you try to give a talk that seems aimed more at amusing than informing? You will be "violating the assignment," but what will actually happen will be more complex than that. Listeners will think such things as "Didn't she understand the assignment?" "Is she trying to see what she can get away with?" "Doesn't she understand what we've been studying and talking about for the last week?" "How's the instructor going to react to this?" "She should have saved this one for another day." Notice two things here. (1) In different ways such thoughts assert that the speech does not fit the "context of persons, events, objects, relations, and . . . exigence" of the situation. (2) A speaker's intelligence and intentions get questioned when a speech doesn't fit its situation. Even if there had been no formal assignment in this classroom, the fact of the recent study of informative speaking would make this speech to amuse seem slightly out of place unless its unusualness is justified in a special way.

Adjusting situations   In many situations unforeseen and unusual treatments of exigences can be fully justified, and in other situations perceptions can be changed so that new readinesses are created. Two examples will illustrate.

One of us taught a speech class where there occurred a group discussion in which several students expressed great concern about preserving wildlife in the United States. A few days later there was a series of speeches, several of which also dealt with ecology. Discussions following those speeches produced many remarks sweepingly critical of disturbers of nature. Criticism was showered on various groups from industries to hunters. At this point a biology major decided privately that the climate of opinion was becoming too one-sided, and, since wildlife management was one of his special interests, he decided to straighten things out by making a speech in favor of regulated hunting of female deer. It happened that doe hunting was then being criticized by some conservationists. What had happened in the class and what was being printed in newspapers and being broadcast all generated a situation in which another speech on ecology could have influence. But a speech endorsing hunting would have to be worked out with care, for a bias against hunting had developed in the class and was being fed from outside it. The biology major adapted so skillfully to this situation that he changed some attitudes.

He began his speech by recalling earlier talk about "management," "protecting the balance," "caring about nature," and the like. Then he said:

> I want you to think some more about "balance." I want you to think about how we are to keep the deer of this state in balance with the space and food we are willing to allow them. I'd like you to think whether you want to protect healthy deer or sick and scrawny ones, whether you want more deer killed on highways, and whether you have any sympathy for the human beings who run the farms of our rural areas. Let me tell you about the balancing problems that affect the lives of deer.

He went on to show that natural reproductive processes would cause deer in his state to overpopulate available wild land every two years unless a certain number of does were regularly eliminated. Fewer than the required number had been killed in past years, he said. The present imbalance was justification for extending the annual doe season. Several listeners' reactions were well expressed by one student who said, afterward: "Now you've got me almost embarrassed. I don't hunt; I don't even like the idea. But the way you put it, it seems like I *ought* to take up hunting deer if not enough other people do. Really, I don't feel too comfortable!"

In this instance a variety of forces inside and outside the classroom had provided a usable exigence for talk about the speaker's *subject*—ecology. The only thing he needed to justify was that doe hunting was in fact a positive ecological matter. This he did by artistically linking hunting with the ecological theme of balance. The biology major had no need to generate a new exigence to justify his speech; he needed only to make the audience believe that his subject, doe hunting, fell within the range of their sense that ecological balance ought to be promoted.

You will find in Appendix B another instance of adjusting the forces that create rhetorical situations. In this case Dr. Lee Upcraft gave additional information about the exigence—arriving at a generally acceptable policy on liquor (paragraphs 1 to 5). By injecting this further information into the situation he paved the way for re-formulating the exigence: an acceptable policy had to be *legally* acceptable, he said (paragraph 7). From that point on he could safely argue that the university's policy was the only acceptable one.

Our first example shows how an existing exigence can be used as justification for introducing unexpected—even initially unpalatable—ideas. The second example shows that if the exigence of a situation justifies a certain person's appearance, as Dr. Upcraft's appearance was justified, the speaker gains the freedom to try to define how the exigence should be understood. In short, the exigences or readinesses of rhetorical situations do not always dictate *what* you may say; they often dictate only that you must *justify* saying what you choose to say. But there are rather rigid situational assignments, too.

Rigid situational assignments The first classroom situation we imagined on page 50 is one so rigid that it is difficult to see how any student speaker could safely try to alter it except in case of an emergency. As other instances of rigid situations think of courtrooms. Law, courtroom customs, the case being tried, and many other factors rigidly prescribe what it is fitting for the judge, for the attorneys, and for witnesses to say. In courts both the exigences and the manners of addressing them are very confining for all speakers. Academic ceremonies are less confining; but normally the fact that they are academic dictates that there are exigences only for talk having something to do with education. Occasionally a speaker may be so much more important than the academic aspects of the ceremony that he or she can disregard the prescribed subject; but this is rare. It happened at Westminister College in Missouri where Sir Winston Churchill was invited to speak at a convocation shortly after the Second World War. The ceremony was staged to honor him as the famed war leader, so Churchill could ignore the academic aspects of the situation. He gave his famous "Iron Curtain" speech describing Cold War tensions. But there are few such occasions where a speaker dominates over the exigences of situations. When in 1977 President Jimmy Carter spoke at a convocation honoring the president of the University of Notre Dame, Mr. Carter had to observe and address the exigence of praising the university's president before he could acceptably invoke his own status as president of the United States and introduce discussion of American foreign policy. The point is that very few speakers have the prestige it takes to dictate exigences to rhetorical situations.

A representative example of misunderstanding rhetorical situations happened at a national conference of officers of college and university women's associations. With student affairs predominantly coeducational and equality of women and men widely valued on campuses, this conference's planning committee proposed a reexploration of the functions of women's collegiate associations. The committee's plan was to hold a series of workshops in which college and university women would consider new directions for women's associations. The planners hoped that the issues for discussion would grow out of a keynote address that they invited a distinguished woman journalist to give. We do not know what explanation of the rhetorical situation the planners gave to their invited speaker, but what happened was distressing to all.

The keynote speaker spoke interestingly of problems and gratifications of professional women, especially journalists. She said nothing about college and university women's associations and their functions. The planners of the conference were deeply concerned, and during the speech audible murmurs of perplexity and dissatisfaction could be heard. The speech was an excellent one for this speaker to make, but whether by the speaker's or the planners' error, the speech failed to address what the conferees saw as the problems to be resolved by the conference. The conference workshops got off to a very slow start because the keynote speech had provided no starting points, and a good many conferees blamed the speaker for not doing what she had been expected to do.

Perhaps this speaker should have inquired more carefully into the rhetorical situation she would face. Perhaps the planners should have made the exigence of the situation clear when they invited their speaker. For our purposes it does not matter who was to blame. The point is that in some situations a whole series of subsequent events can go awry if a speaker does not clearly understand and deal with the exigences that actually exist. A happier rhetorical event grew out of the story we have just told.

One of the planners of the original conference perceived what had gone wrong at the conference and the next year invited the same speaker to give the same speech on a university campus. This time the planner advertised the occasion as a lecture-discussion on "Women in Professional Life." The journalist accepted the invitation, gave substantially the same speech she had given at the conference, and the speech and subsequent discussion were eminently successful. The moral: sometimes you can create situations with exigences that invite the kind of speech you have in mind; at other times you must conform to the readinesses of audiences and the needs of situations that you cannot control or remake.

Not every situation involving people calls for talk. Not every situation that calls for talk calls for the kind of talk *you* feel inclined to give. Then you must be silent, change your rhetorical plans, or wait for a more suitable occasion. But usually rhetorical situations are broad enough to be approached in diverse ways, including redefining exigences or bringing latent ones to the fore. In all circumstances the most complex component of the situation to think about is the audience. What kinds of things does one need to discover about audiences and what questions should guide one's thoughts about them?

WHAT IS AN AUDIENCE?

Audience is a common term about which we often think too sweepingly and too crudely. You have probably read and heard references to "the mass audience" that imply that any large audience is a mass of faceless beings who present speakers with a kind of soft surface on which the speakers can make any imprints they choose. Sometimes it is implied that when people join together to form an audience they lose or abandon their individualities. We contend that those are mistaken and misleading notions. What we are about to say has been debated by social psychologists since the 1890s, but we believe the evidence grows stronger and stronger for the claims we shall make.

We think you will be seriously mistaken if you approach any audience in any rhetorical situation as though the people are anything but highly individualistic, self-controlled persons chiefly interested in their private affairs and the affairs of the groups and individuals they have learned to value. We doubt that there is even such a thing as *crowd psychology* or *deindividuation* or any other process that can strip away individuality and impose group or mob feeling. But it doesn't matter practically whether we are right or wrong. The hard fact is that as a public speaker you will almost never encounter audiences that are composed of other than decidedly self-conscious individuals.

The audiences you will talk to will be small and large groups of people who need to be treated as though they had the following qualities:

1. They will have standards of judgment they feel they can rely on in interpreting what you say and do. They will seldom feel at a loss about how to judge you and what you say.

2. They will be inclined to *question* what you tell them are the "facts" about the

ways things are. They will be especially ready to question what you tell them they ought to think or do.

3.   Even when they can't explain exactly how they evaluate what you do or say, they will still feel that they have adequate ways of "measuring" the worth of what you say.

These are the conditions of mind of people exercising *critical ability*.[6] Our contention is that you can never lose as a speaker if you treat all listeners in all rhetorical situations as people who will listen to you critically in these senses. That certainly applies to your classroom listeners, and we think it applies to everyone who will hear you throughout your life.

The strongest argument against this view is the belief that when people come together as an audience, group pressures for conformity are so strong that individuality disappears. That view deserves at least passing consideration.

Conformity in audiences

There is a large literature in psychology and theory of communication that emphasizes the ways in which group pressures can influence the judgments of people in small and large groups.[7] One of the difficulties in applying this research to the art of public speech is that almost no investigations concerning conformity have dealt with normal rhetorical communication in carefully analyzed rhetorical situations.

Common sense and findings in extensive experimental research make it plain that when small or large groups of people come together for almost any purpose, including hearing public speech, the individuals in the groups respond to and often defer to reactions of other people around them. Hence the concept of "group pressure" or "pressures for conformity" has come into being. Most investigations of how these pressures work have been made using fairly small groups of people who were allowed or encouraged to report their thoughts or feelings directly to one another. It is clear that in those circumstances what the majority seemed to be thinking could influence an individual or a minority. In some of the experimental settings the majority could actually punish those who didn't "follow along." Deviants could be criticized, ignored, or otherwise treated differently from those who agreed. Without much doubt, then, there is such a thing as group pressure for conformity in thought and action. But such pressures are not present all of the time in all communicative situations, and, even when such pressures exist, it has been shown that the way majorities exert pressure, how important minorities or individuals think it is to disagree, what authority or status or personal appeal the deviants have, and how communicatively effective the deviants are determine whether group pressure will be successful or unsuccessful.

What does this have to do with how a public speaker ought to conceptualize an audience? First of all, it implies that a part of any speaker's analysis of his or her rhetorical situation ought to be an investigation of (1) whether minority/majority differences of view exist and will be known in any way that could influence the effect of the speech; (2) whether pressures for conformity, if they exist, assist or get in the way of the goal of the intended speech; and (3) whether the situation ought to be studied further, if pressures tend to get in the way of the goal, to see how alternative views can be made more attractive, authoritative, or otherwise persuasive. Since pressures toward conformity are almost never beyond resistance, a speaker's first concern, where such pressures exist, is whether to *use* them or create plans for countering them. Second, the possibility that group pressures may exist within a rhetorical situation should not be overrated. As a public speaker you have no need to think that if most of an audience has views different from yours you must therefore give up. Experimental studies of conformity contain many instances in which minority views that are positive, artistically expressed, and suited to the exigences of situations have significantly changed majority views.[8]

Whether the views you introduce into rhetorical situations conform to majority views or not, the task before you is to compose and express what you have to say so that listeners will find it natural to attend to and give credence to your message. In later chapters we will deal with specific ways of composing and presenting speeches, but here it is important to note that all such strategies find their justifications in the natures of rhetorical situations and in the general psychology of listeners.

Having dealt with the basic features of situations, we shall turn for the rest of this chapter to more specific psychological facts about listeners. The first such fact is that listeners give attention for reasons that you, as speaker, can adapt to.

GETTING AND DIRECTING ATTENTION

A great German zoologist wrote, "The outside world—the world perceived by the senses—is the source of all that a form of life is and does, thinks and feels."[9] One way to describe listeners is to say that they "form themselves" by what they notice as they hear and see. A speaker's concern, then, is with what his or her listeners *will choose* to hear and see during speaking. We know that in general what listeners attend to is determined by (1) what stimuli impinge on them, (2) what previous experience leads them to expect *now,* and (3) what those listeners think they need and want *now.*[10] From these generalizations we can build some rules of thumb for adapting to audiences. One rule is: what will allow the listener a strong sensory experience (actual or vicarious) will be readily attended to and responded to. This means actions and words that enable listeners to see, hear, feel, taste, or smell in reality or in imagination will draw attention. Vivid words and movements that suggest sensory experience are special resources for getting and holding attention. The word *lightning* can trigger the image of a lightning bolt's zigzag outline seen at some other time. If introduced in a talk about the power of storms, the lightning image can help listeners feel as well as accept intellectually the power you are speaking of. A simple arm gesture upward can help listeners sense the distance to the moon. These are but two of hundreds of ways you can gain and maintain attention by taking advantage of the fact that all people are prone to attend to whatever gives them actual or imagined sensory experience.

Another rule of thumb we can draw from our three principles of attention is that keeping similarities and dissimilarities clearly before listeners will help to maintain their attention. People have learned to expect and to look for comparisons and contrasts. That is how we have learned most of what we know, and it is how we choose between satisfactions for our needs and wants—we check over "more and less" and "like and unlike." Again, there are hundreds of ways you can be both logically clear and satisfying to listeners by emphasizing contrasts and comparisons.

The first of our principles of attention suggests another important rule of thumb: since people can attend to *any* stimulus impinging on them, the job of a speaker is to make the stimuli of his or her speech more interesting and more gratifying to human needs than any competing stimuli. Perhaps you can't kill the fly buzzing in the room, but you can with words and actions make the university budget more important than the fly. For example, you can draw listeners' attention to their tuition charges. The room may be uncomfortably hot, but a good word picture of a ski run can at least temporarily pull attention away from the heat and toward your subject.

Doing all you can to control the stimuli that touch on your listeners' consciousness, using and guiding their expectations and dealing with their needs and wants, are the fundamental ways of getting and directing attention. In our next seven chapters we shall deal with specific procedures by which these necessities can be met. Here we need only add that getting attention is easy; holding and directing attention are the tasks that require careful planning and an active, responsive relationship with your audience during speaking. You have only to stand up or raise your hand or sometimes just draw in your breath to get attention. Holding and directing it toward the ideas important to you require adaptation to how people attend and what they attend to. Some of their grounds of belief and interest are universal and apply in all rhetorical situations. Let us turn to those next.

GENERAL GROUNDS OF BELIEF AND INTEREST

Biological needs

We can begin with the basic fact that everyone in your audiences will be biologically mammalian and have the bodily and organic needs generally found among mammals. All of us want gratifications for hunger, for thirst, for our need for oxygen, for sexual drives, and for security from injury, punishment, and other kinds of painful or depriving experience. But being human we also exercise preferences in many of these matters. We seek gratifications for our physical needs, but we are also capable of deferring or even suppressing some of these needs when we want something else still more. For example, audiences are often willing to undergo a certain amount of physical discomfort—undue heat or hard seats—if they believe that what they will hear and see will protect them from some later harm or pay off in long-range satisfactions.

So if you want to direct listeners' attention and alter their perspectives, one possibility is to show them, if you can, that some of their biological needs can be gratified if they listen to you and accept your ideas. No speaker can do this always, but when it is possible, listeners are very likely to attend at least until they begin to doubt the promise or to suspect that following what you urge will force them to give up still more important goals. Modern advertising constitutes a veritable textbook on how appeals to biological interests and needs can direct attention and motivate choices.

Here are some examples taken from recent magazine advertisements: "I believe an annual checkup is important to my health. I feel the same way about vitamins." "Salad time and the dressing is easy!" "The unique Rolls-Royce automatic air-conditioning will maintain any climate you wish at two levels of the interior, which means that you can enjoy the same degree of comfort from head to toe, from day to night." "Velvet feels like a million." "When you head a one-parent family, you need more than a little life insurance." Some of these appeals you will find too crude or blatant for listeners' tastes, but the examples show the varied, sometimes unique ways in which people's basic interest in their physical conditions can be linked to other kinds of ideas. If you can make such a linkage, it will almost surely increase the prospect of your being heard and heard with favor.

Sex

Sex is a social condition as well as a biological fact that makes for differences in listeners' readiness to attend, believe, and change. You need to try to accommodate your speaking to those differences. There is much argument today about what interests, motivations, and degrees of persuasibility differentiate women and men, but it is undeniable that in Western culture men and women do not react precisely the same to all communicated material. Why should it be otherwise? Female and male roles and experiences are not identical; so any sensible speaker ought to take into account where male and female experiences are apt to have differed. Especially when only one sex makes up an audience, an astute speaker will recognize that special experiences are there to be drawn on in ways that might be quite lost on an audience made up entirely of the other sex.

There is also a growing and fairly consistent body of evidence showing that women are more critical of female speakers than men are, and vice versa. So if you are a woman, you ought to expect more difficulties in directing attention and changing attitudes of women than of men. If you are male, it will be wise to assume that other males in your audiences will be a bit harder to interest and persuade than the women.

A further consideration is that during the past twenty-five years the roles and relationships of women and men have been and are changing continually. Almost no sweeping generalizations can be made anymore about sex roles. The result is that speakers have to give special consideration to just which sex roles and relationships are conventional, accepted, or idealized by each audience they address. The roles of the sexes are certainly a theme that grips attention in most audiences; only situational analysis can tell what kinds of responses the theme is likely to trigger.

Age

Age, too, is both a biological and a socially significant condition that characterizes every listener. When you analyze an audience's perceptions of you and your material especially, it will be important to consider to what extent similarities or differences in age will affect those perceptions.

To generalize across situations about any age group is precarious, and there is not much research on the relation of age to judgments, except in relation to specific subjects. What we do know, however, tends to confirm the suppositions of traditional lore in rhetoric and literature: the young are more persuasible than their elders and the elderly are more cautious; the young, middle-aged, and old tend to give closest attention to different aspects of ideas and issues. What is scientifically known suggests that in speaking you can safely follow the implicit guidelines of Aristotle, unless you know something special about a situation or audience that indicates otherwise. None of the observations we are about to paraphrase from Aristotle has been disproved as a generalization about our own society, and many have been confirmed sociologically.

Aristotle tried to address himself, as few modern psychological studies have, to "the proper means of adapting both speech and speaker to a given audience." He sought rhetorically applicable generalizations about the young, men in their prime, and the elderly. Below is a quick summary of his observations, and if you take the trouble to compare them to the results of public opinion polls that report opinions by age groupings, you will be struck by the modernity of what he said, except for his neglect of women's views.

In youth "men have strong desires, and whatever they desire they are prone to do. Of the bodily desires the one they let govern them most is the sexual; here they lack self-control. They are shifting and unsteady in their desires. . . ." They are "quick to anger, and apt to give way to it," and they are "fond of honor" and even "fonder of victory." Money means relatively little to them "for they have not yet learned what the want of it means." They are not cynical; rather, they are trustful "for as yet they have not been often deceived." Being quick to hope and living much in anticipation, "they are easily deceived." Although brave and spirited, they are also shy. Being idealistic, "in their actions they prefer honor to expediency" and are dogmatic. "All their mistakes are on the side of intensity and excess. . . ."

In middle life, Aristotle thought, people "will be neither excessively confident . . . nor yet too timid; they will be both confident and cautious. They will neither trust everyone nor distrust everyone; rather they will judge the case by the facts. Their rule of life will be neither honor alone, nor expediency alone. . . ." They will temper valor with self-control, and they will be neither parsimonious nor prodigal with their possessions. Generally, "all the valuable qualities which youth and age divide between them are joined in the prime of life." Is it not so of both men and women?

The aged have characteristics opposed to those of the young. Thus, "they err by an extreme moderation" and are "positive about nothing" for they have lived long and been disappointed much. They tend to be cynical and "put the worst construction on everything"; they are suspicious, and sometimes small-minded. They "aspire to nothing great or exalted, but crave the mere necessities and comforts of existence." They are constantly apprehensive and "live their lives with too much regard for the expedient and too little for honor." What other people think means little to them, for they "live in memory rather than in anticipation."

Aristotle concluded: "Now the hearer is always receptive when a speech is adapted to his own character and reflects it. Thus we can readily see the proper means of adapting both speech and speaker to a given audience." [11]

A speaker cannot, of course, always gratify the idealism of youth and the caution of age with the same argument; nor can he or she depend on it that there are *no* cautious youths and *no* radical elders in an audience. But more often than most speakers realize, ideas are at once *right* and *fair* (satisfying idealists) and *practical* (satisfying the cautious). If you look at Dr. M. Lee Upcraft's speech in Appendix B, you will see that he addressed both the issue of fairness and the issue of practicality. His immediate audience was relatively young, but what he said would be publicly reported and must make sense to people of all ages associated with his university. It is well, then, that he spoke as he did. His appeals to "right" certainly struck home with his young audience, but his emphasis on the practicalities of the university's legal position and the students' future prospects seem to have made *some* impression on the immediate audience and also could stand as a strong justification of the university's position for *everyone*.

Our main point here is that as a speaker you can and ought to include something for each prominent age group in any audience. Almost any subject is open to treatment in relation to ideals and also practicalities. Although age groups may differ in the intensity of their interest in one or another topic, their differing interests are seldom in total conflict. Adapting to age groups' special concerns is largely a matter of choosing what to *emphasize* and what kinds of supporting materials to use.

Intelligence

Intelligence is another attribute everyone has to some degree. What is measured by intelligence tests is clearly related to how people respond to speech and what kind of speaking is likely to be most gratifying and influential to them. The abilities that are measured when intelligence is estimated are these: verbal comprehension, handling numbers, spatial perception, remembering, reasoning, fluency with words, and perceptual speed.[12] Notice how important skill in language is in this list! It is not surprising then that most tests that try to measure what is taken in from "lecture material" correlate better with tests of general mental ability than with other tests.[13] This and other evidence argue that the higher your listeners' intelligence, the better they will be able to understand speech; the lower their intelligence, the more help you must give.

There is also evidence that the more intelligent people are, the greater their critical ability, and that less intelligent people have limited powers of comprehension and analysis.[14] On this basis the higher the intelligence of your listeners the more readily you can expect them to understand you, but the quicker they will be to criticize you if you make what they take to be mistakes. Your safe course with highly intelligent listeners is to be careful to justify and qualify your data and your claims. But if you are talking to people of limited intelligence, you ought to make your speech as simple as possible and be especially clear about how one idea relates to another.

To these generalizations another can be added: regardless of intelligence levels, people who have little or no initial knowledge of what is said to them are likely to accept what they hear *first* about that subject. Accordingly you will need to consider what your listeners already know about your subject. If they know the subject well, be careful to leave no doubt that you are in full command of the relevant material—and be doubly careful if you believe your listeners are highly intelligent. On the other hand, if you are clear, plainly well informed, and unpretentious, you can expect both the gifted and the ungifted to pay attention to you, comprehend you, and find you believable. Never make the mistake of supposing that clarity and the greatest simplicity a subject will allow are viewed as weakness by listeners of any intelligence level.

Strength of attitudes

We have said several times that in analyzing a rhetorical situation you need to think about what your audience will probably know about your subject and how they understand their own relations to that topic. There is actually a further consideration: how *strongly* does the audience feel about the matter? If you can find this out, you will be better able to estimate how they will interpret what you say and what precautions you may need to take in order to be understood as you intend. R. E. Lane and D. O. Sears succinctly expressed what any speaker must expect:

> People who differ from you will tend to distort your views. When you differ slightly from your friends, they will think you agreed with them. Your enemies will think you disagree with them more than you actually do. Both tendencies will weaken your capacity to influence them in the way you wish to.[15]

If you can estimate what your listeners believe and disbelieve and how strongly, you can insert additional material to prevent being misunderstood by agreeing or doubting listeners. If agreement or disagreement is minor, you probably don't have to worry about it, but if listeners strongly agree or disagree, you ought to be very explicit about where you stand.

It is seldom possible to change strongly held beliefs very much by means of any one speech. Strongly held beliefs are very easily reinforced—even by just showing that you too agree. But the stronger the belief, the less change you should ask for at any one time. A good guideline is: If you are dealing with beliefs *lightly* held, you can ask for large changes of view; but if you are dealing with *strongly* held beliefs and must challenge them, you should ask for the smallest changes that will serve your purpose or plan. Otherwise you will need to create a fairly long-range series of appeals for change. You are really involved in estimating listeners' *commitments,* and there are three aspects of commitment to ideas that you ought to think about.

Moderation versus indifference   Speakers sometimes make the mistake of dealing with listeners of "moderate" views as though those listeners had no opinion at all or were indifferent to the topic in question. But to hold moderate views—refusing to take a flat yes-no view of a subject—can be to hold that moderate position very, very strongly.[16] People can be very dogmatic about their "open mindedness" [17] or insist strongly that it is too early to make a decision or that only an "independent" position makes sense. You may need, then, to treat the views of "neutrals," "moderates," or "independents" as cautiously as you would a strongly favorable or strongly negative view toward a controversial position you want to take.

Action and commitment   An often helpful way of estimating how strongly a view is held by members of an audience is to ask yourself whether a significant number of the listeners have ever taken any *action* in favor of or against an idea you plan to discuss. There has been a good deal of research on how actions commit people, and it appears that just making a speech or writing an essay or letter to the editor in support of or against something can fix that view more firmly in a person's mind. This being true, it is useful to find out, if possible, whether any of your prospective listeners have joined organizations, given money or time, marched, written, or *done* anything about topics or positions you plan to take up. If any have, you have nothing to lose by assuming that those acts show your listeners have strong, fixed views about the issue on which they acted. If you can use the views on which they acted in support of your own views, you ought to. If you cannot use them, you ought to avoid raising the acted-on beliefs against yourself. If you must alter such views in order to accomplish your goal, remember to ask for only small changes in any one speech.

Proofs of commitment in speech situations   A kind of "measure" of an audience's commitment that inexperienced speakers often forget about is the fact that a listener *comes to hear you*. This is not a major consideration in classroom speaking; listeners are present probably more because they have to be than because they are breathlessly waiting for you to speak to them. Their presence signals no special commitment to you or any other speaker, but speech situations outside of class are different. Consider your own actions. It takes at least curiosity to get you out of your apartment or dormitory and into a meeting where someone talks publicly. Even when you turn your head on campus to listen more closely to someone, you express some special openness to what is being said. The basic point is that when listeners listen *voluntarily*, their action is an expression of a favorable commitment to the person who speaks—unless we know the listener's real purpose in attending is to scoff or oppose. There are many situations in which listeners' presence shows a desire for information or for reasons to believe what the speakers are expected to say. Many rallies, seminars, worship services, lecture-discussions, caucus meetings, testimonial or memorial meetings, teach-ins, and the like are occasions where the presence of a listener is usually a sign that that listener is already committed to the expected speakers and what they will probably say. Where attending, as an action, is a sign of commitment, considerable responsibilities are imposed on speakers. *Not* to be informative, convincing, impressive, or inspiring according to the listeners' expectations will violate expectations in the situation and make the audience feel negatively.

If you work thoughtfully enough and hard enough, you can even turn a classroom into this kind of situation. The acid test of classroom speaking is: can you create a climate of opinion and expectation in which your colleagues will try to attend class just to hear you? We have seen this achieved. It is the ultimate compliment to a speaker when colleagues attend not because they have to, but because they are committed to the speaker as a worthwhile person and communicator.

In this section of our chapter we have been pointing out general tendencies that exist within all rhetorical audiences and which need to be thought about and anticipated in speech composition. To summarize quickly, we have said that *all* audiences in *all* situations will have biological needs, will be male or female, will be of some age or range of ages, will have some identifiable level or range of intelligence, and will hold beliefs with some degrees of commitment that are open to estimation. You ought to inquire into these conditions as they apply to any audience you address. Easily said. But how does one go about such estimations? Basic information about a situation and some common sense will usually serve. Let us illustrate with an actual example.

One of us (Arnold) accepted an invitation to talk with an audience on the subject, "On Listening: What Does Rhetoric Have to Say to Cognitive Psychology?" The topic was proposed by the organizers of a conference on "Cognition and Symbolic Processes." The conference was held on a university campus, and faculty and students from a large number of universities in the United States had been invited. The invitation to appear said that speakers should prepare a formal essay on the assigned subject and submit it in advance of the conference so it could be distributed to conference participants as they arrived. At a designated hour each speaker would then be expected to summarize his or her paper in a talk with the audience. (The rest of this account is in the first person to make it easier to follow.)

This would be only the second time in my life that I had ever made a speech to professional psychologists and those who join them in their conferences. I prepared the requested essay well in advance of the conference, submitted it to one of the sponsors, and was assured that the subject matter was appropriate. Now the problem was to plan the talk version of the paper, which conferees would have had a chance to read before my appearance. I still did not understand the conference or my place in it very well, but reviewing the topics discussed in the preceding few pages allowed at least a partially satisfactory plan for the oral presentation.

Biological needs   Would biological needs play any part or offer any resources by which to adapt to the situation? The time for the speech was 1:30 p.m., following the luncheon period. People would be sluggish, perhaps wanting a nap as much as anything else. To counter this I developed several new examples that would involve the listeners in thinking of themselves in their listening-speaking relationship with me. The aim was to keep the listeners thinking actively about their *own* experiences, right now. I determined that the speech should be extemporaneous so that by my own directness I could counter any tendencies toward tiredness or boredom.

Sex   The audience would be made up of men and women, but the different experiences and roles of the sexes seemed unimportant because the act of coming to this conference would be proof that a common interest in psychology was, on this occasion, more important than any sex-grounded differences of interest. Also, anything I had to say about listening applied equally to men and women.

Age   By reviewing the published program I could see that some people present would be in their sixties and seventies, but I also learned that both undergraduate and graduate students were being encouraged to attend by several departments at the host university. I could expect listeners ranging in age from the late teens to the seventies. On that basis I inserted into my talk some new references to what had been known about listening forty years ago, incorporated some well-known data from the 1950s, and expanded a reference to a brand-new book that present-day students were likely to know about but that had only been cited in my formal paper. The adjustments were not major, but my objective was to include something that would have been part of each age group's academic experience.

Intelligence   Given the nature of the conference and the setting, I could assume that the audience would be highly intelligent and perhaps better informed than I was about psychological research and theory. Frankly, I felt rather intimidated. Accordingly I inserted into my talk new assurances that I was not trying to make sweeping generalizations from the limited data I had to offer. As it turned out, I probably went too far in trying to protect myself against the critical thinking of a well-informed audience. A succeeding speaker criticized me for not having claimed enough! My insecurity about addressing professional psychologists apparently led me to underestimate the degree of agreement there would be for my themes.

Strengths of belief and commitment   Part of my formal paper attacked purely behavioristic conceptions of listening. This criticism was consistent with the views of those who call themselves "cognitive psychologists." Such psychologists consider it as already proved that human behavior cannot be explained in mere terms of stimulus and response. Because of this belief and commitment on their part, I inserted into my talk some comments on recent philosophers' speculations about the complexity of human perception and thought—speculations some of these scientists might not have known about but that supported views they already held. I had, of course, no need to worry about the listeners' commitment to the study of how people think; no one uninterested in this topic would bother to attend this conference. The primary exigence of the meeting was to clarify the nature of perception and thinking. My thoughts about listening related directly to their concern, so I had no need to adjust the situation to secure a hearing.

These thoughts about the characteristics and concerns of the audience were virtually all I had to work with in readjusting the content of an already-written paper for the assigned talk. Discussion following the speech showed that my adjustments had worked well except that I apparently had overestimated the critical tendencies of this intelligent audience. They actually felt my evidence and arguments supported more sweeping claims than I had dared to offer.

We offer this experience as a typical example of how a speaker can improve his or her adaptation to a rhetorical situation by systematically considering how biological needs, sex, age, intelligence, and strength of beliefs and commitments are likely to influence listeners' receptivity. Not all of these factors will need to be adapted to in every situation, but all are *potentially* significant. You need always to think about them all in order to discover where opportunities do and do not lie. The guidelines for speakers that can be drawn from our survey of general grounds of belief and interest can be summarized this way:

1. Treat all audiences as made up of individuals who will exercise their critical abilities; treat them as thinkers.
2. Emphasize how your ideas relate to each other and to the exigences of the situation.
3. When you can, show listeners that you can help them toward gratification of biological needs; when biological needs work against willing attention and belief, show that there are other gains to be had from attending.
4. Expect and prepare for a little more skepticism from listeners of your own sex than from the opposite sex; be alert to any especially significant sex roles about which the audience is sensitive.
5. Include content that will have some appeal for each major age group in the audience.
6. Justify and qualify for highly intelligent audiences; clarify specially for audiences of lower intelligence.
7. Ask for major changes of view only where opinions and beliefs are lightly held; seek change only by small degrees when trying to alter strongly held beliefs and commitments; indicate your agreement with strongly held beliefs and commitments whenever you can.

Just as people's general grounds for belief and interest point us toward certain useful strategies of audience adaptation, people's general receptivity to certain rhetorical patterns—ways of saying things—gives us additional resources we can use regardless of our purposes in speaking and regardless of the kinds of rhetorical situations we encounter.

AUDIENCES' READINESS FOR SPECIAL RHETORICAL FEATURES

When your ideas can be expressed in the ways we are now going to discuss, they will be more readily attended to than if you express them otherwise. These ways of expressing thought and feeling give color and liveliness to speech. They can be *built into* your basic thoughts. They are sometimes called *factors of attention,* but we think it is clearer to say they are special *rhetorical features* for which audiences are always ready—apparently just by virtue of being human beings who have the unique ability to think and speak symbolically.

There are at least nine of these special rhetorical features: activity, proximity, realism, familiarity and novelty, conflict and suspense, vitality, specificity, intensity, and humor. Following is a brief statement of what each of these features is, accompanied by the general reason that the feature is likely to control or direct attention. Brief examples of the features are also given.

Feature	*Basis of influence*
1. *Activity.* Actual movement suggested by the idea itself or by verbal imagery or by activity displayed in speaking. You refer to racing cars, draw a sweeping curve on the blackboard, or you say, "He *scurried* out of his hiding place."	The presence of change or movement always tends to attract attention; real or imagistic movement creates the sense of change; a speaker's movement *is* change.
2. *Proximity.* Showing that things are near in time or space to the listener, or near to one another (actually or figuratively). You draw two shapes close to one another, or you say, "Such a person could be sitting *next to you* on the bus," or "The planet, Mars, is now our *neighbor.*"	Adjacency is among the simplest relationships to perceive, and real or imagined adjacency to a listener implies that the listener is or could be directly involved in experiencing whatever you are speaking of.
3. *Realism* or *vividness.* Pictorial or other sensory qualities introduced by imagistic language or by action or by physical illustration. You say, "I was covered with *black sticky mud*," or you point to where the mud covered you, or you bring some mud and show what it is really like.	Learning through the senses, directly or vicariously, is the basic experience by which knowledge is gained, survival defended, and many of our greatest pleasures experienced.
4. *Familiarity and novelty.* Association of ideas with what listeners know, or presentation of what was either unknown or never perceived in the way proposed. You compare governmental budgeting to family budgeting, or the family budget to regulating the international balance of payments.	All humans prize and attend to what they have experienced before; they also enjoy or are curious about experience that is new.
5. *Conflict and suspense.* Showing either animate or inanimate things in opposition to one another or in competition with one another, the details or the outcome being in either case uncertain to some degree. You create an image of a contest between science and the environment, or you say, "This is a race between ideas and fear," or you inject a "fight image" or illustration when amplifying.	Opposition is the most obvious of differences, hence easily perceived. When competition or an active clash is present, *change* and the *unknown* are both present to draw human attention.
6. *Vitality.* Associating ideas or objects with matters that directly affect the lives	Personal interests and purposes are prime reasons for granting attention; what

Feature

of listeners. You relate the cost-of-living index to listeners' food budgets and breakfast tables, or you make listeners see that *their* future lives depend on the science-environment contest.

7. *Specificity.* Presentation of precise detail. You say "spreading oak" instead of "tree," or you show a model or mock-up instead of just describing, or you give descriptions for which listeners can fill in details, as Dick Barnes did with campus scenes (see pages 46–47).

8. *Intensity.* The force of any aspect of communication—of voice, movement, or energy of language. Speech allows wide variations in intensity levels: of sound, of physical action, of vividness or color in language. You increase loudness for emphasis; you move more abruptly or sweepingly than usual; you lean toward listeners, or point, or you say with deliberateness, "This next point is the most important one," or you say, "The floor was littered with garbage" instead of "covered with debris," which would be less specific and so less intense.

9. *Humor.* Introduction of exaggeration, incongruity, irony, word play, unexpected turns of thought or phrase. You might speak of a small-town mayor as a "monarch" or of football as "agitating a bag of wind" or of jogging as "running with no place to go."

Basis of influence

seems to touch life itself has special significance for all.

The more concrete or specific any concept, the more easily it is acquired by humans—provided the detail does not obscure the nature or meaning of the *whole*.

Within limits too complicated to explain here, the impact of any stimulus tends to vary with the intensity of the stimulus; also, noticeable *changes* in stimuli and *contrasts* between intensities of stimuli draw attention to the *dissimilarities* and to *change*.

The nature of response to humor is not fully understood. Several things seem involved: the attractions of the *novel* or unexpected, the satisfactions of safely regaining the *familiar* after having unfamiliar expectations built up and then reversed, the satisfactions of *contrast* between reality and unreality.

All listeners are psychologically attuned to certain forms of speech content, especially to the forms listed in the columns just given. In view of what we have said earlier in this chapter about the general nature of listening, all talk ought to be as much as possible marked by the nine features we have just described and illustrated. There is virtually no subject and no situation for which the first eight of these features would not be appropriate; only humor can sometimes be out of place. Each of the features has to be *constructed* by a speaker—none is inherent in a subject or a situation.

A measure of your art in speaking is the extent to which you are willing and able to pepper your talk judiciously with activity, realism, specificity, and the rest.

To search for such ideas and language is to be sensitive to the human possibilities of rhetorical situations, subject matter, and language. This takes knowledge of the resources of public speech, of course, but it also requires attitudes that have come to be called aspects of "rhetorical sensitivity." A rhetorically sensitive person is one who:

1. Accepts role taking (functioning differently in different situations) as part of functioning as a human being.
2. Attempts to avoid routine verbal behavior.
3. Is characteristically willing to undergo the strain of adaptation.
4. Tries to distinguish between all information about anything and information that is practically suitable for communication.
5. Understands that an idea can be represented in a good many different ways, i.e., knows that there is never just *one* way of saying anything.[18]

Points 2, 3, 4, and 5 in this list relate directly to using the rhetorical features we have just discussed. To try to introduce them into your speech *is* to avoid the routine; it *is* to adapt to the natures of listeners; it *is* selection of the most communicable aspects of available information; and it *is* to recognize that some ways of saying things are rhetorically better than others.

This chapter has been about the *general* things one must recognize about situations and human beings if one is to be rhetorically effective. One of our hopes is that from reading the chapter you will see why we can never give you formal rules that will work the same everywhere. One can't speak effectively "by the numbers," as we said at the beginning. Every rhetorical situation makes at least slightly different demands, and the only way to effective, artistic public speech is through *thinking out* the allowances of each specific situation and audience as you prepare to meet them. The authors we just quoted have described the task especially well:

> The rhetorically sensitive person is . . . always unsure, always guessing, continually weighing. The rhetorically sensitive person deals with the most slippery of intellectual stuff, the values, attitudes, and philosophical predispositions of others. But once the rhetor understands that he must cope with the contingent, that he necessarily swims in a sea of probabilities when engaging another in discourse, once he appreciates that the complexities and inconsistencies of men are given in the interpersonal equation, then social cohesion becomes possible. . . . [Then] we can begin to grapple optimistically with the problems of rhetorical creation and adaptation that social interactions simply demand of us.[19]

Neither you nor we will ever create the science of audience analysis that Plato dreamed of in the quotation at the head of this chapter. We will not be truly adaptive speakers (or writers!) until we understand that every communication is a *new* problem in probabilities. *What* probabilities have to be taken into account we have tried to state in terms that apply everywhere: the probable influences of biology, age, sex, intelligence, commitment to belief, and the universal preference for some kinds of communicative expression over others. Working out what those forces invite and allow in a particular rhetorical situation is slippery intellectual stuff, indeed. But rhetorical sensitivity and creation of influential speech have their beginnings exactly there—in how one diagnoses and *thinks about* what a rhetorical situation is and what people are like when they are listeners. We have given you the topics and some guidelines for this kind of thinking. What conclusions are accurate for the next situation you will enter, we cannot say. You must figure that out when you get the specific data about the situation and the particular people in it. And so it will be for the following situation, and the next, and the next. What we have given you are directions on *how* to think and *what* to think about. Follow that plan and the probabilities are that you can construct a "fitting" response to each situation.

When you have formed your general judgments concerning your next rhetorical situation, you will need to rework your goals and assemble the ideas that will fit both you and the situation. Traditionally this stage of preparation has been called *invention*. The term suggests what must go on at this stage: discovery, sorting, research, forming proofs and clarifications, and humanizing. Our next three chapters explore the problems and options that arise as you move into this phase of creative activity.

EXERCISES

Written

1. Write a careful analysis of some rhetorical situation with which you are familiar (involving a fraternal group, club, religious congregation, or some specific occasion for speaking) giving special consideration to the following:
    a. the special allowances and requirements of the situation
    b. chief biological wants and needs, if any, that affect the audience
    c. special social wants and needs, if any, that affect the audience
    d. any special characteristics of age, sex, expectation, knowledge, and attitudinal commitment that all speakers should take into account

    When you have completed the analysis, indicate what *special* adaptations any speaker entering this situation will have to make.

2. You are to prepare a short speech using the central idea: "Television should be used as a major resource in general education." Outline the major points you might make in such a speech if it were to be given to audience *a* below; then outline the major points you might try to make if the speech were for audience *b* below. Justify any differences there may be in the two outlines.
    a. An audience of twenty college students aged seventeen to twenty-two, made up of ten men and ten women, assembled for an informal class on study habits organized for students whose academic records do not "meet the potentialities indicated by standardized aptitude-test results."

b.   An audience of twenty college students aged nineteen to twenty-two, all cadet teachers in an elementary school, attending one of a series of weekly seminars. The seminar topic for this meeting is "Motivation." There are eighteen women and two men in the group.

3.   Using the text or a recording of any speech, identify the points at which the speaker seems to have adapted content for the specific purpose of suiting it to one or another of the audience characteristics discussed in this chapter. Identify and evaluate the effectiveness with which he or she took advantage of special resources to make the speech fit the particular situation.

Oral

1.   With four or five classmates work out through discussion an outlined description of your class as a rhetorical situation for the next group of talks to be given in your class. The subpoints of written exercise 1 above may serve as starting points for your descriptive outline.

      Optional. As an exercise in group reporting, assign parts of your completed outline to each member of your group and, together, make a joint classroom presentation of your conclusions.

2.   Do the necessary research and then report orally to your class on one of the following subjects: the psychological process called reinforcement; the psychological process called suggestion; the social (or ethical or other) values of college students today; the expectations of ceremonial audiences; the unique expectations of audiences that have power to make policy or legislate; authority (or evidence) as a source of persuasion; theories of crowd behavior; Sherif and Sherif's concepts of "latitudes of acceptance and rejection" (see note 16 of this chapter).

3.   Prepare and deliver an oral report on the methods of audience analysis and adaptation used by a trial lawyer, preacher, or political speaker you have observed or read about.

4.   Prepare and deliver a talk on some aspect of audience research, advertising or market research, or the relation of market research to industrial design.

5.   With several of your colleagues, conduct a discussion of the human interests appealed to and the special rhetorical features built into this passage from President Ronald Reagan's Inaugural Address, January 20, 1981:

> This is the first time in our history that this ceremony has been held on the West Front of the Capitol Building. Standing here we face a magnificent vista, opening up on this city's special beauty and history. At the end of this open mall are those shrines to the giants on whose shoulders we stand.
>
> Directly in front of me, the monument to a monumental man, George Washington, father of our country. A man of humility who came to greatness reluctantly. He led America out of revolutionary victory into infant nationhood.
>
> Off to one side, the stately memorial to Thomas Jefferson. The Declaration of Independence flames with his eloquence.

And then beyond the reflecting pool, the dignified columns of the Lincoln Memorial. Whoever would understand in his heart the meaning of America will find it in the life of Abraham Lincoln.

Beyond these monuments to heroism is the Potomac River, and on the far shore the sloping hills of Arlington National Cemetery with its row upon row of simple white markers with crosses and Stars of David adding up to only a tiny fraction of the price that has been paid for our freedom.

Each one of these markers is a monument to the kind of hero I spoke of earlier. Their lives ended in places called Belleau Wood, The Argonne, Omaha Beach, Salerno, and halfway round the world on Guadalcanal, Tarawa, Pork Chop Hill, The Chosin Reservoir, and a hundred rice paddies and jungles of a place called Vietnam.

ENDNOTES

1. Plato, *Phaedrus,* pp. 271–72, trans. G. M. A. Grube, in *Plato's Thought* (Boston: Beacon Press, 1958), p. 214.

2. Don Ihde, *Listening and Voice: A Phenomenology of Sound* (Athens, Ohio: Ohio University Press, 1976), p. 182.

3. G. R. Miller, M. Burgoon, and J. Burgoon, "Functions of Human Communication in Changing Attitudes and Gaining Compliance," in C. C. Arnold and J. W. Bowers, eds., *Handbook of Rhetorical and Communication Theory* (Boston: Allyn and Bacon, in press).

4. Giraud Chester, *The Ninth Juror* (New York: Random House, 1970), p. 104. Mr. Chester, once a teacher of speech and broadcasting and later a broadcasting executive, wrote this interesting book to recount his experience as a juror in a criminal case in New York City.

5. Bitzer's "The Rhetorical Situation" first appeared in *Philosophy and Rhetoric* I (January 1968): 1–14. It received the James A. Winans Award for Distinguished Scholarship in Rhetoric and Public Address in 1968. The passage quoted here is from Bitzer's "Functional Communication: A Situational Perspective," in Eugene E. White, ed., *Rhetoric in Transition* (University Park: Pennsylvania State University Press, 1980): 21–38. This later essay offers "some modifications and extensions" of Bitzer's earlier views.

6. These three statements are adapted from Hadley Cantril, *The Psychology of Social Movements* (1941; republished New York: John Wiley & Sons, 1963). The original statements appear on pp. 76–77 of the 1963 republication.

7. The classic experiments on group pressure and individual judgments were conducted by S. E. Asch. They showed that college students regularly gave wrong judgments about the lengths of lines when a majority of the group of eight took what were in fact wrong positions. When these experiments are cited as evidence that people overwhelmingly conform to the behaviors of those around them, it is usually forgotten that *if just one other group member agreed on a judgment,* most of Asch's subjects held out for their own *right* judgments about the lines. See Bernard Berelson and Gary A. Steiner, *Human Behavior: An Inventory of Scientific Findings* (New York: Harcourt, Brace and World, 1964), pp. 335–36. Furthermore, more recently it has been argued that at least 32 percent of the conformity Asch claimed to have found was actually "adoption of a new public position, while the private position remains unchanged from what it was before." See Lawrence S. Wrightsman et al., *Social Psychology for the Seventies* (Monterey, Calif.: Brooks/Cole Publishing Co., 1972), p. 481. Wrightsman and his colleagues list among the "unresolved issues in the study of conformity and nonconformity" the facts that the natures of *non*conformity have been far

less studied than the presence of conforming *overt* behavior, and that psychological research has generally not distinguished overt compliance with unchanged private opinion from compliance in consequence of conformingly changed opinion.

8. Representative examples of such research are summarized by Dennis Gouran and B. Aubrey Fisher, "The Functions of Human Communication in the Formation, Maintenance, and Performance of Small Groups," in C. C. Arnold and J. W. Bowers, eds., *Handbook of Rhetorical and Communication Theory* (Boston: Allyn and Bacon, Inc., in press).

9. Wolfgang von Buddenbrock, *The Senses,* trans. Frank Gaynor (Ann Arbor: University of Michigan Press, 1958), p. 12.

10. Bernard Berelson and Gary A. Steiner, *Human Behavior: An Inventory of Scientific Findings* (New York: Harcourt, Brace and World, 1964), p. 100.

11. From *The Rhetoric of Aristotle,* translated and edited by Lane Cooper, pp. 132–37, bk. II, chaps. 12–14. © 1932, renewed 1960 by Lane Cooper. Reprinted by permission of Prentice-Hall, Inc., Englewood Cliffs, New Jersey.

12. Berelson and Steiner, *Human Behavior,* pp. 212–15.

13. This evidence is reviewed by Robert N. Bostrom and Carol L. Bryant, "Factors in the Retention of Information Presented Orally: The Role of Short-Term Listening," *Western Journal of Speech Communication* XLIV (Spring 1980): 137–45. The authors also make the important point that standard listening tests may not measure *all* of the processes involved in listening.

14. Ralph L. Rosnow and Edward J. Robinson, *Experiments in Persuasion* (New York: Academic Press, 1967), p. 198.

15. R. E. Lane and D. O. Sears, *Public Opinion* (Englewood Cliffs, N.J.: Prentice-Hall, 1964), p. 51.

16. For general discussion see Carolyn Sherif, Muzafer Sherif, and Roger Nebergall, *Attitude and Attitude Change: The Social Judgment-Involvement Approach* (Philadelphia: W. B. Saunders Company, 1965). A particularly inclusive experiment generally confirming the points made here is C. David Mortensen and Kenneth Sereno, "The Influence of Ego-Involvement and Discrepancy on Perceptions of Communication," *Speech Monographs* XXXVII (June 1970): 127–34.

17. K. D. Frandsen found this a clear characteristic of a sample of Peace Corps Volunteers. "Haiman's Revised Open-Mindedness Scale: A Comparative Study of Response Patterns," *Speech Monographs* XXXIV (August 1967): 389–91.

18. Roderick P. Hart and Don M. Burks, "Rhetorical Sensitivity and Social Interaction," *Speech Monographs* XXXIX (June 1972): 75–91. The items listed are adapted from this source. The essay deserves to be read in full by all who are interested in the nature of communicative adaptation.

19. Ibid., p. 91.

CHAPTER 4

... Even in the field of sensation, our minds exert a certain arbitrary choice. By our inclusions and omissions we trace the field's extent; by our emphasis we mark its foreground and its background; by our order we read it in this direction or in that. We receive in short the block of marble, but we carve the statue ourselves.
—William James, "Pragmatism and Humanism" [1]

Invention:
Basic processes

Where can you apply the principles of this chapter in everyday life?

1. Wherever you need to find discussable subjects in situations that don't dictate what is to be talked about.
2. Where you need to know what can be said about a subject you are somewhat familiar with.
3. Wherever you need to do research on a familiar or unfamiliar topic.
4. Wherever you need to decide whether speech or some other method is best for presenting information.
5. Where you need to adapt information to audiences who have limited knowledge or who doubt what you need to tell them.

When evaluating someone else's speech consider:

1. Has the speaker chosen the topics of thought that are most important for accomplishing his or her purpose in this situation?
2. To what extent does the material the speaker uses provide *both* logical support and interest value for what is said?
3. Has the speaker used the most effective media of communication in presenting his or her materials?
4. To what extent has the speaker chosen ideal rhetorical devices by which to make difficult ideas intelligible and doubted ideas credible?
5. What gives this speech the "stamp of originality"?

At this point we begin a three-chapter exploration of principles and methods of discovering what to say in public speech. The traditional name for this topic is *rhetorical invention*. The task is to discover what shall be the *content* of a communication. In this chapter we shall discuss how to uncover and think about ideas that could be useful in speaking. In the next chapter we shall deal with methods of making useful ideas significant for listeners, and in the third of this series of chapters we shall treat ways of specially adapting ideas to specific purposes you may adopt in speaking.

Most of you who read this book will be students enrolled in courses in oral communication. Classroom speaking will be part of your course work. In a class, choosing subjects to talk about often creates a special problem in invention, and because this is so we shall pause to discuss choosing subjects for practice speeches, even though in nonclassroom speaking subjects are usually dictated by the situations or by what the speakers are known to be interested and expert in. In any case what we shall say about choosing subjects will be practical for any occasion on which you are free to speak on anything you choose.

CHOOSING SUBJECTS

A good subject for a speech ought to meet several commonsense tests. The subject ought to be significant for the listeners. It should also be appropriate for you because you are the person who must try to create a purposeful human relationship through and about the subject. And, of course, you should be able to say what you need to say about the subject within the time and within any other restraints imposed by the situation in which you will speak.

These are standard tests of a suitable subject for any speech, but they don't help you to locate a specific, satisfying subject. There is, however, a practical way of locating promising subjects. It is called *brainstorming*. We recommend it to you as a way of discovering interesting topics.

The basic strategy is to let your mind run freely over all kinds of subject matter. Suspend your doubts and critical inclinations temporarily. Try simply to notice what is interesting in the world about you and within you. Our next paragraph illustrates how the process can work. Subjects discovered are printed in brackets following the freely flowing thoughts that brought them to mind. The paragraph is a true account of discussable ideas generated by one of your authors as he sat in his study-recreation room and spent eight minutes looking about and jotting down subjects as they occurred to him.

There is a pool table in the room [kinds of recreation, games, amusement, amusement taxes, the recreation industries]. The walls are lined with books, and the nearest shelf contains books on English literature [famous authors, the study of literature, interesting novels and poetry, England, English versus American literature]. There are some edited typescripts on a small table [problems of writing, the publishing industry, the processes of editing, the requirements of scholarship in any academic field]. A stereo set is at the end of the room [broadcasting, competition between AM and FM radio, the recording industry, favorite recordings and artists, regulation of mass communication media]. An electric clock hangs on the wall [efficient uses of time, clock collecting and kinds of timepieces, historical ways of keeping time, "clocking" athletic events]. The corner of a neighbor's house is visible through the window [architecture, the construction industry as a barometer of the economy's condition, insulation and other methods of energy conservation, engineering advances in methods of heating and cooling]. Some trees and vines are also visible [forestry and horticulture, plant diseases, landscaping, community planning, industrial zoning and pollution control, use of natural resources]. This brainstorming is being done for a textbook [education suggests more possibilities than there is time to pursue just now, but it is a rich topic].

It took eight minutes to look about and jot down these topics for possible discussion. It took twelve more minutes to organize and to type them up. By the most conservative count more than thirty-five discussable subjects were discovered, organized, and recorded in twenty minutes. If you had looked around the same room and outside of it, you would have thought of some of the same topics and of a good many different ones that reflected *your* personal knowledge and interests. Furthermore, you could, if you wanted to, create interesting talks on aspects of several of the topics your author thought of. And if you do your own brainstorming in the same way, wherever you are right now, you will come up with even more promising possibilities that suit you as a potential speaker. Try it. Look up from this page and let your thoughts run freely. Jot down each idea that occurs to you. You will end with several subjects you might make a speech about. A different way of brainstorming is to think about your classroom and the people who will be there. What do the room and the people suggest? Look forward to pages 213–15 where Alma Franco's outline appears. She surely arrived at her so closely adaptive subject and supporting ideas by thinking about her classroom and her class as sources of interesting, discussable subjects.

Brainstorming for usable speech subjects is not daydreaming; it is productive and fun if it has a purpose, for the world reveals most interesting features and problems if we look at it freely. Other ways of using brainstorming in invention include walking along library shelves noting the book titles, or watching closely any group of people, animals, machines, or plants to see what discussable topics their features suggest. Another method is to start with the name of any class of things and enumerate the items that belong to that class. Try "clothing," "vehicles," "monuments," "celebrities," or "inventions." See whether interesting and usable instances come to mind as you think about the things that fall into these classes. The first time we wrote this list of four items, "vehicles" immediately suggested "hang gliding" because we had both watched some hang gliders soaring the evening before. Do you know some odd, interesting, or especially important things about some kind of vehicle or invention—or whatever?

When, by using one of the brainstorming processes we have discussed, you have accumulated a list of available topics, the next step is to cull the list for *live* possibilities —significant topics that interest *you*. Don't worry yet about whether a topic is manageable, and don't worry about whether your audience will automatically be interested. If a subject is significant *for you,* there is probably some way to trim or expand or otherwise adapt it to fit your particular audience and situation. The first test is whether some aspect of a topic holds significance and interest for you. It need not be patently within your present knowledge and preparation. If you can and want to learn more about it than your audience knows, you have a live possibility that you can begin to refine into an appropriate subject for a specific speech. The important thing at this stage is to choose *something* you can begin to shape into a talk. Dawdling and choosing overworked kinds of subjects are two enfeebling faults when you need to find a subject for a speech.

A colleague of ours who studied diaries of more than a thousand college students in speech classes found that a consistent difference between good speakers and poor speakers was that the good speakers chose subjects for speeches carefully but swiftly and then stuck with their choices. Most of their available time went into preparation. Poor speakers consistently reported that they spent days trying to settle on acceptable subjects. We do not know just how indecisiveness is related to poor speaking, but the evidence is clear that good speakers choose subjects promptly and stick with them; poor speakers do not. If indecisiveness is your problem, it could be useful to keep a simple chart of the hours you spend on each phase of speech preparation: choosing a subject, locating your specific purpose, searching for further ideas, outlining, rehearsing. Perhaps if you see in graphic form where you actually spend your time, you will be able to use time more efficiently by setting deadlines for the various tasks.

A second practice that endangers success in speaking is choosing overworked subjects. This comes about in two ways. Some students find *an* article on what is to them an unusual subject and without any further investigation adopt that subject. Then if the subject happens to be very popular in the press, the speakers unknowingly bring to their listeners something everyone already knew—having read about it somewhere else. We think of a period when it seemed every magazine and newspaper feature section was carrying articles on child abuse. One of our students read one such article, based a classroom speech on it, and in the discussion period found that a half-dozen of her classmates knew more about the subject than she did because they had run across better articles than hers. Just a little research in current periodicals would have enabled this speaker to bring some *news* about child abuse because she would then have known her subject more broadly than her peers. It was the narrowness of her research that confined this speaker to the aspects of her subject that were commonplace; there was plenty to be learned about the subject that was not commonplace or overworked.

The other, more obvious kind of overworked subject is the one about which there is little or nothing new to say *if the subject is treated conventionally.* Who doubts that "Advertising Is Big Business" or "Christmas Is Too Commercial" or "Travel Is Broadening" or that "We Need to Keep Physically Fit"? Conceived in the ways we have phrased the subjects here, these are trite subjects that promise no significant news for anyone. However, the *consequences* of massive advertising, what to *do about* the commercialization of Christmas, how to *get the most out of* travel, and how to *evaluate* physical fitness programs are all matters about which almost anyone could profitably use some information and counsel. Our point is simply that to avoid shopworn subjects you need to discriminate needed, interesting, useful aspects of topics from aspects of the same topics about which your listeners have no need to know or already do know. There is probably no overworked subject if you make this discrimination. To make it is actually to begin to fit your subject to the situation you will enter.

The heart of what we have been saying about choosing subjects for classroom speeches is this. If a subject for your next speech is not obvious, the way to move swiftly and efficiently is to brainstorm for possibilities and then cull these possibilities for live options that can be used to focus on a specific goal for a specific speech. Begin your selecting by entertaining seriously those topics that especially interest you and about which you know or can find something that will make them interesting to others. This done, settle promptly on one of your most intriguing options so you can concentrate the rest of your preparation time on shaping a specific speech that suits both you and the requirements of your rhetorical situation.

CLASSROOMS AS RHETORICAL SITUATIONS

A cliché of modern education says that classrooms are artificial settings, unlike the "real world." To the contrary, we believe that a speech class can and ought to be treated as a real-life rhetorical situation, different from others chiefly in the facts that *practice* is understood as part of the business to be carried out and that the audience is perhaps more generous and helpful than most outside audiences. As is true almost everywhere, your classroom audience is eager to learn and to be interested. And it has all the general characteristics of audiences that we discussed in Chapter 3. However, your classroom audience is special in that it is made up of people with a common interest in seeing one another grow as communicators; they will help you to refine your skills if you invite them to. And they offer you another advantage: they comprise an audience you can learn about rather easily because you will be with them for a longer time than is usual with other audiences.

The issue for you as you evolve a speech for a classroom situation is whether you will treat your listeners as the real people they are. This issue will confront you every time you choose an idea for inclusion in your talk, at every step of formulating your central idea, and at every decision about how to organize and express your thoughts and feelings. In every such decision you either reach toward your listeners as real people or you separate yourself from them by disregarding their knowledge, interests, and concerns.

The basis of the art of public speech is discovery of where and how the speaker's knowledge, interests, and purposes *meet* the knowledge, interests, and purposes of the listeners who share the rhetorical situation. We can't say how this "meeting" is to be achieved through a specific subject because we don't know who will be in your audience or what your subject will be, but we can say what your listeners want generally—in a classroom or elsewhere. An eminent psychologist has written:

> ... People want a good opinion of themselves both in their own eyes and in those of others. Self-respect and popular esteem are active needs. If a man is deprived of them he becomes anxious, tense, and restless.... Abilities are rarely useless, and to be able to exercise one's wits may be a means of self-respect and general esteem.[2]

These observations suggest the tests you ought to apply as you shape your central idea and choose lines of thought for a classroom or any other rhetorical situation. Ask yourself: Will this choice respect my listeners' opinions of themselves? Will it contribute to their self-respect? Will it gratify them by inviting them to exercise their own wits? Make these fair and charitable concerns for your listeners your standard tests of what you do as you create speeches, and neither you nor your colleagues will believe the classroom to be an artificial place when you speak.

DISCOVERING LINES OF THOUGHT

When you have committed yourself to a subject for a speech, your next problem in invention will be to find out what you can say about it. Only after you know what is possible to say can you decide what is best to say in the situation you are preparing for. But there is a practical problem here. One cannot know everything about very many things. People spend their lives studying the cells of plant or animal structures or the roles of supply and demand in economics, and the next generation discovers there is still more to be known and understood. It is unlikely, then, that you will ever know everything knowable about any subject you speak on. But that need not prevent you from becoming sufficiently informed *for your purpose in the rhetorical situation* that you will enter. Your task in preparing for public speech is to find out how people think about your subject and then to assemble the ideas that will enable them to think sensibly in those ways. Happily there is a method by which you can efficiently discover the important ways in which people tend to think about any subject you choose to discuss.

The method we propose is actually centuries old. It was recommended and used by such historic figures as Aristotle, Cicero, Francis Bacon, John Milton, as well as by hundreds of lesser speakers, writers, and scholars; it is also a method that is consistent with modern research on learning and concept formation.

The method amounts to this. The things people think and talk about are relatively few. For example, we speak about the *size* of thousands of things. We also consider the *advantages* and *disadvantages* of almost every action we think or speak of. A hundred times in any day we refer to the *causes* and the *effects* of this or that. Therefore, if we can locate the standard ways of thinking listeners are likely to follow in responding to ideas, we will have a checklist, a set of cues or topics, that can guide us in answering the question, What kinds of things could be said about this subject?

A series of experiments has shown that reviewing a list of standard topics of thought helps speakers and problem solvers to think of more and better ideas to use in communication. Even when investigating what they considered uninteresting subjects, students who had brief training in the method we are going to present produced 10 percent more ideas about their subjects than did their peers who thought about the same subjects but without the assistance of any standard list of topics of thought. When the students used subjects they thought were interesting, those who used the list of topics of thought produced an average 17 percent more ideas in a given time.[3] Another experiment using groups of students assigned to solve a social problem showed that the groups who used standard topics of thought as cues in thinking produced significantly more ideas about their problem and developed solutions that were judged superior to those produced by groups working without cues.[4] Additional experiments show that there are a number of different cuing systems that can be helpful to people who want to communicate ideas;[5] the system we are offering you is one of those schemes. In short, if you want to think productively about what you *could* say concerning a subject for a public speech, the steps we are now going to outline and illustrate work and can organize research for a speech so that you needn't spend hours and hours gathering information that, in the end, turns out to be irrelevant to your purpose and your rhetorical situation. The first step in this process is to define the requirements of your situation.

Classify the rhetorical situation

First, you need a way of distinguishing what *kinds* of ideas will be most important in the situation you will enter. By making the kind of situational analysis we have discussed in earlier chapters you can get this kind of assessment. Broadly speaking, rhetorical situations tend to invite one or more of three kinds of ideas. Some situations call predominantly for *advice;* some call predominantly for talk that shows how *facts* ought to be *judged;* some call for *reinforcement* of beliefs and feelings already held by the audience. These are three broad classes of exigences or needs that you will face in speaking. So, if you can decide the dominant kind of content your situation will require, you will have discovered the general types of information you will need most in developing your subject for that situation. You classify your situation as belonging to one of these three types. This tells you which kinds of information are most important for you and which are less important. Here are some illustrations of how you can work.

Whenever an audience has to or ought to decide on a course of action, it is predominantly *advice* that is needed. The basic question for both speaker and listener is: what will be done or left undone, at what cost or benefit? In language we will use later in this book, this kind of situation invites *persuasion about a proposition of policy.* It is a situation in which an alert speaker's central idea is almost certain to contain the words *should, ought to,* or their equivalents. Examples of appropriate central ideas are: "Nurses aides ought to be used more widely in hospital care," or "You should vote in the coming election," or "Internships ought to be given a more prominent place in academic programs."

If you see that you will be entering a rhetorical situation that calls for or allows advice of this sort, you can immediately know that ideas having to do with the expediency (desirability, feasibility, and so forth) of alternative courses of action are ideas you will especially need. These will be facts, theories, experiences, and the like that have to do with rewards and costs in the future and with prospects for happiness for those who act or refuse to act. Most of your initial preparation time, then, ought to be spent finding facts and lines of thoughts that say something about consequences of the actions (and inactions) you expect to discuss. By choosing to talk about "should's" and "ought's" or by recognizing that your situation requires you to do so, you isolate a crucial kind of content your speech must include.

In a second class of rhetorical situations audiences function as judges of facts and events rather than as deciders of future action. Rhetoricians have traditionally discussed these situations by pointing to the situations in courts of law, but modern speakers need to take a broader view. Audiences render judgments about facts and events in many situations. When they seek or are given information, they must judge the accuracy, sufficiency, and relevance of the data they receive. Most of what one needs to say in a speech of inquiry deals with what the facts are and why they are important— though when solutions are considered the situation shifts to focus on policies and future actions. All persuasion about propositions of fact succeeds or fails to some degree according to the judgments of fact that the listeners finally render.

When you need to focus on what is true about something or whether something exists, your job is to get your listeners to interpret facts in light of some code or set of standards. The standards may be the law of the land, the Ten Commandments, the theory of probabilities, the standards of historical research or of doing science, the canons of art criticism, personal standards for distinguishing truth from error, or something else. Whatever the code, your judging listeners will especially need two kinds of knowledge: (1) knowledge about the facts or events they are to judge, and (2) knowledge about the standards they are to use in judging. Once again, as soon as you can see what your listeners will have to *do* in the situation, you will have identified the main kinds of ideas you will need to give.

To restate this guide: If in informing, inquiring, or persuading you are going to ask for *judgments,* you will need ideas that define and clarify whatever is to be judged and you will need information that clarifies the standards to be used in judging. You may need other information too, but these two kinds of content will be essential. And here are three subsidiary questions that can be helpful to you in deciding how much and what kinds of factual-judgmental information you will need to gather for this kind of situation. Ask yourself: What facts must I supply to give listeners enough knowledge of the facts? Will I need to say anything about what is relevant and what is irrelevant to the judgments they must make? Will I have to supply the standards for judging, or will the audience already know the standards and how to apply them? Your answers to these questions further focus the list of especially important ideas you have to find—in your own mind or elsewhere.

There are also situations in which the main exigence or need is to have old beliefs strengthened, familiar beliefs made more firm, convictions deepened, or familiar knowledge rendered important or amusing or diverting. In such situations the audience neither seeks nor very much wants new judgments and new courses of action. Commencement exercises are such situations. So are many worship services, service club meetings, fellowship meetings, banquets, and political rallies. People who go to commencement exercises accept the worth of education; worshipers accept the greatness of their deity; fellowship groups accept the worth of being together. All wish the "good" that brings them together to be magnified, deepened, enriched, or even exaggerated.

This kind of situation invites you to connect your specific subject with what the audience values. In some cases you may need to show that what you are talking about threatens those values. In either case you are reinforcing existing views. This calls for material that connects your subject with well-known virtues such as justice, courage, moderation, gentleness, power, friendship, and devotion. If you need to reinforce views *against* something, you will need to connect the views you oppose with whatever your hearers think of as the opposite of virtues or strengths: meanness, excess, ignorance, weakness, faithlessness, and the like. In short, if you are to enter a situation where reinforcement is the main task, your initial research should center on discovering what virtues are associated with whatever it is that you and your audience are committed to.

To summarize what we have said so far about rhetorical invention, we have proposed that you (1) get an understanding of the rhetorical situation you will enter, (2) decide on the subject you will speak about, (3) classify your situation as one of the three types we have just described, and (4) begin the research phase of preparation by exploring your own mind and other sources for the kinds of material your type of situation uniquely requires. To proceed in this way is not to suppose that you will need no other kinds of material for the final speech. The procedure simply sends you toward your *most important* types of material *first*. That saves time and effort. You do not run around in your thinking or in a library gathering speech material that will not fit your rhetorical situation and your purpose. The time to gather miscellaneous material is when you know you need it.

Here is an illustration of beginning the process of invention as we have proposed. The situation we will imagine occurs annually in most colleges and universities. At some time in an academic year there is an orientation program or a careers day on which students who have chosen their major subjects of study talk to incoming or lowerclass students about what it's like to be a major in this or that subject or academic program. Almost anyone might be invited to make such a talk on what is special about chemical or environmental engineering, journalism, Hispanic studies, speech communication, or any of the hundreds of other concentrations college students can choose. Let us suppose you have been asked to make such a talk to a group of students who have not chosen their majors.

So we can be realistic in our example, we will suppose that you are majoring in environmental engineering—a rather new field in engineering. As you come out of your chemistry lab, a friend hails you. He says, "I just came from Professor James's class in ecology and water resources, and he says there's a meeting of freshmen engineers on Friday in the Forum Building. Each of the branches of engineering is to have an upperclass major talk about the work in his or her department. Professor James is in charge of eco engineering's schedule, and he wants you to speak for eco engineering. So, get to James's office and get the crib sheets on dirty water and foul air!" Since you are reading this book we piously hope you will know better than to take your friend's last bit of advice. There are better ways to prepare than to rush to a professor for help on such a notice.

As someone who has been around your school for a while, you can diagnose the prospective rhetorical situation rather easily. The audience will be a mixture of still-bewildered and clear-eyed underclassmen and underclasswomen. They will all be interested in engineering careers. Some will have chosen their majors; most will not. Yours being a relatively new kind of program, many students will be vague about environmental engineering as a major and as a career. You know, but many listeners will not know, that your program begins with the usual series of basic courses in the general engineering curriculum, and at the junior year you shift into general courses in ecology and then into a concentration on the relation of engineering to problems of (a) air pollution, (b) water pollution, or (c) sound pollution.[6] But your immediate inventional problem is to decide what portions of what you know about this major deserve to be presented in the situation Professor James is going to ask you to enter.

As soon as you know this much about your prospective assignment, you can begin to sort out what you will need to think up for your talk. You will be entering a situation in which the listeners' most urgent need will be for *facts* about environmental engineering as a curriculum and as a career. But you will want to make your major look good, too; so you will be asking your listeners to *judge* the program a *desirable* one, whether or not they elect to enter it. This is a general meeting where all majors will be discussed; it is not a place to sell or advise people on any one major. It is certainly not a situation in which just reinforcing existing knowledge will meet the exigences. This puts you in a position to begin creating appropriate speech material.

Because you will be asking for judgments on facts you will need to supply, you will need to know and be able to explain and adapt two sorts of information: (1) the details about the environmental engineering program as it is organized at your school, and (2) how the underclassmen and underclasswomen distinguish good from not-so-good in thinking about academic majors in engineering. The first kind of information you can get from reviewing your college catalog and from talking with Professor James and others who direct the program. The second kind of information you can probably find out best by talking with representative underclass and upperclass students about how and why they chose their majors.

There you are. You know what information to pursue immediately. You also begin to see where you are apt to find it, if you do not already have it. Merely deciding that your "rhetorical situation" will be a "judgment situation" focuses you on what it will be most important to invent as material for a speech. If you had been invited to talk at a parents' day gathering, you might decide that *advising* parents on whether they ought to encourage their sons and daughters to investigate environmental engineering as a career would be the best way of responding to their expectations and needs. Then, the *future prospects* of engineering in general and environmental engineering in particular and the demands of these career choices would become the kinds of material to search out in detail. Had you been invited to talk to the organization of environmental engineering majors, you would choose to search for ideas about the *worth* and the exciting prospects of careers in that field.

You do not need to know anything about engineering or the relatively new field of environmental engineering to see the point of our illustration. In any circumstance, you can point your search for speech material in useful, not wasteful, directions if you decide promptly *what you will be asking of your listeners and they of you.* What will you want them to *do:* decide about courses of action, make judgments about facts or events, or develop stronger or less strong attitudes toward what they already know or think? Make that decision, and you will know where to go for information.

MAKING THE DETAILED SEARCH

Once you know the general kinds of information your rhetorical situation is likely to require, the natural thing to do is go and get it if you do not already have it. But what is *it?* As our environmental engineer you could get the university catalog and read its description of the environmental engineering major to your audience. Anyone ought to know this would be a mistake. Why would it be a mistake, beside the fact that this is not a situation in which reading is appropriate? If you regurgitated the catalog's information, you would be (1) depending solely on the editor of the catalog for what needed to be said, and (2) failing to ask whether *this* situation and *this* speech purpose call for any special kinds of information. Our example is extreme, but in principle it illustrates the mistake many student speakers make in invention. They let writers who were writing for readers determine what shall be said in a unique rhetorical situation. The *it* that a speaker should search for in rhetorical invention is subject matter that is both true to the subject and specifically fitted to the situation in which the speech will occur. This means that even when you know everything about a topic, you need to review that knowledge to find out what is and is not promising *speech* material.

A way of thinking that we call *topical review* lets you review what you know and what you can find out for *relevance* to each speech situation you enter. It is part of an ancient yet always usable system of invention that has been known since the days of Aristotle, but is too seldom taken advantage of today. Francis Bacon wrote about this system:

> . . . A faculty of wise interrogating is half of knowledge. For Plato says well, "whosoever seeks a thing, knows that which he seeks for in a general notion; else how shall he know it when he has found it?" . . . The same places [topics] therefore which will help us to shake out the folds of the intellect within us, and to draw forth the knowledge stored within, will also help us to gain knowledge from without; so that if a man of learning and experience were before us, we should know how to question him wisely and to the purpose; and in like manner how to peruse with advantage . . . books and parts of books which may best instruct us concerning what we seek.[7]

The "places" or topics Bacon was writing about were simply a set of headings or cues that identified the standard ways in which people think and talk about subjects that interest them. Running through such a list of "sayables" asking, "Will I need to say anything of that sort?" lets a speaker uncover from memory or other sources a wide array of material *pertinent to a particular speech*. As we pointed out on pages 78–79, recent experimental research has shown that this method of topical review helps students get more ideas, even out of their own memories.

Fortunately a self-cuing method of invention for speaking does not have to be long or complex. The reason is that we talk about a limited number of themes. Treatments of these themes vary, but not the basic ideas themselves. We discuss the same types of ideas over and over. This is not a sign of laziness. It is the natural result of our shared ways of thinking about human affairs. Here is a tolerably complete list of topics we constantly think about and discuss with each other, *no matter what the subject.*

A.   Attributes commonly discussed
    1.   *Existence* or nonexistence of things
    2.   *Degree* or quantity of things, forces, etc.
    3.   *Spatial* attributes, including adjacency, distribution, place
    4.   Attributes of *time*
    5.   *Motion* or activity
    6.   *Form,* either physical or abstract
    7.   *Substance:* physical, abstract, or psychophysical
    8.   *Capacity to change,* including predictability
    9.   *Potency:* power or energy, including capacity to further or hinder anything
   10.   *Desirability* in terms of rewards or punishments
   11.   *Feasibility:* workability or practicability
B.   Basic relationships commonly asserted or argued
    1.   *Causality:* the relation of causes to effects, effects to causes, effects to effects, adequacy of causes, etc.
    2.   *Correlation:* coexistence or coordination of things, forces, etc.
    3.   *Genus-species* relationships
    4.   *Similarity* or dissimilarity
    5.   *Possibility* or impossibility

No speech you are likely to make will contain information related to all of these topics. Neither will every imaginable thought or bit of data be suggested as soon as you ask whether you need to talk about one of these attributes or relationships. The values of reviewing these headings each time you plan a speech or are working on ways to develop a point include two major ones: (1) you will discover that your mind, your books, and other people have more help to offer you than you thought, and (2) you will be testing material for relevance to your situation as you pick it up from your own mind or other sources. Simply ask yourself about each cue: will I need any information about *that?* and have I overlooked anything that's important about *that?* Here is an illustration of how you can use the sixteen topics.

Suppose you have decided to speak to your class on the subject of voting. Suppose, too, that you have passed the stage of narrowing your subject and have decided that your central idea will be that your colleagues ought to vote regularly in local and national elections. Obviously this is going to be a situation in which you will be *advising.* This tells you that ideas about future rewards and costs of voting or not voting are what you need most. With that much in mind, what might happen if you ran through the sixteen topics in the list above? (In what follows we allowed ourselves only two minutes of thought about each topic.)

First try *existence.* Will you need any facts or ideas about the existence of anything? The right to vote exists for every citizen over age eighteen. Your listeners will know that. But it might be worthwhile to emphasize it. *Nonexistence* might remind you that this is a relatively new right for people under twenty-one. We have it; our parents didn't. In this sense voting is a special privilege for your younger listeners. Jot that down. It might be worth working into the speech. In two minutes of thinking about this topic we didn't think of anything else useful to say, so we moved on.

Will there be anything important and pertinent to say about *degree*—the quantity of anything? Yes indeed. You will certainly need figures on how many eighteen to twenty-four year olds there are, what proportion of them voted in recent local and national elections, and whether these were high or low turnouts. If you don't know these data, you will have to find them, so make a note of reminder. *Degree* might also suggest that it would be useful to compare data on voting by younger and older groups. Unless the younger vote less frequently, there will be little point in advising your listeners as *young* voters. If the young vote as much as elders, you ought to speak to your audience as part of the total population. Notice that this topic of *degree* is suggesting several specific kinds of statistical information you will certainly need. There is no question about whether or not you will require this sort of supporting material, and the topical review is indicating *which* statistics will show you how to advise the young voters.

Now try *spatial attributes*. An almost random but potentially useful thought might pop up: how *far* is it to a polling place? If you could find out that none of your listeners would have far to go to cast a vote in the next election, you could make the claim: "See how easy it is!" Make a note to investigate where most of your classmates live and where their polling places would be. (If yours is a residential school, getting this information will be easy; if most of you are commuters, it may be impossible to get the information.) In any case, this line of thought ought to remind you that the cost in inconvenience is something to be dealt with. *Spatial attributes* also ought to suggest that you think about or find out whether there are any special voting patterns in the area or areas from which most of your listeners come. There might be a basis for arguing, "We ought to top the competitors in voting" or "In our area the record is shameful." Make a note about trying to get some comparative, regional figures.

Try *time* as a topic. Some lines of thought are obvious. Elections are set for specific times. Are those times convenient for college students or not? Are there grounds for encouraging get-out-the-vote drives on your campus? To do so might be a good proposal if important elections occur during your regular sessions.

Does *motion or activity* suggest anything sayable or any information you will need? Two minutes of thinking about it produced nothing for us, but maybe you will think of something pertinent. Good luck. One should not worry if a cue does not trigger useful ideas. Go on to the next cue.

Form, either physical or abstract, can suggest registration forms. If one of your listeners is not registered to vote, how does he or she get registered? What forms must be filled out? Sent to whom? By what times? This is going to be crucial information to include in this speech, for your goal is to get an action. Then you must be prepared to show your listeners *how* to act in the way you are advising. Make a note to get all of this kind of information and, if possible, a sample of the registration forms (if there are any) your listeners must have completed if they are to be eligible to vote.

Now, *substance:* physical, abstract, or psychophysical. That can suggest that voting is a right, and perhaps you will want to argue that it is an obligation of citizenship. Jot down that possibility. You may or may not want to use it, but keep it for future consideration. Nothing else comes to mind as this paragraph is being written. So we move on.

Capacity to change seems rich as a topic. What changes can a higher voting level bring about—particularly in the areas where your listeners would vote? What changes have been brought about by students' votes? A number of mayors have been elected by the votes of eighteen to twenty-four year olds. This is a line of research you should surely follow. Write down the reminder. *Change* also suggests one of the mental obstacles you are going to have to overcome: the notion that "one vote can't change anything." You must find material to refute that. Remind yourself to see if you can find instances of close votes on bond issues, ordinances of concern to college students —housing codes, regulation of entertainment, law enforcement, and the like.

Potency or capacity to further or hinder anything may suggest that a high level of voting by eighteen to twenty-four year olds could prevent something they would prefer to prevent in their areas. Graft? Overrepresentation of one party or a clique? Some ecological danger? If anything like that is suggested to you, jot it down for future consideration. Would you have any use for a slogan like "youth power"? Make note of that; you may want it.

Desirability in terms of rewards or punishments can remind you that no ideas about the costs of *not* voting have cropped up yet. Any of the desirable features of voting could be turned around into losses if that seems wise when the speech is finally shaped, but that can wait. The loss of your voice in public affairs might make a theme worth developing briefly, so that ought to be jotted down. In the specific areas where your listeners would vote, there may be special losses if the young do not vote. You ought to remind yourself to check into that when you have found out about their voting areas.

Feasibility brings up the old problem of being in one place and being registered to vote in another—voting is not feasible because it is so awkward for some people. If your audience is mainly living away from their permanent homes, you must be ready with precise information about two things: how to change one's voting registration and how to secure and vote by absentee ballot. If you do not know about these procedures in your state or the political units that make the rules for most of your audience, you must find out about them. Also try to think and make note of who or what would be the best source to consult on this. That it is feasible for everyone, or nearly everyone, in your audience to vote is a point you will have to establish or you will be unlikely to secure a genuine commitment to act from your listeners.

Turn now to the relationships in the list of topics. For any subject and purpose, certain of these relationships are likely to be crucial ways of showing how your ideas fit together so as to lead to conclusions. This will be true of how details relate to major points and how major points add up to support your central idea.

Causal relations: is there anything important to be known and said about them? Unquestionably. What are the consequences if college-age voters stay away from the polls? What happens if they vote in large numbers? In other words, what are the causal relations between voting and other facts? This is a crucial relationship to be shown in your speech. Failure to vote at least causes a part of the population to go unrepresented in public affairs. You will need to show how losses *follow from* not voting and how benefits *arise from* voting. Thinking about the topic of causation quickly reveals that for your case to be strong you must show *direct* causal relations between voting and specific public consequences.

Correlation, or the coexistence of things, does not suggest much. All we can think of is that you might reasonably tell listeners that a satisfying sense of having done something worthy and responsible goes with voting. Is anything more suggested to you?

Genus-species relationships are especially important when you are defining things or differentiating things from each other. If your speech were about civil rights in general instead of voting, it would be important to talk about what specific *rights* (species) properly fall under the *class* (genus) of *civil* rights, and *civil rights* would need to be differentiated from *civil privileges.* But for a speech advising a class to exercise their rights to vote, no such differentiations seem important. Everyone will know what voting is. It might be important to make some differentiations between voting regularly and voting as an absentee, but that will depend on whether you find out your listeners are or are not familiar with the voting laws of their areas.

Similarity-dissimilarity as a topic ought to remind you that you must investigate whether most of your listeners come under the same voting regulations or fall under different ones. If most are from the same state, you will have little trouble; if considerable numbers come from different states with different voting regulations, you will have to find out what those differences are and decide later how important it will be to talk about their similarities and dissimilarities. This topic could also suggest looking into the ways in which the rights and the voting records of your listeners are like and unlike the rights and records of other groups of young people in other parts of the country, among young people not attending college, and of young people in other countries. Maybe there will be ways of making your listeners feel proud or ashamed or responsible if you have such comparisons and contrasts to use.

Finally *possibility or impossibility* can suggest at least one very important idea for your speech: it is very seldom impossible for a citizen of the United States to vote. Only a very recent change of residence, conviction of crime, or total physical incapacitation prevents voting in most places. You could build an impressive point from this: Every listener, virtually everyone, *can* vote; the only issue is whether each one cares enough and wants to vote. A fairly persuasive case for "obligation" could be made, as we have seen; if you were to connect it with the theme that there are very few real excuses for not voting, the argument could be still stronger.

These are examples of the directions in which thought and research can be guided by reviewing sixteen familiar topics in the earliest stages of speech preparation. This whole review can be completed thoughtfully in twenty minutes to a half-hour once you know your subject and the kind of situation you are going to enter. What does our example show you can get from such a review? At least these things:

1. recovery of some bits of fact and other information about your subject and the nature of your audience
2. some specific *ways* of presenting data and ideas that will have to be covered
3. a list of specific information you ought to gather now that the review is finished

4.   a list of some problems of audience adaptation you will need to consider at a later time in your speech preparation
5.   perhaps, as in the case of the ballots, some notion of what would be desirable visual aids and other materials for demonstration
6.   a list of some things it will be very important to find out regarding your specific audience
7.   recognition of where some of the problems are going to arise in composing this speech—eradication of indifference and the one-vote-can't-change-anything attitude will be a major task in achieving persuasion

From such a review you gain much more than simply a retrieval of data from your memory bank. You get a preview of the research you must do and a preview of some promising ways of building units of the final speech. What you will gain more than repays you for the short time it takes to make a topical review as an early move in rhetorical invention.

FURTHER RESEARCH

Books are among the best places to go for information, but they are *not* the only wells of knowledge. We repeat that *you* are always one of your most valuable sources of information. Perhaps instead of talking about research for speeches, we ought to speak of "recovery, inquiry, and research for speeches." As you prepare to speak, never forget to ask yourself: What have I already read about this? What have I ever heard about it in conversations, in lectures, on radio or television? Have I seen anything firsthand or in photographs? Such questions often stir the memory. You ought thus to explore your memory and check your notebooks as an early step in research.

Other people are excellent resources. What photographer is not happy to answer questions about photography? What traveler is not all too pleased to reminisce about what he or she has seen? What professional person is unwilling to talk about the problems and accomplishments of his or her profession? We all know people who would be happy to supply information; yet, just as we often forget to probe our own minds, we neglect convenient, willing resource persons.

Public officials, teachers, business people, and others are often overlooked as sources of valuable information. One must be careful about seeking assistance from such persons because of the heavy demands on their time, but even the busiest people are frequently willing to grant limited aid to those who know what they want and are able to draw out needed information efficiently. The busier these people are, the more likely they are to have responsible aides and researchers who can provide you with factual information even more readily than their principals. We recall a speech student who wanted to cite a statement the president of her university had made in an unpublished address. She went to the president's personal aide, hoping to see the president. She did not need to see him. The aide was able to produce within minutes a mimeographed copy of the speech the student needed; he was also able to give her a quick review of the occasion and audience for the speech. She had the key information needed for her speech—and at no trouble to the president. Congressmen and other officers have staff members specifically assigned to care for requests for service from their constituents—and this includes supplying documentary information. Many major corporations maintain public-information departments whose business it is to supply data to people interested in their operations. To draw on such resources you need chiefly a very clear idea of what it is you want and knowledge—from prior research—of who is most likely to know what you want to know. Carefully planned, prearranged interviews or clear and precise letters are the usual ways of securing help from busy people. Such interviewing and correspondence ought to be a normal part of an effective speaker's preparation.

Personal investigation is another neglected avenue of research. We would think ill of a person who, after urging us to read Judith Guest's *Ordinary People,* turned out to have only seen the movie. What then of speakers who deplore the low level of television programming without having checked the full program listings and explored the viewing options open to their particular listeners? To take other examples, you are fortunate if you have never been subjected to speeches on juvenile delinquency by speakers who had never visited a youth court, a settlement house, or even talked with young people of the kinds they discuss. One need not be an ex-convict to speak of prisons or a parent to discuss children, but to neglect obvious and convenient opportunities for firsthand inquiry is to miss vital and immediately relevant information.

Do not overlook your friends as resources. Discuss with them ideas you think of presenting to an audience. At the least you will have a test of how these thoughts go over; at best you may come away from such conversation with new information or new directions in which to look for information.

When your subject is one about which your information is limited, it is best to begin research by looking at general books, encyclopedia articles, and survey articles. These will give you background material; usually they will show you the major subtopics under which your subject is normally treated. If you already have a good general background about your subject—as you might well have for the speech about voting that we just imagined—you will probably have no need to consult the general sources. But suppose you wish to speak about the classical Greek theatre, or Greek scientific theories, or Greek politics, or Greek rhetoric. Your topical review of possible ideas and lines of thought would remind you that you will need some general knowledge about the Greek world in which these ideas and institutions were set. Some brief, general, authoritative essay or book on ancient Greek society is what you ought then to seek. Edith Hamilton's *The Greek Way* is a book of this sort that is readily available. You could read it in an evening. Or an encyclopedia article on Greek society could serve your needs. On a different kind of subject it might be important to remember that there are excellent specialized encyclopedias. On any topic concerning modern social psychology the *Handbook of Social Psychology* edited by Gardner Lindzey and Elliot Aronson is almost sure to have an authoritative, general essay. Many other fields have similar encyclopedias and handbooks: philosophy, biological sciences, theology, and social work are just a few.

Whatever the source you use in gathering general material at the outset of research for a speech, your objects in reading should be two: (1) to get an overview of the topic and (2) to secure good leads to other, more detailed information. A dividend you will gain from such reading is a sense of which *aspects* of your subject interest you most and will interest your listeners. It sometimes happens, too, that from checking general sources one finds out that a subject that seemed promising isn't, because it is either too complicated to deal with or there is just too little known and knowable about it. For example, any encyclopedia article on the subject of relativity will quickly show that in most respects this subject is too technical for easy, popular discussion. And any good, general article on the Greek theatre will reveal that the aspect of this subject about which almost nothing is known with certainty is how the actors dressed and moved.

When you search general works you hope you will be led toward specific kinds of information that will complete your understanding and perhaps give you a better idea of where, within your subject, you ought to focus a speech. Here is a hypothetical example and a real example of how this kind of investigation works.

Suppose you have decided that you want to make a public speech about advertising in the United States. Anyone but an expert on that subject ought to begin by looking at some general article. If you consulted the fourth edition of the *Columbia Encyclopedia,* you would find a brief essay under the heading "advertising." You would learn that advertising is discussed under the subheadings of who buys most advertising (food marketers, drug companies, and so forth), the medium of communication used (newspapers, radio, TV, and so on), and the business of advertising agencies—"Madison Avenue business." This breakdown of the subject can show you what you would need to touch on in a talk that tried to cover the whole subject of modern advertising; but more usefully, it shows you some specific aspects of the subject on which you can focus a less comprehensive speech. The same article will give you the names of the leading trade associations (sources of further research material). It also gives the titles and authors of four major, general books on advertising. With just this limited amount of information you are equipped to (1) decide whether and how to narrow your intended speech subject and (2) look at one or more of four authoritative books on your subject.

To give you an actual example of initial research for speaking, one of your authors (Arnold) performed an exercise which we shall now describe.

I imagined I had been assigned to make an informative speech on a subject of my own choosing. Since I had brainstormed for possible subjects (see pages 74–75), I looked back at this record of possibilities. "Clock collecting and kinds of timepieces" was on the list. As I looked at the item this time, I remembered that a few months earlier I had visited a clock museum and found it very interesting. Here was a live possibility, so I decided my subject was clocks and that my central idea would be to inform my listeners of some significant features of clocks—features I must wait to choose until I learned more about clocks. With the assigned purpose of informing, I knew also that what I must gather would be chiefly *facts* about clocks and reasons why those facts should be judged significant and interesting for nonspecialists like my listeners.

These things decided, I entered my university's library and went directly to the reference room. It had just been rearranged! I couldn't see the encyclopedias in their usual place. A reference librarian was glad to show me the new encyclopedia section, and I took down the *Encyclopedia Americana* because it is recognized as a good source and was in the first shelf I came to. Under the heading "clocks" I found a long, well-written article that defined a clock and discussed the history of sundials, water clocks, sand glasses, weight-driven clocks, spring-driven clocks and watches, electric clocks, and quartz-crystal and atomic clocks. There was also a bibliography of twelve books. Some seemed very technical, but two had titles that sounded general enough for my use. They were: G. H. Baillie, *Watchmakers and Clockmakers of the World,* published in 1947, and W. I. Milham, *Time and Timekeepers,* published in 1941. Titles like *Electrical Timekeeping* and *Time Measurement* seemed unpromising except as reference sources to look at later.

Thinking that it is always prudent to check more than one general source to see what information is "standard" and generally thought important by experts in the subject, I turned next to the most famed of encyclopedias, the *Encyclopaedia Britannica.* Again the heading was "clock." The definition given was much the same as in the *Americana,* and subsections of the article were organized, as before, by kinds of driving mechanisms used. However, the *Britannica* article gave detailed explanations and drawings showing how various of these mechanisms worked. Much of this, I thought, was too technical for me to handle in a speech or for a classroom audience's interests. The *Britannica* article also had a section on "The Clock in Decoration." It made the interesting point that as soon as housings were put around the mechanisms of clocks, artists began to develop decorations to suit the shapes and the housing materials. Here was a topic I had not thought of before: our clocks are cultural facts as well as timepieces. One could focus an entire informative speech on that central idea.

The *Britannica* article had a bibliography of thirty items, including most of the books cited in the *Americana.* Again, many were highly specialized, but G. F. C. Gordon's *Clockmaking, Past and Present,* second edition, 1949, seemed a promising source if my speech finally assumed the historical bent that was increasingly suggested to me by what I had read. And were I to make this talk at my own university in Pennsylvania, I certainly ought to check G. H. Eckhardt's *Pennsylvania Clocks,* 1969—a work important enough to make *Britannica*'s bibliography.

At this point I had spent forty minutes in the reference room. I needed to make at least one other check before leaving there. How are clocks and other timepieces being treated *currently* in popular literature? In other words, what's *new* about clocks, watches, etc.? The obvious source was the *Reader's Guide to Periodical Literature.* Moving to that section of the reference room, I looked first at the *Cumulative Guide to Periodical Literature* where entries for the period between 1973 and 1978 were printed. Under "clocks" I found four columns of articles, listed under such subheadings as "clocks and watches," "design and construction," "history," "maintenance and repair," "marketing," "test reports," "antique," "digital," "atomic," and "floral—see environmental art." I was not yet prepared to gather specific information, so I simply studied the entries for (1) what I could learn about current topics about clocks and (2) leads to articles relevant to the specifically historical-cultural view of clocks that I was developing. On the first point I learned two things that were new thoughts: almost four dozen entries had to do with building your own clocks, showing that there must be a strong hobby interest in clocks today, and the word *digital* cropped up in almost a third of all the titles given. Apparently clock building is a feature of our leisure culture today and the digital mechanisms have a technical importance I at this point did not understand. Closely related to the first of these points was the fact that the only historical-cultural articles listed had to do, again, with collecting clocks and building clocks. Here was the hobby theme again. Here, too, was some justification for talking about the history of clocks. With this much background knowledge I left the reference room and went to the other great resource every library has—the card catalog of books held.

Under the heading "clocks" were well over 100 cards. (Had I first looked under "time," I would have found works on mathematics, philosophy, and physics, and a cross-reference card reading "see also clocks.") First, I checked these cards to see whether Baillie's, Milham's, and Gordon's books were in this library. Only Milham's was. Next I thumbed the 100 or so cards, looking for other fairly recent, inviting works that might help me at this stage. I found a most interesting one. It was H. A. Lloyd, *Old Clocks,* fourth edition, 1972. This book had been revised and reissued every seven or eight years since its first appearance in the 1950s. (Always look at library cards for this kind of information!) It must have a good deal of merit. If it were of a historical-cultural character, it would be the kind of source I should read next.

The library was an open-stacks library, so I had to hunt the books I was "betting on" myself. I looked first for Lloyd's book and found it. It had chapters on the mechanical development of clocks, types of clocks (for example, mantel and long-case), European and American clocks, evolution of clocks by chronological periods. Furthermore, the book had a twenty-seven-page first chapter on timekeeping from the beginning of history to the discovery of the pendulum, and the book had eighty plates illustrating technical and stylistic features of clocks. It appeared to be an "all you want to know and more" book on clocks through the ages. Would it be authoritative? Yes. A note in the acknowledgments said that the author of *Americana*'s encyclopedia article had been the final proofreader of the book. He, it turned out, was associated with the Museum of Science in London. Clearly this was a book I should study for the speech I was imagining, but what of Milham's *Time and Timekeepers?*

When I found Milham's book, it was less up to date than Lloyd's but gave a more detailed history of timekeeping. With Lloyd's popular book and Milham's detailed one, I was sure I could build the outline of a sound, interesting speech on any of several aspects of the history of clocks. If I needed still more details later on, it would be easy to find them in the specialized books and magazine articles I now knew how to locate in the encyclopedia articles, the card catalog, and the *Reader's Guide to Periodical Literature.* There was clearly plenty of interesting information for me to learn, organize, and sharpen into a closely focused speech on selected historical-cultural aspects of clocks. The two comprehensive books I had found would be my starting points.

All that I learned in this research expedition was acquired in one hour and fifty minutes. There was no doubt that I had a rich and interesting speech subject that is much discussed today—at least in hobby literature. There was plenty of material available to support a focused, informative speech about historical-cultural developments of timepieces. And it was clear that in a few more hours I could learn enough to prepare that speech.

Had I pursued the inventional processes for this imagined speech further, I would probably have settled on a central idea such as, "Humans have kept time by the sun, water, weights, springs, and electricity," or "Timekeeping has followed the growth in human understanding of energy sources," or "When people encased the clock, engineering and art were wed," or "How your quartz (or digital) clock (or watch) works." The encyclopedia articles and books I had located would give me basic information for any of these speeches. Quite probably, however, they would not furnish me with every detail needed for any one of these speeches. Bits of exact information would have to be gathered from other kinds of sources. Our earlier experiment with a topical review of possibilities for a speech on voting by college students illustrated this. For a speech on voting or about clocks, or almost any other kind of speech, one discovers that specialized information not available in general sources must be located.

For a speech about voting one would need bits of information about when the constitutional amendment lowered the voting age to eighteen, how many people there are in the eighteen- to twenty-four-age (college) group, how many of them had voted in recent elections, what the local laws are concerning registering to vote, and voting records of other countries and other areas of the United States. A speech about timepieces might require details about when and where electricity was first used in timepieces, who discovered that pendulums could be used to regulate clocks, what is meant by Greenwich Mean Time, and so on. When you need these kinds of information, it is time to explore some of the many volumes of classified data: *The World Almanac*; *The Statistical Abstract*; *Facts on File*; the specialized encyclopedias; compendiums of statements like *Bartlett's Quotations*; and other specialized sources like Gavin's *Foul, False, and Infamous: Famous Libel and Slander Cases in History,* and Jane's *Ships of the World* or *Aircraft of the World*. These are sources of isolated, classified facts. Your reading in them will of course be far more selective than in any of the general works.

There is another resource in almost every college and public library that students and faculty members too seldom use. On the library staff is probably someone designated "reference librarian," often with a staff of assistants. These people are hired to help *you* solve research problems, find useful information, and conquer the many indexes and other research facilities of the library. Overwhelmingly they *want* to help you, but they have to be asked—asked clearly so they can understand your needs precisely. Appeal to these people when the routines we have described do not work; they are experts on aids to research.

In all exploratory activities connected with preparing speeches, you should never forget that the purpose of it all is to extract what is necessary to create a *communication that will serve as your personalized way of getting a particular set of responses* from a specific audience. One does not assemble a speech; one collects specific kinds of raw materials out of which one can mold a personal message—a unique composition. Re-

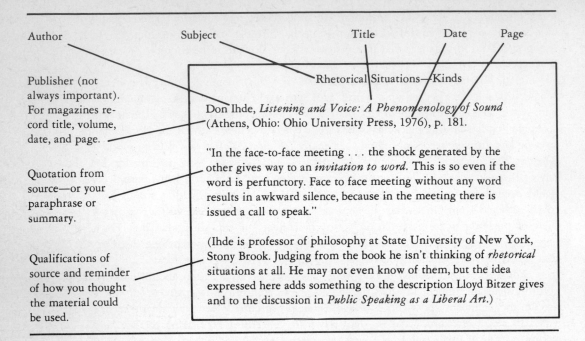

Author   Subject   Title   Date   Page

Publisher (not
always important).
For magazines re-
cord title, volume,
date, and page.

Quotation from
source—or your
paraphrase or
summary.

Qualifications of
source and reminder
of how you thought
the material could
be used.

Rhetorical Situations—Kinds

Don Ihde, *Listening and Voice: A Phenomenology of Sound*
(Athens, Ohio: Ohio University Press, 1976), p. 181.

"In the face-to-face meeting . . . the shock generated by the
other gives way to an *invitation to word*. This is so even if the
word is perfunctory. Face to face meeting without any word
results in awkward silence, because in the meeting there is
issued a call to speak."

(Ihde is professor of philosophy at State University of New York,
Stony Brook. Judging from the book he isn't thinking of *rhetorical*
situations at all. He may not even know of them, but the idea
expressed here adds something to the description Lloyd Bitzer gives
and to the discussion in *Public Speaking as a Liberal Art*.)

FIGURE 4-1 *Note card*

search for speaking properly ends whenever you have collected most of the raw materials for weaving together an original, informed communication that will serve a
specific purpose with the audience that will hear it.

In all research an important but technical matter is: how should you *record*
information you find as you reflect, converse with others, and read? So many speakers
compound their difficulties during research by jotting information randomly on page
after page of notebook paper. If you pause to think how you are going to use such
information, you will take your notes in a very different manner.

The material you acquire in research finally has to be woven together to make
a personal message suited to a particular rhetorical situation. Doing this kind of arranging is clumsy business if you have to turn notebook pages back and forth to re-
discover what you have collected. Suppose you have collected a reasonable amount of
material on cancer and, in thinking about your speech, you decide you should identify
the different *types* of cancer. If all your notes are scattered through a notebook or
on sheets of paper and are ordered as you found them, your information on types of
cancer will be mixed in with other kinds of information about causes, methods of
control, tests for, and so on. But recovering the data on types would be simple if all
your notes were on individual slips of paper or cards, each labeled according to the
subject covered. You could then in a few moments shuffle the cards marked "Cancer—
Kinds" out of your full pack of notes, examine what you have, and decide whether
and how you should discuss this topic.

There are many satisfactory forms for recording information for convenient use during speech composition. Figure 4–1 illustrates one way and identifies the kinds of information you should record.

What you need from any record of information is clear. Your record should be complete enough so you need not make a second trip to the original source. You will want an accurate record of what you found; it must allow items of information to be separated, sorted, and compared in any conceivably useful way. As far as we know, only recording individual units of information on individual slips of paper meets the last requirement. So we say: note separate bits of information on separate slips and put the complete reference to your sources on all slips, or work out some code system for identifying exact sources. Also, note on each slip the qualifications of the source, if you know them, and what it was that made you interested in the item when you took it down. Doing all of this can become tedious, but it saves steps and the bother of wondering later why you wrote something down in the first place. We know from experience the extra steps we have taken in consequence of sloppy note taking, and we have wondered too often why in the world we took down a note. Be forewarned!

When have you collected enough material from thought, conversing, and reading? The general answer is: when you believe you can support or adequately clarify a central idea that suits you and your situation. When you think you can do that, stop researching and put together an outline such as we illustrate in Chapter 8. At this point you don't need to worry about your Introduction. What you need to test is whether you have the needed ideas and back-up material to make your central idea and its subheadings interesting, clear, and credible. We can illustrate this testing process using a central idea and two main points that might contribute to its development.[8]

Central idea:
Buying on credit often has important advantages over immediate payment.

	I. Whenever there's inflation you pay your debts with less costly dollars.
(Idea and support found in research.)	A. L. C. Thurow (MIT economist) says: "Borrowers can now repay their debts with dollars worth just 63 cents in 1975 terms."
(Outlining shows point is undeniable but adaptation to audience is lacking.)	B. [More specifics needed here to make vivid and involve listeners. Get data on how "cheaper dollar" would work for a person who borrowed to pay tuition.]
	C. Reagan Administration forecasts we'll still have 5 to 6 percent inflation in 1983 even if their plans work (UPI story, June 3, 1981).
(Idea from common knowledge.)	II. For most people, buying a house or condominium *must* be a credit purchase.
(General data are missing.)	A. [Get figures on percentage of home purchases on credit.]

(Data from research.)

(Outlining shows data
applying to audience
are needed.)

(With average income
data, entire point
can be clinched.)

(How much is proved
so far is foreseen.)

B. Average price of a home in 1980 was $76,000
(AP dispatch, June 1, 1981).
1. Average income of college graduates in the
U.S. was $_____ in 1980.
2. Average home costs almost _____ times
the average income you and I can expect
a few years from now.

C. Obviously home ownership must be a credit
affair for you, me, and the vast majority of
people.

III. As long as there's inflation, you pay necessary
and optional purchases in ever-declining currency
though your amount is fixed in the debt.

Roughing out an outline in this fashion will enable you to (1) discover where
the gaps are in the information you have so far collected, (2) see spots (for example IB)
where special information that will involve the listeners needs to be collected, and
(3) observe whether you have or can get enough material to make each main point
cogent and complete and, taking all the main points together, support or fully clarify
your central idea. You know your research is completed when you are satisfied with
both the logic and the appeal of a full outline of this kind. However, there may still
remain some adjustments of your basic material—needed because *talk* is your medium
or because of unique characteristics of your listeners.

ACCOMMODATING AUDIENCES

In the example of buying on credit, two kinds of adequacy could be checked at the same
time: (1) what further facts were needed to support the claims made, and (2)
whether the available material would fit the interests of the specific audience to be addressed. It is essential that both of these considerations be in your mind throughout
research and speech composition. Being rhetorically sensitive in research and composition means looking for the best material to support *your* views or purposes and
treating it in ways that will *appeal to your listeners* in the situation you will share
with them. Treating ideas this way may require some accommodations and adaptations
we have not yet discussed: adapting to the medium of talk, adapting to the alternative
ways most material can be treated, and adapting to conditions of doubt.

Adapting to the medium of talk

Talk is not the ideal medium for every kind of material. This means that you need
to present data in the ways that communicate them best. Our courts recognize that some
content is better presented in print than in speech. Hence an attorney normally pre-
pares a written brief of the case and also makes an oral argument. The judge can study

the brief at his leisure, when there is time to check on precedents, review the law, and otherwise handle the technical side of the case. Speech is simply not the best medium for processing technicalities. We see this in other professions too. Engineers and architects almost always need to use sketches, sectional drawings, and models as well as speech if they are to communicate their subject matters with full effect. The point is, then, that you too should review your material for a speech to discover where you will need to reinforce what speech can convey with communication using other auditory and visual means.

For what kinds of content is speech most effective? Attitudes toward propositions and persons are much more effectively communicated through speech than through pictorial or written media. Feeling and emphasis are more effectively conveyed in person than in print. Speech is also the best medium for communicating the relationships between ideas and human experience. Hence aspects of an idea or event that have strong human significance are naturals for oral communication, and ideas that lack human significance need to be associated with matters of human concern or presented through some other medium than speech alone.

These facts do not limit you as much as you may think, for public speech is both auditory and visual communication. Never forget that you are your most convenient and versatile visual resource. A shape or a sigh or a process like cutting or tearing may be hard to convey by words alone, but you can illustrate or suggest any of these by bodily action. Nonetheless, you will be wise to review material you have available for any speech with a view to making the most of the content that lends itself to oral communication and subordinating or excluding the materials least effectively communicated through speech and action.

RESHAPING IDEAS

Don't give up too soon on ideas and data that at first seem difficult to adapt to speech. There is seldom only one way of handling subject matter. For example, there are many qualities of a piece of music or a painting that are scarcely communicable through words, but you can still talk about either if you deal with the work's structure or form or its history. And you can often reinforce your words by playing brief excerpts from the music or referring to a reproduction of the painting as you discuss its form or analyze the use of colors in it. The point is that if one attribute of a subject doesn't lend itself to oral presentation, there are probably other aspects of it or lines of thought about it that do. When you can't effectively present everything you would like to, cut back your treatment to those matters readily presented through speech.

And consider various rhetorical devices that will help you become clear and interesting even though your subject seems difficult to present orally. Very seldom is there no usable analogy, no example, no familiar principle, or no easily imagined experience that will create at least an approximate impression of the concept you must deal with. If you have seen the astronomer, Carl Sagan, present such television programs as *The Cosmos,* you will recognize how an astute speaker can reshape even the most complicated ideas into terms and forms ordinary people can understand; his primary methods are using careful analogies, giving specific examples, and relating everyday principles and processes to astronomical events. In the speech we quote in our next section, Saint Paul adopted the methods of philosophical deduction when he wanted to show the superiority of his "unknown god" to philosophers who were used to this pattern of discourse. Thomas Huxley once explained the principles of scientific investigation to an audience of English workers by showing that this kind of investigation resembles investigations of crimes. Huxley's speech is still used as a model of clear exposition. So be on the lookout for forms other than traditional ones in which to put difficult concepts.

Often ideas need reshaping, not because of their inherent complexity or the limits of listeners' understanding, but because their significance might not be clear otherwise. Some years ago Professor Laura Crowell made a careful study of the complicated changes President Franklin Roosevelt and his team of speech writers made in developing an address to the Congress, delivered on January 6, 1941. The speech went through seven different drafts before it was given, beginning with five pages Roosevelt composed to show his assistants what he wanted. (It is testimony to his art as a composer that 60 percent of this material was appropriate for the final, seventh version of the address.) What Professor Crowell found was that Roosevelt and his staff at first *added* ideas to the initial draft. Then they went through a stage of shifting ideas around in the speech to get the right ones into the important first and last positions. In this process they also began to drop out details and to reduce paragraphs to pithy statements. In the last drafts they seem to have concentrated on sharpening the language—inserting alliteration, parallelism, reconstructing statements to get just the right emphasis, and rearranging statements to achieve climaxes. It was not until the fifth of the seven versions that the final, overall shape of the address began to appear clearly.

As Professor Crowell says, "Often these alterations are not matters of finding appropriate expression for ideas so much as of finding the appropriate ideas for expression." Often only a few words had to be found to add major new dimensions to ideas, as in these instances:

> ... Immediacy of the crisis is not the only time relation developed in the preparation of the manuscript. The claim that before 1914 no foreign war "constituted a real threat against *us* or against *any other American nation*" is changed to read "constituted a real threat against *our future* or against *the future of any other American nation*." ... The time shadow is lengthened differently in regard to the danger of enforced isolation for future generations: "thinking of our children" is amended to read "thinking of our children *and their children*." [9]

Crowell sums up her tracings by indicating that the process was actually one of fitting "Roosevelt's truths" to "truths of and about American listeners":

> The cumulative effect of these sentences—built to express Roosevelt's concepts of governmental function and relationship, shifted to place the climactic idea in the climactic position, altered and trimmed to add force and effect by the very words chosen—is powerful indeed. Considering that the first wording of the ideas was done by writers with long training on scores of earlier addresses and thus the first sentences embodied much of the style desired, considering that each sentence, each

word, underwent severe scrutiny not only in itself but in the light of changes made elsewhere in the address, one begins to understand the power of the final draft.[10]

Roosevelt was perhaps the most expert public speaker to hold the presidency in this century. If experts such as he needed to plan and revise in this kind of detail to "get it right," the rest of us should expect to do considerable planning, adaptation, and revision just to be adequate in communication. And we can do it. Student speakers can do exceedingly well at adapting material in order to solve their communicative problems, as the following true narrative indicates.

Bob Barth was one of a class of fifteen students, all but four of whom were college freshmen. Nine were women and six were men. In conference with his instructor Barth revealed that he would like to explain the operation of jet aircraft engines in his next speech to the class but, he said, this probably would be unwise since it was clear that only two of the fourteen students who would be his audience had even an elementary knowledge of mechanical and physical principles. Barth's judgment on his audience was exactly right; most knew nothing and seemed to care nothing for the world of physics and mechanics. Nonetheless, Barth's instructor contended that this was a golden opportunity for an experiment with what careful selection of ideas and methods could accomplish with a difficult audience. Barth reluctantly agreed to do what he could and set doggedly to work designing a speech that assumed little interest and no mechanical knowledge on the part of his hearers.[11]

On the day of his speech Barth began by saying:

I am going to talk to you today about jet engines. I suspect you think you aren't interested. Probably what's in your minds now is something like this.

Here Barth uncovered a rough but clear drawing of a jet engine "pod" covered with words such as "dangerous machine," "complicated," "for mechanics only," "expensive." He continued:

The fact is that in principle at least jets aren't complicated. They're rather simple. If you've ever blown up a toy balloon and then let it out of your hands to watch it shoot through the air as the wind escaped, you not only know something about jet propulsion, you've used it. Let's begin right there—with the air escaping out of the balloon.

In this vein Barth covered simply but accurately the elemental facts about the construction and operation of two types of jet engines. There was nothing unusual about his delivery, except that it was not as direct and forceful as it ought to have been. The language of the speech was simple and the examples were always from everyday life, but there were few other marks of artistry. Even the charts and sketches that communicated things hard to put into words were freehand crayon drawings on cardboard sheets of different sizes. Yet when Bob Barth ended his talk there was a ripple of applause—the first applause heard in that public-speaking classroom. At the end of the hour two young women who had been in the audience exchanged these observations as they walked from the room. "I learned more today than I do in most class periods," said one. Her companion replied, "Yes. And imagine! I even thought I understood that engine!"

What happened? A speaker accepted his audience as he found it, adjusted to its limitations and its needs, and gave it as much information as their little knowledge, his inventiveness and art, and the time would allow. Without fanfare Barth offered his listeners two always alluring reasons for attending: I can help you understand what's been mysterious to you, and you'll find the whole experience much easier than you expect. Scarcely any subject is unusable in speaking if speaker and audience approach it in this spirit.

Adapting basic ideas for doubters

In Chapter 3 we discussed the principle of asking for only small changes of opinion when addressing doubters. Particularly in persuasion it is important to remember this principle. And it may require that one not say everything one knows or thinks. One of the most famous examples in literature is found in the story of St. Paul's sermon on Mars Hill in Athens. As it is told in the book of Acts in the Bible, Paul came on a missionary journey to Athens, Greece. There he became upset at the many idols he saw in the city, and he argued strongly in synagogues and on the streets against idol worship. However, there was in Athens a group of philosophers and religious thinkers who held regular discussions in an open meeting place called the Areopagus at the top of Mars Hill, overlooking the city. One day these men invited Paul to come to speak with them. The rest of the account, including a summary of what Paul said, runs this way in the Revised Standard Version:

> And they took hold of him and brought him to the Areopagus, saying, "May we know what this new teaching is which you present? For you bring some strange things to our ears; we wish to know therefore what these things mean." Now all the Athenians and the foreigners who lived there spent their time in nothing except telling or hearing something new.
>
> So Paul, standing in the middle of the Areopagus, said: "Men of Athens, I perceive that in every way you are very religious. For as I passed along, and observed the objects of your worship, I found also an altar with this inscription, 'To an unknown god.' What therefore you worship as unknown, this I proclaim to you. The God who made the world and everything in it, being Lord of heaven and earth, does not live in shrines made by man, nor is he served by human hands, as though he needed anything, since he himself gives to all men life and breath and everything. And he made from one every nation of men to live on all the face of the earth, having determined allotted periods and the boundaries of their habitation, that they should seek God, in the hope that they might feel after him and find him. Yet he is not far from each one of us, for
>
> 'In him we live and move and have our being';
>
> as even some of your poets have said, 'For we are indeed his offspring.'
>
> "Being then God's offspring, we ought not to think that the Deity is like gold, or silver, or stone, a representation by the art and imagination of man. The times of ignorance God overlooked, but now he commands all men everywhere to repent, because he has fixed a day on which he will judge the world in righteousness by a man whom he has appointed, and of this he has given assurance to all men by raising him from the dead." [12]

The story of this speech closes with these words:

> Now when they heard of the resurrection of the dead, some mocked; but others said, "We will hear you again about this." So Paul went out from among them. But some men joined him and believed....[13]

This account of a missionary's speech carefully designed to win a hearing within Greek culture suggests the problems speakers must solve when talking to audiences whose ideas are different from the speaker's. St. Paul found it necessary to suppress his strong personal distaste for the Greek religion in order to make this speech. This was his first opportunity to talk to some of the most important religious and philosophical thinkers in Athens. He deplored their religion, but to get a hearing he chose not to say so directly (as he had apparently been doing in the streets). He actually used a facet of his listeners' paganism as a means of getting to his own central idea. His choices were rhetorically wise; had he not moderated his criticism of paganism and had he not used the entire situation delicately to assure that he would be heard out, he would have undermined his whole reason for going to the hilltop to talk. If he wanted to convince any leading thinkers in Athens, he had to treat them as we said in Chapter 3 that doubters must always be treated. They must be moved from their strongly held positions and commitments by slow degrees. Generally, although not at every point, that was how Paul approached his task. The account says some listeners rejected the message because Paul still went too far for them when he talked of resurrection. But we are told others were moved far enough to be willing to hear more. Later, it appears, some who heard more came to believe Paul.

There are few records of persuasion that illustrate so clearly the delicacy of judgment you and all speakers have to exercise to get even *some* acceptance from those who doubt your truth. No matter how convinced *you* are, a doubter simply will not see the merits of your ideas if you only proclaim them. Doubts and counter opinions are truths too. Real communication occurs only when "speakers' truths" and "listeners' truths" are accommodated to one another—in the best way rhetorical art allows.

ORIGINALITY

It is in the *re*-creation of research materials that you become original, truly an artist. We close this chapter with some observations on originality, for much of which we are indebted to one of our former colleagues, an expert teacher, the late Herbert A. Wichelns.

Once your information is gathered, you must reflect on it and stamp it with your own personality. Then you must present it in your own words. *To be original you must be able to discover and convey fresh meaning in known matters.* Rarely does even the greatest speaker discuss what was totally unknown before his speech. To realize a truth clearly because you have experienced it in your own mind produces a degree of originality gained in no other way, even though the base for such originality is to be found in readily accepted axioms.

As *you* do when listening, your listeners will be demanding in exchange for their attention that you have actively thought for yourself, have reached your own point of view, and have reacted as an individual to information you have digested. To be heard with attention and confidence you must exercise judgment in sifting the materials to which you have exposed yourself, and you must test your own reasoning. You must say what you have to say in your *own way,* choosing your *own* words. Since individualized choices in both matter and structure are involved, you should be extremely wary of constructing speeches based on a single source. If you rely heavily on outlines found in debate manuals or study files or on ideas expressed in a *single* book or magazine account, you cannot hope for originality even though you actually speak the words conveying the final message. If talk is not a fresh accommodation of yourself and your thoughts to *these* listeners in *their* situation, your human relationship with them will surely be tarnished.

Systematic preparation with full consciousness of your listeners' natures and needs is the key to originality in speaking. You must become intimately acquainted with the facts of your subject, and their humanized meanings. You must judge your material with keen awareness of the speech situation into which you will bring it.

Sifting the important from the unimportant takes time and reflection, and for this reason the likelihood of discovering fresh significance in a subject will increase if you begin work early. Ideally, a period of several days should elapse between the period of research and final organization and rehearsal of any important speaking—whether delivered in formal or casual settings. During this gestation or cooling-off period you should explore—perhaps using such a topical system as we have provided —the meanings and possibilities of what you know. Ideas about your subject should be forced to grow within you; only thus can they flower into some final form that is right for you, for the speech situation, and for your particular listeners.

It takes imaginative thinking to bring freshness to a subject. You must strive to find the distinct shapes and the potential uses of the materials you use. You must try to see what is unique in your relation to these materials and in their relation to the lives of your hearers. The function of imagination here is not to create the unreal or imaginary but to bring to particular listeners a personalized understanding of your version of reality. Imagination ought to reinforce and animate fact and probability by revealing what happens *in life* if these facts and probabilities are accepted or rejected.

What are some tests of originality? You should be able to defend what you say. You will know more than you have had time—or thought wise—to tell in an initial statement. You will be able and eager to trace ideas to their sources, crediting and evaluating these sources during your talk and afterward. Although you may have borrowed—with acknowledgment—you will always be stating your own ideas, for selection and evaluation of the ideas are yours.

If you are original in speaking, you will not rely on others to the extent of repressing your own individuality. You will avoid the hackneyed and be free of clichés because you will say nothing that does not uniquely fit the speech situation. Like any other work of artistic merit, your work—your talk—will be the product of personal experience, personal insights, and intense awareness of the natures of those with whom you seek to communicate.

1.   Assume you are to speak to a classmate or to your entire class in favor of major-
     ing in the academic subject that interests you most. Identify three lines of
     thought (topics) that it would be useful to discuss with the audience you have
     decided on. Identify three other lines of thought that are relevant to your sub-
     ject but that you would *not* choose to discuss with the listeners you have in
     mind. Explain the grounds on which you include and exclude each line of
     thought you cite.

2.   Assume you are to give a classroom speech on "consumers ought to educate
     themselves." Which of the sixteen lines of thought (topics) listed in this chap-
     ter suggested the most promising lines of research for this speech? Explain why
     the remaining cues are not potentially useful as guides to promising informa-
     tion for this speech.

3.   Identify the lines of thought (topics) used in some brief, familiar speech such
     as Lincoln's "Gettysburg Address," Shakespeare's version of Mark Antony's
     speech over the body of Caesar in *Julius Caesar,* Dr. Martin Luther King's "I
     Have a Dream" address, or Dr. Upcraft's speech in Appendix B of this book.
     Defend or criticize the speaker's choice of these lines of thought. Were there
     other topics he or she might as wisely have chosen? If so, illustrate how one
     of them might have been incorporated into the speech.

1.   Give a short speech in which you explain two ways a proverb or a maxim (for
     example, "Haste makes waste," "If anything can go wrong, it will," "Small is
     beautiful") can be interpreted.

2.   Choose a simple process (for example, playing a golf ball out of a sand trap,
     shuffling a deck of playing cards, checking out a book from the library, pre-
     paring the cover for a term paper). Now plan and present two one-minute
     speeches, each explaining the process in a different way. Discuss with your class
     which way was better and, most importantly, why.

3.   Give a brief report on a speech or editorial you have heard or read and in
     which you believe the creator made exceptionally inventive use of the lines of
     thought (topics) available—or failed to take advantage of lines of thought
     open to him or her.

4.   Form a committee with three or four of your colleagues. Compose an outline
     or sketch of a speech, editorial, or other practical message intended to accom-

plish a specific purpose with an audience your committee imagines and describes. When the committee has settled on purpose and audience, use the cuing terms in this chapter to construct a committee's list of *all* the things it might make sense to include in the message. Then cut this list down to the topics that *ought* to be covered, and prepare the committee's sketch or outline of the whole message.

5. In anticipation of the next round of speeches in your class, divide into groups of three or four. In each group brainstorm, using the topical system of this chapter, for things that might be said about each member's intended speech subject. If time permits when this is done, have each group review the results of the brainstorming to single out the discovered items that each speaker ought to touch on in his or her speech.

6. To intensify your awareness of the many ways most subjects can be treated in speech, divide your class into groups of three; assign a *noun* to each group (trees, girl, car, Eskimo, etc.); have each group member choose a cue from page 84 and then prepare and give a two-minute talk on the assigned subject, using chiefly lines of thought (topics) suggested by the chosen cue word. You should discover that there are more interesting things to be said about simple subjects than you supposed.

ENDNOTES

1. "Pragmatism and Humanism" is Lecture Seven of James's *Pragmatism* as originally published in 1907. See William James, *Pragmatism* (Cleveland: World Publishing Co., Meridian Books, 1955), p. 161.
2. Robert Thomson, *The Psychology of Thinking* (Baltimore: Penguin Books, 1959), p. 155.
3. William F. Nelson, "Topoi: Function in Recall," *Speech Monographs* XXXVII (June 1970): 121–26.
4. This experiment was conducted by William F. Nelson and John L. Petelle and was reported as "Topoi: Functional in Group Problem Solving," a paper read at the International Communication Association convention, Montreal, Canada, 1973. The findings are also summarized in John L. Petelle and Richard Maybee, "Items of Information Retrieved as a Function of Cue System and Topical Area," *Central States Speech Journal* XXV (Fall 1974): 191.
5. For a good summary of the findings and their implications for a theory of how we store and retrieve information, see Petelle and Maybee, "Items of Information," pp. 190–97.
6. These are the options in one program we know about. There are, of course, many other ways in which concentrations in this kind of program are divided.
7. Francis Bacon, *De augmentis scientiarum*, V, p. 3, *Works*, IV, p. 423.
8. This outline is based on one prepared by Robert L. Carlton, a student at the University of Colorado-Boulder.
9. Laura Crowell, "The Building of the 'Four Freedoms' Speech," *Speech Monographs* XXII (November 1955): 266–83.
10. Ibid., p. 282.

11.   This speech was delivered by Robert Barth to a beginning public speaking class at Cornell University.

12.   From the Revised Standard Version of the Bible (New York: Thomas Nelson, 1959), Acts, 17. 19–34. Copyrighted 1946, 1952 © 1971, 1973 by the Division of Christian Education and the National Council of Churches of Christ in the U.S.A. Reprinted by permission.

13.   Ibid., 32–34.

CHAPTER 5

Invention:
General tactics

Where can you apply the principles of this chapter in everyday life?

1. Wherever you need to know just what "supports" an ordinary bit of persuasion.
2. Wherever you need to "prove" something about a debatable subject.
3. Wherever you want to make a favorable impression on someone else through verbal communication.
4. Wherever you need to make some idea clearer or stronger.
5. Wherever audiovisual equipment is to be used in support of other communication.

When evaluating someone else's speech consider:

1. Did the speaker have a single, clear goal in speaking? If not, why not?
2. What uses did the speaker make of the listeners' established patterns of thinking and feeling about the subject matter of the speech?
3. Was the reasoning attempted full enough to seem convincing to this audience? Was there too much or too little reasoning at any point?
4. Did the speaker establish himself or herself as intelligent and trustworthy on this subject? If so, how was this accomplished? If not, how could more have been done?
5. Did the speaker sufficiently clarify and amplify all major ideas so listeners would understand them as intended? If so, what tactics were well used? If not, what opportunities were missed?
6. If audiovisual aids were used, were they well designed for the purpose and well used to serve the speaker's ends? If such aids were used but poorly, what lessons did you draw from that?

Do you like conversationalists or public speakers who insist on telling you *all* they know about violins or economics or scuba diving? We have heard an audience of students utterly bored by a remarkably informed speaker who tried to tell them how to pick a race horse to bet on. He tried to tell his listeners everything about race horses. He was thoroughly prepared to talk, but did not fit his talk to his situation. He had neglected three basic, tactical activities of planning that any rhetorical situation requires: setting a precise goal, sorting and building available materials into *rhetorical proofs* that fit the situation, and then finding ways of clarifying whatever information deserves to be presented. These three tasks are the principal concerns of this chapter.

A simple way of describing effective talk is to say that it makes pertinent points and justifies them. Let's assume, then, that you have completed the basic inventional processes of choosing a subject and gathering appropriate information about it. You ought next to reconsider exactly what you want to accomplish in this speech.

PURPOSIVENESS

You set goals for yourself before you began investigating your subject, but speakers often find that their goals change as general preparation proceeds. You therefore need to take stock again—to reset your central idea and to express it, now that your research is completed.

What will special thought about your central idea do for you at this stage? It will force you to decide finally which of several kinds of speeches on your subject you really want to make, now that your research is about finished. Any subject can be treated in more than one way. Usually the more we learn about a subject the more possibilities it presents. It is time to reexamine your initial plans, for you dare not be vague or indecisive. "I want to talk about rock formations" doesn't settle which of many talks about rocks you want to frame now. By contrast, "I want to show my listeners what forces produced each of three rock formations" identifies a specific speech about three aspects of geological processes. "I shall explain the three rock formations that are most common in this area" identifies another speech. You could make a coherent, influential talk on either of the last two statements. If you have done some research on rock formations, you could probably speak on either. But now you must decide. To make the decision efficiently, frame a precise sentence that expresses (1) your exact aim and (2) exactly what limits you will finally put on your subject. We discussed the standards for this kind of sentence on pages 28–30.

We do not mean that your sharpened statement of your central idea cannot be rephrased as you work over the material you will use. You should always feel free to redirect your overall aim as you think about what you can do with what you know.

What is important is that in every moment of building a speech *some* precise central idea and goal should be utterly clear to you. If it is not, you are apt to ramble in preparation and in speaking; then listeners are likely to lose their way too.

Rethinking your central idea in preparation will be a service to your listeners. As we have said, listening is not a very efficient way of acquiring information and belief. Listeners need what help they can get to extract the right ideas from talk. All experiments testing what happens when speakers assert their central ideas and purposes in so many words show that this practice helped the listeners to understand and retain what they heard.[1] This argues that you ought to tell your listeners exactly what your purpose is, unless more will be lost than gained from early revelation of your central idea.

When auditors are doubtful or hostile, it is sometimes wiser to pave the way for acceptance before asserting directly what conclusions you want drawn or actions performed. However, even in such cases, *you* cannot afford to be without a precise sense of your overall purpose, and you should not seem to your listeners to be talking without at least a short-range objective. When experienced speakers withhold revelation of their central ideas, they usually try to indicate that they have some lesser, uncontroversial goals in mind as they move through the preliminary matter that leads to the overall goal they will finally reveal.

As always in speaking, you must exercise judgment about what is the tactically sound way of revealing purpose in speaking. There is no formal rule to follow except the rule that *you* need a clear statement of your central idea *all of the time,* whether or not you reveal it fully to your listeners. Therefore you ought to pause, following research for speaking, to reset your central idea precisely. When that is done, the next task is to assemble your material in ways that will make what you say credible. You must build the proofs that will support your central idea and attain your purpose.

CONSTRUCTING RHETORICAL PROOFS

The central idea governing a well-conceived speech does not accomplish the work it forecasts. Ideas, language, and behavior are deployed to do this work. That is what we mean by *proof.* The somewhat military connotations of the words *tactics* and *deploy,* which we are using, deserve to be taken seriously; it is indeed the mix and the placement of forces that will determine the proof power of any speaking you do.

Your goal is to get someone else to accept information and use it if you are to inform them; to experience heightened desire to investigate if you are to provoke inquiry; to revalue their prior knowledge if you are to reinforce beliefs and attitudes; to accept *your* interpretations of data and their own interests if you are to persuade; or to suspend a good many serious concerns if you are to entertain. Whatever you attempt as a speaker, you ask your listeners to shift their outlooks to some degree. So it is important to think about what people demand as the price of shifting their views.

People change views because they think they have found sufficient reasons or proofs that to shift would be a good thing—from *their* vantage points. What they think of as reasons may or may not involve much private reasoning. What seem sufficient proofs of something may have been decided by much logic or by scarcely any at all. In short, the reasons or proofs that suffice in rhetorical situations are not all logical, though they are not *il*logical either.

There are three kinds of proof that listeners in any situation demand before they will change views in response to talk.

1. They demand that either the talk itself or their own experiences show there is a *connection* between what they are asked to do or think and their own personal interests.
2. They demand that either the talk itself or their own experiences give *rational* justifications for believing what is said.
3. They demand that the source of the communication (the speaker and his or her sources and sponsors) seem *worthy of confidence*—on the subject of communication, in this rhetorical situation.

A whole speech and all its main parts must satisfy all three of these general demands if there is to be change in the attitudes and beliefs of those who listen. To check this, consider yourself as a listener. You constantly make these demands of speakers, although the demands are probably expressed in your mind as questions.

Suppose someone is talking to you about a curriculum in business administration. Such questions as these pop into your thoughts. Why should *I* care about business administration? Why bring this up *now*? Why should I believe the curriculum really *is as you say it is*? Why is what you are saying *wiser* or *truer* than some other version? Why should I listen to *you* on this matter? A major part of listening to anyone is getting clear, satisfying answers to these questions—either from what is said or from your own knowledge and experience.

Notice that some of these questions ask whether the listener's personal interests are going to be satisfied (Why should *I* care? Why bring this up *now*?); some ask for rational justifications (Why should I believe things *are as you say they are*? Why is what you urge on me *wiser* or *truer* than an alternative?); and another asks about the speaker's qualifications (Why should I listen to *you* on this matter?). If you see to it that these five questions are satisfactorily answered either by what you say and do or by what your listeners are already aware of, you will have built the needed proofs for effective public speech.

To explain how one builds these justifications or proofs we will have to discuss them separately, but in practice these influences never operate separately from one another. Again, you can demonstrate this by examining your own behavior. When a speaker shows you that something is in your own interest, don't you also think better of him or her? And don't you think trusted friends more "reasonable" than people you dislike or distrust? Haven't you said, "I don't see any flaws in the reasoning, but I still don't believe it because I don't trust the guy"? We are dealing, then, with how to build proofs that intricately influence one another, even though we shall have to discuss them separately.

"Why should *I* care?" and "Why bring this up *now?*" ask for attention to the questioner's personal interests. We raise such questions out of concerns about ourselves and our personal affairs. But they are not unimportant for that reason. We saw in Chapter 3 that it is normal for listeners to be concerned about things that affect their private interests and that people see no point in attending to things that have no perceivable bearing on their lives. So every speaker needs to give listeners some satisfying answers to why *they* should care about what is said *now*.

People's inclinations are difficult to account for in detail because they are subjective. Individual interests usually have different explanations; they arise from distinctive experiences and preferences. You cannot, therefore, predict individuals' motives precisely. Consider an apparently simple instance.

Suppose someone says to you, "Here's a thousand dollars." It is easy to say that person "appeals" to your need for and perhaps love of money. But that is almost meaningless. What would motivate you would be some notion of how you could gratify yourself through *use of* the money, and you would have to think fairly hard to pick out just what personal need or interest you would most like to gratify by using the cash. However much you may need money or like what it can do for you, the person who offers it cannot be sure how you as an individual rank the various gratifications that having money can provide. It is seldom that any offerer of money—or any speaker—can touch a recipient's or listener's basic, private value system directly through words. What one can do through words is awaken images—set off a scenario—of the gratifications the listener has learned to connect with possessing money or whatever a speaker offers. Words can point a listener's thoughts in the direction of specific interests or desires and kinds of gratifications, but the details of these and the choice to be made among them are the listener's internal affair. In other words, no one *inserts* beliefs or choices or preferences into others' minds. Using speech, one can cause listeners to envision personal gratification that might follow from believing or acting according to what is being said. Any speaker, then, ought to try to evoke gratification-justified images within listeners' minds so that what the speaker offers becomes justified in the listeners' thoughts by at least some personally rewarding possibilities. Let us look more closely at the processes involved.

Modern social psychologists argue that we behave as we do in consequence to internal forces. Depending on the psychologists' theories, these forces are referred to as needs, drives, tensions, goals, and motives. Whatever they are called, they are conceptualized as forces that internally stimulate us to act. They direct our activity toward simple or complex goals. The goals are attainment of conditions we believe will satisfy our needs and desires. They may be conditions we pursue for the sake of satisfying physiological needs (for food, drink, warmth, and so on), or conditions in which we can expect social rewards, or conditions in which we can gain both sorts of satisfaction. For example, our basic desire for physical safety and our learned need for social approval may cause us to strive toward the goal of associating with other people in hiking clubs or labor unions or karate classes. Over time, experience teaches us that certain kinds of behavior tend to yield fairly predictable satisfactions, and so we acquire fairly stable patterns of activity that we regularly follow when we experience recurring patterns of need-produced tensions. We learn, for example, that to drink a cup of coffee or a cola at midafternoon "picks us up." So when we feel tense or tired, we go through an activity that satisfies thirst, even though we are not particularly thirsty. And we are gratified directly in one way and indirectly in another: we feel more relaxed or we feel "picked up," and at the same time we have enjoyed the pleasures of taste, of warmth or cold, and of sipping and swallowing. So, the next time we feel tense or tired, we will get coffee or cola again because we believe a whole complex of gratifications will flow from drinking it.

In similar ways we develop attitudes toward and patterns of thought about a host of ideas and ways of doing things. Out of experience we build what might be called prefabricated patterns of thought about the way things are and about what thoughts and actions can satisfy and gratify us. It is these patterns that speakers can work with. Consider two instances. People learn that experienced advisers are more reliable than inexperienced ones. If a speaker reminds them that a quoted authority is thoroughly experienced, this reference to experience sets off a quick chain of reasoning, ending in something like "I can believe that." Suppose someone has been told that Midwesterners are more friendly than New Englanders. Then a speaker says social life will be more pleasant in Winona, Minnesota, than in Pittsfield, Massachusetts. The learned formula—Midwest equals friendliness—may come into play to make the statement believable and the unknown (Winona, Minnesota) desirable.

Everyone has thousands of such ready patterns of feeling and reasoning. The formulas are seldom verbalized, and they are often contradictory, but we all carry them about as ways of deciding within ourselves "what is right for me" and what promises pleasure or pain, truth or fiction.[2]

Listeners will think and feel in these learned, predisposing ways about what you say. That is not the only way they will respond, but it is one of the ways. So part of your task in providing proof for whatever you say is to build speech so that it will touch off the kinds of predisposing patterns of thought and feeling that can support your ideas and make them personally attractive to your listeners. Let us see how this can be done.

Below are a few lines from a speech by Dr. Daniel J. Boorstin, Librarian of Congress. Dr. Boorstin was addressing the Associated Press Managing Librarians' Association on "Dissent, Dissension, and the News." Early in his speech it was important for him to distinguish between *debate* and *dissent*. Ordinarily, defining terms is not a very exciting or emotional business, but even in this task Dr. Boorstin systematically triggered first a series of favorable, private feelings toward debate and then a series of negative feelings and "reasonings" about dissent. We have broken the passage into individual thought units and opposite each unit we have placed the kind of private feeling/reasoning we think Dr. Boorstin's words probably evoked in the audience of editors.

Statements	*Probable responses*
A debate is an orderly exploration . . .	*Order* and *exploring* are desirable, so debate is desirable.

Statements	*Probable responses*
of a common problem that presupposes the debaters are worried by the same question.	Sharing concerns and focusing on questions are desirable—the method of debate is therefore reasonable and desirable.
It brings to life new facts . . .	*Facts* and *newness* are "good"; they are our editorial ideals. Debate serves the same "goods."
and new arguments that make possible a better solution.	The whole object of having freedom of information is to allow all arguments to be heard so *better* solutions can be found. *Debate* serves the same goals we already have.
But dissension means discord.	*Discord* is not constructive.
As the dictionary tells us, dissension is marked by a break in friendly relations. It is an expression not of common concern . . .	*Breaking friendship* is socially destructive and to be avoided if possible.
	This is opposite to the end of journalism, to focus on concerns that are common.
but of hostile feelings.	*Hostility* is the opposite of agreement, one of the "goods" that *debate* fosters, just as good journalism does.
This distinction is crucial.[3]	[Dr. Boorstin missed an opportunity to clinch the pattern of thought and feeling he had triggered. He could have concluded: "Debate is productive; dissension is discordant, unfriendly and unproductive."]

Dr. Boorstin offered no formal reasoning here, though he did cite the authority of the dictionary. He made no special attempt to show himself to be uniquely qualified to say what he did, but his reputation may already have done this. The thought he wanted endorsed was that debate is valuable but dissent is not. He justified—made the thought believable—by trying to activate a series of favorable and unfavorable formulas for deciding what is and is not valuable in public discussion. Notice especially that what is valuable in public discussion is a matter every editor thinks and feels about while devising editorial policies and passing on what news and comment deserve publication. Boorstin's editors were sure to have special, professional interests in this topic and probably some long-used formulas for thinking about it. Boorstin gave the editors opportunities to assign *approved* qualities to debate, *then* disapproved qualities to dissent. In setting up his statements in this way, he arranged matters so that every negative response toward dissent could also remind the listeners of the contrasting merits of debate—to which they were already committed by training and profession. If Boorstin's scheme worked, the listeners experienced an increasing intensity of approval of debate as their estimation of dissent was pushed lower and lower. Nonetheless, the passage illustrates that ideas borne on language can be arranged to trigger a mixture of already developed thoughts and feelings and special interests that will be favorable to a speaker's purpose. If you have made a preliminary analysis of your listeners' established patterns of thought and feeling, you can invent similar proofs that appeal to self-interest and established attitudes.

You will speak on many matters for which the strongest proofs exist within your hearers, needing only to be awakened and organized to support what you say. For example, it would be silly to introduce statistics, quotations, and formal arguments to establish the point that students need special study spaces in which to work—especially if your audience were made up of students! The listeners' experiences and feelings about study would supply proofs more potent than any data from outside sources. Students soon learn attitudes and develop feelings such as: you have to be able to spread out your materials when you study; it's hard to study when others around you are doing something else; I need protection from interruptions; and having the right atmosphere helps you to concentrate. Such beliefs and feelings would only need to be brought to your listeners' consciousness to become powerful proofs for the proposition that every school must provide special study spaces if it is to claim to have adequate educational facilities. On the other hand, exactly *how much* such space is needed for each student is not something that can be proved by drawing on personal interests and established attitudes and feelings. For this a good deal of outside data and rational argument based on the data would be required.

When listeners' personal experiences and interests can do the *proving* for us, how do we find out what experiences and interests are present to be used? To identify all the significant attitudes of even a single audience would require research by a corps of social scientists. Some political and other figures have the benefit of this kind of research, but most of us must try to communicate effectively without such advantages. Even so, we are not without resources. We can use such generalizations about how people feel and think as were discussed in Chapter 3. These will help us estimate what self-interests reside in listeners generally. In addition we can learn specific facts about specific audiences and situations and so derive specific estimates about a particular audience's standard ways of thinking and its special, shared interests. And if the audience is one you associate with over some time—as is the case with your classroom audience —you can know a great deal about that group's thought patterns and interests.

You will not, then, need the Gallup polling organization to tell you what resources of self-interest you can draw on. A little thought should remind you that young people in your audience are more disposed than their parents to endorse idealistic and unqualified propositions. Nor do you need to be a social scientist to predict that people who live in communes are less likely than people who live in fraternities and sororities to feel strongly about the worth of "organization." You also know that it will be fairly easy to evoke admiration of mechanical ingenuity in an audience of males, and that people who have difficulty in supporting themselves will be more ready to think about personal economics than those who have no money worries. To compose effective proof based on established attitudes and self-interests, you need to ask what your prospective listeners identify as "good for me and mine" and what they think of as "not so good for me and mine." To ask and answer that question is to make a simple survey of attitudes and special interests. Your answers will show you where you can evoke established thoughts and feelings favoring what you want to say or disapproving of what you oppose. Your answer may also tell you which thoughts and feelings you need to skirt lest they leap into a hearer's consciousness as proofs against you.

Remember when you use this kind of proof that your listener might call it up spontaneously. If not, you will need to remind that listener that his or her ready-made attitudes and interests *apply here*. Rousing applicable thoughts and feelings is one of your best ways of teaching a listener to care *now*. What is needed is to direct caring toward the conclusions you have in view. You may do this suggestively or directly. It is also important to keep the audience's personal caring from subsiding or from becoming attached to ideas that do not support your point. The biology major whose classroom speech on hunting female deer was described in Chapter 3 and Bob Barth, whose speech on jet propulsion was cited in Chapter 4, illustrated how effective, ordinary analysis of preset feelings and ways of thinking can yield powerful forms of *proof* based on listeners' habits of thinking and feeling. Dr. Boorstin's address to the editors is another illustration. You should notice that none of these speakers used existing attitudes simply to get the listeners to reaffirm what they already believed; each speaker taught new beliefs and feelings by connecting old patterns with new information. Thus they caused their hearers to generate new sorts of feelings and thoughts—as proofs for what the speakers were urging. You need to do this kind of proving too, wherever it is possible on any point of any speech.

Developing rational justifications

As you sort out the points you want to make in any speech, you will come to those about which your listeners may have doubts or simply not understand as you do. On those points you will need to justify your views rationally, that is, by argument. The questions you must answer for the listeners are: why should I believe things *are as you say they are?* and why is what you say *truer* or *wiser* than some other version? As a matter of fact, there will be few occasions when listeners will have no uncertainties or doubts about some things you want to say, so some amount of rational proof, of argument, will need to be built up in almost every public speech. In this section, then, we shall discuss what rational proving is in rhetorical speech, how it works, and how you should think when building such a segment into a speech.

Even though we sometimes talk as though *good reasons* were easy to identify and were the same for everyone, the fact is that it is not easy to say what is a rational ground for accepting an idea. The first bothersome thing is that on most topics there are good reasons for accepting any of several different judgments. What we discuss most are things about which there can be more than one reasonable view. That is why we discuss them—in order to choose the *most* reasonable answer from among several possible ones. Consider how many answers and reasoned justifications could be presented in response to such questions as: What is the most reasonable way to use nuclear energy? What are good reasons for getting married? Are you right about the last movie you saw, or is the newspaper critic who disagreed with you right? The list of such highly debatable questions could go on and on. Even in matters of philosophy or of law we cannot say with finality what *the* rational answer is.

How many different views there can be about "what is reasonable" was illustrated in 1971 when the Supreme Court heard and decided a case in which the federal government sought to prevent the *New York Times* and the *Washington Post* from publishing excerpts from allegedly stolen secret documents that came to be known as "The Pentagon Papers." The Court rejected the government's case by a six-to-three vote. The vote was decisive, but *not one justice agreed totally with any other justice on the proper reasons* for voting on one side or the other. Every justice felt compelled to write his own distinct reasons for voting as he did; so six rational justifications were issued for voting as the majority of the Court did and three sets of reasons were issued for voting with the minority. Why? Because the justices, like all of us, used different evaluative standards in determining what was most reasonable. Different perceptions of what was fact, different interpretations of the law, different estimates of what could or would happen in the future, and different personal preferences entered into each justice's reasoning. These kinds of differences are always in play when any of us makes judgments. Consequently speakers and all other makers of rhetorical communication need to remember that almost nothing they say will seem certain to everyone who hears them. On most matters what is a reasonable or rational proof depends on who is doing the estimating. The result is that to give another person rational justifications is always to satisfy *that* person's standards of rationality and sufficiency of evidence.

Before we come to how you can judge when a rational proof is sufficiently strong for your purpose, we need to see what such proving looks like in actual talk. Following is the ending of a college student's speech to his class on the state of scientific knowledge concerning marijuana and its effects. His concluding point was that allegedly scientific findings about marijuana should be accepted only after examining the methods and purposes of the research. This kind of proposition could be supported best by reasons and evidence—rational proof. The quality of research on marijuana was not familiar to everyone, and some might have thought that if the research was "experimental" it *must* be "scientific" and so credible. These were views Steve Mayhew, the speaker, undertook to dispose of.[4]

Mayhew ended his speech as follows:

Let me say something finally about some major drawbacks concerning laboratory tests on the effects of marijuana. There is often a problem with the validity of the tests that are made.

Marijuana raises emotional issues and, unfortunately, objective data are sometimes spiced with subjective interpretations. For example, some tests haven't even had control groups, yet dramatic interpretations have been made. There was one experiment involving sperm counts where men were locked up for about four weeks in isolated rooms, without seeing any women. Their sperm counts dropped. Now, don't you think if there had been a control group without any marijuana, and these poor people were locked up for four weeks, their sperm counts would drop too?

Also, hybrid rats have been used in some of the experiments. These are rats that can be bred to be susceptible to almost any disease there is. They can be bred so as to allow medical examiners to make such reports as that drinking water leads to cancer. How were the rats used in marijuana experiments bred?

So, what I want to say in conclusion is that the public must be wary of medical reports about marijuana and only regard seriously those which have been replicated and which have been done under proper experimental conditions.

Mayhew was trying to convince his listeners to approach "scientific" research on marijuana cautiously. He needed to show there were good reasons for such caution. How does a speaker do this? The speaker shows that the principles of logical reasoning that the listeners already have in their minds *require* such caution from all reasonable persons. Let's examine how Steve Mayhew worked out this process in actual talk.

The English logician Stephen E. Toulmin has devised a way of laying out arguments that can help us see the various features of Mr. Mayhew's rational justifications.[5] Professor Toulmin contends that in rational argument we present some—sometimes all—of six kinds of material. Among them will be **data, warrant, backing for warrants,** and **claim.** Sometimes, also, we offer **qualifications** of our **claims** to forestall or take account of real or anticipated **conditions of rebuttal** that, if not guarded against, might make our **claim** seem more sweeping than the evidence justifies. Using these concepts we can show from Mayhew's speech how one builds proof when an idea must be backed up with evidence and logic.

The first **claim** Mayhew wants accepted in this section of his talk is that there is often a problem with the validity of laboratory tests of marijuana. It seems clear that his listeners' basic question will be, Why? The audience of students can't be presumed to be fully acquainted with the research on marijuana. Their lack of knowledge makes a rational support of the **claim** necessary. So Mayhew says the "problem" arises because subjective interpretations creep into findings due to the researchers' emotional feelings about marijuana. Using Toulmin's concepts as convenient labels, we can diagram this argument as in Figure 5–1.

From Figure 5–1 we can see what Mayhew gave his listeners to justify his **claim** and also what he did not give them. He gave them some "facts," or **data,** about the research and then stated his **claim** as a plausible inference drawn from the **data.** But he said nothing to explain *why* subjective interpretations of data make tests of questionable value. He did not explain by what principle of reasoning he could justly derive his **claim** from the **data** he gave. A logic professor might rightly tell him that his argument was incomplete. But was completeness necessary in this situation? Probably not. Mayhew was talking to an audience of college students. He could expect them to know enough about experimentation to understand that interpreting experimental data subjectively or emotionally would tend to produce questionable conclusions. If his listeners were likely to think that "subjectivity makes for invalidity in experiments" or that "you shouldn't let your emotions creep into scientific interpretations," his argument, incomplete in *words,* would be completed in the listeners' minds. And if it were, Mayhew's **claim** would seem soundly rational.

The first thing we learn about building a reasoned proof, then, is that when

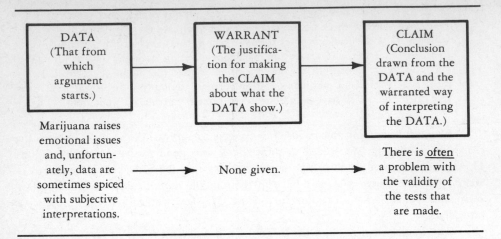

FIGURE 5-1 *Toulmin system*

listeners have the needed knowledge and principles of reasoning in their heads they can be trusted to understand unspoken parts of arguments, much as they can be trusted to "understand" the words "Do you" as part of the question, "_____ want to go with me?" In building a proof that is rational, then, one problem is to decide how much of the needed information and reasoning the listeners can and will supply for themselves. In Toulmin's language Mayhew's listeners were quite likely to "fill in" the missing **warrant** (Figure 5–1) and to perceive that he had supplied a proof that his **claim** was sound.

There is something else we can see from Figure 5–1. The word *often* appears in Mayhew's **claim**. Toulmin calls this kind of term a **qualifier** of a **claim**. *Often* says the "problem" exists frequently but not everywhere in research on marijuana. Other common **qualifiers** you will find in arguments include "probably," "at least half the time," "in 10 percent of the cases," "sometimes," and so on. Such qualifications are needed when some question could reasonably be raised about a **claim**. Here, the **data** Mayhew gives do not show that emotionalism and subjectivity *invariably* enter into research. That limitation is what Toulmin calls a **condition of rebuttal,** and to meet it Mayhew has qualified his **claim**—findings are *often* but not invariably suspect. Figure 5–2 shows the full logic of the argument as it was stated.

Here we need to notice too that by using the term *often* Mayhew not only made the logic of the argument tight but also may have earned some credit for *himself* as a proof by tightening up his logic. Some listeners may have noticed his care and taken it as a sign of intelligence, perhaps putting more trust in him as an adviser on what one should think. He didn't claim too much.

If Mayhew had stopped his argument at this point, he would have been rhetorically unwise (1) because the information he had offered **(data)** about research on marijuana was merely an assertion that reasonable listeners might doubt, given the respect most people have for science; and (2) because the material so far presented

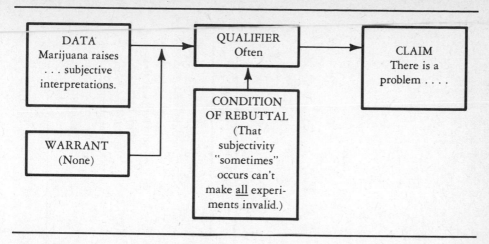

FIGURE 5-2 *Toulmin system refined*

was so brief that listeners might not have had time to grasp the point. So Mayhew went on to support his **data** by adding specific instances. By the time he had finished he had presented the extended argument we have summarized in Figure 5–3.

By adding examples to show that some experiments were poorly designed—presumably out of carelessness or bias on the part of experimenters—Mayhew was able to incorporate *specificity*, which gains attention and gives enough time to the argument to signal its importance, while greatly strengthening the force of reasoning. If emotionality, subjectivity, and defective design mark any scientific studies of the effects of marijuana, there is almost surely reason to sense a "problem" with the research and ample reason to "be wary" in evaluating all such medical reports. The final result was a chain of arguments, all of which directly or indirectly supported the final **claim** Mayhew wanted to impress on the listeners: the public must be wary and take seriously only what has been replicated and done under proper experimental conditions. Assuming that his listeners would not immediately question his **claim** that a "problem" exists, Mayhew used that **claim** as **data** for the broader **claim** that we ought to "be wary." But the chain of argument would work *only* if the listeners were ready to supply the **warrants** Mayhew left unspoken in the two arguments. As we have already said, whether that would happen would depend entirely on listeners' familiarity with the normal tests of scientific research: objectivity, replicability, and control of conditions. Whatever listener was familiar with these standards could easily fill in the missing parts of the arguments and be logically forced to agree that there is a "problem" and that we would be wise to "be wary." We think Mayhew's college audience would be equipped to do this, but what would the **warrant** of the second argument sound like if Mayhew had decided to state it himself? He might have said: "You can't have a reliable experiment unless you have some 'natural' group to compare to your 'experimental group,' as Donald Campbell pointed out in his essay, 'Factors Relevant to the Validity of Experiments in Social Settings.' " (Citing the

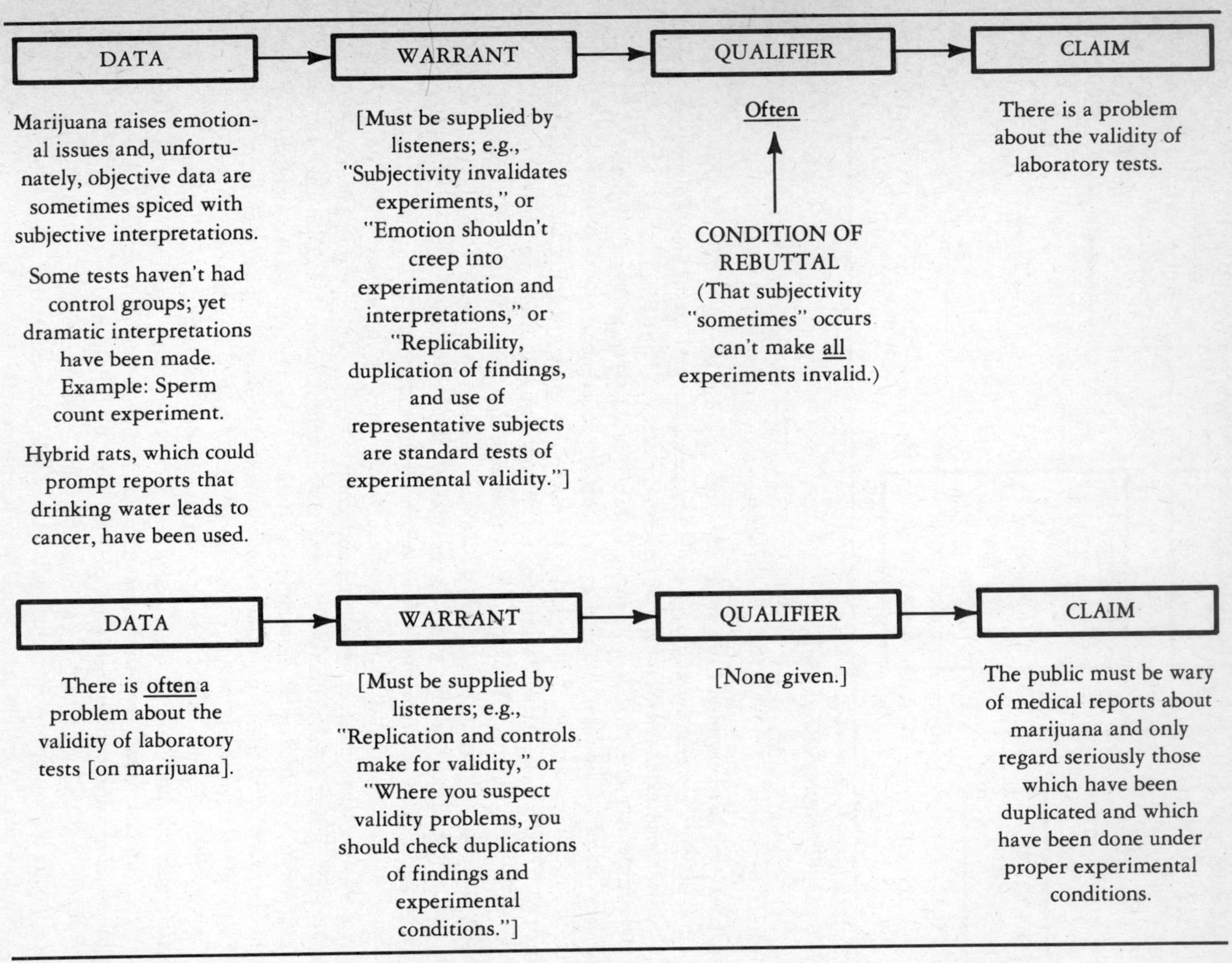
DATA
WARRANT
QUALIFIER
CLAIM
Marijuana raises emotional issues and, unfortunately, objective data are sometimes spiced with subjective interpretations.
Some tests haven't had control groups; yet dramatic interpretations have been made. Example: Sperm count experiment.
Hybrid rats, which could prompt reports that drinking water leads to cancer, have been used.
[Must be supplied by listeners; e.g., "Subjectivity invalidates experiments," or "Emotion shouldn't creep into experimentation and interpretations," or "Replicability, duplication of findings, and use of representative subjects are standard tests of experimental validity."]
Often
CONDITION OF REBUTTAL
(That subjectivity "sometimes" occurs can't make all experiments invalid.)
There is a problem about the validity of laboratory tests.
DATA
WARRANT
QUALIFIER
CLAIM
There is often a problem about the validity of laboratory tests [on marijuana].
[Must be supplied by listeners; e.g., "Replication and controls make for validity," or "Where you suspect validity problems, you should check duplications of findings and experimental conditions."]
[None given.]
The public must be wary of medical reports about marijuana and only regard seriously those which have been duplicated and which have been done under proper experimental conditions.

FIGURE 5-3 ***Toulmin system illustrating extended argument***

authority would provide what Toulmin calls **backing for warrant**.) Adding such words would have completed the second argument, in Toulmin's terms, but the practical question for Mayhew—or for you—is: do I need to *say* it, or will the listeners supply it? If the listeners can be trusted to supply any part of an argument, you may bore them by saying it in words. We suspect that Mayhew would have lost little by saying the sentence we have just put in quotation marks, but we doubt that he lost anything by leaving the notion to be filled in by his actual audience. However, if he had been talking with immature listeners—say, fifth graders—or with listeners of low intelligence, it would probably be important to say something like "You can't have a reliable experiment unless you can compare the group you're testing with some other group that isn't given the drug you're testing; if you want to see how a drug works, you need to compare what happens to the people who take the drug with what happens to people who don't take it." Our point is simply that in building a rational proof, *how much* you need to say about each part of each argument depends on what the audience knows and does not know. What they don't know needs to be supplied in words. Rational proof is "complete" only when you are confident that all of its parts are present either in the heads of the listeners or in your words.

From the example of Mayhew's arguments we can draw several guidelines that should direct you in trying to prove anything rationally.

1. You need this kind of proving whenever a **claim** you want to make is unfamiliar to your listeners or whenever you have reason to think the listeners might doubt it. In either of those two circumstances your task is to show that some **data** exist to justify your conclusion or **claim**. Then, the crucial things are to show that the facts or **data** that support you are true and significant and that there is good *reason* (stated as **warrant** or left to be understood by the audience) for drawing your particular conclusion or **claim** from these facts. If there is any danger that your listeners will doubt or deny the **data** you base your conclusion on, you will need to add to and defend those **data** until it seems unlikely that any listeners can miss their truth and importance. If *the way* your **claim** grows out of the **data** is apt to be obscure or doubted, you will need to state that **warrant** in so many words, and perhaps supply additional reasons **(backing)** to show why it is legitimate to draw the kind of conclusion you do. When there will be doubt or uncertainty about anything you claim, you need rational proof to support what you say.

If no one will doubt what you want to claim, you may need to amplify the point and make it more vivid, but you don't need to build a rational proof for it. This is your guideline for deciding when rational proofs are needed at any point in a speech and when they are not.

2. When rational proofs *are* needed, how *much* proving is required depends on (a) your listeners' knowledge of the point in question, (b) the kinds of tests these listeners are used to applying when matters of this sort come up, and (c) your relationship (as authority, equal, or inferior) with the audience in your particular rhetorical situation.

A mistake speakers make is to give only their own validations for ideas. The real audience sometimes applies more exacting standards than the speaker is prone to. You may feel strongly that the Denver Broncos are a better football team than the Los

Angeles Rams, but if you say that to an informed football enthusiast, you are going to have to give reasons. On the other hand, if your listener is not a sports enthusiast, the same set of reasons would tell him or her "more than I want to know." To avoid either underproving or overproving, we suggest that you ask yourself two questions whenever you begin to build reasons into a speech: (a) Are the evidence and reasons sound enough so *I* believe them, for myself? and (b) How much *more* or *less* than this will it take to satisfy my listeners in the situation where I will meet them? If what you *know* is sound enough to satisfy you when you make your own judgments, you will meet your responsibilities as a conscientious speaker. If you tailor what you know to your listeners' interests and needs, you will meet your responsibilities and aspirations as a well-received communicator.

3. Our example of Mayhew's speech should remind you that on decriminalization of marijuana and on thousands of other arguable topics there is little that we can prove *finally*. The maximum goal in most rhetorical proving is to invent structures of thought and evidence that will prompt listeners to think, "That's more reasonable than anything else I know of." For the most part, the arguments you will need to build will be arguments about what seems most *probable*. You can seldom show that what you say is absolutely true; your goal should be to show that the reasons for believing what you say are stronger than those for disbelieving it.

4. Because rhetorical arguments are seldom conclusive, their attractiveness and their sources enter into listeners' judgments of them. Your reasoned proofs will therefore be strongest if you present them in ways that also appeal to listeners' established ways of thinking and feeling and in ways that reflect credit on *you* as their source. It is almost always possible to find rational justifications that rouse the special interests of listeners and at the same time reflect your own intelligence and consideration for your audience. Remembering to qualify his **claim** with the word *often* was not only logically necessary for Mayhew; it also showed he knew what he could claim and what would be too much to claim. Illustrating another way of appealing to listeners while giving them reasons and evidence, a student at the University of Colorado at Boulder spoke to her classmates on the need for preventative medicine as a hedge against skyrocketing medical costs.[6] In showing that costs were truly rising, she was careful to cite both national costs and costs in the city of Boulder where her listeners were living. And to illustrate these costs she amused the listeners mildly by quoting the hospital charges for "what some people call a 'routine procedure,' having a baby," and for such "replacement parts for your body" as "a new plastic finger" and "a silicone breast replacement." She forcefully supported her **claim** that medical costs were becoming exceptionally high but at the same time was considerate of her listeners by selecting **data** that were "close to home" and by relieving the possible tediousness of statistical data through injecting a bit of irony: "routine" for childbirth and "replacement parts" for prostheses. In sum, as you assemble evidence and reasoning for points you must argue, you should give some attention to which ways of handling the material will put you in the best light and appeal to the personal interests of your listeners.

5. We have said several times that few rhetorical arguments can be *certainly* true. Then what are the standards by which their adequacy is judged? What measures

do listeners and critics apply to your rational proofs? The tests listeners apply are largely a series of cultural "should not's." Listeners will doubt your arguments, intelligence, and good will toward them if you seem to:

a. contradict yourself. Consistency in all reasoning is counted as rational justification, inconsistency as irrational.

b. draw on **data** that have no clear relevance to what you are claiming. Introducing material not clearly connected with the **claims** made is counted as illogical and often as a sign of the reasoner's ignorance.

c. use examples that are unrepresentative or unfairly chosen. Listeners then tend to think you either "don't know any better" and so are undependable or that you are deliberately unfair and so are untrustworthy.

d. use **warrants** the listeners do not understand or deny. If they cannot see *why* **data** lead naturally to the **claims** you make, listeners will consider the reasoning faulty or consider you obscure, or both.

e. claim *more* than your **data** justify. Careful **qualification** of **claims** is taken as a sign of sound logic and of intelligence, as in Mayhew's case. Failure to qualify appropriately is taken as a sign of faulty reasoning and, perhaps, of ignorance or intent to deceive.

f. use incompetent or unqualified sources for **data** or as **backing** for **warrants**. Again, such choices are counted as signs of ignorance, intent to deceive, or both.

These are the general lines along which listeners of our culture evaluate rhetorical proofs that purport to be rational. A point you should notice is that when fault is found with an argument, it is also likely that the arguer will be faulted as a person. You will be wise to recheck each bit of reasoned proof you build against these "should not's" and to check all of your rational proofs, taken together, to see that there are no inconsistencies among them.

If you check your proposed reasonings as we checked Steve Mayhew's, you will be able to judge when the support for a **claim** is sufficiently complete and convincing for the kinds of listeners you will address. For a good example of simple but carefully developed rational proof, look at paragraphs 5 through 8 of Dr. Upcraft's speech in Appendix B. Upcraft's audience did not really want to believe that their university ought to adopt a stern policy concerning drinking in residential halls, yet Upcraft built a powerful, logical argument for why the policy must be adopted. (See Figure 5–4.) There was no doubt about the **data** here. The issue was whether or not "legal trouble" was a likely consequence of the university's position's being neglected. Upcraft backed his unexpressed **warrant** in ways even a reluctant listener must accept —with reason and with legal authority. It is hard to conceive of a stronger argument, for only if Upcraft's logic (**backing** 1) can be denied and/or the legal opinion (**backing** 2) can be countered with an equally authoritative contrary opinion could the **claim** be challenged. It seems unlikely that the listening students would be able to do either. Upcraft was therefore right in judging that this unit of rational proof would be sufficiently complete and convincing for his audience and rhetorical situation.

The rational proofs you build for your **claims** in speeches need to be tested in the

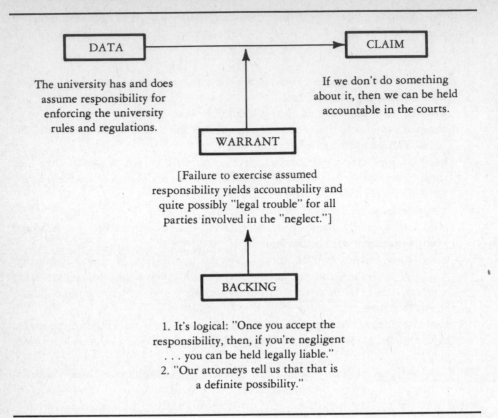

FIGURE 5-4 *Toulmin system applied to Upcraft speech*

same commonsense ways. Avoid the pitfalls we identified on page 123 and test convincingness in the way we have done with Dr. Upcraft's argument, and you will have done what a speaker can do to appear convincingly reasonable.

Making yourself a justification for ideas

"Why should I listen to *you* on this matter?" is something asked about every speaker, and often. Aristotle pointedly stated the reasons for the question.

The character of the speaker is a cause of persuasion when the speech is so uttered as to make him worthy of belief; for as a rule we trust men of probity more, and more quickly, about things in general, while on points outside the realm of exact knowledge, where opinion is divided, we trust them absolutely. This trust, however, should be created by the speech itself, and not left to depend upon an antecedent impression that the speaker is this or that kind of man. It is not true, as some writers on the art maintain, that the probity of the speaker contributes nothing to his persuasiveness; on the contrary, we might almost affirm that his character is the most potent of all the means of persuasion.[7]

It may seem strange to call on so ancient an authority to explain the influence of speakers as their own justifications. The fact is that, although no topic has been more diligently studied by experimenters interested in rhetoric, there is still no more succinct and defensible statement on the practical role of a speaker's *ethos* than Aristotle's. He wrote:

> As for the speakers themselves, the sources of our trust in them are three, for apart from the arguments [in a speech] there are three things that gain our belief, namely, intelligence, character, and good will. Speakers are untrustworthy in what they say or advise from one or more of the following causes. Either through want of intelligence they form wrong opinions; or, while they form correct opinions, their rascality leads them to say what they do not think; or, while intelligent and honest enough, they are not well-disposed [to the hearer, audience], and so perchance will fail to advise the best course, though they see it. That is a complete list of the possibilities. It necessarily follows that the speaker who is thought to have all these qualities [intelligence, character, and good will] has the confidence of his hearers.[8]

Modern scientists have devoted a good deal of effort to exploring the dimensions of *ethos,* the speaker as justification for ideas. On the whole their findings argue that what listeners look for and weigh in speakers is a pair of attributes Aristotle called "intelligence" and "character" and investigators of the past forty years have variously called "competence-trustworthiness," "expertness-trustworthiness," "authoritativeness-character." Something similar to what Aristotle called "good will" or "the beginning of friendship" [9] turns up in other studies, suggesting that we look for and respond to personal qualities we like and can identify with.[10]

How does one build into a public speech proofs of intelligence, trustworthiness, and good will toward listeners? Virtually every choice you make in composing and presenting public speech will "say" something about whether you do or don't possess these qualities. What is it you want to show then?

Intelligence   Your material and your treatment of it must show that you know your subject well and can treat it accurately but appropriately to the situation you are in. The University of Colorado student who presented both national and Boulder, Colorado, data on medical costs (page 122) showed that she knew enough to collect both general and specific information relevant to her rhetorical situation. Ample, precise, but not overwhelming information signals that you know your subject and that you know it exactly. In talking about conservation to a persuasion class, a University of Delaware student said:

> If you ever go up into the area of the Creek, what you'll find is a quiet, scenic, very beautiful forest. I was there recently and, believe me, it is, indeed, beautiful. There are over thirty varieties of wildlife present—ranging from deer and foxes to the rare flying squirrel. And some 143 species of birds and twenty different types of reptiles and amphibians. Plant life is just as richly abundant—more than 250 species —forty-three kinds of trees and well over 200 varieties of wildflowers.[11]

We think this speaker established himself as specially qualified to discuss the future of this area because he showed quickly, precisely, but selectively that he knew it in detail. And whenever you can unpretentiously reveal that you know your subject first-hand, you will build further credit with your listeners for knowledge and intelligence about the subject.

Being clear and explicit about what is most important and playing down what is trivial or not exactly to the point are two other ways of displaying intelligence and in consequence generating trust. A segment from a panel discussion that took place in one of our classes illustrates this. A group of students decided to investigate apartment leasing in their university community. When they had finished their investigation, they made a presentation to advise their classmates on renting apartments. The group gave a series of formal speeches and at the end invited questions. Here is a transcript of a few minutes of that question-and-answer period.

Questioner 1 in audience:	Did anything especially surprise you in your study?
Panelist 1:	One thing that amazed me was that when we made a survey of students who rent apartments, we found an astonishing number of people who didn't even read their leases. That was one of our questions: "Did you read your lease? If you did, did you understand it?" There were an amazing number of people who hadn't read them at all.
Audience questioner 2:	But isn't it the situation that if you don't sign the lease, whether you read it or not, you don't get the apartment?
Panelist 1:	These people signed the leases without even trying to read them.
Questioner 2:	But even if you read it, you could hate it.
Panelist 2:	That's just the point. There are important degrees of what's said in leases. And we found great differences in both leases and how renting companies treated them. We found one company that went over the leases with the renters, but another one had contract terms that were really bad, in fact amazing. Yet people didn't read, so they couldn't pay any attention to the differences.
Panelist 3 (to questioner 2):	I don't think you have the picture right. Leases can be full of tricky clauses. Now, when you look for an apartment, you have to file a lease application. At that time you'll *see* the lease. You file the lease application and you put down half of the required security deposit—it's either that or you deposit one month's rent. Now they'll send you the lease, and if you read it for the first time at this point and don't like it, and refuse to rent, you forfeit your deposit. That's all perfectly legal because you signed the lease application. But you're stuck simply because you didn't read the lease when you had the first chance. It *costs* not to read!

| Questioner 3: | I take it then that you found marked differences among leases. |
| Panelist 2: | Besides the differences in requirements that we've talked about, another major difference was that some were long and full of details and others were short, direct, easy to read, and easy to understand. |

In these exchanges the panelists impressed their listeners because they so obviously knew the facts about leases and leasing and were clear in their own minds about the precautions renters should take. Panelist 1 was entirely clear on why failing to read leases was always a mistake. Questioner 2 missed or ignored what was said, but panelists 2 and 3 refused to be drawn away from the central point; they restated it and reviewed, with special emphasis, why and when it was important to read a lease. And when questioner 3 restated what the panel had already said (panelist 2 had said that differences were great), panelist 2 took the opportunity to restate the general idea and add a further fact about the differences.

In these short public speeches the speakers on the panel made *themselves* supporting proofs of their ideas. By what they said and by their insistence on not straying from the main points they showed they were fully informed—at firsthand—and that they understood the whole subject well enough to separate the truly important from the less important. Still more, by trying to make a main point clear to questioner 2 they communicated their concern for all listeners' understanding, a sign of their good will toward the audience. In sum, by clearly focused communication they displayed their intelligence, trustworthiness, and good will.

Another way to show that you are intelligent enough to be believed and trusted is to treat your subject accurately but with no more detail and technicality than is necessary for your purpose with your audience. The possibilities here are too varied to enumerate, but the kinds of adaptations that show a speaker's concern for the limits of listeners' understanding can be suggested by comments two different instructors wrote to student speakers who had artfully adapted technical material to their classroom audiences. To a speaker who had talked on the need for and possibilities of solar energy for home use, an instructor wrote:

> You seem in command of the facts, and you seem reasonable. Nothing you say makes extreme claims, so we're more inclined to trust what you say. Your research shows, but you didn't overload us with information. We can also see that you gathered some of your information specifically for *us*. As your student-critic said, "statistics were used when we needed them"; and so it was with everything: you didn't tell us more than we needed to know to understand the immediately possible uses of solar heating.

At another university a student talked on the ground preparation that must precede any airplane take-off. His instructor wrote:

> Even though your subject was complicated, you simplified it for us and related it to us. Your analogies helped us. The comparison of giving directions on how to get to Arby's with the way a flight plan is filed was especially good for those of

us who don't understand flying. Your language was easy to understand because you explained any technical terms you *had* to use, and you didn't use such terms when simpler language was possible. It was also wise to have your map–visual aid specially marked so we would focus on the spots you wanted us to look at. We could follow your step-by-step description of preparation because you told us when you were beginning each step and when you had finished with it. That you could be so direct, informal, and concerned about just how much we would be able to understand showed that you had prepared this talk specifically for *us*, not for just anybody in the world.

These evaluative comments identify a variety of things you can do with materials for speeches in order to show that you are not only intelligent about your subject but are also intelligent about listeners' interests and abilities. You will also have noticed that the kinds of compositional choices that earn credit for being informed and intelligent earn credit for trustworthiness too. We trust those who show us that they know *both* what they are talking about and *to whom* they are talking.

Trustworthiness   Trustworthiness is attributed to a speaker when a listener thinks the speaker (1) knows what he or she is talking about and (2) shares and respects values that the listener prizes. We have seen this in the examples just discussed, but a further point needs to be made about shared values in communication. It is easy to say and it is to a considerable degree true that if you can show your listeners that your interests, goals, and values are like theirs, those listeners are likely to be attracted to you and what you say. Show them that you are not interested in what interests them or that you deplore what they value, and you will almost surely "turn them off." To earn trust, then, you need to work into your speech evidences that you *are* interested in your listeners and in the things they value highly. However, this is not the entire process of encouraging others to trust you as a speaker.

After an extended review of research on how persuaders persuade, Herbert W. Simons wrote:

> What emerges from this review is that persuaders should be similar to the audience, yes, but they should also be different in ways that increase their credibility. By what they say and do they should appear as "superrepresentatives" of the persons they are attempting to persuade.[12]

The point is an important one, for persuaders or any other speakers. The most trustworthy speaker on any subject is the one who knows most about it, provided the speaker also has good intentions toward us. As listeners, we trust most those who know *more* than we do, who understand *better* than we. As Simons says, we extend our fullest trust and belief to those who represent us but in a superior way, who are like us in interests and values but know more and are more experienced than we.

In composing a speech, then, you ought to reveal your special qualifications, directly and indirectly but in an unboastful way. The panelists we quoted earlier are good models. They said directly that *they* had personally read and compared the leases, *they* had surveyed student renters, and *they* had investigated how renting companies dealt with prospective renters. By firmly but unoffendingly correcting a listener's "picture" of the renting process, panelist 3 indirectly claimed that he and his colleagues understood the process best. But all the while these panelists were treating the subject of leasing from the point of view of student renters, the point of view that would most interest this audience of students. The student who cited medical costs in Boulder, Colorado, dropped the remark that she had gotten these figures from the community hospital. The student who discussed flight preparations mentioned early in his talk that he was a licensed pilot. All of these tactics and more are valuable ways of letting listeners know that you deserve their trust because you have acquired some *special* qualifications for speaking on your chosen subject.

Revealing your qualifications as a "superrepresentative" for your listeners is a delicate business. If you are obvious about it or give your own qualifications too much attention, you will seem boastful and therefore too insensitive to your listeners' intelligence to be trusted. If you hide your special qualifications, what you say will lack some of the influence it could have had. The best ways to hit the golden mean in claiming your right to be trusted are: (1) study your subject thoroughly so the depth of your knowledge will be reflected in your natural choice of the best sources, best arguments, and truly significant back-up information; (2) let it be known what special efforts you have made to insure that your ideas are sound (for example, you double-checked surprising statistics, consulted an especially well-known source, or made an experiment); (3) let it be known if you have some relevant firsthand experience; (4) if you have no special qualifications, show that your data and interpretations are agreed to by people who are experts; and perhaps most important, (5) make it clear both directly and indirectly that you are speaking in your *listeners'* interests, not just your own.

Good will   According to Aristotle, good will is an aspect of personal proof. Modern investigators have not been able to identify this dimension of credibility when they have performed factor-analytic experiments. We think a reason may be that what Aristotle had in mind as "good will" is so entangled with what we moderns think of as "trustworthiness" that there is no clear separation of the two in our minds. However, Aristotle's notion of good will can be helpful in building the kind of personal proof or image of self that can win listeners' adherence to ideas. Aristotle conceptualized good will not as a quality of a person but as a quality *attributed* to a person. He believed we feel good will in someone when we think we perceive "some merit or goodness" and that the feeling of good will is a feeling of "undeveloped friendship." [13] We suggest that it can be very helpful to you as a speaker to ask yourself constantly: how must I treat this material to *show* my listeners that I am at least a *possible* friend to them and their interests?

Far more often than should be the case, we hear undergraduates and adults speak as though they were talking encyclopedias or writers for posterity. Speaking-listening is an intimate relationship if fully realized, yet speakers often make too little effort to show their wish to achieve person-to-person communication. It is not difficult. We heard an engineering student speak on satellite television in the home, using a set of main headings that clearly showed he had thought of his listeners' interests as he composed his speech.[14] His headings were:

I.   What is satellite TV reception?
II.   Why should you want this kind of reception?
III. What do you need to receive these signals?
IV.   What will it cost you?
V.   Are there any legal problems you could run into?
VI.   It's worthwhile to watch these developments; you'll soon be able to choose satellite reception against cable or antenna reception.

Mr. Baker had organized and adapted information about this technical development to suit the concerns of his consumer-oriented listeners. They were bound to respond to him as a person friendly to them and their concerns.

Bob Barth, whose speech on jet propulsion we discussed in Chapter 4, also earned personal credit for adapting to his listeners' limitations. And the pilot who spoke on preparations for flight displayed his consideration of his nonspecialist listeners.[15] He interspersed in his speech such remarks as:

> A flight plan is simply the detailed directions for getting from one place to another. Suppose you were telling a friend how to go from the State College Hotel to Arby's. What would you have to put in the directions to make them exact? . . . The pilot uses a device like this—a kind of circular slide rule—to figure out how much fuel he will consume in his flight. You needn't worry about how the calculation is done, but I do want you to remember that the plane's rate of fuel consumption, the time the flight will take, and the weather conditions he expects must all be known and entered into this preparatory step in planning.

By recognizing what was not essential to this audience and emphasizing what was essential, the pilot showed plainly his thoughtfulness concerning the specific audience he addressed.

Each of these speakers adjusted raw material to fit the particular interests, limitations, and needs of a specific audience. These special adaptations showed themselves in what was said. Each gave listeners reasons to feel that the speaker was friendly and considerate toward them. The listeners had proof that each speaker had thought about them as he prepared. That proof could become a reason for trust as well as for general friendly feeling. The speaker's rhetorical invention had been *for them*. Thereby each speaker showed he was intelligent about speaking as a relationship as well as about his subject.

In closing this section on the kinds of justifications or proofs speakers use to support their ideas, we repeat what we said at the beginning. We have had to discuss separately justifications accomplished (1) by calling up listeners' personal interests and habitual ways of thinking and feeling; (2) by providing data and reasoning; and (3) by displaying one's own intelligence, trustworthiness, and good will. But as our examples have shown, these ways of proving intertwine. Each kind reinforces or weakens the others.

A brief excerpt from a defense speech by a man who is still probably unmatched as a legal pleader in English will illustrate what we mean. Almost 200 years ago Thomas Erskine was pleading for his client, a defendant in what under modern laws would be called a divorce case on grounds of adultery. Erskine was already famed as both a prosecuting and defense attorney, and his opponent in this case had cautioned the jury that Erskine would try to sweep them out of their senses with rhetorical eloquence. Erskine's problem was to convince the jury that he would *not* become a spellbinder and that the proofs that his client had not seduced another man's wife required no eloquence from him but only the listeners' interests in getting at the truth of the matter and their understanding of the facts and the logic of the case. At one point in his plea he said to the jury:

> Now, to show you how little disposed I am to work upon you by any thing but by proof...I will begin with a few plain *dates,* and as you have pens in your hands, I will thank you to write them down. I shall begin with stating to you what my cause is, and shall then prove it—not by myself, but by witnesses.
>
> The parties were married on the 24th of April 1789. The child that has been spoken of, and in terms that gave me great satisfaction, as the admitted son of the plaintiff..., that child was born on the 12th of August 1791. Take that date, and my learned friend's [the plaintiff's attorney] *admission* that this child must have been the child of Mr. Howard [the plaintiff], an admission that could not have been rationally or consistently made but upon the implied admission that no illicit connection had existed *previously....* On this subject, therefore, the plaintiff must be silent. He cannot say...[his] parental mind has been wrung....[16]

All three kinds of justification or proof operated in this bit of speaking that probably took less than two minutes to deliver. The listeners' interest in not being led astray and their confidence that "facts" could not mislead them were used. Erskine's claim and *demonstration* of his reasonableness were offered as refutation of the other attorney's warning that Erskine would appeal to feelings only. Erskine's reasonableness intertwined with evidence of his considerateness and confidence in the jury when he invited them to figure out for themselves what the dates and the opposing attorney's admission proved about the child's conception and parenthood. If the listeners accepted Erskine's dates and thought about them in their usual ways, they must feel that Erskine was respecting, not misleading, them and that the plaintiff had no claim on their sympathies—at least prior to August 12, 1791. Ordinary ways of thinking and feeling, the logic of the dates, the opposing attorney's concession, and Erskine's evident regard for the jury's good sense all contributed to the same result for the jurors: there was no reason to think that Erskine's client had had an affair with Mr. Howard's wife at any time before August 1791. Neither was there reason to feel sorry for Mr. Howard, the plaintiff, or fearful of Mr. Erskine as a pleader.

This is such a fabric of interrelated proofs as you should try to weave as you compose speeches. Your central idea—whatever it is—needs the support of *all* the means of rhetorical proving.

CLARIFYING AND REINFORCING IDEAS

When you have constructed the skeleton of a speech showing the ways logic, listeners' interests, and evidences of your intelligence, trustworthiness, and good will support your central idea, there may be still further content you need to insert. Reasons and attitude-awakening statements may not in themselves give listeners all the knowledge they need nor sufficient time to think over the full meanings of what you have to offer. The speech you are planning may need no more proof, but points may need further *amplification*. It may be useful to expand your treatments of some ideas. Just the core statements may not be quite enough to make an idea clear, emphatic, or memorable. Thoughts that you add for these purposes we call *amplifying* procedures or tactics. These additions may strengthen proofs, but their chief functions are to clarify and/or reinforce ideas for which you have already constructed enough basic proof.

There are at least nine standard ways of clarifying and reinforcing ideas. We discuss them below, showing how each clarifies, reinforces, and incidentally proves.

Introducing anecdotes

An *anecdote* is usually a brief narrative illustrating an idea with which it is connected. To clarify or emphasize the force of a tornado you might narrate how a storm picked a house off its foundations and dropped it in a field a half-mile away. Fables, parables, imagined episodes, or real incidents allow you to amplify and clarify by narrating briefly. Narrating also allows you to dramatize the idea or event you have in mind. The chief things to consider when introducing anecdotes are that they need to be kept short and listeners must understand precisely what point or points they clarify or amplify.

An anecdote, like any other example, offers some rational proof about what it illustrates and clarifies. More importantly, an anecdote sets events before hearers actively and vividly. This invites listeners to exercise their customary ways of thinking and feeling, involving them in the subject as it is being clarified. Consider the following instance of an extended anecdote that sets many kinds of feelings and images working in order to communicate the depth of a man's gratitude.

William Howard Armstrong was trying to say how genuinely he appreciated the Newbery Medal awarded him at the American Library Association's convention at Detroit on June 30, 1970, for his story *Sounder*. "The boy" in *Sounder* has no other name. Armstrong used both his book's phrase "the boy" and an anecdote from his own life to amplify how and why it meant a great deal to him to receive the equivalent in children's literature of the Pulitzer Prize. He said:

> And now I find myself in the precarious position of having won a prize for a book called *Sounder*, written for anyone who might like to read it.
>
> Until I received a telephone call from Mary Elizabeth Ledlie some time in February, the word Newbery had *not* meant to me a man in England who stocked his bookshop with stories for children. [The award is named for such a man.] But Newberry had been a word to stir the deathless joy and remembrance of a small boy's Christmas. Because if that boy were especially good from somewhere around October 27th or November 12th until Christmas, his father would take him to Newberry's five-and-dime store in town. And after he had looked at all the bows and arrows and red wagons, he could ask the jolly, red-coated Santa Claus—enthroned amid the incense of chocolate and peppermint—to leave them under the Christmas tree for him.

But Newberry's Santa Claus never brought the bow and arrows or the red wagon. So out in the back pasture the boy would cut a maple sapling with his two-bladed barlow pocketknife that he had won for selling Cloverine Salve— guaranteed to cure shoulder-gall for horse and chapped lips for man. Then with sapling and binder twine from the hayloft, the boy would make his own bow.

But tonight it is real. The boy will not have to go home and hammer the Newbery Award out of the top of a Campbell soup can or out of a washer off the axle of his father's hay wagon.[17]

Many people have said thank you, but few have said it with more grace coupled with intense speaker-audience involvement than Mr. Armstrong—through the powers of anecdote.

To the extent that Armstrong's anecdote proves, it expresses his character as a sensitive and unpretentious man, even though he is a famous author. For a different, far simpler use of anecdote, look back at panelist 3 responding to a questioner in the audience (page 126). By putting his explanation in brief narrative form, having his questioner imagine going through the steps of leasing an apartment, he quickly involves the questioner in a set of experiences taking place through time. By this simple means he injects *action* into his explanation and proves by invoking the questioner's own self-interests, involving *her* in the action of failing to read the lease when she could have.

Finding or inventing an appropriate anecdote to show your idea or claim *in action* is especially wise when what you must talk about is abstract, as Mr. Armstrong's sense of gratitude or the act of "renting" that the panelist had to clarify.

Comparing and contrasting

Comparisons and contrasts clarify, vivify, and often *argue*. One may offer metaphors, similes, or antitheses, or compare and contrast anecdotes, examples, whole arguments, or descriptions. Since we acquire many of our new concepts by comparing or contrasting the new with the old, these methods are especially valuable because they use familiar learning processes. Since conflict and similarity are fundamentally interesting to people, all contrasting and comparing vivifies.

An important distinction is that a comparison or contrast, used primarily to *prove*, needs to be developed with much more attention to the *literal* likenesses and dissimilarities than do comparisons and contrasts used merely to intensify or clarify. Consider this sentence from President Jimmy Carter's Inaugural Address in 1977:

We will be ever vigilant and never vulnerable, and we will fight our wars against poverty, ignorance, and injustice, for those are the enemies against which our forces can be honorably marshalled.[18]

Carter did not mean wars in any literal sense. The goals he set for government were couched in war language for emphasis and to give listeners a sense of the activity and determination he hoped to instill in government. Everyone would recognize that the comparison of domestic action with war was figurative. Mr. Carter was under no obligation to show how his administration's policies would be literally like *war* policies. The comparison was a promise, not a claim requiring literal support.

However, the requirements were very different when Lady Barbara Ward Jackson, a British scholar in economics, addressed an audience at Herbert H. Lehman College in 1973 and undertook to show her audience that underdeveloped countries of the world had made great strides forward *under exceptionally difficult circumstances.* To prove this she built up a comparison between economic development in Europe and America in the nineteenth century and the more difficult economic circumstances in which underdeveloped countries must grow in the twentieth century. Here is the basic part of her comparison-contrast:

> Nineteenth-century industrialization created jobs, and the jobs, quite frankly, called for hands, mill hands. (Why mill hands? Because they only wanted their hands. They certainly did not want their brains.) In short, in the nineteenth century massive labor-intensive industry was the dominant technology. But in our century we have splendid, sophisticated, automated machines run by computers (which only break down about three times a year!). We have dispensed with the need for large reserves of manpower. And what is the result? The population curve goes up and the employment curve goes down. And on the edges of every major city [in developing nations] are the shanty towns where the environment for humans combines the worst of two centuries: nineteenth-century urban blight—bad sewage, cholera, and water-borne disease, and, added to all this, generally, the fancier sophistications of twentieth-century pollution—thermal, chemical, even nuclear.[19]

The speaker was presenting rational proof that developing countries have made their progress despite unusual difficulties. Her proof was the comparison-contrast of industrialization in two centuries. Each similarity and each difference she identified became **data** for the **claim** that development in the twentieth century is exceptionally difficult. Whether her **claim** was believed depended on how *literally* listeners accepted the similarities and differences Lady Jackson identified. Obviously Lady Jackson could not have met her situational needs by such quick, allusory, comparisons and contrasts as served President Carter's needs.

When you introduce comparisons or contrasts you will need to consider whether you want them to bear the weight of rational proofs or simply lend vividness and interest to what you say. If your purpose is to prove by comparison or contrast, you must be careful to supply enough detail so listeners will see and believe the *literal* similarities and differences.

Defining

When terms or concepts to be used in your speech could be obscure or ambiguous to your listeners, you may want to insert definitions of them. Defining is accomplished in several ways, not all equally effective in public speech. Ideas can be defined (1) by classifying them; (2) by differentiating them from other ideas that belong to the same class; (3) by exemplifying them; (4) by inferring their natures from the contexts in which they normally occur; (5) by referring to the etymological derivations of their names; (6) by explaining what they are not; (7) by describing or explaining them from some special vantage point (such as specifying what a musical note is if we view it as a complex of sound waves); (8) by specifying functions, as when a child defines an automobile as a thing to ride in.

The most formal kinds of definition are overused in speaking. This is particularly true of dictionary definitions that classify terms and define them etymologically. Definitions that compare, contrast, or exemplify are far more interesting and easier to understand. Classifications and derivations usually demand that the listener think abstractly; therefore it is a good rule to offer these definitions only *after* other modes of amplification have been provided. The formal definitions can then function to sum up other, easier-to-understand definitions, as in the first example below.

> To understand what a barge is, think of a railway coal car. [Example.] Take the wheels off the coal car and imagine the ends of the car are well sloped back toward the bottom. [Further detail by example.] Now imagine the wheel-less car floating in the water—a river, a canal, or possibly the sea. You have what is basically a barge: a floating cargo hauler, unpowered, low, and bulky. [Functional definition with characteristics that classify the barge.] A barge, then, is typically an unpowered cargo vessel used for hauling heavy freight. [Most abstract, classifying definition.]

Here is another definition of the same idea—a formal, classifying definition. It is less easy to take in at a single hearing and is so less suited to speech:

> A barge is a large, flat-bottomed boat used for transporting goods. While there are powered barges, most are towed. Modern barges are usually bulky vessels for hauling heavy freight.

The two explanations are the same in basic content, but the first proceeds from specific examples and comparisons to a concise, classifying statement. The second proceeds in the opposite order, confronting the listener with a difficult-to-absorb classifying statement at the outset and only afterward providing specific, concrete information.

Only occasionally do etymological definitions interest and genuinely clarify. It does not help very much to know that the English word *define* comes from the Latin *definire,* meaning "to limit." It is better to say that *define* means to "explain or set forth the limits of something." On the other hand, if you are trying to explain what *habeas corpus* means in law, the shortest, quickest, and most vivid way to do it is probably to tell your listener that the literal Latin meaning of *habeas corpus* is "you may have the body." In short, etymological definitions are always available to you, but they ought to be used or rejected according to the *practical* help they will give your particular audience. Discussion of derivations is not inevitably clarifying or interesting. Definitions that exemplify, describe, or compare and contrast are your best resources when you need to add brief explanations of difficult terms or concepts.

Describing

When Aristotle noted that people like communications that set pictures before their eyes, he pinpointed the chief standard by which to judge the value of a description. Telling anecdotes, comparing and contrasting, and defining emphasize the special details of whatever is being talked about, but describing usually sets the *whole* of something before a listener. Unless intended to be humorous or ironic, description ought to focus attention on significant rather than trivial aspects of what is being described. It should also clarify interrelationships or patterns that give the subject its special character, and it should be as pictorial as the content will allow.

You need to insert descriptions into speech when an example or two or a concise definition cannot provide enough detail or show fully the relationships that your listener needs to understand. Describing also gives you an opportunity to argue indirectly concerning the nature of what you describe. Since any describer fits together the elements that go into his or her description, the describer always implies that this is the best way of understanding what is described. If we accept a speaker's description, we accept that version of what is true.

Here is a fairly long description of imaginary circumstances used partly for clarification of a problem but more as an argument in favor of a policy. It was used by a science fiction writer testifying before a House of Representatives committee on the subject of copyright laws:

> I am a science fiction writer, so I spend quite a lot of time thinking about the future, including the future of the publishing business. I'm not so sure that's a cheerful thing to think about. I have a great respect for books and for the printed word, but the traffic may be going all in the other direction.
>
> It's easy to imagine a time, perhaps not very far in the future, when every work of art—every story, every poem, every book, every painting—is stored in some great galactic computer, and when you want to read *War and Peace* or *Lust for Life* or *Slaughterhouse-Five* you can just punch a few buttons and it will appear for you on a cathode tube—in your bedroom, if you like, so you can watch it between your toes like the Johnny Carson show. Well, that might not be so bad. But from there it's only a step to having the computers write or compose or draw the things in the first place, and then we're all out of business. . . . The prospect of electronic information storage and retrieval will produce serious difficulties for writers.[20]

Obviously Pohl was pictorializing an amusing prospect for readers of the future, but it is likely he created the description as a *support* for the **claim** made in the last sentence of our excerpt. The difficulties he implied and asserted in connection with his description were, in fact, supports of the final claim he made in his full statement:

> I think we're probably the only country of importance in the world that doesn't already have, or isn't about to get, a copyright law that protects the writer for his life plus 50 years. I think it's about time we did have one.[21]

When your primary goal is to provide information, not to argue, the best descriptions for you to use will be those that allow you to create clear and precise images in the listeners' minds. What follows is an excerpt from a classroom talk by an engineering student on "Acoustic Control." In the single, short passage you will see David Kaneda using brief description and then a two-sentence anecdote to pose a problem that will allow him to define and exemplify what a "sound leak" is. Mr. Kaneda has said that two major problems acoustic engineers must learn to control are (1) too much sound and (2) too little sound. Now he says:

First, I want to talk about too much noise. Now, fellows, try to picture this. It's Saturday night and you've come back to your apartment with your date. You've laid in a bottle of wine for this moment. All is mellow, or soon will be. Then, all of a sudden the guy next door decides he wants to listen to Lynyrd Skynyrd in stereo. The sound becomes so loud it seems it's in the same room with you. There goes your mood—and your date's. Now, assuming you had the door closed, how did the sound get into your room with you and your date? It came through paper-thin walls. Right? Wrong. Actually a lot of sound comes through what we call "sound leaks." A "sound leak" is just some place where there's no barrier to sound. For example it could be where the walls join.[22]

As you review what your research justifies you in saying, look for opportunities to amplify arguments through description of real or imagined scenes and for places where you can focus attention sharply by vivid images.

Introducing examples

Using examples is probably the most readily available and most useful of all modes of amplification and clarification. Whether factual or hypothetical, examples can focus listeners' attention on just those features of a subject that the speaker most wants understood. All of us have said perplexedly, "Can you give me an example?" We seem to understand specific cases more easily than generalizations, and most of us gain more satisfaction from specific data than from abstractions. Exemplifying, whether as a part of defining or in the form of anecdote or as an element in description, is the speaker's ultimate weapon where clarification and vivification are his principal concerns.

When you need only to illustrate, as David Kaneda did with his very brief anecdote of the neighbor turning on a Lynyrd Skynyrd record, your exemplification can be very brief, and it may take the forms of anecdote, comparison, contrast, a statistic, or some other. But if your point needs considerable expansion, you may want to insert a series of examples. The student who spoke on satellite TV reception for the home (page 130) developed his entire second point, "Why should anyone want this kind of reception?" by means of examples, listing a number of different kinds of programs receivable from satellites but not from ordinary sources of television programs. Often you will need only to identify some specific instances to make clear the reality or the importance of a general idea. At other times you will need to treat your examples as specific instances that prove a generalization you want to offer.

When your object is to *justify* a conclusion by citing examples, you need to choose examples that are typical—in no way out of the ordinary—for an instance must be representative to justify a generalization. You might illustrate the qualities of imported cars by citing the qualities of Datsuns and Fiats, but referring to Jaguars and Rolls Royces would be to cite unrepresentative cases. Furthermore, examples can become so interesting in themselves that even the points they are supposed to support or illustrate are lost. One of our students tried to illustrate "spot reporting" in radio journalism. His example was a tape recording of a network news reporter's on-the-scene, almost hysterical account of the unexpected murder of Lee Harvey Oswald (assassin of President John F. Kennedy) as Oswald was being transferred from his jail cell in Dallas, Texas. As the student might have foreseen, no listener remembered that this was supposed to be an instance of on-the-spot reporting. Predictably, all questions at the end of the student's talk had to do with details of President Kennedy's assassination and of Oswald's murder. Examples have great fascination for listeners; they need to be chosen to do exactly what you require of them—no more and no less.

Quoting

Quoting other sources can lend justification to what is said. This is especially true and important if your listeners do not consider you a person of authority on the matter you are discussing. Here's a clear example. We are not complete authorities on how this kind of evidence works in speech, but Professor James C. McCroskey has conducted a number of studies on the matter. So we will cite his statement:

> ...We found that a communicator with moderate-to-low ethos could increase his ethos by including factual material and opinions attributed to qualified sources. This effect, however, was not found in connection with all topics. Whether the audience is familiar with the evidence the communicator uses, or with similar evidence, appears to determine whether the communicator may build his ethos by including evidence in his message. If the evidence is unfamiliar to the audience, it has a favorable impact. Otherwise it has no effect. It is important to observe, however, that the inclusion of evidence has never been found by experimental researchers to lower a communicator's ethos, even if the evidence has been internally inconsistent.[23]

If on reading our quotation and noticing our note you tend to think we probably are giving you solid information on the uses of quotation, we have made our point. Not we, but the better authority, supports our claim that quoting other sources can lend justification to what is said.

Sometimes you will want to quote someone, not because the person is a major authority, but because he or she said things better than you could. For example, if you were talking about ambition you might conclude that the importance power has for ambitious men was especially well expressed by Oliver Wendell Holmes, Jr., when he said, "The reward of the general is not a bigger tent, but command." If you think so, that line might be a good one to quote in amplifying your own views. But as a *proof,* the quotation would not function as strongly as our quotation from McCroskey. If Holmes had said, "A general in the army is more interested in the size of his command than the size of his office or his tent," there would be no point in quoting Holmes. You could say the idea in your own words as well as he. On the whole, it is never worth quoting other people's words unless the quotation carries more authority than you can give or expresses ideas more clearly and wittily than you could.

Repeating and restating

Repeating and restating are important amplifying tactics. To give their hearers second and third chances to perceive and understand, speakers need to use these resources often. Research on the usefulness of repetition suggests that with each of your first three repetitions of a thought or fact you further increase the likelihood that your listeners will actually grasp what you say. It appears that after the third repetition, the gains achieved by each succeeding repetition diminish. There is also evidence that repetitions work best when you distribute them through other material rather than repeating the same item two, three, or more times in rapid succession. Apparently this is not true with restatements—phrasing a given idea in several different ways. These *re*phrasings have strong impact if given in rapid succession. Notice the restating function of these two sentences from a talk by the president of Deere & Company to an audience of industrial analysts. Both sentences say the same thing, but the second says it differently from the first:

> Our second goal is to achieve a more stable rate of growth than we have managed in the past. We want to lessen the downside swings which periodically have affected our earnings. . . .[24]

Obviously the corporation's president wanted to emphasize that steadier profits were the company's goal, not just stability for stability's sake. Restating the meaning of "stable rate of growth" as "lessen the downside swing" not only let him emphasize the policy but allowed him to touch the *financial* experts' special interests at the same time.

It is a good idea to consider what phrases or sentences you should use in moving listeners' thoughts from one of your main points to the next. These transition points offer good opportunities to work in restatements of the point being left, as you forecast what you will turn to next. If you have just completed showing that deficit spending contributes to inflation, you can move to the next point with a transitional statement such as: "Deficit spending contributes to inflation, but it's not the sole cause, so let's see how management of interest rates affects the economy." You will have used a natural opportunity to restate the thrust of your earlier point one more time, and you thereby improve the likelihood of its being remembered. As you flesh out each talk, look for such opportunities to repeat and restate without seeming to do so *just* for the sake of emphasis.

Any repetition—whether in the same or in different terms—increases the probability that the repeated idea will be perceived by a listener. Even unvaried repetitions tend to make listeners accept what they hear as true; so in this sense repeating and restating tend to justify the idea advanced even though the content may not change. You see and hear this principle used much in advertising, as slogans are repeated, sometimes in the same way and sometimes in different ways. The same practices are usually part of every propagandist's arsenal; Adolph Hitler wrote specifically that this was the way to sell "the big lie." True or false, it seems that what we hear often, we attend to and tend to believe. No speaker should forget this, but you should be equally alert to the fact that sheer repetition tends to irritate people if done unimaginatively.

Quantifying

Statistics clarify and often support or prove because they express quantity in the language of numbers. Therein lie the strengths and weaknesses of statistics as amplifying materials.

The danger of highway travel can be variously expressed. We can dramatize it through anecdote or example; we can compare it to the danger of air travel; we can describe congestion and consequent dangers. We can also express this danger statistically; but now we shift from word symbols to numerical symbols. By this shift we gain much in precision, but we lose much in imagery. We may say there were 500 traffic fatalities in Powhatan County, which has a population of 1,500,000 people. This is a precise expression of traffic deaths in that county. But to get this precision, the conditions under which 500 people died, all the consequences of their deaths, and much other information have to be dropped out of the story. We have chosen to represent people and things by numbers. Moreover, the language of numerical expression has specialized rules—a kind of special grammar. What is it the numbers represent? Considering what they represent, and how the counting was done, what may not be inferred? What kinds of statistical manipulation are allowable, given these numerical representations of reality? Such are the normal questions any use of numbers raises. Unless you tell your listeners—in so many words—how your statistics may and may not be interpreted, there is a strong possibility your statistical amplifications will confuse or even mislead. This means statistics alone are not very useful to listeners; listeners require numbers plus analysis of their meanings. If your research material contains important statistical data, you may need to insert comparisons or other clarifying tactics to emphasize their meanings. It is not immediately striking to say that in 1960 Kennedy defeated Nixon for president by 118,550 popular votes. But the significance of that number can be made instantly clear if you add that this voting margin represents fewer people than live in Topeka, Kansas, or about the same number as live in Savannah, Georgia. Such localized comparisons would emphasize the *narrowness* of the margin—which would be the real point of citing the figure.

Though they have limitations as supporting material for public speech, statistics are invaluable for showing quantitative attributes and relations. Because they are so valuable, it is important to remember that they not only need interpretation but that you may have to compensate for their abstractness. One good way of compensating for the burden statistics put on listeners is to round off the numbers; for example, let "1,611" become "slightly over sixteen hundred." You can help, too, by presenting any series of statistics visually as well as orally. Also, try not to concentrate a great many figures in any single part of your talk. This is not always avoidable, but if you must present several statistics at some single point in your speech, try to ease the situation by emphasizing comparison and contrast and by reinforcing the numerical data with such visual aids as graphs, charts, and tables.

Using audiovisual aids

Rightly used, audiovisual aids can give clarity, vividness, and appeal to personal interests and can provide rational justification for what you say. The trouble is that audiovisual aids are often unwisely introduced or clumsily used. The sensible reasons for using aids in public speech are to save or reinforce words, to bring ideas closer to listeners' live experience, to enhance attention by introducing change (but not for its own sake), and to relax listeners by letting them get information from a "new" source.

The audiovisual resources open to modern speakers are becoming more and more numerous. Every one of the following has been used to advantage in our speech classes: photographs, maps, charts and graphs, models, mock-ups, blackboard drawings, assistants who help with demonstrations, sound movies, slides, videotapes, musical instruments, disc and tape recordings, even the entire room in which the speaking was taking place! But with all these resources, it is still a fact that the most versatile and convenient audiovisual aid any speaker has available is his or her own body. You ought never to forget this as a speaker. What else bends, smiles, points, sounds off, never gets out of focus, and keeps on communicating even when the electricity goes off?

The basic principle you should apply when you think about whether an idea ought to be clarified or supported with audiovisual aids is this: Unless you can create an aid that is less complicated than the idea it is to clarify or support, *don't use one*. A useful aid makes understanding *easier* or it interferes with your message.

Despite the difficulties they can introduce, there will be many times when the basic material for a speech can be communicated best with the help of audiovisual resources. Then the following considerations come into play. Any aid you use ought to be relevant to whatever point you want to clarify or amplify. Consider the facts about your speaking situation. Whatever audio aids you use must be hearable or they will be worse than nothing; visual aids must be seeable or there will be no point to introducing them. In sum, take thought of the sight lines and the acoustics of the place where you will meet your audience. A good classroom exercise would be to discuss with your classmates what audiovisual aids would be appropriate in each of the settings we have sketched in Chapter 10, pages 264–267. What problems would be encountered with each kind of audiovisual aid you can think of, in each situation?

Another specific problem that needs consideration in deciding whether to introduce audiovisual aids is the time they will consume. Take a pair of extreme cases: There is nothing wrong with an hour-long documentary film or a twenty-minute segment of an opera, but what public *speech* could *contain* these audiovisual units? To be more practical, think of the judgment the students whose critique is presented in Appendix B had to make. They decided Dr. Upcraft's speech was not too long to present to their audience in full. They had thirty minutes for their presentation. Dr. Upcraft's speech was approximately twelve minutes long. That left the six panelists about eighteen minutes for their analysis of it. We leave you to judge whether they were wise to use the entire speech as an audio aid. What would you have done in their position had the speech been twenty minutes long?

There seems almost no end to the ways in which audiovisual aids can be misused in speaking situations; almost all misuses grow out of disregard for the fact that audiovisual aids potentially endanger the speaker's own mastery of purpose, audience, and occasion. "Who is in charge?" is always a pertinent question when audiovisual aids are brought in. The following true story presents a set of extreme circumstances, but it illustrates how and why unsophisticated use of audiovisual amplification can turn a speech into something very different.

The student's chosen subject was "The Treatment of Snakebite." Having introduced his subject, he startled his audience by releasing a white rat from a cardboard canister. The speaker announced that the rat's name was Maudie and whipped out a hypodermic needle. Plunging the needle into Maudie, he explained that he was giving the animal an injection of snake venom. Maudie would expire within a few minutes. Meanwhile, he would explain what steps a human being should take if bitten by a poisonous snake. To clarify these steps the speaker now drew grease-penciled lines and circles on his forearm to indicate where incisions should be made in cases of snakebite. But Maudie was dragging herself about, gasping her last breath in full view of everyone. Naturally, her troubles drew even the speaker's attention away from his explanations. He interrupted himself to comment: "Oh, yes. Bleeding at the mouth—quite natural at this stage." The speech, of course, was a failure, as any thoughtful person could have foretold from the moment this speaker decided to introduce poor Maudie as an aid.

We charge this speaker with cruelty and bad taste, but what is more to the point for our present purposes, he exercised no rhetorical, situational sense at all. The poisoning of a rat was foreseeably irrelevant to his purpose. It was certain to set in motion situational forces he could not control. It was predestined to draw attention away from what he alleged was his main message. Movement, attitudes of revulsion, surprise, the life-death contest, suspense—all these would predictably work to grip listeners' attention. No comparable forces could be arrayed to work for the speaker's message—however good his grease-pencil drawings or his exposition of them. Had one of us not actually experienced this event, we would have thought such rhetorical stupidity about audiovisual resources could not be found on a college campus. But we know lesser degrees of poor judgment are found everywhere. You have certainly seen speakers introduce charts so detailed you could not understand them. You have seen speakers pass items through an audience while trying to talk to the audience at the same time. You have seen models and mock-ups whose many detailed features so drew away your attention that you did not hear the two or three simple points their introducer wanted to make about them. You have been, then, in the presence of the fundamental mistake made by Maudie's executioner: poor judgment with regard to the rhetorical potency of an aid.

What we want you to see is that audiovisual materials used for their own sakes can overwhelm speaker and speech. "A picture is worth a thousand words," it is said. But if pictures or other nonspeech content can convey one's entire message, the speaker ought to send the pictures and omit the speech.

We have no desire to minimize the values of audiovisual devices as clarifying, vivifying, and amplifying resources for speakers. Very often they are invaluable, even essential. How many people know where Izmir is without having it pointed out on a map? What is the best way to enable an audience to understand the differences between an emu and an ostrich? To show pictures, of course. To differentiate a diatonic from a chromatic musical scale? Let them hear the two. Audiovisual means of clarifying and amplifying are invaluable, rightly chosen and used. To remind you again of their variety here is a partial list:

the object itself
models: complete, cut-away, and mock-up
motion-picture film clips
photographic slides
photographic enlargements
maps
blackboard or other sketches, diagrams, and outlines
graphs: bar graphs, pie graphs, and pictorial graphs
schematic representations: organizational charts, genealogical charts, and so on
sound tapes and disc recordings
videotapes
other people: as demonstration assistants, examples, and so forth
staged scenes

The list could be extended. Any device whatever that will present an idea to the five senses—sight, hearing, touch, taste, and smell—may help you clarify, vivify, and prove what you want to tell through speech. But to summarize our cautions as well as the potentialities of such aids, here are a few do's and don'ts it will be useful for you to remember:

1. Introduce visual and other external resources where you think your best verbal-personal presentation is likely to fall short of complete clarity.
2. Always *verbalize* what it is your listeners are *supposed* to see, hear, and understand from any audiovisual resources you introduce.
3. Where more than a few seconds are to be devoted to an aid, let your hearers know what they are to learn from it *before* introducing it; then restate what should have been learned *after* using the aid.
4. Design or edit all aids to eliminate or hide objects and material that are irrelevant to your immediate purpose. Eliminate whatever might send listeners' thoughts in directions you do not wish them to go.
5. Use your aid where you need it; then get it out of sight and hearing so your audience cannot dwell on it when you want them to attend to something else.
6. If possible, pretest sight lines and sound levels from all positions in which listeners will be during your speech. Pretest the workings of your aid if it has to operate in any way.
7. Give *your* attention to the audience when using audiovisual aids, not to the devices. You are still the main communicator, and your listeners need your attention even though they are receiving part of your message through another source.
8. Always choose the *simplest* form of audiovisual stimuli capable of doing what you need done. For the same reasons, keep machinery to the minimum for getting your task done.

The most important advice for all speakers who take advantage of audiovisual resources is: *keep yourself in charge and maintain the closest possible personal relation with your hearers.* You are still the chief messenger!

In the latter part of this chapter we have identified nine ways of adding clarification, amplification, and reinforcement to basic ideas that will be parts of speeches you plan. As we have shown, most clarifying tactics also support ideas rationally, psychologically, or both. We cannot give you formulas for adopting these tactics. We can only say that when you are composing any public speech, review all the points you feel you must make and ask yourself whether one or more of these special procedures would make the points clearer and stronger for your listeners. In addition to clarity and reinforcement, frequent use of these methods will give your talk the kinds of variety in development that audiences like.

The function of this chapter has been to show you the resources of proving, clarifying, and reinforcing that are open to every speaker's use. Once your research is completed and your central idea refined, your tasks are to build the proofs and add the clarifications and reinforcements that your presentation allows and needs. We have shown you that rhetorical proofs are of at least three kinds: those rooted in listeners' standard ways of thinking and feeling, those that assert rationally supported claims, and those that arise from listeners' perceptions of you as an intelligent, trustworthy guide of good will. These forces *will* operate as you speak; the question of how favorably they will operate for you is answered by your wisdom in deciding how to manage the raw materials that form the core of your message. One aspect of that management is proof building, which we discussed in the first part of this chapter; another aspect is adding vivifying, clarifying, and reinforcing procedures, nine of which we have just identified and illustrated. What blend of proofs and reinforcements is best for the next speech you will give, we cannot know. We hope to have shown you *ways of thinking* about proofs, clarifications, and reinforcements. If, as you flesh out each plan for a speech, you keep your listeners' needs, interests, attitudes, and goals in mind, you are likely to come to sound conclusions about where to evoke their feelings, their trusted ways of reasoning, and your own credibility in support of your central idea and the points that develop it. And the same regard for your listeners must guide your decisions about where and how to clarify and reinforce those proofs.

What you want to accomplish with your audience puts some special constraint on your rhetorical invention, of course. We therefore complete our study of invention by considering in the next chapter what special tactics are yours, depending on whether you plan to inform, inquire, reinforce views, persuade, or entertain.

EXERCISES

Written

1.   Before beginning other preparation for your next speech write out a "Choice of Subject" paper containing the following information: (a) an exact statement of your proposed speech subject; (b) an exact statement of your central idea;

(c) a brief essay explaining why your subject and central idea are timely, significant for you and your audience, amenable to oral presentation, and manageable in the time available. Present this paper to your instructor for evaluation, or have two or three classmates read it over and tell you whether they understand exactly what you plan and whether it seems a wise plan for the audience you will meet.

2. Evaluate each of the following statements. Indicate how well each meets the criteria for good expression of a central idea. Properly rephrase any statement you find unsatisfactory in wording.

   a. Don't adopt the sales tax.

   b. This is a speech to clarify the processes by which committee chairpersons are chosen in the United States Senate.

   c. I want to explain that women ought to receive the same pay as men when they perform the same jobs and that in general their equality with men should be universally recognized.

   d. Economic and social effects of the growth in the United States' tourist industries since 1960.

   e. It takes study to appreciate the art of motion pictures.

3. As you prepare your next talk, label in the margins of your outline what *kind* of supporting or amplifying material you are planning to use at each point. Then write a short paragraph contending that you have achieved the best degree of *variety* in supporting material that is open to you. Discuss your defense with your instructor or one or two of your classmates.

4. Identify and evaluate (a) the kinds of proof and (b) the kinds of clarification-amplification used in the following excerpt from Leonard Bernstein's lecture, "The World of Jazz":

> But I find I have to defend jazz to those who say it is low-class. As a matter of fact, all music has low-class origins, since it comes from folk music, which is necessarily earthy. After all, Haydn minuets are only a refinement of simple, rustic German dances, and so are Beethoven scherzos. An aria from a Verdi opera can often be traced back to the simplest Neapolitan fisherman. Besides, there has always been a certain shadow of indignity around music, particularly around the players of music.
>
> I suppose it is due to the fact that historically *players* of music seem to lack the dignity of *composers* of music. But this is especially true of jazz, which is almost completely a player's art, depending as it does on improvisation rather than on composition. But this also means that the player of jazz is himself the real composer, which gives him a creative, and therefore *more* dignified status.[25]

Oral

1. With a group of four or five classmates choose a subject to talk about. Almost any subject will do. Assign to each member of the group *one* of the nine ways

of clarifying and reinforcing ideas discussed on pages 131–143. Have each member of the group prepare a one-minute statement about the agreed-on subject, using primarily the single method of clarifying and reinforcing ideas that was assigned to him or her. After each group member speaks, discuss the advantages and disadvantages *any* speaker will face when he or she chooses to amplify ideas by that method.

2. Working in groups as suggested in oral exercise 1, assign each group member the task of using *one* of the three ways of building proof discussed on pages 109–131 in a one-minute talk about some aspect of the topic the group has chosen. Following each presentation discuss how the one-minute talk could have been made stronger (a) by using additional kinds of justification for what was said and (b) by better use of the particular kind of justification assigned to the speaker.

3. Using a group like that suggested in oral exercises 1 and 2 above, choose a subject for an imaginary speech to be given in a situation you have imaginatively worked out. In group discussion phrase the ideal central idea for the imaginary speech, agree on what main points ought to be made about it, and make a list of what tactics of invention would be especially important in developing each point.

4. Prepare and deliver a one-point informative speech in which you use at least four forms of amplification.

5. Prepare and present a short speech on some aspect of a subject you know your classmates disagree about. Try to build enough rational justification into your speech to satisfy a skeptical listener. After the speech, invite a listener who agrees with you and one who still disagrees with you to evaluate how well you proved your point. Conduct a class discussion of their evaluations of your proof.

6. Present an oral report on an advertisement or advertising campaign. Discuss how established ways of thinking and feeling, rational support of claims, and the credibility of sources were used in this advertising.

7. With a group of three or four others in your class, or alone, choose one of the figures in Chapter 10 (Figures 10–1, 10–2, 10–3, or 10–4): (a) analyze whether the setting makes visual aids desirable and if so why; (b) determine what sight lines a user of visual aids needs to be especially concerned about in this setting; (c) decide what would be the best *kinds* of visual materials to use in this setting if any at all proved desirable. When you have made your analysis, report your conclusions, with reasons, to your class.

ENDNOTES

1. Among experimental studies supporting this proposition are Donald L. Thistlethwaite, Henry deHaan, and Joseph Kamenetzky, "The Effect of 'Directive' and 'Non-Directive' Communication Procedures on Attitudes," *Journal of Abnormal and Social Psychology* LI

(July 1955): 107–18; Donald K. Darnell, "The Relation Between Sentence Order and Comprehension," *Speech Monographs* XXX (June 1963): 97–100; Ernest Thompson, "Some Effects of Message Structure on Listeners' Comprehension," *Speech Monographs* XXXIV (March 1967): 51–57; John E. Baird, Jr., "Effects of Speech Summaries upon Audience Comprehension of Expository Speeches of Varying Quality and Complexity," *Central States Speech Journal* XXV (Summer 1974): 119–27.

2. For a concise outline of a general theory of attitude change, see Irving L. Janis, Carl I. Hovland et al., *Personality and Persuasibility* (New Haven: Yale University Press, 1959). Parts of the summary we have presented derive from C. W. Sherif, M. Sherif, and R. E. Nebergall, *Attitude and Attitude Change* (Philadelphia: W. B. Saunders, 1965). We have also drawn on Ch. Perelman and L. Olbrechts-Tyteca, *The New Rhetoric* (Notre Dame: University of Notre Dame Press, 1969), and Vernon E. Cronen and William K. Price, "Affective Relationship Between Speaker and Listener: An Alternative to the Approach-Avoidance Model," *Communication Monographs* XLIII (March 1976): 51–59.

3. The complete text of this speech appears in Wil A. Linkugel, R. R. Allen, and Richard L. Johannesen, *Contemporary American Speeches,* 2nd ed. (Belmont, Calif.: Wadsworth Publishing Company, 1969), pp. 203–11. The excerpt quoted appears on p. 205, as "paragraph" nine.

4. The talk was given by Stephen T. Mayhew, then a sophomore in business administration at The Pennsylvania State University. It was one of a series of speeches given in a basic speech course; the title the students chose for the series was "The Case of Marijuana: To Decriminalize or Not?" Used by permission of Mr. Mayhew.

5. Stephen E. Toulmin, *The Uses of Argument* (Cambridge, Eng.: Cambridge University Press, 1958). See especially Chap. 3, "The Layout of Arguments."

6. Ms. Mary Lou Figley was the University of Colorado student.

7. From *The Rhetoric of Aristotle,* translated and edited by Lane Cooper, pp. 8–9, bk. I, chap. 2. © 1932, renewed 1960 by Lane Cooper. Reprinted by permission of Prentice-Hall, Inc., Englewood Cliffs, New Jersey.

8. Ibid., pp. 91–92, bk. II, chap. 1.

9. *Ethics,* trans. J. A. K. Thomson (New York: Penguin Books, 1976), p. 296, bk. IX, chap. 5.

10. A good summary of contemporary research on the *ethos* of speakers and the credibility of sources in general appears in Gary Cronkhite, *Persuasion: Speech and Behavioral Change* (Indianapolis and New York: Bobbs-Merrill, 1969), pp. 172–78. For a general discussion of the role of identification between speaker and listener, see Herbert W. Simons, *Persuasion: Understanding, Practice, and Analysis* (Reading, Mass.: Addison-Wesley, 1976), chap. 8, "Establishing Common Ground."

11. Robert Dike was the University of Delaware student.

12. Simons, *Persuasion: Understanding, Practice, and Analysis,* p. 162. For Simons's full discussion see pp. 152–67.

13. *Ethics,* pp. 296–97, bk. IX, chap. 5.

14. The speaker was Maurice Baker, an electrical engineering student at The Pennsylvania State University.

15. The speaker was Alan Kominsky, a premedical student at The Pennsylvania State University.

16. Thomas Erskine, "On Behalf of Mr. Bingham," a trial for adultery, the court of King's Bench, February 24, 1794. Text adapted from Chauncey A. Goodrich, *Select British Eloquence* (New York: Harper and Brothers Publishers, 1880), p. 709.

17. William H. Armstrong, "Newbery Acceptance Speech," delivered June 30, 1970, and published in *The Horn Book Magazine* XLVI (August 1970): 352–55. Printed by permission of the publisher.

18. Inaugural Address, January 20, 1977. Text as reported by United Press International news service.

19. From "Proposals for a Planetary Community," Herbert H. Lehman Memorial Lecture,

Herbert H. Lehman College of the City University of New York, April 10, 1973, by Lady Barbara Ward Jackson, then Schweitzer Professor of International Economics at Columbia University. Text as published by Lehman College Publications, Number Nine.

20.   Frederik Pohl, science fiction writer and editor, testifying on June 18, 1975, The Gold Room, Rayburn House Office Building, Washington, D.C. Text as in *An Author's Symposium for Congress,* published by the Coalition for Fair Copyright Protection, no date or place indicated. Mr. Pohl's statement, from which this is an excerpt, appears on pp. 6–7 of the text of the symposium.

21.   Ibid., p. 7.

22.   This speech was made by David K. Kaneda, an architectural engineering student at The Pennsylvania State University, in a basic speech course.

23.   James C. McCroskey, *An Introduction to Rhetorical Communication,* 2nd ed. (Englewood Cliffs, N.J.: Prentice-Hall, 1972), pp. 72–73. Most of the findings referred to here come from McCroskey's "Experimental Studies of the Effects of Ethos and Evidence in Persuasive Communication," D. Ed. dissertation (The Pennsylvania State University, 1966). See also McCroskey, "A Summary of Experimental Research on the Effects of Evidence in Persuasive Communication," *Quarterly Journal of Speech* LV (April 1969): 169–76.

24.   Remarks of E. F. Curtis to members and guests of The Machinery Analysts of New York, May 26, 1976. From the text of "prepared remarks," published by Deere & Company, Moline, Illinois.

25.   From Leonard Bernstein's televised lecture "The World of Jazz," in *The Joy of Music,* p. 97. © 1959. Used by permission of Simon and Schuster, New York.

CHAPTER 6

Invention in relation to purposes

Where can you apply the principles of this chapter in everyday life?

1. Wherever you need to give someone an extended explanation.
2. Wherever, as a committee member or other group leader, you need to pose a problem for discussion.
3. Wherever you need to intensify someone's beliefs or feelings.
4. Wherever you need to persuade someone to share your views.
5. Wherever you would like to entertain someone through talk.
6. Wherever you need to pick out material specifically suited to one rhetorical purpose rather than to another.

When evaluating someone else's speech consider:

1. Did the talk have a clearly dominant, overall purpose?
2. If informing was the primary goal, was the information accurate, sufficiently complete, and unified?
3. If inquiry was the primary goal, was the audience (a) prepared and (b) motivated to answer a clearly posed question?
4. If reinforcing beliefs and feelings was the primary goal, were familiar ideas related to listeners' values in interestingly fresh ways?
5. If persuasion was the primary goal, did the speaker support his or her positions with *all* three kinds of proof? Did he or she appeal to attitudes and feelings of the listeners, use rational proofs, and give evidence of intelligence, trustworthiness, and good will toward the listeners?
6. If entertaining was the primary goal, were ideas treated in unusual ways that would especially interest or amuse the listeners?

This chapter concludes our study of discovering and refining what will be useful to say in public speech. In Chapters 4 and 5 we focused on the problems of invention that all speakers face, no matter what their specific purposes. But as a speaker's purpose becomes more and more precise, the options in choosing subject matter narrow. The normal purposes for speaking tend to emphasize informing, inducing inquiry, reinforcing, persuading, or entertaining. If you focus clearly on what you want to accomplish in a given rhetorical situation, you will find that one of these goals dominates your aims. And depending on which purpose dominates, some inventional moves become more important than others. It is on these special requirements that we focus now, looking at the constraints of each conventional goal in speaking.

With your basic thinking and research completed and your material sifted, sharpened, and enlivened to serve your central idea, it is wise to reassess your preparation a final time to see whether you have done all that your special aim allows and requires. You are at the stage of final stock taking in rhetorical invention. What should you think about and recheck, depending on your overall purpose in speaking?

SPEAKING TO INFORM

There are times when speakers are fully satisfied if their hearers understand what is said. If that is what you aim for, your dominant goal is *informative* or, in other terms, explanatory or expository. A teacher's lecture and a physician's explanation of how a disease must be treated are examples of this kind of speaking. To a considerable extent the committee of students whose presentation appears in Appendix B had this kind of goal. But Dr. Upcraft, when he addressed the mass meeting of students on his university's drinking policy, could not be content with mere understanding.

Whether understanding is your aim for a complete speech or only for a section of a talk, certain kinds of material are called for and distinctive standards have to be met.

Any material that clarifies such attributes and relationships, as listed on page 84, is potentially appropriate for informing, except the attribute of *desirability*. If you get to talking about desirability, you will be moving out of the realm of informing and toward some degree of persuasion. Desirability as a topic implicitly or explicitly raises questions about debatable matters: "good," "bad," "better," "poorer." There is nothing inherently wrong with informing about a subject and then persuading your audience of its desirability, but you should know that when you do so you assume obligations beyond those of simply informing.

The standards listeners apply to talk that seems predominantly informative are: (1) *accuracy,* truth to fact in both detail and proportion; (2) *completeness,* sufficiently comprehensive to cover the subject; and (3) *unity,* intelligibility as a whole. When a speaker indicates that he or she wants us to understand, we begin watching whether what is said seems true, whether there is enough detail to allow us a full understanding, and whether what we are being told adds up to anything that fits together. If we think all those standards are met, we experience the satisfaction of "being informed." This being the case, you will be wise to recheck the whole of your speech plan to see whether you have in fact assembled enough material to meet these three tests.

Mistakes in explaining

What you promise in your central idea defines what you become obligated to be accurate and complete about. Promising more than you mean to cover or treating something different from what you seemed to promise are psychological mistakes. Listeners will hold you responsible for being accurate and comprehensive concerning as much as *you* say you mean to cover. Suppose you say you will explain "the nature of the modern bicycle." You will be thought inaccurate if you say or imply that all bicycles have several speeds; someone will know that racing and other bicycles do not. You will err by ignoring an important feature of modern bicycles if you neglect to point out that modern bicycles are specially designed for different uses. One cannot understand the varieties of modern bicycles without this important fact about the principles of their design. And your listeners' sense of the central, unifying principle of bicycle design will be less than ideal if you neglect to point out that no matter how designs differ, the goal of all designs is to relate human strength to speed of movement on some preconceived range of surfaces. However, you will be free to promise less than full information about all bicycles. If you say you will exclude racing bicycles from your explanation because they are so specialized, your listeners will no longer hold you responsible for their treatment. The important point is that your promise defines what you must explain accurately, comprehensively, and in a unifying way. Let your central idea express *exactly* what you intend to explain; then do that much, no more and no less.

Failure to provide listeners with a sense of unity or wholeness is frequent among information givers. A way to protect yourself against this is to recheck the statement of your central idea to see that it expresses all, but no more than, you want your listeners to understand. A very good practice is the following. Write the words: "When I finish I want my listeners to understand that. . . ." Insert after *that* a single clause expressing what you want to accomplish. "When I finish I want them to understand *that* the Battle of Gettysburg was a battle of maneuver rather than of firepower" is a precise statement that will express for you and for your listeners exactly what comprises the whole that you promise to explain. "When I finish I want my listeners to understand the Battle of Gettysburg" is too sweeping and too loose to define *what* unity you will focus on. A statement of this sort cannot define the boundaries of what your listeners are to comprehend. "What is the coherent whole to be explained?" is the question you need always to answer directly to yourself and directly or indirectly to your listeners if your informative communications are to have the quality of unity.

Maintaining interest in informing

Maintaining interest is sometimes difficult when you speak to inform. Some material that needs explaining lacks inherent qualities that will draw attention. Explaining the nature of a chemical compound can present this kind of problem. What, then, can you do? You may need to search for special materials that can add interest. As we showed in Chapter 5, specific examples, comparisons, contrasts, and brief narratives are possibilities. So are all facts that are close to the experience of your listeners. Build in examples of the uses of the compound; compare or contrast it with other kinds of mixtures the listeners know about; or, to illustrate chemical bonding, personify the elements of the compound so you can "introduce them to one another" or give them a "torrid" or "cool" relationship. Such special treatments of dull facts can enliven them.

The physical features of a one dollar bill scarcely seem subject matter for an engrossing speech, but we heard a student give a most interesting speech on this subject. He did it by finding unusual, concrete, and newsworthy facts associated with dollar bills. First, he presented a blowup of a dollar bill, showing the details of both sides. Then he related some unusual historical details and some long forgotten interpretations of the specific words and images on the bill: that it was copied from the Spanish dollar; that beneath the scales of justice are thirteen stars—representing, of course, the original states; that the Latin phrases mean "one nation out of many states," "God has favored our undertakings," "the new order of ages," and the last two are borrowed from the Roman poet Virgil; that the pyramid was chosen as a symbol of the Union; and so on. For each feature of the bill the speaker had some informative and interesting datum to establish for his listeners that "the design of our dollar bill has significance dating back to the time of George Washington."[1] When so commonplace an item can be given significance by careful addition and treatment of ideas, it seems clear that speakers *can* compensate for remoteness, technicality, or ordinariness in matters that need lucid explanation.

Some subjects are difficult to explain because they are inherently complex. Acoustics is such a subject. But David Kaneda (page 137) showed how technicalities can be simplified and associated with listeners' personal experiences. He also made a good move in this direction in the way he introduced his subject. He opened by saying: "I want to talk to you today about acoustics. 'Acoustics' is just a fancy word for *sound*. I'm really going to talk about *sounds* to show that we can control them." Substituting an ordinary term for a technical term can sometimes make understanding easy. Another way of clarifying the difficult is to treat the subject *as if* it were other than it is. We can illustrate again with sound.

No one has ever seen a sound wave. But everyone has seen the water waves we call ripples. Therefore it has become customary to explain part of the behavior of sound waves *as if* these waves acted the way ripples do in spreading outward when a stone is dropped into water. This analogy works very well and is fundamentally both true and clear as long as we confine ourselves to how sound waves spread out from their source. But if we move to the topics of amplitude and duration of sound we shall have to invent a new set of comparisons. The point of hunting for useful *as if* treatments for difficult subjects is that people build new knowledge on knowledge they already have. Comparison and contrast are basic ways of learning; listeners are used to them, so they work well in presenting information. Some aspects of a steel-rolling mill can be made both clear and interesting if we think of the steel *as if* it were dough and the mill *as if* it were equipped with kitchen rolling pins. When your subject is hard to understand, look especially for fresh *as if* treatments as you complete the processes of invention.

Informing as a subordinate purpose

We have been discussing informative speaking as if information giving normally occurs apart from other purposes for speaking. It seldom does, but we can talk of but one thing at a time. Clear explanations persuade us to believe; they encourage us to seek more knowledge; they reinforce our feelings; and they are often entertaining in the sense that new learning is pleasing. Good informative speaking is also often a necessary preliminary to persuasion. When President Reagan announced his economic policy in February of 1981, he *explained* the policy and also sought to persuade people to accept it. An explanation can also imply commitment and intention to persuade. A speaker who explains methods of contraception will almost surely be interpreted as endorsing their use. Thus sex education programs in schools are repeatedly attacked as encouraging permissiveness and even sexual promiscuity. On especially controversial matters such as these, "pure" explanation is almost impossible because speakers are naturally thought to stand with and for whatever they present. Nor is this wholly illogical, for the strongest persuasion is often the clearest exposition of how and why things are as you say.

For these reasons we cannot separate the informative neatly from the persuasive or reinforcing, but your immediate goal at any moment of speaking ought to be clear to *you*. Knowing that the important thing is to clarify in some particular part of a speech will draw your thoughts to the strategies of clarification: examples, narratives, comparisons, and contrasts. With a subpoint so clarified, you may then want to try inducing inquiry about it or persuading your audience of its desirability. That further goal does not change the fact that *for those moments when information giving is your immediate aim,* you must provide ideas that meet the basic tests of informing: accuracy, completeness within the boundaries you have put on the thought unit, and unity. The tests applied are the same whether the whole or a part of a speech is predominantly informative.

SPEAKING TO INDUCE INQUIRY

Even when you don't "have the answers," it is sometimes necessary to speak. A chairperson meeting his or her staff or a planning commission raising a problem with its community or a student trying to get a study session started must raise and clarify problems *for discussion*. Solutions will be found through the discussion, if at all. Explaining problems for the purpose of getting others to study, reflect, and create answers is a common function of public speech; to carry it out requires at least some information giving and some persuasion. Speaking to induce inquiry is thus a mixed form of communication.

Creating a spirit for inquiry

If you look about you, you will see more speech aimed at inducing inquiry than you may have expected. One apartment mate may notice a sink drain is slow. What shall we do? Consult the landlord or superintendent? Let it go? Try to fix it ourselves? Call and pay a plumber ourselves? The person noticing the problem may bring it up with his or her partners, describing and estimating the problem, expressing what ought to be, and reviewing the possible actions. Now take a different social situation. A single person or a committee is asked to investigate what a group's choices are. What are the best options for repairing the fraternity or sorority's sound system? One investigator or several may speak for a few moments, informing the audience about the options uncovered, probably outlining the advantages and disadvantages of each. The extent of the persuasion may be merely to make others see that the different options deserve serious discussion *now*—perhaps that the decision should not be put off.

What does the audience need when occasions like those we have described arise? Generally speaking, the audience needs: (1) a clear understanding of what the problem is, (2) some notion of what must be accomplished in order to eliminate or ease the problem, (3) knowledge of what the *realistic* options are, and (4) knowledge of the main advantages and disadvantages of each choice. You can see that *informing* is a major task given to whoever speaks in this kind of situation. But there is more: whoever speaks must also make the problem significant for those addressed, or else there will be little motivation to discuss and make a choice. Unless the problem has the proportions of a crisis, ways must be found to create a wish for a solution (for example, reminding the audience of how pleasant it was to have a sound system that really worked) and to create sufficient perplexity about the solution so that the audience will be willing to think about the relative worth of their options.[2] The first step in motivating listeners to think seriously about something perplexing is to confront them with a clear, unambiguous question that cannot be answered without making a choice.

Posing questions for deliberation

The central idea of any remarks to induce inquiry ought to express a precise question that the listeners can probably answer if they think over their options carefully. Such a central idea might be put thus: When I finish, I want the audience to be prepared and motivated to answer the question, "What is the best plan for getting our sound system repaired?" On a different problem the statement might be: When I finish, I want the audience to be prepared and motivated to answer the question, "What is the best method for teaching elementary school children who do not yet have a full command of the English language?" The words *prepared and motivated* will remind you of your dual tasks—to inform *and* to motivate. You will need to explain the nature of the problem, and if possible you ought to suggest the directions in which you and the audience ought to look for a workable solution. These aspects of your task will be primarily informative, and you should review your plans at these points for accuracy, completeness, and unity. But somewhere you will also need to answer your listeners' ever-present question, "Why should *I* care?"

There are at least two ways of motivating listeners to think about a problem. One is to amplify the seriousness of the problem, connecting it as directly as possible with listeners' self-interests. The other is to show them that they *can* do something about the problem. If the problem were repairing a sound system, it would be possible to emphasize that repairs are possible without spending too much and that the job could be done within a short time *if* the listeners make up their minds *now*. Sometimes the penalties of failing to make a decision can be stressed. Sometimes the opportunity "to make a difference" can be stressed, as when a committee chairperson urges his or her group to decide on a specific recommendation "or the decision will be made without our having had any input at all."

Questions of policy and of action arouse inquiry better than questions about fact or value. If you want to open practical inquiry instead of lengthy philosophical discussion and debate, you will need to be careful in phrasing the questions you pose in speeches of inquiry. If you pose questions such as, "What are the inalienable rights of women?" or "Is racism eradicable in America?" you are apt to invite interminable debate about definitions and values. But if you try to motivate and prepare your listeners to discuss narrower policy and action questions, the discussions you can generate are likely to be much more practical. "What can *we* do that could enhance the day-to-day rights of women?" or "How can racial discrimination be minimized or eliminated on this campus?" are the kinds of narrowed, practical questions listeners can most easily be brought to see the utility of discussing inquiringly.

Material and organization of speeches of inquiry

The kinds of ideas that are pertinent when you intend to induce inquiry are those appropriate to informing, with one exception. If the problem you want to raise is one of policy or action, the topic of *desirability* must be treated—though it would not be were you simply to inform. For example, whether athletic scholarships should be identical for women and for men finally becomes a question of whether such equality would be *desirable*—say financially, in maintaining overall athletic programs of good quality, on grounds that we should treat the sexes equally, and so on. At some point the desirability of anything we think of *doing* or *changing* is bound to come up, so you must be prepared to discuss that topic whenever you choose to ask listeners to consider actions or changes.

The distinctive pattern of organization for main ideas in a speech of inquiry is discussed in Chapter 7 (pages 194–195). The divisions proposed there constitute final guidelines to the special sorts of material this kind of speaking requires.

Inquiring speech normally begins with discussion of a problem and proceeds toward solutions deserving consideration. This kind of movement of thought is not inherently interesting. The major reason is that in inquiry judgment is suspended; we hold ourselves back from making decisions until we have command of all the relevant facts and options. There are few natural climaxes of thought until the very end of discussion; only then comes the satisfying release from tensions. In return for asking listeners to defer judgment and to sustain the tensions of inquiry, speakers ought to repay them by using the most interesting clarifying material available. For this purpose the amplifying tactics that do most to aid auditors (see Chapter 5, pages 131–143) ought to be reviewed to be sure you are prepared to sustain interest as fully as possible.

To sum up, questions, not propositions, stimulate inquiry. The central ideas of speeches to induce inquiry ought to express answerable questions, preferably of action or policy. Any individual or group presentation intended to evoke inquiry ought to pose a question listeners can see the practicality of discussing. The speaker's functions in this kind of speaking are to inform listeners so they *can* think sensibly about the problem posed and to motivate them to think about it.

SPEAKING TO REINFORCE BELIEFS AND FEELINGS

From time to time rhetorical situations require that we speak to reinforce beliefs and feelings that listeners already have. We speak of values of education on commencement day; we emphasize the importance of equality at a women's rights meeting; in a part of a speech we need to build up listeners' dislike for taxes before trying to get them to vote against a bond issue. At such times we aim to make the listeners feel or believe something more strongly than ever, or perhaps we speak to inspire confidence or faith in what is already believed. Indeed, some authors treat this kind of speaking under the heading of "the speech to inspire."

Speaking of this kind is a form of persuasion. For two reasons we are considering it apart from what we shall shortly call *persuasion*. The material you need in order to reinforce is unique, and when you develop points and themes in this kind of speaking you will amplify more than you will prove.

Appropriate ideas

As you prepare to reinforce beliefs and feelings, your need is primarily for ideas your listeners already have some knowledge about. Whether you talk about education, physical fitness, or science, your task is to amplify existing beliefs about that subject. One of the most important ways of doing this is to connect what is known about the subject with important values the listeners share. The essential process of reinforcing is to associate familiar ideas with *high* values, or if you are reinforcing negative feelings to associate the familiar with what the listeners hold in *low* esteem. To the extent that you work chiefly with the familiar, speaking to reinforce allows you the least

intellectual freedom of any type of speaking. This is why speaking to reinforce can
be heard in all societies, no matter how repressive. There are always some approved
ideas and some "proper" values that can be extolled, and there will be certain "improper" ideas and values that can be connected in denunciation. Hence, speaking to
reinforce (positively and negatively) occurs in all known cultures and social systems,
though inquiry and free persuasion do not.

Uses of reinforcing speech

Despite its limitations, speaking to reinforce has usefulness everywhere. Through this
kind of speech religious congregations are sustained and such sociopolitical virtues as
pride and mutual respect are maintained as active forces. Indeed, the shared values
that bind us into social groups continue to exist by virtue of being continuously repeated and reinforced through public speech. Without such speech our social bonds
would atrophy and society would drift toward anarchism. Other forms of speech become agencies of change and diversion; it is chiefly speech to reinforce that gives us
and our communities the sense of cohesiveness we cannot comfortably do without.

But people need different kinds of reinforcement at different times. Those who
attend meetings of ethnic groups indicate by attending that their beliefs about nationality or race are, just then, of high importance. Whoever addresses them must recognize
that this is an occasion where thoughts of nationality or race are to be reinforced, not,
say, thoughts about commerce or education. However, the same persons who attend
the ethnic meetings will also be members of business, educational, and political groups;
they may on another day gather as business people or as political partisans, wishing
then to have those other beliefs reinforced and appealed to. In sum, just what deserves reinforcement in a rhetorical situation is normally determined by the shared
values and interests that brought the audience into that situation.

Rhetorical situations that invite speech that reinforces are often ceremonial, but
they are not always so. Anniversaries, religious and other observances, rituals of various sorts are ceremonial and invite reinforcing speech, but kick-off meetings for cam-
paigns, locker-room half-time sessions, corporate sales meetings, and gatherings of
conservationists are among the many nonceremonial settings where reinforcement is
likely to be appropriate and appreciated. Even dating and lovemaking can be occasions
for reinforcing talk, though hardly for public speech.

Preparation

Assuming a moderately formal circumstance for reinforcing speech, how does one
prepare for it? You ask what the exigences of the situation are—its special needs—
and you select a theme or general subject that has some connection to those needs:
faith for the religious gathering or competition for the sales meeting. Next you formulate a tentative central idea that can guide you in searching for special materials. At
this point you will help yourself and ultimately your listeners if you adopt the fol-

lowing formula for framing central ideas for speeches to reinforce. Write the words, "When I finish I want my listeners to believe (or feel) more (or less) strongly *that* . . ." Compose a clause to follow *that*. Let it express precisely the belief or feeling you want to intensify or diminish, and insert either the word *more* or the word *less* according to your intention. A finished central idea might read, "When I finish I want my listeners to *believe more* strongly *that* it is worthwhile to take personal steps to diminish pollution." Another might read, "When I finish I want them to *feel less* strongly that inflation is desirable."

The unique feature of a central idea for reinforcing is that it needs to express the *degree* and *direction* of change you will seek. Our formula will remind you to make clear decisions on both points.

In preparation for speaking to reinforce you will be searching for ideas about which your listeners already have knowledge and feeling. Any of the attributes and relationships we commonly discuss (see page 84) can suggest potentially discussable themes that justify greater or less belief and feeling. Since you will try to intensify attitudes, you will need material that arouses. For this purpose the imagistic, the memorable, the quotable, and sometimes the poetic are especially useful. Your objective is to link your ideas to listeners' impressions of such qualities as justice or injustice, courage or cowardice, prudence or foolhardiness, gentleness or aggressiveness, prosperity or depression, honesty or dishonesty, and so on. But you should look for fresh, unhackneyed ways of making these links because your main task is to make ideas more important. They will be so if they have the "virtues" or "vices" your listeners admire or deplore. The links will be interesting if you find and develop until-now unnoticed associations between the listeners' values and the already-familiar subjects you are trying to make impressive.

It is best to develop a single train of magnifying or diminishing thought than to try to make an idea impressive in several different ways. Enlargement of an idea is preferable to multiplying its features. An ancient Greek speech is still a good model in this respect. In his famous funeral oration commemorating the bravery of Athenians who had died in the first year of the Peloponnesian Wars, Pericles expressed the pith of his whole speech thus:

> Taking everything together then, I declare that our city is an education to Greece, and I declare that in my opinion each single one of our citizens, in all the manifold aspects of life, is able to show himself the rightful lord and owner of his own person, and do this, moreover, with exceptional grace and exceptional versatility.[3]

His whole address, as Thucydides reports it, merely amplifies these tightly related thoughts concerning the city for which the dead had fought. A lesser speaker might have insisted on discussing the way the heroes died, the justice of the way, the qualities of victories and defeats, and the gratitude of living Athenians—all in a misguided effort to multiply listeners' feelings of gratitude to the dead. Pericles wisely chose a single theme and amplified it: Athens' worth ennobles its fallen soldiers. His speech had focus.

What makes a speech to reinforce successful? Usually it is the freshness of the connections you make between the idea you reinforce and what your listeners value. Your
opportunity for originality lies in finding *hitherto unnoticed significance* in already
familiar materials. Some examples will illustrate ways by which speakers do this.

Speaking before the Seattle Shriners in 1976, the bicentennial year of the United
States, Charles Boyle, a writer and consultant, turned his listeners' negative memories
into supporting material for the proposition that "this age" will deserve to be looked
on as "the good old days." In the major portion of his speech Boyle contrasted the
"good old days" of pre–World War II (which many of his middle-aged and older
listeners were fully aware of) with 1976. On topic after topic Boyle argued or suggested that the world was better off now than then. Finally he arrived at his conclusion that the United States has never been without serious problems but *thrives* on
adversity, so the "drummers of despair" should be distrusted because if "people . . .
do their jobs one step at a time" their "great grandchildren will be looking back at
this age and saying, 'Those were the good old days.' " We may suppose that this was
what Boyle's middle-aged and senior listeners wanted to believe; his reminders of their
former "hard times" were calculated to encourage their inclinations to endorse the
status quo.[4]

Winston Churchill used the same general methods of associating values, making
vital and important the rather platitudinous notion that the British and the Americans should "never cease to proclaim . . . the great principles of freedom and the
rights of man which are the joint inheritance of the English-speaking world." To reinforce this idea he said:

> . . . This means that the people of any country have the right . . . to choose or change
> the character or form of government under which they dwell; that freedom of
> speech and thought should reign; that courts of justice, independent of the execu-
> tive, . . . should administer laws which have received the broad assent of large ma-
> jorities or are consecrated by time and custom. Here are the title deeds of freedom
> which should lie in every cottage home. Here is the message of the British and
> American peoples to mankind.[5]

Undoubtedly Churchill's careful choice of value-laden words helped to make the virtues of self-government, freedom of speech and thought, and independent courts
dignify the importance of "proclaiming."

Abraham Lincoln used the same general methods at Gettysburg; however, he
found the virtues he spoke of by studying the *setting*. It was a dedicatory scene, but,
he thought, simply to "dedicate this cemetery" would not sufficiently dignify the occasion. So to the ordinary act he attached the value-laden concept "dedicate ourselves."
Then he associated that idea with still more important *national* goals. Thereby he
established the notion that the military cemetery had importance as both a personal
and a national symbol. Many other dedicatory speeches—of buildings, laboratories,
works of art—have used this theme of "dedicating ourselves to higher goals" to make

the occasion more impressive. Similarly, the importance of a charitable organization can be made more impressive if a speaker dwells on the fact that its services reach far beyond its membership.

Although magnifying and diminishing ideas are functions frequently associated with ceremonies, purposiveness and clarity are not thus any less essential. The point is worth emphasizing because speakers participating in ceremonies often tend to ramble among topics not closely related to one another. Perhaps they do this because so many familiar things seem possible "talking points." But listeners have no less desire for focus and clarity at ceremonies than elsewhere. So wherever you speak to reinforce, your tasks are (1) to amplify familiar ideas and values in ways that make some central point by (2) highlighting not-so-familiar attributes and relationships.

From this specialized form of persuasion we turn now to more general problems of persuasive speaking.

SPEAKING TO PERSUADE

When you try to change people's thoughts, feelings, and actions, it is not always possible to accomplish all that you would like. You cannot always ask for great changes. To do so when listeners hold firmly to views different from those you advocate is almost certain to turn them off, as we pointed out in Chapter 3. If you are realistic, you will recognize that to achieve less than you wish were possible is not necessarily failure in this form of speaking. The measure of effectiveness in persuasion is taken by comparing what you actually achieved with what was reasonably possible considering all the circumstances. Dr. Upcraft was successful in the speech reprinted in Appendix B; he was able to turn his audience around. But a persuader like the conservative speaker-writer-broadcaster William Buckley must usually be satisfied with achieving small changes in public opinion. Buckley speaks very effectively for a set of political and religious principles that many Americans refuse to accept. In these circumstances we must count Buckley successful if he reinforces views of those who already agree with him (arch-conservatives and devout Catholics) and induces *a few* changes in the views of political liberals. One of our students, Beth Wallingford,[6] faced comparable limitations in classroom speaking. In late 1980 she decided that voluntary military service was a failure in the United States. She also knew that three-fifths of her audience would be college-aged males "who just won't *want* to believe me" if she pressed for the solution she had become convinced of—restoration of the compulsory draft. She decided it was more important to win general support for a lesser conclusion: that *some* changes must be made in conditions of military service. So she deliberately set out to persuade her audience that they must *either* endorse much higher pay and better conditions for people in military service *or* admit that restoration of the draft system was the only way out. She had little trouble accomplishing this limited goal, and in the process she established in everyone's mind that existing military policies were inadequate to the nation's needs. She was successful because this was as much as could reasonably be expected from a single speech. In like manner Joycelyn Clarke (see pages 215–218) asked for tolerance but not endorsement of cults. In persuasion you set your sights on what is practically possible in your situation. To persuade need not be to convert.

Special requirements in persuasion

You will not always try to convert people when you persuade, but you will always be asking for *some* shifts of beliefs and attitudes. What special demands are imposed on you by such an aim?

Justifying through listeners' feelings is always essential. Because some persuaders overlook the importance of justifying change by evoking the special interests of listeners, we shall consider that kind of justification first. The point was forcefully put by the Scottish rhetorician George Campbell. His language and psychological theory seem quaint, but his point concerning motivation in persuasion is unmistakably sound:

> ... When persuasion is the end, passion also must be engaged. If it is fancy which bestows brilliancy on our ideas, if it is memory which gives them stability, passion doth more, it animates them. Hence they derive spirit and energy. To say that it is possible to persuade without speaking to the passions, is but at best a kind of specious nonsense. The coolest reasoner always in persuading addresseth himself to the passions some way or other. This he cannot avoid doing, if he speak to the purpose. To make me believe it is enough to show me that things are so; to make me act, it is necessary to show that the action will answer some end. That can never be an end to me which gratifies no passion or affection in my nature. You assure me, "It is for my honour." Now you solicit my pride, without which I had never been able to understand the word. You say, "It is for my interest." Now you bespeak my self-love. "It is for the public good." Now you rouse my patriotism. "It will relieve the miserable." Now you touch my pity. So far ... [is it] from being an unfair method of persuasion to move the passions, that there is no persuasion without moving them.[7]

A twentieth-century psychologist might reject Campbell's technical distinctions among fancy, memory, and passion, but would agree there can be no changing of attitudes or feelings without engaging the desires that Campbell called "passions." The modern psychologist would agree with Campbell that "the coolest reasoner" must certainly fail to change views unless aided by feelings. This necessity of enlisting active desires is one of the special demands the persuader's aim imposes on you.

In order that active drives may operate within hearers, it is sometimes necessary to refrain from expressing all that you believe. You may avoid asking for all the opinion change you would really like, in the manner of Beth Wallingford, because your listeners do not yet understand the problem well enough to see all that they must do. Or their habitual ways of thinking may prevent them from grasping the belief system that lies behind what you would like to persuade them of. This was

St. Paul's problem when speaking to Athenian philosophers on Mars Hill (pages 100–101). A persuader *must* get the listeners' feelings running in the direction of the change persuaded for, but what these listeners *can* feel, what they know enough to feel, is the only emotional justification you can energize on your behalf. As George Campbell said, there is no persuasion without moving people's feelings, but in weighing your resources you need to consider seriously which feelings are present to be moved and which are absent or undeveloped.

Justifying rationally is also essential in persuasion because people will not change their views unless they believe there are good reasons for changing. One of the best ways of learning what arguments you can offer is to consult all sides of the subject as you prepare. The ideas we try to persuade others of are controversial, or we would not need to persuade in the first place. This means that (1) there are opposing views to learn well enough so that you can persuade rationally against them and (2) there is little likelihood that you can get a full, clear view of the issues and evidence by consulting just one side. One does not expect to receive the whole story about a labor dispute at the labor union headquarters or from officials of the disputing corporation. Nor is one likely to get all the facts from hearing the witnesses for only one side in a court case. Less obvious but equally biased sources of information abound on almost all controversial issues.

You need to consult all sides in your research: read *The Nation* and *The National Review,* the *New York Times* and *United States News and World Report* if your subject involves a liberal-conservative controversy in politics. See that you get the positions of union and management if your subject concerns a labor dispute. Getting both sides will not necessarily give you the whole story. You are likely to come away from this kind of investigation with a good deal of extraneous information. But you will know where opponents differ and where they agree. Where they agree you will find your most impressive proofs; where they disagree, you must make your own decision, consulting other less partial sources and applying the tests of responsible argument that we discussed in Chapter 5 (page 123). Perhaps the most important profit obtained from studying all sides of a disputed issue on which you want to persuade is that you will come away knowing what the alternative arguments are. If you are convinced of one point of view, you can then argue it defensively as well as affirmatively; if you are, at the end, not convinced of any specific position, perhaps this is not a subject for you to persuade about. Perhaps in your state of mind a speech to induce inquiry is the appropriate goal.

Offering yourself as justification in persuasion is so closely related to showing you are acquainted with all sides of an issue that the two can scarcely be separated. Of all speakers, the inquirer and the persuader must be most jealous of their reputations for integrity, for both presume to lead and advise. They thereby place their own reliability at issue. What persuadees want to see in advisers is consistent evidence of full understanding, sound reasoning, and sincere interest in the persuadee's well-being. Hence, if you show that you are fully acquainted with all the positions that could be taken about your subject and reason carefully, you will be showing that the position you have chosen is one that *you* have arrived at *fairly.* Your evident knowledge and reasonableness then become proofs that you have your listeners' interests at heart and are an adviser worth following.

Making it clear that you have considered alternative answers in arriving at the position your persuasion supports also has very pragmatic advantages. Experimentation has almost uniformly shown that recognizing opposing views while persuading has longer-lasting influence than has one-sided persuasion. Only when an audience already agrees with you or when they will never be exposed to other views does it seem safe to be one-sided.[8] It is wise, then, to let your audience know that you are aware of and able to refute or otherwise dispose of views different from your own. It also seems better to present your own views *before* introducing and disposing of counterviews. Research on this point is not definitive, but two things seem clear: (1) what we hear first affects how we respond to what we hear afterward, and (2) it is less efficient to build up an opposing idea and then knock it down than to build up one's own position so it can stand against others.[9]

Your best strategy in persuasion, then, is to present your position on any point strongly and then recognize conflicting views, showing that they are less credible and less satisfactory from your listeners' points of view than are your own. This arrangement of arguments will, if done justly, establish you as a speaker of intelligence, trustworthiness, and good will toward your listeners.

The blended proofs of persuasion

In the previous paragraphs we have repeatedly said that one kind of persuasive proof reinforces another. Let us now reinterpret that notion in terms of procedure rather than principle. You will carry out your inventional processes for persuasion best if you check your plans closely to see that you have material with which to accomplish the following:

1.   You must satisfy your listeners that you have not taken your persuasive positions irresponsibly. You must give some evidence that there are essentially rational reasons for the position (see Chapter 5, pages 121–123).
2.   Blended with the rational reasons for your positions should be reasons you provide that show how your listeners' concerns and special interests will be served by their accepting your position in preference to any other position they may know of.
3.   The implicit message of each unit of your persuasion ought to be, "On this point the most logical and most gratifying view that you the listeners can adopt is the one I am offering you."

What chiefly distinguishes the persuasive speaker from the informant, inquirer, or entertainer is that the persuader's primary test in choosing materials for inclusion in his or her speech is: will this material offer some reasonable promise or threat that could bend my listeners' thoughts toward the conclusions I want them to reach? *Change,* but not necessarily conversion, is what all persuasion aims at, and a persuader has not found the right kinds of material until all major units of speech *invite*— rationally *and* psychologically—shifts in the direction of the persuader's central idea.

SPEAKING TO ENTERTAIN

A speaker who decides to *entertain* assumes an obligation to hold attention agreeably by diverting listeners' thoughts from matters of high seriousness. Often, although not invariably, the task is to provide amusement. Another way of defining entertaining speech is to say it so completely interests listeners that they have almost no sense of working to acquire the full significance of what is said.

Notice that entertainment *may* be amusing but is not invariably so. A first-rate travelogue can be entertaining but not basically amusing. Many narratives and descriptions entertain us with varying degrees of humor. So a speaker planning to entertain listeners should recognize that being humorous is not the only option open.

Any subject—any theme that will hold attention agreeably in a diverting rather than highly serious way—is a potential subject for entertaining talk. The *treatment* of the subject is the distinguishing mark. Treat any subject lightly, divertingly, and you can make it entertaining.

Occasions for entertaining

Typical occasions for entertaining talk allow extraordinary latitude for choosing subjects. These occasions tend to be convivial gatherings or situations where no stronger motivation than curiosity has brought people together. Wherever listeners are willing to be diverted from the usual and the serious, there is a rhetorical situation for entertaining speech.

Where casual curiosity has created the speech situation, there is occasion for entertaining speech that is not predominantly humorous. Light, straightforward treatment of whatever subject is the speaker's specialty is usually expected. Consider two of many possible settings. A Rotary club invites the public to a postluncheon period during which Mr. So-and-So will talk about his recent visit to India. A sorority invites Miss Blank who won a gold medal in Olympic competition to speak at a coffee hour. Obviously Mr. So-and-So's trip and Miss Blank's Olympic achievement prescribe each speaker's subject. Few listeners in either place will be deeply informed or consumingly interested in either India or Olympic competition. Most will be there chiefly to see the traveler or the champion. The traveler has to say things in a fairly formal way because of the structure of his situation. Miss Blank will doubtless be asked to "tell us" at some point or points during the coffee hour. But in both places the speaker's task will be to give special information in popular terms that will satisfy the listeners' casual curiosity. This dictates that each should be prepared to give prominence to whatever is most colorful, most human, most tantalizing about the prescribed sub-ject. Whatever discourse has these characteristics is almost certain to be entertaining. It need not be as objective or as comprehensive as a speech on India or Olympic competition prepared with the purpose of informing.

Treatment of subjects

From what we have said, one may draw several important inferences. First, *speech that entertains differs from other speech primarily in the way subject matter is treated.* The more agreeable and diverting the amplification and delivery of ideas, the more entertaining speech will be. The difference between informing, inquiring, and per-suading on the one hand and entertaining on the other is chiefly a difference of manner, not of matter. A second inference is that *to be entertaining a speaker must regard the pleasure of his or her audience more highly than the logic of the subject.* This does not mean that to be entertaining one must be inaccurate; on the contrary, accuracy at least in some details is essential. What arrests us is usually some disproportion of attention to specific details: detailed attention to the colorful garb of Indian women without much attention to, say, the social significance of their dress, or ludicrously detailed attention to the rigors of training for Olympic competition without much at-tention to the results of it. The entertaining speaker must remember that the inter-esting *parts* of the subject are often more important than the *whole.* In this sense the logic of a subject is sacrificed to the pleasure of the audience. A third inference to be drawn is that *although good humor is always entertaining, entertainment does not necessarily depend on the presence of humor.* This inference has been amplified by our earlier examples.

Since it is the *treatment* of material that makes speech entertaining, you will want to give special attention to stylistic resources in developing speech to entertain. (See Chapter 9, pages 239–47.) However, to create entertaining language you first find ideas that lend themselves to entertaining treatment. Once again, a review of the attributes things and people possess and the relationships that may exist among these attributes (page 84) can suggest potentially entertaining thoughts. Any attribute of anything has potentially humorous possibilities if examined in enough detail or distorted in some fashion. Charlie Brown and Lucy and Linus in the comic strip "Peanuts" constantly create humor by treating the *existence, nonexistence, forms,* and *possibilities* of things absurdly.

Treating something as belonging to a class (*genus*) to which listeners don't ordinarily assign it can be entertaining and sometimes highly informative too. Tom Nobile, an engineering student at The Pennsylvania State University, delighted and seriously informed his classmates with a speech on "Economizing on School Materials." To his colleagues' surprise, he recommended rescuing academic supplies from the university's trash dumpsters. In the segment of the speech that follows you will see that the entertaining qualities arise from his "reclassifying" dumpsters and stressing the *feasibility* and *desirability* of rescuing *trash.* Said Nobile:

These temporary resource receptacles [*laughter*]—no, that's the best descriptive term for them because everything you need for class is in them. [*More laughter.*] Really, I'm serious, and I'd like to make the further point that dumpsters in the academic section of the campus don't have garbage in them. They just have trash. So it's not like you were going to be rummaging around in really foul-smelling stuff.

Next, let me make the point that it's legal to explore them. You can rummage in these dumpsters all you want. I've been stopped a few times by campus security. They ask what I'm doing, and I tell them, "I'm looking in these dumpsters trying to find something useful." Sometimes they're impressed by my thrift, and sometimes they think I'm off my rocker.

I know it's hard to imagine that people do this scavenging, but I've brought some concrete evidence of what's to be found. You know how sometimes professors ask you to turn in term papers in folders [*holds up a handful of clean manila folders found in a dumpster*]. And sometimes you just need something to hold stuff, so you need filing envelopes like these [*holds up several large filing envelopes*].[10]

Nobile continued his display of practical items he had found and concluded with a further twist in his reclassification strategy. He unrolled a large "Comparison Shopper's Guide" (on paper rescued from a dumpster) showing retail prices for items he had displayed and, in a column headed "Dumpster," the word *free*. He ended with, "And there's my final point. If you extrapolate these figures you'll find that over a year's time you can save about $30.00—which is roughly equivalent to three cases of Michelob." He had now converted the dumpster from "temporary resource receptacle" to a competitor for academic supplies stores.

Nobile treated the dumpsters as belonging to the *genus* supply sources rather than to the *genus* trash-disposal bins. He furthered the entertaining qualities of his speech by surprising the listeners with the *desirable* things he had found and by demonstrating the *feasibility* of searching dumpsters (it was legal). His listeners were most conscious of having been entertained, but in fact they had learned something interesting about those lowly dumpsters and about trash disposal in general.

"The Conspiracy Against Lefty" was the title of another, this time subtly persuasive, talk given by a left-handed student who made her plea for more consideration for left-handed people while she exaggerated what it is like to be left-handed in a right-handed world. She assured that her speech would be considered more entertaining than deliberately persuasive by deftly jumbling *causes* and *possibilities* as she contended that the entire horse-breeding, training, and equipping establishment is governed by conspiratorial "right-wing plotters" who "brainwash" every newborn foal to resent all left-handed persons who try to approach in "a natural and convenient manner."

In entertaining it is *treatment* that counts. Any subject—idea, person, object, experience—has or can be given entertaining relationships to other ideas, persons, objects, and experiences. Speakers hunt for *conceivable* attributes and relationships when their goal is to entertain.

Unique aspects of content in entertaining

Three other, interrelated points need to be made concerning the content of speech that entertains. They can be stated briefly, but their importance is considerable.

1. *Only in entertainment is it sometimes advantageous to make no sense.* Sometimes the nonsensical bears just enough similarity to the sensible to amuse us. Here lies much of the fun of Lewis Carroll's *Alice in Wonderland* and David Brenner's outrageous "analyses" of noses, air travel, and South Philadelphia customs.

2. *What entertains in speaking is that which is quickly and easily understood.* Private jokes or asides and private experiences are not entertaining. In entertaining speech all meaning is public—familiar and easily grasped. Even nonsense must contain a semblance to sense, or the response is not amusement, only bafflement. It is true that working puzzles can be entertaining, but puzzling speech is not. The reason is that speech moves swiftly through time, leaving listeners no opportunity to work puzzles as they appear.

3. *An entertaining speaker may properly disregard or even do violence to the natural logic of a subject, but he or she will please the audience most if the speech has some kind of thematic unity.* This will give the audience the satisfaction of having been pleased by *something,* not just some *things.* Even the nightclub gag man recognizes this audience demand for structure in entertainment. If artful, he will separate his mother-in-law jokes from his insurance-company jokes, giving each group the status of a thought unit within his patter. As though further adapting to the preferences of modern audiences, more and more comedians now develop entire monologues around single themes treated humorously. In so doing they emulate the practice of the best among entertaining speech makers.

Entertaining speech can carry subordinate notes of informing or persuading, as our examples of the speech on rummaging in dumpsters and the speech on "The Conspiracy Against Lefty" showed. In comparable ways entertainment can be injected into speeches with serious intent, provided that entertainment does not seem the dominant function of the speaking. Four famed political figures of this century have earned admiration for sprinkling witticisms, quick and amusing analogies, and entertaining ironies through their speeches: Sir Winston Churchill, Franklin D. Roosevelt, Adlai Stevenson, Sr., and Ronald Reagan. But when the intention in speaking is serious, such astute speakers as these inject entertainment as quick relief but maintain their serious goals in the forefront.

In our three-chapter survey of how content for speeches is discovered, selected, and blended we have examined the opportunities and the constraints that are yours when you set out to inform, induce inquiry, reinforce beliefs and feelings, persuade, or entertain. In this chapter we have shown how these various purposes limit the range of ideas from which you can draw content and that each kind of purpose imposes its special manner of treating ideas once they are found. A generalization to be drawn from what we have said here is that you cannot be wholly successful until you have determined what goal will dominate in your speaking. Only when you know your specific, dominating aim can you finally sort out the useful and the less useful from all you have learned in inventive investigation.

Having said that—and it is true—it is still a fact that mixed or combined purposes do occur in effective speech. We have illustrated with students' speeches how entertaining can be mingled with informing or persuading. Also, in long speeches such as legal or political speeches, informing may be preliminary to persuading or inquiry preliminary to persuasion in behalf of a preferred course of action. But if public speech is first-rate, there will be no doubt about which purpose *dominates* the whole communication or any part of it. If your primary intention is to persuade, you will see that your informing sections finally stand as *grounds for* believing as you urge. If your goal is other than to entertain for entertainment's sake, you will see to it that entertaining subsections provide momentary diversion without distorting your information-giving processes, your ultimate objective of conducting an inquiry, or your persuasive proofs.

EXERCISES

Written

1. Write a brief essay on differences between speech materials that prove propositions and those that amplify ideas.
2. Choose a general topic such as "The Cost of Living" or "Clothing" and outline three kinds of speeches that could be given on some aspect of the topic. For example, outline a persuasive, an informative, and an entertaining speech on "The Cost of Food Is Rising."
3. Read a speech of your own choosing and write a critique in which you:
   a. Identify what seems to have been the speaker's dominant purpose in speaking.
   b. Identify any subsections of the speech in which the purpose of communication seems to have shifted temporarily (for example, from a dominant purpose of informing to a subordinate purpose of entertaining or persuading).
   c. Evaluate the speaker's success in making shifts from primary to secondary aims and back to the primary aim. (Did the speaker indicate to the listeners that the purpose was shifting? Was there indication of why the shifts were made? How successfully was the dominant purpose kept clear despite shifts? Was the total impact of the speech strengthened or weak-

ened by temporary changes of purpose? If weakened, how could this have been avoided?)

Oral

1.   With two other members of your class choose a simple topic such as earth, tools, or books. Let each member of the group prepare and give to the class a two-minute talk that makes three points about the chosen topic, one talk giving information, another persuading, and the third entertaining. Afterward compare and contrast the different kinds of materials each speaker used and the different ways he or she had to use them.

2.   Prepare and give to your class a short speech of inquiry on a question such as "What is the best way we could conduct our class to get helpful feedback from the audience in our next formal speeches?" When you have opened the problem and suggested directions in which a solution might be sought, preside over a class discussion seeking to devise a plan for handling feedback and criticism during a forthcoming set of classroom speeches.

3.   Among the more difficult topics on which to inform are those in which abstract or aesthetic concepts have to be made clear. For practice with this kind of speaking prepare and give a two-minute talk on how people should go about understanding or appreciating some specific artistic object (a statue, piece of jewelry, architectural form, bit of poetry, or other).

4.   Prepare and present an oral report on the kinds of content used in some speech to entertain. Indicate also what special treatment was given the content. (Speeches by Mark Twain, Will Rogers, or recorded monologues by such entertainers as Joan Rivers, Bob Newhart, or David Brenner could be chosen for this exercise.)

5.   Prepare and present a brief talk on one of the following subjects or some variation on one of them:

   a.   It is unwise for speakers trying to inform to color their content with extensive use of personal opinions.

   b.   A speaker seeking to persuade needs to reveal his or her own attitudes toward subject matter.

   c.   What are some differences between appropriately expressing attitudes toward information in speeches seeking to induce inquiry and speeches seeking to persuade.

   d.   What kinds of proof are especially useful in reinforcing beliefs in the value of the family (or any other subject you choose)?

6.   With four or five colleagues assess why some allegedly good speaker failed in a major attempt at persuasion. (Certain campaign speeches by, say, Adlai Stevenson, Jimmy Carter, or Ronald Reagan might be examined. Or you might consider a television editorial you have recorded, or any other short unit of oral persuasion.) When your group has completed its assessment, organize a group presentation like that illustrated in Appendix B. Your purpose, as a group, could be either to persuade your class that your group's judgment is "right" or

just to inform them of what happened. As you plan your group presentation, pay attention to the specific purposes of your different speakers and to the different materials each needs in order to accomplish his or her specific purpose.

ENDNOTES

1. This talk was given by Anthony Damiani of Herbert H. Lehman College as a classroom speech in a basic speech course.
2. The philosopher-psychologist John Dewey expressed the importance of perplexity thus: "The occasion for deliberation is an *excess* of preferences.... We want things that are incompatible with one another; therefore we have to make a choice of what we *really* want.... Choice ... is the emergence of a unified preference out of competing preferences." *Human Nature and Conduct* (New York: Random House, The Modern Library, 1930), p. 193.
3. Thucydides, *The Peloponnesian War,* trans. Rex Warner (Baltimore: Penguin Books, 1954), p. 119.
4. Charles Boyle, "The Bright Side of Adversity," *Vital Speeches of the Day* XLII (May 1, 1976): 436–38.
5. "The Sinews of Peace," delivered at Westminster College, Fulton, Missouri, March 5, 1946. The text of this speech (also called "The Iron Curtain Speech") is available in many sources. Quoted here from *The Sinews of Peace: Post-War Speeches by Winston S. Churchill,* ed. Randolph S. Churchill (Boston: Houghton Mifflin Company, 1949), p. 97.
6. Ms. Wallingford was a biology major at The Pennsylvania State University.
7. George Campbell, *Philosophy of Rhetoric,* ed. Lloyd Bitzer (Carbondale, Ill.: Southern Illinois University Press, 1963), p. 77, bk. I, chap. 7. Originally published in 1776.
8. The classic studies of one-sided versus two-sided persuasion were reported by Carl I. Hovland, Arthur A. Lumsdaine, and Fred D. Sheffield in *Studies in Social Psychology in World War II,* vol. 3: *Experiments on Mass Communication* (Princeton: Princeton University Press, 1949). A much later study showed that "subjects will be less influenced by counterpersuasion in a small group communication setting if an initial persuader employs a two-sided, refutational message than if he employs a one-sided message." See James C. McCroskey, Thomas J. Young, and Michael D. Scott, "The Effects of Message Sidedness and Evidence on Inoculation Against Counterpersuasion in Small Group Communication," *Speech Monographs* XXXIX (August 1972): 205–12.
9. The once-popular notion that what is heard first "inoculates" against counterviews has been significantly challenged in recent years. See Michael D. Miller and Michael Burgoon, "The Relationship Between Violations of Expectations and the Induction of Resistance to Persuasion," *Human Communication Research* V (Summer 1979): 301–13.
10. Mr. Nobile titled his talk "Economizing on School Materials." Used by permission of Thomas D. Nobile.

CHAPTER 7

... Form is the creation of an appetite in the mind of the auditor, and the adequate satisfying of that appetite.—Kenneth Burke, "Psychology and Form" [1]

Disposition: Organizing materials

Where can you apply the principles of this chapter in everyday life?

1. Wherever you feel the need for communicating in speech or writing in an especially orderly manner.
2. Wherever you need to orient others to a subject.
3. Wherever you wish to summarize what someone has said.
4. Wherever you wish to report processes or happenings to others.
5. Wherever you feel the need to raise a question or pose a problem and you do not know the solution.

When evaluating someone else's speech consider:

1. Was the overall pattern of organization that the speaker used clear?
2. What different patterns of ideas were effectively used within the overall structure?
3. Were the introduction, body, and conclusion of the speech easily perceived? What elements did the speaker include in each of these main divisions? Did the speaker omit the introduction or conclusion? If so, was there justification for doing so?
4. Did the overall pattern help to reveal the rhetorical purpose of the speech?
5. Did the way the speech was organized make it easier to listen to?

In his book *The Image,* Kenneth E. Boulding points out that one modern view of the universe assumes an ever-present tendency "for things to run down." He continues by saying, "The end of the universe, according to this picture, will be a thin, uniform soup without form. It is toward this comfortless end that all physical processes are moving." Boulding insists, however, that history exhibits another tendency, "the tendency for the rise of organization":

> It is the capacity for organizing information into large and complex images which is the chief glory of our species. . . . Our image of time . . . goes far beyond that of the most intelligent of lower animals, mainly because of our capacity for language and for record. . . . Closely associated with the time structure of his [man's] image is the image of the structure of relationships. Because we are aware of time, we are also aware of cause and effect, of contiguity and succession, of cycles and repetition.[2]

The organization of a message is an application of this human capacity and appetite for organizing the environment. We all yearn for structure in what we deal with, and when language is our method of acquiring information, we organize almost instinctively. For example, test your own impulses on this list of words:

dive	cookout	sun
hot	pool	shade
cool	music	water

Does the list please you as it is? Probably not. Aren't you inclined to try to see some system or pattern among the words? Now suppose we say, "Use these terms in a story about a *party.*" Using *party* as a "key," or rudimentary central idea, enables you to build an organized, satisfying image. Our own image is this:

> It was a hot day, just right for a party by the pool where we could enjoy diving into the cool water, lounging in the sun, or taking refuge in the shade. Good music filled the air, and the smells of the cookout just beginning filled us with satisfaction.

What's your version? A list of ideas is fundamentally unintelligible until you see in it or impose on it some structure that gives the items organized meaning *for you.* Because the same thing is true of the ideas in any public speech, we devote this and the next chapter to the subject of how to choose and plan agreeable, effective, *structured* speech.

Before we proceed, however, we need to make a point about *when* one organizes speech. We have just spent three chapters discussing inventing the substance of speech. Now we turn to organizing that substance. Though we are considering the two topics separately, you should understand that in actual practice the steps of inventing and the steps of organizing alternate as you compose speech. At some moments of preparation you will find yourself thinking about what to say (invention) and at next moments you will begin thinking about how to order those ideas (organization). Then you may shift to inventing again and afterward to organizing. There are two distinct kinds of thinking involved here: finding *what* to say and deciding *how* to put those things together. You will not ordinarily do all of the first kind of thinking before beginning the second kind, so you must understand that what we shall say in this and the next chapter applies whenever you turn your mind to organizing, for however brief a time. With that in mind, let us consider what ought to concern you in *any* moments when you focus on organizing ideas.

INFLUENCES ON ORGANIZATION

Happily, on most matters that we speak about we generally share concepts of relationships through which we connect ideas with our listeners. We are used to connecting things by time, cause and effect, contiguity, cyclical succession, repetition, and similar conceptions. Even listeners with poor perceptions can see such relationships, a major fact that allows us to communicate with one another. As cautions, however, speakers must remember: (1) listeners do not take in as much detail as readers, so speakers must show relationships very plainly; (2) the object of all organizing is to give a set of thoughts some pattern that a particular audience will recognize; and (3) it is foolish to try to organize ideas before most of them have been located and a central idea has been identified.

Organizing is necessary for intelligibility, but it is also necessary for listeners' psychological gratification. Listeners lose interest when a speech does not seem to be advancing toward some meaningful goal. They like progression they can recognize. They want cumulative, psychologically satisfying effects. A speech, then, must build, point by point. Somewhere a climax must be reached. This high point is usually near the end of the discourse, but it may and sometimes does occur earlier. In either case it will be psychologically satisfying if points along the way are given time, detailed development, and intensity proportionate to their relative weights within the total structure. Listeners anticipate that somewhere in your speech all the necessary information will be in, all arguments developed to the point of acceptability. They expect, in short, that all roads will lead to Rome. In this they are simply displaying the chief glory of their species.

Not all decisions about organizing derive from the natures of audiences. Much depends on your own understanding of your ideas. If you try a plan and it seems too complicated to be easily remembered in speaking, you ought to look for another plan that you can manage readily. This is important because uncertainty about organization is often a major cause of lack of confidence in speaking. On the other hand, when you are satisfied that *you* understand how each piece of supporting material is related to each other piece and to your central idea, you will be able to proceed with assurance.

Subject matter can impose patterns of organization too. As material is discovered and gathered, you will begin to sort it. Sorting may show that materials such as anecdotes, questions, examples, and statistics tend to group under particular patterns. Thus materials about topography or scenery will lend themselves to spatial organization, producing description. Historical materials may virtually demand to be handled in narrative, chronological form. The organization of many sections of your speeches will be governed more by the nature of the material than by any other single influence.

How materials ought to be weighted in relation to one another may also be determined by your research. As you move through the inventional processes we discussed in Chapters 4, 5, and 6, you may evolve an image of your speech that you will have to change when you undertake to structure all you know. You may be startled by how little there is to say about a pet idea, for example. Then you have the choice between discarding a seemingly weak contention or backtracking to search for new information.

You will often find that you have too much material for the available speaking time. It is paradoxical but true that beginning speakers tend to fear that they will not have enough to say but end up belaboring their rhetorical situations with too much detail. Sifting ideas and paring them down is an important part of organizing. If you discover that you have support for a dozen ideas that seem significant, you should discard the least fruitful points or organize the material in another way. No listener can remember a dozen different points, and the likelihood is that if you have located that many points some are main points and others are secondary. In that case, identify or create a few major headings (usually not more than three or four for a short speech) and reduce the other points to supports or amplifications of the major headings.

The processes of elimination and reorganization are sometimes painful. But if you reduce your speech to essentials, cutting can be advantageous. Sometimes you may have to cut on short notice; for example, if your speaking time has been encroached on. It happens even to the famous. Franklin Roosevelt found it necessary to cut his 1932 speech accepting the presidential nomination. The plane in which he flew from Albany to Chicago was hours late, which meant that he would appear before an audience wearied by waiting to hear him. He wisely decided that his speech would have to be shorter than he had planned. Samuel Rosenman, who assisted him with the speech, writes:

> With each radio report, we were falling further and further behind schedule; and more and more paragraphs came out of the acceptance speech. This lopping off of material on which we had worked so long and so hopefully was a painful process. I know that there were some jewels dropped on the airplane floor that day. It is likely, though, that the cutting process hurt us more than it did the speech.[3]

Such may be your feeling; yet rejection and red penciling will often result in conciseness and sharper focus. The tightening that comes from excision usually enhances the organic unity of a speech.

When you have decided which main points are to be amplified or supported, questions arise about how to order them. Knowing that audiences are likely to pay closest attention to and be least tired during the early part of a speech argues for putting your strongest point first. But knowing that listeners are also likely to remember the ideas they have heard most recently argues for placing your strongest point last. Despite numerous experiments, there are no rules by which you can choose between these alternatives.[4] All you can be sure of is that the first and last positions in any series are more impressive than the other positions. Therefore, it is sensible to place ideas of lesser importance in the intermediate positions. Experienced speakers employing three points favor placing them in 1–3–2 or 2–3–1 orders of strength. In dealing with four points they favor 1–3–4–2, 1–4–3–2, 2–3–4–1, or 2–4–3–1 orders of strength. Your final decision has to be one of *judgment*. It ought to rest on whether special features of content or situation lead you to "bet" that primacy or recency will here be the position of greatest emphasis for your particular audience.

We suggest that the strongest point be put first when it is also least familiar, when the audience is already very receptive to the point, or when some other activity—such as the tour of a building or a banquet—may beckon to your listeners. On the other hand, the strongest point might be put last when you know that part of your audience may be late in arriving or when your final argument will be followed almost immediately by the signing of a pledge or some other private or public commitment or action.

Although we usually think of organization or disposition of entire speeches, the principles of clear organization also operate for the various points within discourse. If you use narrative, chronological order is almost inescapable. Interrupting narrative for expressions of personal opinion almost always diverts attention from the main movement of thought. Yet there may be circumstances where spontaneous insertion of definitions or other clarifying details is necessary if you are to adapt to your audience. The questions to be asked about any break in an established order of ideas are: "Is this departure relevant? and will this deviation from the thought pattern *help* to achieve my purpose?"

Occasions and settings influence organization of ideas less often than do audience, speaker, and material. The occasion may require initial acknowledgments or personal greetings, but these are minor adaptations. A setting may also more severely narrow your choice. For example, a Washington's birthday celebration may call for a eulogy of George Washington. Speakers have found that eulogies are successful when the praise is structured by recounting incidents in that person's life or describing his or her traits of character. When speakers depart from a pattern because the occasion itself is unexpectedly changed by some distraction, such as the rattle of jackhammers outside the window, a sudden power failure, or the unexpected appearance of an important personage, modification of the message is as much a matter of audience adaptation as of adaptation to the occasion.

Plainly, the ordering of ideas for speech cannot be done randomly. Nor can it be done by rule. Organizational choices are wisely made only after careful consideration of the audience's expectations, the speaker's capabilities, the nature of the data used to achieve the speaker's purpose, and, incidentally, the circumstances prevailing at the time of delivery.

MAIN COMPONENTS OF A SPEECH

The number of *parts of a speech* has been an issue of debate for centuries. Today's convention is that a speech should have an introduction, a body, and a conclusion *unless* there are strong reasons for building it otherwise. The proportions of these parts depend on the subject matter, the situation, and the speaker, but most often they depend on the audience's expectations and motivations. There will also need to be clear connections that link the three main portions. These linking parts are transitions. A speech has a beginning, a middle, an end, and internal transitional elements. We will consider these separately.

Introduction

The introduction to any speech or series of interrelated speeches ought to establish the relationship of what is to be said to the rhetorical situation. It must (1) attract initial, favorable attention; (2) provide necessary background for the audience so they may comprehend what follows; (3) be suitable to the occasion; and (4) contribute to your own ease as a speaker during a crucial period of adjustment. In addition, the introduction ought to be coordinated with and must relate to the body of the speech. It is not a preamble or a prelude without relation to what follows.

At the outset you must gain attention in such a way that your listeners will want to go on listening. Any of the methods for achieving attention may be employed, but the most useful ways are to refer to something familiar or something novel. You may start with a reference to the occasion, to its purpose, or to other things about which the audience already knows. You may begin with greetings, an anecdote, or analogy. Tradition may dictate what you will say. Or you may need to awaken the audience by sharpening the focus of their attention. Where this is so, unusual facts or stories, shocking or startling assertions, unfamiliar statistics, telegraphic headline fragments, or other striking materials may enable you to create curiosity or suspense. Reference to your own interests and needs, especially if they are similar to those of your audience, may create common ground and cause your audience to want to listen. A modest statement of your qualifications for speaking on the subject you have chosen can make your listeners want to hear more.

Most audiences want to be given reasons for listening. They are always ready to ask, "Why should *I* listen? What's in this for *me*?" Often they want directions about what to listen for. The ways in which you can touch off an audience's powers of concentration are limitless; yet none is truly useful unless it will at once seize attention and favorably dispose your audience to what follows.

If you will look in Appendix B at Joe's introduction to his group's presentation, at Dr. Upcraft's introduction to his speech (paragraphs 1–4), and at Kathy's analysis of Upcraft's introduction, you will see most of the functions we have just enumerated being carried out, then pointed to by Kathy. The function given least attention by Joe and by Dr. Upcraft was attracting attention to the subject. Given their situations, this is understandable. The classroom group was *scheduled;* the audience knew beforehand that the group was to present a critique, although the listeners did not know what speech was to be examined, nor did they know that Dr. Upcraft himself would be present. It was background and indications of how the group's subject related to the audience that Joe needed chiefly to focus on. Before his audience Dr. Upcraft scarcely needed to establish attention because the meeting he addressed was about his subject. More for his own purposes than for the audience's feelings or interest, he needed to give the historical background of the policy he had to defend. He needed also to acknowledge the audience's invitation to him, which he did in a single sentence. However, in neither Joe's nor Dr. Upcraft's situation was there need to do what you may have to do in a classroom speech: draw an audience's attention *away* from other things *to* a subject for which only you can prepare them.

Your subject may make it important to give certain preliminary information in your introduction. It may be necessary to define unfamiliar terms that you must use later or to explain special meanings that you will have to assign to familiar terms. A short historical review such as Dr. Upcraft offered may be necessary for full understanding of your speech. For Dr. Upcraft past events had given rise to the policy he must defend. In other circumstances, such as when you must argue from some precedent or when your listeners have thought little about your subject, a fuller history of the question may be needed.

Definitions and histories are sometimes supplemented or replaced by statements of matters that you must deal with or that you will not deal with in the body of your speech. Items specially singled out because you intend to pass them over or because they seem irrelevant are often called *waived materials.* You simply state that you will not consider them and give your listeners your reasons. Giving main points to be developed later is what the Romans called *division;* today it is sometimes called *initial partition.* The tactic is useful when your audience needs to know the path you intend to take. Of course, you would not offer such statements if you wished to preserve suspense or feared that revealing your entire plan so early might make some listeners defensive. Initial partitioning is not a useful introductory tactic in speeches developed inductively or in those designed for unfriendly audiences. Even then the central idea is often withheld until some later, more strategic moment—possibly even the end of the speech.

In speeches constructed on a deductive pattern you ought to include the central idea of your speech as a final item of your introduction or as an initial item in the body of the speech. Whenever it appears, it ought to be carefully expressed in a single, economical, unambiguous sentence, as was pointed out in Chapters 2 and 5.

Not all the items we have mentioned will be included in any one introduction. What your listeners *need* to know before you proceed should dictate how much and what kinds of orientation material you offer. In addition to the illustrative introductions in Appendix B, an introduction for a speech appears in the exercise section of this chapter (written exercise 2). In each example you will find the speaker taking some of the steps we have just discussed, omitting others because of the nature of the situation, the subject matter, or the speaker's role in the situation.

The introduction is a part of the speech that, given the right circumstances, may be omitted altogether. It is not necessary if an audience is already attentive and interested in your subject, if they expect you to speak, if they already possess the background information, or if they are highly motivated. College professors can often dispense with introductions after the first few lectures. If their audiences are oriented and motivated, introductory remarks become superfluous. You, however, should be cautious about omitting introductions. Rarely can an introduction be omitted when you speak to an audience for the first time; never, when your audience is not entirely ready to pay attention from the outset.

Body of the speech

The body of a speech comprises (1) the main points, (2) the material that supports or amplifies these points, and (3) transitional phrases or sentences. The same requirements hold for a group presentation of a subject. Consider the extent to which Kathy, Ron, Patti, Greg, and Stephanie fulfilled these obligations in presenting the body of their group's report (see Appendix B).

Earlier we discussed sorting and sifting materials to arrive at main points and determine their psychological weighting and placement.[5] Whatever your decision regarding their order, internal organization should always be so devised that neither you nor the audience loses sight of the point you are proving or clarifying. You should be clear about the relationship between *the material used to prove* and *the point being proved*. When these stages of preliminary analysis have been completed and you know your main points, you next word the main ideas.

Where possible, main points ought to be worded in parallel phrasings to provide balance, thus making them easier to remember. They should also be worded to elicit the responses you seek from your audience. Main points for informative speeches should be simple, clear assertions. In speeches of inquiry the main points are often worded as questions that are then explored or answered with information. Main points for persuasive speeches should be assertions, slanted in wording to express your point of view and to support the main proposition embodied in your subject sentence. These main points should be *contentions,* reasons closely linked to the subject sentence so they become the foundation stones on which the core idea rests. Main points for speeches of reinforcement are framed in essentially the same ways as those for other persuasive speeches. For speeches designed to entertain, main points usually take the form of assertions.

The ways of arranging these points into patterns are discussed later in this chapter. Under the discussions of the various patterns of organization you will find some examples of wordings for main headings adapted to the different purposes.

Transitions[6]

Listeners cannot easily review what you have said after it has been spoken, as they might turn back and reread the pages in a book. Therefore, you will need to provide careful transitions if your speech is to be clear at all points. *Transitions* are words, phrases, sentences, or groups of sentences that join ideas together. If clear and smooth, they contribute to the organic unity and the clarity of your speech.

Transitions are like signposts. They tell your audience where you have been, where you are, or where you intend to go. They are most frequently needed at the completion of a main idea, before you move on to the next one; but you may also need them as connections between subsidiary points or phrases leading to the ideas in single sentences.

Extended transitions are sometimes called *internal summaries*. They are especially useful as you complete one major point to open up another. They serve the functions of any transition, but if carefully constructed, they can also review or clinch the point just completed. There is an old saying that "first you tell 'em what you'll tell 'em; then you tell 'em; then you tell 'em what you told 'em." It is hackneyed, but if not followed too mechanically, the saying carries good advice. Quickly restating the gist of the point you are completing "tells 'em what you told 'em" and gains for you the advantage of repetition or restatement as a means of emphasis. This can be joined to a brief statement of why that thought leads naturally and logically to your next point or topic, which you can now preview ("tell 'em what you'll tell 'em") in a clause or sentence. Thus, you create an *internal summary* that clinches one main idea as it justifies and announces the next step in presentation. These are the functions of all transitions whether brief or expanded. Some examples of how transitions are normally phrased follow:

Since we have already considered that . . . , we should adopt . . . .

In addition to . . . there is another outstanding reason (element, factor, consideration, fact) . . . .

We have seen . . . , yet it remains for us to observe . . . .

But . . . is only one important viewpoint. Equally important is . . . .

I have shown you that my proposal is socially sound and politically desirable. Furthermore, it is economically beneficial. Let us look at this last contention.

Since . . . is so, what can be said of . . . ? (Questions can often be useful as transitions.)

Where the connection to be emphasized is between subpoints, or where the thought relationships are easy to comprehend, a phrase or even a single word such as *so* or *yet* may be adequate to tie ideas together. Some examples of such phrasings are:

More important than all this is the fact that . . . .

In contrast to . . . .

Looked at from a different angle the problem seems to be . . . .

This last point raises a question: . . . ?

What was the result? Just this . . . .

On the other hand . . . .

When this has been done . . . .

And so you can see that . . . .

When more than one person participates in presenting a report or argument, transitions become very important as the flow of talk shifts from one speaker to another. For the speakers' total message to hold together for the listeners and have a strong impact on them, it is necessary that someone emphasize how the several parts of the presentation relate to one another. Sometimes this is done by having a chairperson make transitional connections between subtopics developed by different speakers; sometimes, as in the presentation in Appendix B, it is left to the speakers who precede and follow one another. Either way, good transitions here and within individual speeches should (1) show that communication is moving from one idea to another,

(2) demarcate completed ideas, (3) indicate the relationships between the ideas involved, and (4) remind speaker and listener of the overall sequence of thought.

Seek variety in transitions. Avoid using only stock phrases or repeating the same few phrases over and over. And do not be too brief. The whole point of making a transition is to show a connection clearly. A mark of an unpolished speaker is the tendency to use only *and, also,* or *like* as transitions. This gives the impression that the ideas have only been tacked together instead of joined according to their natural or logical relationships. But even such a speaker communicates better than one who vaguely gropes his or her way, melting from point to point, as it were.

Conclusion

The final segment of your speech, its conclusion, performs functions that serve the audience, you, the occasion, and the material itself. At the end of a talk listeners normally expect at least (1) a restatement of your core idea or (2) a summing up of main points. Both restatement and summary may be needed. Almost any body of material needs a final rounding out that fuses subject matter with intent. To emphasize a detail or simply to fade into silence obscures meaning. The audience should not feel at the end of a speech that they have been left hanging, that the speech ended too abruptly, or that the subject is still up in the air. *The final moments of a speech ought to be used to drive home the central idea.* The audience should know that you have finished, and you should feel satisfied that you have accomplished your purpose and produced a final impact. This does not mean that your final sentence ought always to be a restatement or summary. Recapitulation is the main function of most conclusions, but your last sentences are often strongest if devised to challenge the audience. Final sentences may echo the beginning sentences or constitute a return to a text or refrain, thus providing a frame for all you have said. A "thank you" at the end of a speech may detract from the central idea and an otherwise strong final impression. Indeed, any remarks of appreciation used as last sentences ought to be carefully considered since they may destroy the focus of an otherwise effective conclusion.

Joe's conclusion (Appendix B) illustrates some general and special points about concluding a presentation. This conclusion would have been more effective if Joe had reviewed *which* rhetorical processes his group had shown contributed most to Dr. Upcraft's rhetorical achievement. He neglected this and so missed the opportunity to reinforce the group's findings. Not unlike many other speakers, Joe had the additional concluding task of controlling *what was to happen next.* He could have been far more incisive in directing the next happenings. Did he want Dr. Upcraft to respond to the criticism or did he want questions from the audience? He left this unclear. Fortunately Dr. Upcraft chose to make some impromptu responses. This particular example should remind you that in concluding any communication you need to make sure—by what you say—that you leave the rhetorical situation exactly as your purpose requires.

Occasionally, but rarely, you will speak in a situation where you need not utter concluding words. Sometimes someone else will conclude what you have said, as when one person explains that the treasury is empty, knowing that a colleague will immediately make an appeal for money. Dr. Upcraft had the special circumstance that a hearing would continue. He had only to be available, having spoken.

Introduction, central idea, body, transitions, and conclusion will, with rare exceptions, be parts of every speech you will deliver, though you will give these sections of each speech quite different forms. You will, for example, organize the introductions and the bodies of speeches according to one or more of the following different patterns.

EFFECTIVE PATTERNS OF ORGANIZATION [7]

Four conditions will usually determine the most appropriate pattern for a given speaking situation: (1) the particular type and degree of response you seek from the audience; (2) whether the audience is favorably, unfavorably, or apathetically disposed toward your subject, your central idea, and you as a speaker; (3) how much knowledge your listeners possess about your subject; (4) how you can best relate your central idea to the interests and desires of your audience.

The *patterns* commonly used in structuring ideas in practical speaking include: (1) chronological, (2) spatial, (3) topical, (4) ascending and descending orders, (5) causal, (6) problem-solution, or disease-remedy, (7) withheld proposal, or indirect sequence, (8) open proposal, or direct sequence, (9) reflective sequence, or pattern of inquiry, (10) Monroe's motivated sequence, and (11) elimination order. Each is explained in some detail in the sections that follow.

Patterning ideas is imposing structure on content. You should bear in mind that none of the patterns we are about to discuss needs to be followed rigidly or in its entirety to be useful as a general scheme for organizing speech. Also, any of these patterns can be used for the organization of a whole speech, for a major segment of it, or for relatively brief developments of arguments, explanations, or amplifications. For example, you might develop the introduction of a speech chronologically but in the body argue from cause to effect or present a problem and then offer its solution. The schemes of organization from which experienced speakers select most often are these.

Chronological pattern

The *chronological pattern* is a time order, enumerating occurrences in the sequence in which they happened or giving directions in the order to be followed. Material will often dictate this kind of ordering. Narration—the recounting of events—unconditionally demands it.

Chronological patterns may be used in all kinds of speech units and are common when the purpose is to inform. The time sequence usually allows climactic development, arousing curiosity and creating suspense. Examples may be found in the narrations of circumstances leading to crime in Clarence Darrow's famous summation at the trial of Loeb and Leopold, or in Daniel Webster's classic speech for the prosecution in the Knapp-White murder case. William Armstrong (pages 132–133) used a short narrative as a means of amplifying how different receiving a literary prize was from the unfulfilled dreams of his childhood. Within the total structure of the group presentation in Appendix B, Patti and Greg develop their particular points by following the line-by-line or time sequence of Upcraft's speech. In many eulogies, speeches of nomination, historical lectures, demonstrations, and instructional discourses, the entire body of the speech is chronologically organized.

One weakness of chronological patterning is that important considerations such as cause, effect, desirability, and form cannot easily be emphasized without interrupting the movement in time that gives chronology its chief interest value.

Spatial pattern

The *spatial pattern,* as the name implies, is based on the relationships of parts of a whole as they exist in space. Here you proceed systematically, describing how something looks or functions. Normally you will describe from left to right, top to bottom, bottom to top, or front to back. Sometimes you will describe by moving from the center to the periphery. For instance, you might describe the control panel in an airplane by pointing first to those centered instruments most often used before moving out toward the surrounding instruments less frequently used. You would then be using a pattern of descending importance, which happens here to become identical with the pattern of spatial description. In all spatial arrangements you will need to mention each part or aspect *according to plan;* haphazard coverage makes spatial relationships hard to understand.

Spatial structure is especially useful in giving information. A space rocket on its launching pad might be described from top to bottom, a painting from right to left or left to right, the floor plan of a house from front to back or story to story. The order in which to proceed when describing spatially will ordinarily be up to you. Your decision on which space to take up first ought to hinge on your estimation of how you can be clearest for your audience while highlighting the important relationships among parts. If these standards leave you more than one good way of describing spatially, choose the one that is easiest for *you* to present.

Topical pattern

The *topical pattern* is really one in which there is no easily labeled speech structure. The label *topical* is assigned to organizational schemes that otherwise cannot be accounted for. Some call them *classification orders* to denote that some kind of orderly categorization accounts for the patterning. Some would say topical patterns are those that arise from the subject matter, that these are patterns evolving out of the natural parts of the subject, its aspects, types, or qualities. The word *topical* gives us a clue. A communicator trying to order his or her ideas asks where the places are to which we go for argument or clarification and comes up with an answer such as, "We often look at social, political, or economic aspects of arguments." Thus the speaker *invents* a *special* classification of materials. It may be only one of several schemes of organizing data. Another might have been public interests versus private interests. Dr. Upcraft (Appendix B) developed a series of aspects of his policy problem from paragraphs 5 through 10. In the students' discussion of Upcraft's speech Ron presented two points that were: (1) use of examples and (2) Upcraft's argument that the university had no choice. The points are related only by the fact that they both "redirect the hostility," and in that sense they constitute topics of proof.

In this way we think of the topics we might use and select from them; they, as we choose them, become the bases for organizing ideas. A topical pattern is an arbitrary grouping of themes pertinent to a particular subject and speech purpose. Topical patterns are not very interesting in and of themselves. At times the topics chosen may arouse feelings of curiosity or need, but the order in which the topics are treated cannot be depended on to attract the attention of listeners. The pattern is adaptable to any purpose but inquiry. The only constraint on such a pattern is that the audience accept the divisions as reasonable and comprehensive.

Ascending and descending orders

When you choose to use *ascending* and *descending orders,* you place patterns, aspects, types, or qualities in sequence according to their increasing or decreasing importance or familiarity. That is, you move from the most to the least important or from the most to the least familiar points or vice versa. You start with the strongest argument and move to the weakest or start with the weakest and move to the strongest. You may start on common ground and move into unfamiliar territory, or you may begin with an unusual aspect or argument and lead the audience to what they already know or to what is already uppermost in their minds. In the case of descending order, for example, you would explain how pulp is processed for the manufacture of paper by taking up the most commonly used process, the ground-wood process, and move through your speech to the soda, sulfite, and alkaline processes, which are used less frequently and are less familiar to most people. Similarly, in a speech on population control, the familiar argument that natural resources of the earth will soon be used up would precede less striking arguments about political and cultural consequences of an exploding population. If you simply reverse the sequence so less well known or weaker arguments come first, you achieve ascending order.

Ascending-descending orders are suitable in speaking to inform, to persuade, or to reinforce. The pattern might also be adapted for use in a speech to entertain. The choice and construction of ascending and descending orders hinge on your judgments of the relative importance of your materials; on your estimate of what will help your listeners remember and give them a sense of climax; and, sometimes, on whether you have time to develop enough points to make ascent or descent psychologically meaningful.

Causal sequence

Causal patterns are used in situations where one set of conditions is given as the cause for another set. In such cases you may begin with a given set of conditions as the cause and allege that these will produce certain results or effects; or you may take a given set of conditions as the effect and allege that these resulted from certain causes.

In most uses of this pattern the specific purpose is to urge elimination of those conditions that function as causes. To achieve this specific purpose, however, you may need to persuade your audience of one or more of these things: (1) that the effects are really undesirable to them; (2) that the alleged causes are truly responsible for these effects; and (3) that elimination of these causes will not result in other undesirable consequences. The first two concerns must either be evident to the audience or must be proved. The third may sometimes be safely disregarded.

The most common use of this pattern is one in which a speaker points out that certain undesirable conditions (*effects*) now exist and then explains that these are caused by certain other conditions (*causes*). The speaker *may* carry the reasoning through a chain of two or more effect-cause relationships to get the present undesirable effects to the cause the speaker asks the audience to eliminate. This kind of development might run thus:

I.   Crime has increased sharply in America during the last two decades. (Stating present undesirable effect.)

II. This increase is partly caused by unemployment. (Establishing first effect-to-cause relationship.)

III. Lack of law enforcement in our communities is also responsible for the increase. (Establishing second effect-to-cause relationship.)

IV. Crime will be reduced by increasing the number of jobs and providing for more police action by establishing a national task force on crime. (Urging audience to adopt proposal eliminating prime causes and thereby eliminating effect.)

Frequently, a speaker will point out that certain existing conditions will cause undesirable effects in the future and so should be eliminated. The normal sequence is to begin with the present causes and then describe the anticipated future effects. Sometimes a more artistic sequence can be achieved by visualizing the future effects for the audience first, then linking these effects to removal of the present undesirable causes. One might structure a unit of speech thus:

I.   The world is drifting toward exhaustion of its fossil fuel supplies. (Portraying future undesirable effects.)

II. This drift is caused by unmanaged consumption of these fuels. (Establishing that present conditions cause the future effects.)

III. Therefore, all nations should be required to submit fuel conservation programs to a United Nations planning commission. (Appealing to audience to support a policy to eliminate present causes to avoid the future effects.)

Sometimes a speaker draws an analogy between a cause-effect relationship and another similar cause-effect relationship already accepted by his or her audience:

I. Efforts to preserve the endangered species, the timber wolf, are failing despite commitments to preserve them made by the United States Department of the Interior. (Establishing present conditions as a potential cause.)

II. Because India failed in the past to provide for the enforcement of game laws, the Bengal tiger was allowed to become virtually extinct. (Referring to past cause-effect relationship.)

III. In a similar way the government's lack of enforcement could result in the extinction of the timber wolf. (Drawing parallel undesirable effects from parallel causes.)

IV. Therefore, the United States Department of the Interior should rigorously prosecute citizens who violate laws regulating treatment of the timber wolf. (Appealing to audience to eliminate present causes to avoid future effects.)

Although causal patterns are generally used to advocate the removal of some condition, they can be used to advocate that certain conditions be encouraged. In this use you would show how something desirable to your audience (effect) results from other things (causes); therefore, the audience should set these causes in operation to secure the effect. Such a pattern might run:

I. We want lower inflation rates in the United States. (Establishing condition, effect, as desirable to the audience.)

II. Diminished inflation is possible only if government spending is reduced. (Establishing a cause as capable of producing the desired effect.)

III. Therefore, let us insist on less government spending. (Appealing for audience support for conditions designed to cause the desirable effects.)

Causal patterns are also often used in informing to describe the relationships of parts of what is being explained, such as the causes of inflation or the effects of X-rays on human tissue. On occasion, speeches to reinforce and entertain are cast in this pattern.

The biggest difficulty in using causal patterns is in making clear that a valid causal relationship actually exists between the two sets of conditions. If the plan is to be effective, listeners must see that genuine and significant (for them) causalities do exist. Naturally, then, the material you use must be open to causal analysis.

Problem-solution sequence

The *problem-solution pattern* presents an audience with a problem and proposes a way to solve it. This pattern is also called the *disease-remedy* or the *need-remedy pattern*. Here, you point first to the existence of a problem or evil and then offer a corrective program that will be (1) practicable and (2) desirable. The corrective program must be capable of being put into effect, and it must be capable of eliminating the problem or the evil in question. It must also be one that will not introduce new and worse evils of its own. For example, this is an issue long debated regarding the legalization of marijuana. Would legalization result in more widespread use and greater evils than we have at present?

The specific purpose of speaking in a problem-solution pattern is to urge listeners to adopt the conditions embodied in the solution. This type of organization usually serves well in the following situations.

1. When the audience is aware that a problem exists and is interested in finding a solution to it, you may advocate one solution as the best of several possible answers. Although you will generally describe the problem briefly, you will be primarily concerned with showing how your particular solution will solve the problem in the best possible way and how any alleged disadvantages of your solution may be avoided. This latter concern, avoiding new difficulties, will frequently involve you in anticipatory refutation, which means you will have to dispel arguments against your proposal even though they have not yet been advanced by anyone.

2. Where the audience is only dimly aware of a problem or need, the problem-solution pattern still serves well. Listeners can be made aware of the problem's exact nature; then, perhaps, the solution will become evident. This is what Dr. Upcraft does in paragraphs 4 through 9 of his speech in Appendix B. Here the goal is to focus listeners on crucial aspects of the problem. They must see that their interests are involved in both problem and solution. The concern is to show that a specific, serious problem does exist. When your audience is not initially aware of their difficulty, it is unlikely that in a single speech you can do more than establish a precise sense of need; but not even in these circumstances can you disregard the solution section of your sequence completely. If you do, you will leave the hearers up in the air. You must at least indicate that there *are* ways of solving the problem.

3. There are situations where the major concerns of both the preceding settings are combined. Sometimes you can carry your audience from awareness of a problem through to a readiness to act on a particular solution.

Now your task is (1) to sharpen awareness of the problem and (2) to show why your solution is the most suitable. Such speech might be structured thus:

I. A serious problem of unemployment now exists in the United States. (Referring to felt need.)

A. This problem poses a threat to our national economy. (Establishing importance of problem to audience.)

B.   This problem costs us millions of dollars in unemployment insurance. (Again, establishing importance of problem to audience.)

C.   The problem is particularly acute for those under twenty-five years of age and ethnic minorities. (Focusing felt need on particular audience.)

II.   The problem of unemployment can be solved by providing jobs through government and private industry for those who need them. (Stating solution to the problem.)

A.   With a government program that provides jobs that will do things such as rehabilitate slum areas, improve our national parks, and ease the work loads in government agencies, we can help solve the problem. (Showing *how* proposal will solve problem.)

B.   Private industries can also help by expanding plants so more jobs are available. (Also showing *how* proposal will solve problem.)

C.   Since both sectors of the economy will participate, the solution would not result in a socialistic system as some may fear. (Meeting objections to proposal.)

Variations on the problem-solution pattern are sometimes used. One variation is that of alternating or staggering portions of a problem with portions of the solution. For example, the cost of a project may be seen as one aspect of a problem, the workability of the project as another. Finding time for the project may be a third. Taking each up in turn and providing the solutions for cost, workability, and time as you present these aspects of the problem may psychologically satisfy your audience better than if you had discussed all of the problem and then its total solution. This is sometimes called an *alternate problem-solution pattern*. (Such alternation is also sometimes used in causal sequences.) A second variation occurs in informing, as when you *show how* people were faced by a problem and how they solved it. You might report how halfway houses came to be established to meet the problems faced by people seeking to overcome drug addiction. Or, like Dr. Upcraft in Appendix B, paragraphs 8 and 9, you may offer a solution already arrived at as the only one possible. The pattern may be used to inform even if the solution is not yet in effect, provided the answer has been decided and is no longer a question for debate. Problem-solution arrangements may also be adapted to reinforce belief and feeling or, more rarely, to entertain.

It can be seen, then, that problem-solution patterns are direct responses to audiences' needs. An audience must feel or be made to feel that a problem exists or that an evil is present before it will accept a solution. You may have felt personally the need you propose and, as a consequence, almost instinctively chosen this pattern. When this is true you must make the audience feel that the needed action is justified in terms of their interests as well as yours. Speech materials also affect your choice of this organizational pattern. They must lend themselves to division into clear-cut problems and solutions. The occasion may determine which items you select to depict a problem and to explain a solution. Thus all forces in the communicative situation are at work in your deciding how and whether a problem-solution pattern ought to be used.

Withheld proposal, or indirect sequence

The most important characteristic of the *withheld proposal,* or *indirect sequence,* is that when using this pattern you give your audience examples, or some basic assumptions and facts, before you present any generalized inferences or conclusions of your own.

This inductive pattern is especially useful when you speak to a hostile audience. Logically the pattern is usually inductive; psychologically it leads listeners gradually toward a conclusion. This is why it is sometimes the only pattern that will enable you to persuade. It permits you to begin an argument with material your audience knows to be true or with assumptions they accept. A common ground of agreement is established with the audience; when inferences are drawn logically from these accepted materials, the audience must either attack the logic involved or admit that you may be right. This pattern is also effective because it reflects man's normal thinking processes —reasoning from examples and assumptions to reach decisions.

Indirectly structured speeches generally operate in one of two basic patterns. In the first a number of examples is given and a generalization is inferred. The plan might be:

I.   Our city was charged with polluting the lake through improper sewerage control during last year.
II. Regulation 73 on smoke abatement was enforced against only three companies in the city during the first six months of this year, although fourteen complaints were filed.
III. Days on which air pollution alerts were officially announced to city residents increased during the last six months by 35 percent over last year.
IV. Three of five retirees from the pollution-abatement office of the city were not replaced last year.
V.   This city administration is not living up to its pledge to improve the quality of our physical environment.

In using this pattern it is essential that your induction meet your own and your listeners' logical tests for acceptable generalizations.

In a second type of indirect pattern you first give basic assumptions or premises acceptable to your audience; then you give the facts of the specific case about which you are speaking; finally you apply your basic premises to the specific case.

I.   The property tax is our primary source of public support for education.
II. Property taxes have more than trebled since the 1960s.
III. The property tax particularly oppresses the elderly.
IV. The property tax oppresses low-income workers who own their own homes.
V.   We have no choice but to shift tax burdens away from the property owners.

Several specialized, indirect patterns usefully support central ideas. One of these is the *applied-criteria pattern* in which propositions of fact or value are argued by first setting up criteria or standards and then showing that the alleged fact or value matches them. Another specialized use of indirect presentation develops when what at first appears to be a pattern of inquiry (described in a later section) concludes by showing or strongly implying that only one solution solves the problem. The so-called implicative pattern resembles an incomplete, indirect pattern in that description, narration, and exposition are used for persuasive purposes. Word pictures, stories, and explanations hint at conclusions. Arguments presented may or may not be stated in formal fashion. In any case, the method is implicative because the audience is left to draw its own final conclusion or application.

As we have noted, indirect sequences are useful in dealing with hostile audiences and where materials can be divided into acceptable and known, unacceptable and unknown. Concerns of speakers also invite use of this pattern. If you are more adept at presenting material indirectly, in the soft-sell manner, than at approaching audiences directly, you may favor this pattern. Furthermore, indirect presentation is feasible regardless of a speaker's purpose.

Open proposal, or direct sequence

The *open-proposal* or *direct-sequence pattern* of organization is in one sense a deductive order and stands in contrast to the indirect sequence. In using this pattern you urge the audience to accept a proposition on the grounds that its validity, morality, or practicality necessarily follows from accepted axioms or principles.

The direct sequence is simple to use. Essentially, it consists of telling your audience what you intend to prove or explain and then giving the arguments or clarifications that support your thesis. On many occasions you will use several different arguments or divisions of clarification supporting your central idea, and these can be grouped into categories. A person advocating certain legislation might develop arguments showing that it is morally right, legal under the constitution, of economic benefit, and practicable. A speaker explaining road building might cover route planning, grading, and surfacing. These divisions could form the main heads of the body of a speech. They could be arranged in a sequence that gave additional climactic or logical force to the development (the proposal is *desirable;* it is *also practical;* moreover it will have *no significant disadvantages*). Your major concern in applying the open-proposal sequence should be that the subpropositions be arranged in the clearest, most natural, and most logical order.

The direct, or open-proposal, sequence includes among its variations the topical arrangements so common in giving information. It also includes the *list-of-advantages pattern* for persuasion. In this scheme the case for a proposition of policy is structured to present a list of benefits arising out of the proposed policy. This variation is closely related to problem-solution organization in that each alleged advantage implies or demonstrates a problem and solution.

In general, an open-proposal sequence is most suitable when listeners are fairly familiar with your subject and when they have favorable or open-minded attitudes toward your position. There are at least two significant advantages in this system of organization. First, you can give a number of arguments or kinds of clarification efficiently while keeping your audience always aware of what you are trying to prove or clarify. Second, the very openness of this way of organizing can enhance your credibility because there seems little possibility that you are hiding anything.

As in the case of the indirect sequence, whether you adopt or avoid the direct-sequence presentation depends on the outlook of your audience, the way subject matter may be reasonably divided, your skill with direct versus indirect presentation, and the tone or spirit of the occasion.

Reflective sequence, or pattern of inquiry

The *reflective sequence* or *pattern of inquiry* is a pattern of organization based on five steps in reflective thinking outlined by the philosopher John Dewey—(1) locating and defining a problem, (2) describing and limiting the problem, (3) suggesting possible solutions, (4) evaluating and testing the solutions, and (5) selecting the preferred solution.

To use this pattern you and your listeners must be willing to suspend judgment about a problem. This willingness comes from experience and reflection; life teaches us that snap judgments are often wrong, and that sound opinions are usually based on careful consideration of numerous factors. An inquiry and its reflective pattern of organization are appropriate when you are willing to assemble information and ponder various solutions with your audience before reaching a decision.

In a state of mind touched by doubt you invite your audience to join you in a quest for the best solution or the best answer to a question. You develop your speech so your listeners feel the problem is their problem, not yours alone. You do all you can do to give the audience and yourself a better basis for coming to a sound decision. This is the function of a speech of inquiry.

Such speaking is obviously both informative and persuasive. It persuasively asks hearers to ponder, to weigh and consider, to explore; but it does not ask audiences to adopt all of your opinions.

An inquirer both resembles and differs from an informative speaker. The person who gives us information is conversant with the subject and aims to impart that understanding. An inquirer, on the other hand, does not enjoy the same degree of certainty. An inquirer is experiencing a degree of discomfort about the subject. He or she either is unable to settle on a really satisfactory choice among competing solutions or for some reason is determined that the listeners must think their own ways through solutions. Such a speaker is certain of some things, having studied and thought about the problem that vexes. Usually the inquirer is ready (or can get ready) to do these things in communication: (1) formulate and clarify the question that poses the problem; (2) explain the background, causes, symptoms of the problem, and the forces at work to intensify or diminish it; (3) explain what criteria a satisfactory solution to the problem ought to meet; and (4) identify and explain some or most of the solutions that seem to be available. This kind of speaker either has doubts about the relative worth of the solution or, like a teacher or counselor, has decided not to give *the* answer but to encourage his or her audience to choose for themselves. The speaker's aims are thus to impart information and to enlist the listeners in the task of choosing final answers.

To orient listeners to his or her subject, an inquirer first provides them with an understanding of the problem they share. He or she informs them of its troublesome symptoms, its causes, and the forces at work to aggravate or ease it. In this process it will be especially important to help the listeners see the differences between the symptoms and the cause(s), else they will be inclined to cure symptoms rather than actual causes. This process of informing the audience may also require a review of historical developments and how controversies, if any, have grown up around the issues.

The speaker does not stop there, however. He or she next considers the criteria an acceptable answer must meet. This is an important and often-missed step. The speaker must be satisfied that he or she has formulated the right criteria, since the acceptability of any solution will depend on what standards are chosen. Although he or she must consider criteria in every case, inquirers do not always find it necessary to present and justify them in the speech. Some are obvious and readily taken for granted: safety on the highways, democracy, speed in settling legal cases. Such standards hardly need formal presentation, and if they do, they require no justification. Sometimes criteria need to be presented but are too complex for explanation apart from discussion of solutions. This might be the case with the aims of a foreign policy or with the nature of the good life. In such cases criteria will be presented piecemeal as various solutions are discussed. But consideration of criteria is integral to inquiry.

Having clarified a problem and said what is necessary concerning standards, an inquirer using the reflective sequence turns to the alternative solutions or answers. This is generally the most important element in the speech; hence you should allow sufficient time for it, restricting preliminary sections to what is absolutely essential. For each solution you explain and assess, do so thoroughly and fairly in light of the pertinent criteria.

In concluding a speech an inquiring speaker should try to make the audience continue to inquire. Their reflection on the subject should not stop when the speaker stops. In fact, inquiry on a large scale—group inquiry—often begins after a speech of inquiry has been delivered. The speaker may well conclude by presenting the salient questions his or her listeners should consider as they continue their search for the best solution. Or the speaker may point out the *direction* in which he or she thinks the best answer will be found.

A speaker who would really inquire may suggest, but would not urge, acceptance of a special solution. He or she may omit Dewey's fifth step altogether. All five steps need not be included in every inquiry. Indeed, some inquiries go no farther than steps 2 or 3. Others omit step 1. The pattern, in short, is subject to considerable variation according to the requirements of speaker, audience, and occasion.

The speaker's own state of mind comes first in justifying this pattern of organization. The readiness of the audience to accept a pattern that does not provide for the conclusive settlement of a problem may also be a consideration. The occasion is a determinant in that the situation must be one in which people can deliberate. An atmosphere of puzzlement, of careful consideration, will most often suggest to you that a pattern of inquiry is your best scheme of organization.

Monroe's motivated sequence

In treating the five basic purposes of speech: to inform, to convince, to activate, to inspire, and to entertain, Professor Alan H. Monroe of Purdue University developed the motivated sequence pattern of organization, which bears his name. Based on the normal process of human thinking, the *motivated sequence* is thought to be especially effective in motivating listeners' responses to speakers' purposes. The sequence consists of five steps: attention, need, satisfaction, visualization, and action.

In persuasive speeches, which Monroe also sees as speeches to actuate and to inspire, all five steps are used. The speaker (1) gains attention; (2) establishes a need for change of some sort; (3) shows how the change needed can be brought about or satisfied; (4) visualizes what will happen if the need is or is not met—that is, pictures the good or bad results of following the suggested course; and (5) appeals directly for action, either mental or physical.

In the speech to inform only the first three steps are used, and the "need" step becomes the "need to know" rather than the "need to believe" or the "need to act." In the speech to entertain only the "attention" step is used, or others are used as the entertainment becomes a parody of informative or persuasive speaking.

This sequence, more than any other, is psychologically planned to lead your audience's thinking naturally and easily from a vague interest in your subject to a definite acceptance of the attitude or action you are advocating. Each step in the sequence is built on the preceding steps. The motivated sequence can be used in a variety of speeches, but it is chiefly useful when you face an audience that has little interest in your subject or when you want to arouse a strong and specific response in your listeners. Here is how the pattern might be developed:

I.   A recent survey shows that the average shopper can squeeze as much as 14 percent more out of his or her shopping dollar by becoming a smart shopper. (*Attention*)

II.   You really need to save money in these days of severe inflation. (*Need*)

III. By reading ads skillfully, by knowing what questions to ask before you buy, and by buying at the right time you can save those precious dollars. (*Satisfaction*)

IV.   If you do as I suggest you may be able to take that trip to Europe you've been dreaming about, buy that motorcycle you've had your eye on, or replenish your wardrobe and become the best dressed person on campus. (*Visualization*)

V.   Although you cannot stop inflation, you can outflank it by starting *today* to follow the tips I've given you so you won't continue to throw your dollars away. (*Action*)

You will notice that you have been exposed to and perhaps have used this pattern of ideas before. But do not miss the fact that the structure is psychologically sound for promoting international cooperation, rousing lethargic voters, showing people how to study better, or even giving a speech to entertain.

Because it is both logically and psychologically based, Monroe's motivated sequence is in whole or in part usable with most kinds of material, in a wide variety of situations, and by any speaker willing to work his or her ideas into the most psychologically inviting form to which they are amenable.

Elimination order

Elimination order is a pattern of organization wherein several or all possible interpretations of a subject or solutions to a problem are considered, and all but one are eliminated as undesirable, impractical, or incorrect. This strategy is sometimes called the *method of residues* because whatever remains at the end is the matter to be accepted by the audience.

The method of elimination is often used as the fourth step of what is otherwise a reflective sequence. This adaptation is especially advantageous when you wish to present an investigation for the purpose of persuading rather than inquiring. At the point of considering solutions you may eliminate all known solutions except the one you advocate. The same pattern may be applied during the second half of a problem-solution speech when more than one solution or remedy must be considered. Thus this pattern may be thought of as a variation that can be incorporated within either reflective or problem-solution systems, or it may be treated as a scheme of organization applicable to a whole speech.

Whether you choose this organizational system will depend on the situation and your own concerns. Both you and your audience must be willing to investigate more than one kind of "answer." The situation must allow discussion of more than one course of action or possibility. Time must be available for full explanation and for testing the possibilities, and the atmosphere must favor a several-sided consideration of the subject.

We began this chapter by considering human beings' special need to find relationships and speakers' consequent needs to clarify and show the movement of thought. Disposition of the content of a speech is further adaptation. It is adaptation to the natural human tendency to search for structure and unity in all things. Our examination of the normal parts of speeches (introduction, body, and conclusion) and of patterns of organization has been a survey of various ways by which speakers have learned to answer the universal demand for organization.

Most of the time a reasonable adaptation to the rhetorical situation will make it necessary to begin a speech by orienting the listener to speaker and subject (introduction). Properly adapted speech will continue with a message that makes listening easier and surer by offering a structural pattern familiar to both listener and speaker. It will conclude with some reinforcement of the total experience of hearing the speech.

We have discussed the standard patterns of organization for two reasons. First, public speech is an art form through which relationships are exhibited in familiar, public terms. The standard patterns of organization are simply the most familiar—the most public—systems our society uses in verbal communication. Second, although not all speech can be effectively structured according to one of the patterns we have discussed, all speech will have at least a segment that can be best conveyed according to one of them. These patterns, then, are optional systems among which you will constantly choose. We hope that by understanding what they can accomplish and what they cannot, you will be able to choose wisely.

EXERCISES

Written

1. a. Choose a subject area, such as air pollution, current methods in secondary education, or the Democratic party in America today.
   b. Carefully write out three subject sentences for the subject chosen. One sentence should be devised for a speech of *information,* another for a speech of *persuasion,* and the third for a speech of *inquiry.*
   c. Write out the main heads for each of the three subject sentences you have composed.

2. Write an essay in which you evaluate the following introduction according to the requirements for a good introduction found on pages 180–181.

DRUNKEN DRIVERS

From the wreckage of the crash, two persons extricate themselves. The first seems to be an elderly, well-dressed businessman, who, after surveying the wreckage, pulls out a young man and helps him to his feet. The young man obviously needs help; his gait is unsteady, his eyes are bloodshot and bleary, and his speech is almost unintelligible. The onlookers are convinced by these signs that he is drunk, which is confirmed by the strong smell of alcohol which is obvious a few feet away.

As the police cars pull up, the crowd is assured that the young man will get what is coming to him. He can get out that his name is William Schultz, and he is a taxi driver, but he is unable to give the police his address, does not know where he is by a few miles, yet insists that he had nothing to drink. The officers dutifully administer a test commonly known as the "Balloon Test" to him. After the balloon is blown up, the contents are passed through a tube containing a purple liquid on what looks to be a wad of cotton. The purple color disappears if the air passing through it is filled with alcohol, the policeman explains, and the faster the color disappears, the drunker you are. At the end of the test, however, the purple color is still there, causing some bewilderment among the spectators and the policemen. Some more tests will be taken down at the station.

It is now the older man's turn for examination. As expected, he gives a good account of himself. He is Milton P. Jones, an executive, on his way home from a business conference. He admits to having had a few drinks two hours earlier with his lunch, but the policemen are unable to smell alcohol on his breath. He is also asked to take the balloon test, and, within a fraction of a minute, all color disappears in the glass tube. Befuddled, the policemen take them both down to the station for further examination.

From the evidence before you, every person in this room must have some thoughts as to who the guilty party is. Young Mr. Schultz appears to have all the physical attributes of a drunk, while Mr. Jones is surely the victim of this terrible crime. We'll come back to these men and their particular case in a few minutes.[8]

3. Assume the following sets of main heads have been taken from the bodies of outlines for speeches. Evaluate each set for (a) the wording of the main points and (b) the overall pattern of organization. Give detailed reasons for your judgments.

    a.   I.   Every speech should have an introduction, body, and conclusion.
        II.   Should the introduction get attention and make the speaker's purpose clear?
        III.   A conclusion should summarize and put the entire speech into focus.
    b.   I.   The social, political, and economic instability of underdeveloped countries is a potential breeding ground for communism.
        II.   We must increase our financial aid and technical assistance to these countries to head off the threat.
    c.   I.   Economical and efficient means of smoke prevention have been devised.
        II.   Heavy smoke darkens the sunlight.
        III.   Smoke is harmful to public health.
        IV.   Smoking is a bad habit.
        V.   The annoyance, filth, and unhealthful effects of smoke have caused an agitation for smoke prevention in large cities.
        VI.   Gas and electricity may replace coal for many domestic uses.
        VII.   Imports of residual oil cause much unemployment in coal fields.
        VIII.   Since smoke is injurious and preventable, immediate steps should be taken toward its elimination.
        IX.   Efficient smokeless furnaces have proved a success.
        X.   Smoke hinders good ventilation.
        XI.   Smoke prevention in large cities should be compulsory.
        XII.   Electric locomotives may be used in place of diesels.
        XIII.   Many fires are caused by faulty furnaces.
        XIV.   Coal smoke damages the lungs.
        XV.   One important step is to sign the Anti-Smoke League petition.

4. Below are the transitional portions of four speeches. Read them carefully and decide where they fall on a scale of poor to excellent. Rewrite those you feel are less than acceptable.

    a.   . . . And also I would like to say that another thing to do to prevent fire in the home is to check all wiring. Also store combustible liquids in a cool place children cannot get to. And also never smoke in bed. . . .
    b.   . . . Now that you're aware of the important qualities that go into the making of a leader, namely intelligence, speaking ability, courage, luck, and

health, you just have to be aware of one more thing before you set out to be one yourself. And this is that the reward for leadership may be slim. . . .

c.   . . . The people of today, haunted by this security neurosis, are seeking security from war, security of income, security for old age and against the penalties of ill health, and security of opportunity. And the questions remain, "What can be done about it?" "How can we attain a state of satisfactory serenity?" One answer is through collective government action. Certain types of security must be achieved in this way. . . .

d.   . . . It is easy to construct a bomb. You can get information through the government, and one paper in Washington, D.C., printed plans for a bomb in one of its editions. Or you can find plans for bombs in other places such as encyclopedias. I know a boy who did that. Also I know of a manual put out by a radical organization. . . .

5.   Locate the text of a speech in an anthology of speeches, an issue of *Vital Speeches,* or a volume of the Reference Shelf series (H. W. Wilson Co.) devoted to speeches. Read the speech carefully. Identify the structure or structures. Defend your labeling of the patterns in a paragraph or two in which you cite specifically what led you to choose the labels you did.

Oral

1.   a.   In class discussion choose several central ideas for impromptu speeches. Sentences such as "The automobile is primarily a vehicle for human transportation," "Donation of blood to the Red Cross is worthwhile," and "Everyone should have a hobby" will serve.

b.   Assign each of the central ideas chosen to three members of the class, and also assign to each of them *one* of the usable patterns of organization discussed in Chapter 7, for example, chronological, spatial, problem-solution, or causal.

c.   Allow time for each of the three students to prepare two- to three-minute impromptu speeches using the patterns assigned.

d.   After hearing the speeches, discuss the suitability of each pattern to the central idea assigned. Also evaluate the speaker's ability to produce a recognizable pattern of organization on short notice.

2.   Make a two-minute speech about a classroom you are familiar with.

Treat *at least* these main headings:

- Blackboard areas
- Lighting
- Seating arrangements
- Virtues and flaws as a classroom

Determine and be ready to defend the sequence in which you order your points and your choice of a central idea. Be sure to append appropriate introductory and concluding remarks.

3. Here is a problem in isolating a usable central idea and in arranging main points and amplifying material. The miscellaneous facts below have (or can be given) relationship to one another. Using them as your basic material, give a two-minute talk in which you have at least two major points amplifying whatever central idea you choose. Be sure to show by clear transitions how the main points relate to the central idea (and to each other if that is important). Here is your basic material:

> In dealing a hand of 13 cards from 52 in bridge, the probability of drawing a perfect hand (13 spades) is 1 in 635,013,559,600. In a four-handed poker game, the chances of getting the highest possible hand (royal flush) are 1 in 649,739. If you are a white, female American, aged 19, insurance companies estimate that you have 57 more years to live. If you are a white, male American, aged 19, the estimate is that you will live 51 more years. If you are a girl and 19, there is 1 chance in 8 that you will marry within a year, but if you are a male and 19 there is but 1 chance in 25 you will marry within a year.

ENDNOTES

1. From Kenneth Burke, *Counter-Statement,* originally published in *The Dial* LXXIX (July 1925): 34–36, quoted from Morton D. Zabel, ed., *Literary Opinion in America* (New York: Harper & Row, 1962), II, p. 668.
2. Kenneth E. Boulding, *The Image* (Ann Arbor: University of Michigan Press, 1956), p. 25. See chap. 2, "The Image in the Theory of Organization."
3. Samuel I. Rosenman, *Working with Roosevelt* (New York: Harper & Brothers, 1952), p. 75.
4. Ernest Thompson, "Some Effects of Message Structure on Listeners' Comprehension," *Speech Monographs* XXXIV (March 1967): 51–57.
5. See pages 177–179.
6. This section is based in part on an explanation of transitions originally written by Harry P. Kerr, University of Maine, Farmington, Maine. Used by permission.
7. The descriptions of the cause-effect, problem-solution, withheld-proposal, and open-proposal patterns in this section are based on explanations originally written by James A. Wood of the University of Texas, El Paso. Donald E. Williams, University of Florida, prepared the original explanation of the reflective sequence. Used by permission.
8. This introduction was composed by Renee Ehrlich for an introductory course in public speaking. Used by permission.

CHAPTER 8

Disposition: Outlining

Where can you apply the principles in this chapter in everyday life?

1. Wherever you have to submit clearly organized plans on paper.
2. Wherever you must prepare for oral reports.
3. Wherever you decide to use notes during an oral presentation.
4. Wherever you are called on to provide bibliographical sources for academic courses or for writing submitted for publication.
5. Wherever you must be in total control of a pattern of ideas.

When evaluating an outline consider:

1. Are the basic divisions of the speech—introduction, body, and conclusion—clearly indicated? If not, is there justification for not having them so?
2. Is the central idea appropriately symbolized and clearly marked?
3. Does a consistent system of symbolization and indentation show the importance of ideas and reveal their relationships?
4. Are there any cases where only one piece of proof is offered when in fact the single item yields insufficient proof or clarification?
5. Is the principle of discreteness observed by allowing only one symbol per thought and only one thought per symbol?
6. Are important transitions and internal summaries clearly identified?
7. If the outline being considered is to be used during speaking, is it written so as to be readable at a glance?

Constructing an outline insures that your ideas will be arranged and sufficiently supported or amplified to meet the needs of your rhetorical situation. Outlining further insures that you will consider the logical relationships among ideas and the weights and emphases you need to give them. Finally, the act of outlining and the use of an outline are exceptionally helpful in setting your ideas firmly in your mind so you can command them confidently as you speak.

The detail in which you outline for public speech depends primarily on the uses you are going to make of the written plan. You may need only a skeletal map of the talk—of the kind we illustrate on page 219 in this chapter. On the other hand, if you want a comprehensive representation of all of your planning or are going to submit an outline as proof of the thoroughness of your preparation, you may need an outline so complete it falls just short of being a manuscript record. Such an outline is illustrated on pages 213–15 below.

FUNCTIONS OF OUTLINES

Your own needs and preferences and the requirements of assignments will determine what kinds of outlines you prepare. In a class you may be asked to construct *content* or *technical outlines* to show a teacher a full record of your preparation. For your private use you may use some combination of *full-sentence, phrase,* or *key-word* outlining. In any case, you will surely need to outline each speech in some degree of detail. To do so is a far better procedure than writing a talk in full as a first stage of preparation. It is much easier to inspect and improve organization if you work with an outline than with a full manuscript.

If you are a beginner, you will find sentence outlines most helpful. Full sentences express complete thoughts, and using them enables you to frame each thought fully and to think out its proper relationship to all other complete thoughts in your speech plan. Thoughts may, of course, be symbolized on paper by single words or phrases or, indeed, by symbols even simpler than words, such as crosses, circles, and the like. But most beginners and most of the expert speakers we know find themselves handicapped in speech planning if they use shorthand outlines of very abbreviated sorts. Experienced speakers do, of course, often speak from very abbreviated sets of notes, but somewhere in the planning stages there is usually a more comprehensive, outlined plan.

Fundamentally you outline to serve *yourself.* Audiences seldom see outlines, so usefulness to you is the most important criterion for a good outline. Outlining is part of dealing with the inescapable problem the ancients talked about under the heading of *memoria.* You will find this general subject discussed at some length in Appendix A, "Rhetorical Theory: A Heritage." (See pages 332–34.) Whoever speaks has the problem of foreseeing where he or she is going, of keeping ideas organized for the listeners' sake, and of generally executing a plan while under the tensions of speaking. All kinds of aids—goof boards, cue cards, and mnemonic patterns—have been used to help speakers remember their plans; the procedure of outlining is simply the most modern and most practical of your alternatives. In learning situations, however, outlining may serve additional purposes.

You are likely to be asked to submit an outline to your teacher. The reason will be to allow you to receive constructive criticism. Your outline, then, is no longer a private paper. It is, instead, a record of preparation to be shared with another interested person who is to make suggestions. This shared paper must be understood by your teacher as well as by you. Since this is so, you must take special care to make ideas and their relationships clear both visually and verbally. You and your critic must agree on a system of outlining. You may be asked to employ full sentences, at least to begin with, because your reader can understand them better than phrases or words. A single word offered in support of another single word may not be comprehensible to your teacher, and it will not indicate whether you have thought through your ideas. For instance, you may know what you will say when you have written the word *economic* and listed *cost* and *profit* as supporting ideas, but your teacher may not see clear-cut connections between these sketchy symbols. He or she may be led to conclude that at this particular stage of speech preparation your ideas have not been fully enough refined, that they are still in vague or fuzzy condition. In fact, you may really have slipped in your own thinking. For your reader's sake and for your own you must take care in preparing your papers so your ideas and their relationships are beyond misunderstanding.

For teaching purposes your instructor may ask you to construct a content outline showing the ideas for your speech and then to add technical labels identifying your kinds of proof, methods of amplification, and the like. When you add such labels to an outline, you have in reality two outlines. One maps ideas; the other maps strategy and tactics. In outlining simple, one-point speeches in Chapter 2 we illustrated technical outlining by identifying the kinds of support proposed for development of a single point. Here is what a full technical outline might look like—probably set side by side on the page with the content outline to which it applies:

Introduction

I. Story—using novelty, stereotypes, familiarity; chronological order
II. Central idea
III. Definitions
   a. By function
   b. By classification

Body

I. Argument—open-proposal pattern
   a. Quotation—familiar
   b. Statistics—visual aids
II. Argument—developed inductively
   a. Report of experiment
   b. Report of second experiment

Conclusion

I. A summary

Such an outline of methods to be used can show you or your teacher how fully you are aware of your own strategies. But notice that a record of this kind will not guide you or an instructor in checking on the *logic* of the plan nor will it remind you of precisely what to say at a given point in a speech. Do not, then, mix the two forms of outlining.

COMMON PRACTICES

No hard and fast rules can be made about outlining, but certain practices promote clarity, organic unity, and the adaptation so necessary in successful speaking. They yield a practical, visual image of a speech plan—one you or anyone else can follow easily. Here are practices it is wise to follow:

A clear indication of the basic divisions of the speech: introduction, body (sometimes labeled discussion or proof), and conclusion   Since these labels are not parts of the idea structure of the speech but are technical notations, they will not normally be given symbols. Numerical and alphabetical symbols ought to be reserved as indicators of relationships. Usually the names of the basic divisions of your speech are centered on the page and go unsymbolized. These labels insure that you have an introduction and a conclusion and that you are aware of what constitutes these portions of your speech. In those infrequent instances when no introduction is used, its absence is readily apparent if one forms the practice of identifying each division actually included.

A consistent system of (A) symbolization and (B) indentation   This aids in clarifying relationships and in helping you to remember those relationships. The system of symbols you use is up to you; consistency in their use is essential. It matters little whether Roman numerals, capital letters, or Arabic numerals are used to indicate main heads and subheads. What matters is that each time a type of symbol occurs it signifies that the ideas thus identified are of approximately the same importance or weight. Uniformity in symbolization will indicate clearly the values you assign to your material, and the different symbols assigned will show which ideas are subsidiary to which. Since you will be working out a structure idea by idea, you should place only one symbol before any one idea. This serves as a caution against composing compound sentences containing more than one thought. If you follow the rule of one symbol for *each* idea, you will be reminded to break compound statements in two. You will need to check very carefully in making a phrase outline to see that each symbol stands beside an idea rather than beside a fragment of one or a phrase that represents—for you—several ideas.

Indentation further reveals values assigned and stirs the memory. If each new idea has a clear indentation, that fact announces to you when it is time to embark on a new phase of your thought structure. Ideas subsidiary to other ideas should be indented under the subsuming thought. In this way it will be easy to see supports and amplifications as subordinate points. Your visual image of your speech will then be of a network of ideas with the least important ones indented farthest from the left-hand margin of the page. Although none of the ideas you set down on the page is, ideally, expendable, it will be less a calamity should an idea given minor weight (one farthest indented) be forgotten.

Sparing use of single subpoints   Whenever one idea is subordinated to another, this indicates a splitting of the subsuming idea for purposes of amplification or support. Usually more than one piece of information is needed to develop a point adequately. Yet one definition, one example, or one opinion sometimes may suffice to clarify or prove to an acceptable degree. Point I.B. in the body of the outline for a speech on "A Slice of the Bronx" on page 214 is an illustration of this. Neither the speaker nor the audience needs to know, for this speech, any more about Mrs. Philipse's loyalism than that the bridge was taken from her. But usually a single subordinate item needs the reinforcement of other, parallel items; otherwise, it ought often to be combined with the idea to which it appears to be subordinate. In any case, any outline containing many single subpoints should be viewed suspiciously. It is likely that the ideas contained in it have not been developed to the point of audience acceptance and that necessary information and proof have been overlooked. Only when you are absolutely sure that one and only one piece of proof is necessary should a subpoint stand alone.

Discreteness of ideas   In outlines ideas should not be lumped together, nor should they overlap. An outline is a structure intended to display relationships clearly. This fact dictates that each idea stand separately within the structure. The need to reveal the relationship of each idea to other ideas is an additional argument for full-sentence outlining. Sentences, if correctly constructed, are expressions of complete thoughts. Be wary of the compound sentence in outlining; it contains more than one idea, making it impossible to follow the principle of one symbol, one idea. Therefore, *and* and *or* should rarely appear in the sentences of an outline; they bear special checking when they do appear.

Appropriate symbolization and placement of central ideas   Since the central idea is the most important idea in the speech, it deserves the highest rank in symbolization. The central idea should stand out unmistakably in your outline. Because it is of highest rank in the hierarchy of ideas symbolized in the outline, it is sometimes not given a symbol but is simply labeled.

In the sample outlines at the end of this chapter and in the diagram on pages 208–09 we have both symbolized and labeled the central idea, indicating that either method is acceptable and that both are common in outlining. No matter which of these practices is followed, the central idea should never appear as a subpoint nor should it be indented under any other point. In deductive patterns it will usually appear near the end of the introduction or near the beginning of the body of the speech. Graphically, it should at least be accorded the same rank as the other most important items in the section. The same is true in symbolizing or labeling and in indenting the central idea when outlining inductive patterns, such as the withheld-proposal sequence. The symbol and/or label used, and indentation, ought to show that this statement is not outranked by any other ideas in that section of the speech. Whether the central idea appears in the introduction, body, or conclusion, it is the most important idea in that division of your outline.

Clear transitions Transitions, including internal summaries, should be clearly and uniformly indicated and set off from the rest of the structure. This is more than a mere technical matter. It is at the points of shift from one line of thought to another that your memory is most likely to fail you while speaking, and it is at these points that listeners are most likely to lose the connections between ideas. If transitions are symbolized and indented in the same manner as other parts of the outline, they should be given technical labels such as "transition" or "internal summary." A common practice is to treat these portions of the speech differently from main points or subpoints, omitting symbols but marking them off by enclosing them in brackets or parentheses. This practice shows how you will move from one point or subpoint to another, and it will remind you of the necessity for repetition and review in speaking.

If you observe these practices, a diagram of your outlines will look like the one that follows. For a short speech you may not need to outline in as full detail as this diagram indicates, but we have included the fullest detail we think you are ever likely to need.

Title

INTRODUCTION

I. _____

    A. _____

    B. _____

II. (*Central idea*) _____

    (*Transition*: _____)

BODY

I. _____

    A. _____

    B. _____

        1. _____

            a. _____

            b. _____

        2. _____

            a. _____

            b. _____

    C. _____

        1. _____

        2. _____

            a. _____

            b. _____

(1) _____
(2) _____
(*Transition*: _____)
II. _____
  A. _____
    1. _____
      a. _____
      b. _____
      c. _____
    2. _____
      (*Transition:* _____)
  B. _____
    1. _____
      a. _____
      b. _____
        (1) _____
        (2) _____
        (3) _____
          (a) _____
          (b) _____
      c. _____
      d. _____
        (1) _____
        (2) _____
    2. _____
      a. _____
      b. _____
      (*Internal summary*: _____)
III. _____
  A. _____
    1. _____
      a. _____
      b. _____
    2. _____
  B. _____
      (*Transition and/or internal summary* _____
_____)

CONCLUSION

I. _____
  A. _____
  B. _____
  C. _____
II. _____

BIBLIOGRAPHY
(OR STATEMENT OF SOURCES)

―――

―――

―――

―――

―――

Two items appearing in this diagram remain to be considered: title and bibliography, or statement of sources.

TITLES

The final act in composing a speech ordinarily is to select a title. Informal situations make titles less necessary than situations in which you will be introduced, but a title provides a label anyone reporting your speech, recording it, or referring to it can use handily. Of course, if your talk is part of a group's public presentation, it will be the group's subject that will need to be titled.

Whether it is an individual or group presentation that you are seeking a label for, you ought to make the title *brief, relevant,* and *provocative.* You will want it to arouse interest and reveal to some degree what the talk or report is actually to be about.

A title needs to be brief for practical reasons. An audience will stop listening before the end of a title such as "The History and Significance of the Carnival of Mardi Gras in New Orleans between 1800 and 1980 with Special Emphasis on the Role of the King in Presiding over Parades and Balls." At first glance that looks completely ridiculous, but it actually might represent the substance of a talk or a symposium at a historical society. However, a title that would serve practical purposes and not suggest that speaker(s) lacked rhetorical sense would be "The Mardi Gras in New Orleans Since 1800." This would be practical for publicity purposes, short enough to fit on a poster or program and into a one- or two-column newspaper head for a report on the presentation.

When a presentation has no title or a long and unarresting one, chairpersons are apt to invent one. One of our students told his classroom chairperson, "Oh, I'm going to talk about fishing, you know." The chairman brought him on with, "Now you all know the trout season opened this week, so John's going to tell us what those people are doing out there along the trout streams." Actually, John had an excellent speech on how tie-flies, artificial lures, are made. He, of course, had to correct the chairperson's announcement before he could begin his talk—a problem he would not have had if he had formed a clear title of his own and had given it to the chairperson. Famous speakers get into similar difficulties. President Franklin D. Roosevelt once gave an untitled speech to the Teamster's Union in 1944. It was a broadly ranging political defense of his policies in conducting the Americans' part in World War II. Reporters, needing a *short* title to fit their headlines and reports, seized on one small segment of the speech and created a title from it. In this part of the speech Roosevelt referred to his black Scottie dog, Fala. The title "The Fala Speech" has stuck to this address ever since, although that title quite misrepresents Roosevelt's subject matter and the rhetorical situation in which he gave the speech.

Titles for presentation, whether by individuals or groups, ought to fairly characterize the presentation and arouse some curiosity about it. Two kinds of mistakes get in the way of these goals: using vague, "umbrella" titles and using titles that are all but riddles. "A Hope for the Future," "You Ought to Try," "A Happy Solution," are not only vague, but they might announce any number of speeches on utterly diverse subjects. They cover everything and nothing. Some other titles we have heard offered in classrooms have drawn attention—but to what? Consider these: "Little Fences and Barriers," "Pins and Needles," "A Slice of the Bronx," and "How to Be Fit." Each is unnecessarily a riddle. "Little Fences and Barriers" could have been "Fences and Barriers of Prejudice." "Pins and Needles" might have been "Healing Pins and Needles," since it was the title of a speech about acupuncture. "A Slice of the Bronx" might have been "Kingsbridge Road: A Slice of the Bronx." A title for any presentation ought to do specific work: convey a promise that can be understood and do it briefly and provocatively.

BIBLIOGRAPHIES

In classrooms and elsewhere some speaking has true significance only if based on research conducted specifically for the purpose of enhancing the speech. "A Slice of the Bronx" is such a speech. So is "Cults Can Care" (both in the next section). So, too, are most lectures, reports, speeches on public policy, and many others we hear outside academic halls. On the other hand, new research is not invariably necessary for effective speaking. New research was not necessary for Alan Kominsky's speech to inform a class he knew well about flight planning (pages 127–28), for he had proved his understanding when he earned his pilot's license. Tom Nobile's entertaining-informing speech on the academic supplies that can be found in university dumpsters (pages 167–68) was not dependent on anything but his own knowledge and firsthand investigation. In short, effective speaking often, but not invariably, entails special investigation for the specific event, and when it does there are reasons to keep a record of what was done. Bibliographies or "statements of sources" are such records, and you may be asked to append them to outlines submitted to your instructor. The instructor, as critic, wants to know what you investigated, what you found useful, and where you found it. Moreover, you yourself may want to relocate these sources at some future time.

Bibliographical entries are expected on many other documents you will prepare: term papers, research reports, essays, and the like. We therefore offer you some fairly detailed advice on preparing such records whenever they are asked for.

There are many forms for bibliographical entries. The important objectives are to be complete and consistent. The following forms meet those tests and follow generally acceptable stylistic practices. Comments on the scope and value of unprinted material are given in informal description, while comments on printed material follow the references to sources and are placed within brackets.

Observation:
During the week of August 12–19, 1982, I took part in NROTC naval maneuvers and saw the things I describe under Point I of the introduction.

I have drawn at several points in the body of the speech on courses I have taken in business, economics, and oral and written communication.

Interview:
On May 12, 1982, I talked with President J. B. Smith of X Company for about an hour and got the ideas on management's problems, which appear in section III of this outline.

Book:
Johnson, Bonnie McDaniel. *Communication: The Process of Organizing.* Boston: Allyn and Bacon, 1977.
   [The first chapter, "Images of Organizing," gave me the idea for my first main point, that this university is organized on "classical" or "design" or "machine" notions. I also used Johnson's criticisms of this organizational theory and others throughout the speech.]

Articles:
A.   From Periodicals:
   Wiley, Richard E. "Family Viewing: A Balancing of Interests." *Journal of Communication* XXVII, no. 2 (Spring 1977): 188–92.
   [The first part of this article was my main source for how "family viewing" came to be a programming concept in network TV programming. The author participated in some of the negotiations.]
B.   From Books:
   Kauffmann, Stanley. "The Film Generation." In Allen Kirschner and Linda Kirschner, eds., *Film: Readings in the Mass Media* (New York: Odyssey Press, 1971), pp. 151–63.
   [Some of the material I used concerning the role of sex in current films (see point II) is taken from this essay.]
C.   From General Reference Books:
   "John Donne." *Encyclopaedia Britannica,* 9th ed. (New York, 1878).[1]
   [Most of the biographical material in my speech came from here.]

Newspapers:
A.   From Signed Articles, Editorials, and News Accounts:
   Fairlie, Henry. "Our Misguided Defenders of the English Language." *Washington Post* (May 29, 1977), sec. B, p. 8.
   [My argument that grammatical mistakes are not in themselves the sources of

failures in communication is based on Fairlie's argument that what you have to say is the most important thing in communication.]

B.   From Unsigned Articles, Editorials, and News Accounts:
Our Colleges and Universities Today, Pennsylvania Department of Education, Harrisburg, 1980.
[*It was from this source that I got my information on the percentages of all minorities and blacks who graduated from Pennsylvania colleges and universities from 1974 to 1979.*]

Pamphlets (where the author or editor is not credited):
"Scrooge & Humbug." *The Pittsburgh Press,* August 11, 1981, p. B–2.
[*This editorial gave me the figures on how many retired federal employees on adequate pensions also draw the minimum Social Security benefit.*]

SAMPLE OUTLINES

The two outlines that follow illustrate good outlining procedures and preparatory methods. The first is an outline for a speech of information five minutes in length. It not only is a good example of organization and the mechanics of outlining, but it illustrates exceptionally careful adaptation of material to a specific audience in a specific rhetorical situation. (See note 2 for details.) You will profit by reflecting on the large amount of material the speaker must have excluded from her talk because it would not fit closely enough the audience and even the room in which she would speak.

Both outlines furnished here are probably as detailed as any you will ever make. Your own needs and your instructor's expectations may allow you to prepare less comprehensive outlines than these, but the principles of outlining and of documenting source material are fully illustrated here because at some time you may need to prepare in this much detail.

A Slice of the Bronx[2]

INTRODUCTION
I.   Kingsbridge Road is familiar to all of us in this classroom because it lies just outside the room we are in.
A.   But do we really know about it?
B.   For instance, it was not until January of 1874 that even the township of Kingsbridge became a part of New York City.

(*Central idea*)
II. I want you to understand some of the interesting historical facts about Kingsbridge Road and vicinity.

BODY
I.   Let's first examine how Kingsbridge Road received its name.
A.   In 1693 Fredryck Philipse was granted a ninety-nine-year franchise to build the twenty-nine-foot King's Bridge over Spuyten Duyvil Creek.

1. Philipse was allowed to collect tolls from everyone crossing the bridge except for the king's troops.
2. Only this bridge connected Manhattan Island with what is now the Bronx, so Philipse tended to overcharge.
3. Nonetheless, the bridge remained the Philipses' property until near the end of the Revolutionary War.

B. Unfortunately Mary Philipse was a Loyalist in the Revolution.
1. All her property, including the bridge, was confiscated by the patriots.

II. The bridge, the road, and the area played further roles in the Revolutionary War.
A. British General Howe had a plan to trap General Washington and his troops on Manhattan Island.
1. He was to sail up the East River, march to Westchester County, and then block the King's Bridge.
2. This would cut off Washington's only means of escape.
3. Washington outsmarted Howe by cutting him off in Westchester.

B. Howe did eventually capture Manhattan by other means and held it for seven years.

III. In the 1800s the Kingsbridge Road area was affected by the construction of the New York and Harlem Railroad.
A. This brought in new people who were trying to escape a congested Manhattan.
1. The railroad had a stop near where Fordham University is today.
2. One of the people who moved into the area was Edgar Allan Poe, who lived in this area from 1846 to 1849.
a. Poe's cottage was across the street on the east side of Kingsbridge Road near 192nd Street.
b. The cottage was moved to the new Poe Park in 1902 and in 1966 was declared an official city landmark.

B. The fast-growing community around Kingsbridge Road needed medical care, of course.
1. Thus, the first hospital established in the Bronx was Fordham Hospital.
a. It was then located on Valentine Avenue near Kingsbridge Road.
b. It had a maximum of twenty-five beds and was open chiefly for accident and emergency cases.
2. The United States Veteran's Hospital building on Kingsbridge Road was purchased by the government in 1921 for use by veterans suffering mental and nervous disorders.

C. Another project with which you are familiar was begun in 1895—the Reservoir.
1. The Reservoir, as you know, is located right behind Lehman College.
a. It has two basins capable of holding 2 billion gallons of water.
b. As it was being dug, many Revolutionary War relics were unearthed: cannon balls, bayonets, swords, and even what turned out to be the skeleton of a British soldier.

D. If you ride the train to school, you have passed the Armory on Jerome Avenue and Kingsbridge Road.
1. It houses the 258th Field Artillery regiment of the New York State National Guard, and that group has an interesting history.
a. Its original organization was as an artillery company founded in 1784.
b. Part of the original company formed the honor guard for George

Washington when he was inaugurated president of the United States.

E. In other days you could not only get to this area of Kingsbridge Road by train, you could come by trolley.
   1. The trolley climbed up Kingsbridge Road west of Sedgwick Avenue.
   2. The trolley was one of the 1701 series—among the last models of trolleys to be built.
      a. The car was so long that it was often derailed.
      b. This trolley was finally retired in 1942.

CONCLUSION

I.   Kingsbridge Road, the street we are on, had interesting roles both before and during the Revolutionary War because it was a means of access to Manhattan Island.
II. The Kingsbridge area became a historic suburb of New York City.
III. As the area flourished, it became the site for a variety of historic and curious projects that have contributed to making the Bronx now a city-within-a-city.

BIBLIOGRAPHY

BOOKS:

Scharf, John F. *History of Westchester County, New York including Morrisania, Kings Bridge, and West Farms, which have been annexed to New York City*. Philadelphia: L. E. Preston & Co., 1886.

Van Pelt, Daniel. *Leslie's History of the Greater New York*. New York: Arkell Publishing Co., 1898, vol. 1.

Wells, James L. *The Bronx and Its People*. New York: Lewis Historical Publishing Co., 1927.

PAMPHLETS:

Peterson, Everett A., and Smart, Mary F. *Historical Handbook of the City of New York*. New York: City History Club of New York, 1934.

Ulton, Lloyd. *The Bronx in the American Revolution*. New York: Bronx Historical Society, 1975.

OBSERVATION:

On Saturday, October 16, I visited the Bronx County Historical Society at 3266 Bainbridge Avenue in the Bronx. There I studied several displays depicting the involvement of the Kingsbridge area in the Revolutionary War and secured other overall information about the area.

Cults Can Care[3]

INTRODUCTION

I.   The Moonies, Salvation Army, People's Temple, Rastafarians, and Mormons, among others, are classified as "cults."
   A. Cults may be defined as groups having exclusive theologies and special rites, practices, and symbols that set members apart from general society.
   B. Most of us don't really know very much about cults.
   C. The Jonestown Massacre in Guyana in November 1978 prompted a widespread revulsion against cults.

(*Central idea*)
II. Cults fulfill needed functions for some people in society.
     (*Transition:* Let me tell you why I think this is so. First. . . .)

BODY

I. Cults offer attractions for those people who need to be taken care of.
    A. The cult can serve as a refuge for some people who cannot cope with the pressures of society.
        1. By close, all-inclusive organization a cult can supply social, spiritual, and material security.
            a. The Moonies and the People's Temple illustrate cults that take over virtually all aspects of life.
            b. The Mormon church doesn't go that far but does provide its own social welfare programs.
        2. The services I have mentioned free individuals from decision making about the aspects of life the organization manages.
        3. For people who can't find ways to order their lives and to succeed in the competitions of life, belonging to a cult can answer their needs for orderliness and predictability in everyday affairs.
    B. Cults can function as a family, providing people with a sense of belonging, dependable relationships, and organized parental controls.
        1. An individual who has not outgrown the need for this kind of dependency can assume an almost childlike status within the all-embracing organization.
        2. For those who lack family or who reject or have been rejected by their real families, a cult can become a "substitute family."
            a. We all know that Jim Jones was "Father" to the members of the People's Temple.
            b. The Moonies, members of The People's Unification Church, stress their role as the divinely ordained "Family" of the members.
        (*Transition:* Yet, the father figure is not an essential in cult life, and that leads to my next point.)
    C. Some cults, such as the Rastafarians, fulfill social needs without a living leader.
        1. This cult, an old one that originated in Jamaica in the West Indies, holds that the dead King of Ethiopia (Jah) is God.
        2. The Rastafarians think of themselves as a chosen people, as do many other religious groups.
        3. A special bond that holds the Rastafarians together is the belief that they will be repatriated to Africa, a right that their "chosenness" confers on them.
            a. They must remain banded together in anticipation of the "great day."
            b. They express their familial unity, their mutual, intragroup support in very pragmatic ways that also reinforce the cult's separation from all others.
                (1) They refuse to work for "the Babylon system," those outside the cult.
                (2) Their work establishes a kind of mutual security system for all members.

(*Transition:* This cult, however, is the exception rather than the rule insofar as the role of leadership is concerned.)

II. Most cults provide leaders for people who need to be identified with a superior being.
  A. Ordinarily, such leaders claim to be and are seen as messiahs or prophets or, at the very least, *specially* ordained men or women of God.
    1. The leader is thus the highest and final interpreter of the cult's doctrines.
    2. His or her judgment cannot be questioned.
    3. The leader can, and usually does, preside over constant, brain-washing infusions of doctrine.
  B. Complete loyalty and submission to the holy leader is, of course, a condition for membership in the group.
  C. Subservience to leadership is what accounts for the isolation so characteristic of cults.
    1. Traditional religions allow their followers to live within the secular world and to respond to it.
    2. Cults pursue some Eden or some "second coming," ignoring the secular world.

(*Internal summary:* We have seen that cults fulfill needed functions for some people by taking care of them and by providing charismatic leaders; yet many persons object to them on the grounds that they end up tragically. Let us look carefully at this charge.)

III. Despite unhappy events in some cases, cults do not always end up tragically, as the Jonestown incident might suggest.
  A. The Mormons suffered repeated attacks by "Gentiles" when they tried to settle in Illinois in the nineteenth century; yet today they are an internationally respected community that has made major contributions to the development of the United States.
  B. Shaker communities in the United States have become extinct because, with celibacy as one of their tenets, they dutifully refused to reproduce, yet they never suffered anxiety or bloodshed.
    (*Transition:* On the other hand. . . .)
  C. The Oneida Community, a society of "Perfectionists," established a thriving silverware industry in upstate New York.
    1. Eventually, they became a joint stock company.
    2. You can still buy Oneida patterns in silverware.
  D. The Salvation Army's social endeavors are applauded by many.
(*Transition:* You can see, then, that. . . .)

CONCLUSION

I. Cults do shelter people who feel lost or otherwise vulnerable to the pressures of "outside society."
  A. They provide homes for many who could be of use to themselves and others in, perhaps, no other way.
  B. Powerful leadership, whether tragic, as was Jim Jones's, or farsighted and constructive, as was the Mormon leader Brigham Young's, seems necessary for their continuance.
II. Cults will exist as long as people think themselves unable to withstand the pressures of society.

III.   We need not join or even applaud any cult.
IV.   We should recognize that cults do fulfill functions for certain of our contemporaries.

STATEMENT OF SOURCES

Anonymous. "Following the Leader." *Time* CXII (December 11, 1978): 36. [Some of the information on the role of the leader (point II in the body) came from this article.]

"Brigham Young," "Mormons," "Oneida," "Salvation Army," *The Columbia Encyclopedia,* 3rd ed. New York, 1963. [Points III.A. in the body; I.B. in the conclusion; III.C. and D. in the body were amplified from this source.]

Douglas, P. "Cults: When God Is Troubling the Waters." *Essence* X (March, 1980): 81–132.

Lowenthal, David. *West Indian Societies.* New York: Oxford University Press, 1972. [Most of my information on the Rastafarians came from this source.]

Morrow, L. "Lure of Doomsday." *Time* CXII (December 4, 1978): 30. [This one-page article provided general information on my subject.]

Rose, Stephen C. *Jesus and Jim Jones.* New York: Pilgrims' Press, 1979. [This book provided information for my introduction and points II and III of the body as well as the conclusion.]

Simpson, George E. *Black Religions of the New World.* New York: Columbia University Press, 1978.

Sparks, Jack. *The Mindbenders: A Look at Current Cults.* Nashville: T. Nelson, 1977. [Most helpful for point II.A.3. of the body.]

Thomas, P. "Targets of the Cults." *Human Behavior* VIII (March, 1979): 58–59. [Point I of the body relied to some extent on this account.]

Train, J. "Moonie Game." *Forbes* CXXIII (March 19, 1979): 134–35. [Information in my speech on the People's Unification Church came from this article.]

Woodward, K. L. and others. "How They Bend Minds," *Newsweek* CXLII (December 4, 1978): 72. [See point II.3. of the body.]

SPEAKERS' NOTES

It is unwise to try to speak extemporaneously from outlines as detailed as those with which we have illustrated outlining. They would consume too much of your attention. The functions of such detailed outlines are, as we have said, to provide a full, visual representation of a complete speech plan, enable you to test the sufficiency of each part of a plan, and generate a report you can submit for review and criticism by another person. When you are satisfied with your detailed plan, you are ready to convert it into an *oral* communication. If you were to speak from manuscript, you would expand the ideas of your outline into fully developed prose that would sound to listeners like *talk*. Much more often you will be expected to speak extemporaneously. Then you will need to *reduce* your detailed plan to a brief set of reminders that you can follow with glances, keeping yourself on track during speaking. Notes of this kind should be designed as cues. For this purpose most of us prefer verbal cues, so those are the kind we will illustrate.

On page 162 we referred to a talk by Beth Wallingford on improving conditions of the military services. Here in adapted form are the speaker's notes Beth used when she gave that speech in a basic speech course.[4]

I.   Intro.
    A.   Volunteer force—started 1973. Nixon withdrew troops from Vietnam
    B.   Main problems now
            Financial
            Quality
            Numbers
    C.   Some changes must be made in the ways we recruit and treat military personnel
II. Financial problems
    A.   Too little funds to armed services now
    B. $ shortage affects equipment & pay—all branches
    C.   Salaries—sliding since 1972—inflation makes worse
            1st term enlistee gets $3.10 an hour. McDonald's pays better!
            200,000 military families qualify for welfare
            $10 million food stamps given on military bases last year
    D.   Fringe benefits can't make up
    E.   So, *the skilled leave, and the unskilled come in*
(*Transition:* These financial problems lead to *quality* problems.)
III. Fewer people of high quality enlist
    A.   % of high school dropouts is growing
            Lowered standards allow them
    B.   But equipment is *more sophisticated*. Results:
            Example: radio test by recruit who couldn't read
            Example: recruits who mistook Soviet for American tanks
(*Transition:* This is our "protection"! This is what limited financing has done with a volunteer system. So now what?)
IV. Solutions
    A.   Pay raises and better benefits could "buy" high-quality volunteers
    B.   The alternative: *draft* the quality we have to have
            Military could then be selective
            Draft would encourage more people to join Reserves
V.   Conclusion
    The main point is that the volunteer service lacks money, so it produces too few people and lowers the quality of the people who are supposed to defend us.
    We can't ignore the trouble we're in, if America is to be a world power.

Ms. Wallingford wrote these notes on three 3″ × 5″ cards. Items were indented as we have shown here. Thus she reminded herself of the ranks of her points, and the symbols and indentations made the points easy for her to notice as she spoke. All her main points were shown in the notes; *some* details, statistics, dates, and cues to examples were included so she wouldn't have to worry about remembering them. Since she had rehearsed her speech, she knew approximately where each major part appeared on the cards. A quick glance would tell her, then, what subordinate points were to be discussed under each. Knowing that speakers forget most often at transitional points, she wrote out the main transitions in a specially marked way.

By keeping her notes brief, Beth avoided temptations to look too much at her notes and too little at her listeners. In speaking she attended far more to the audience than to these notes. And that is what any good set of speaker's notes should allow and encourage.

As you can see from Beth's notes, a good deal of idiosyncrasy can characterize speakers' notes. Only *you* have to be able to read them—but *don't be careless; you can confuse yourself!* Our advice is that you prepare a special set of speaker's notes for every speech situation and that you keep your cues to speech organization and to facts as brief as confident control over your general plan will permit. Too many notes, ill organized for quick visual inspection, keep speakers from establishing the close human relationship with listeners that effective speaking requires.

Detailed outlines are the basic tools by which speakers fix the designs of their speeches as compositions and test the sufficiency of various parts of those designs. A completed outline is a visual representation of how speech materials are going to be handled in the speech to come. Specially prepared speaker's notes are distillations of those fuller plans. Only *cues* to the now-familiar, overall plan are recorded, so the speaker's mind can be free for the business of direct communication while his or her spirits are comforted by assurance that guidance is always there in the brief notes.

Making an outline, reviewing it, and converting it into speaker's notes are aids to what ancient writers on rhetoric had in mind when they used the Latin term *memoria*—the art of attaining command of material, plan, and immediate thinking processes during the moments of delivery. These are the justifications for outlining and preparing speakers' notes. The mechanics of these processes are good or bad in proportion to how well they help you to command the content and the structure of what you mean to communicate.

EXERCISES

Written

1. Arrange the eleven statements below as an outline for a main point in a speech. There is no title, introduction, or conclusion. Select the sentence containing the main point and give it proper place and status in your outline.
   - Political bribery may be increased considerably due to heart transplants.
   - Some feel the poor man deserves it.
   - The families of the poor cannot afford prolonged private care without surgery.
   - *Saturday Review* of February 3rd reports an incident in which a prominent

New York politician used his influence to have a half-hour conference with Dr. Christiaan Barnard when he was in Washington, D.C., to discuss the possibilities of his securing a heart transplant.

- Heart transplants are ethically questionable.
- Some feel the rich man who can afford surgery should receive it.
- The poor are the only means of support for their families.
- The January 6th *Science News* states, "A million dollars could buy a patient almost anything . . . including a new heart."
- There are inequalities shown in deciding whose lives are to be saved through the miracle of heart transplants.
- How many other unreported incidents of this sort will be revealed in the near future?
- Some feel it should be the man or woman with special talent.

2. Make a list of suggestions for improvement in the outline entitled "Cults Can Care" (See pages 215–18).

3. In a sentence or two evaluate each of the following speech titles:
   a. "What You Must Do"
   b. "Acres of Diamonds"
   c. "Elvis Presley—Rock and Roller?"
   d. "The Case for Abortion in the United States Today with Special Emphasis on the Mother's Rights in the Particular Case"
   e. "Klee"
   f. "From Trees to Paper"
   g. "Drug Addicts: The Living Dead"
   h. "An Empirical Analysis of the Relationship between Information Processing and Feedback Utilization in Dyadic Communicative Systems"
   i. "The Land of the Kilt and the Haggis"
   j. "The Eternal Verities"

Oral

1. Outline a speech by one of your classmates as you listen to him or her deliver it. Arrange for a conference during which you compare the outline you composed with the outline he or she used. Look for similarities and differences between the outlines and discuss why these occurred as they did.

2. Compose an outline for a six-minute speech of information or persuasion. Observe the suggestions made in this chapter and in Chapter 7.

3. Here, in proper order, are the items of a blank outline. Choose a suitable subject, organize the items of the outline with proper symbols and indentations, and fill the blanks with ideas appropriate to the subject you have chosen. Be prepared to give this short speech extemporaneously at your next class meeting.

I wonder whether you have thought enough about _____(subject)_____ .

I would define _____(subject)_____ like this: _____ .

You can see what I mean by thinking of these examples:

My first example is: _____ .

Another example is: _____ .

What causes (or results from) _____ is this:

_____ .

An example of how this happens is _____ .

Another example is _____ .

We usually think of _____ as something remote from our everyday lives, but there are cases where it makes a lot of difference to people like you and me.

One everyday influence it has (had) is (was) _____ .

Another influence is (was) _____ .

My conclusion is that the next time we hear people talk about_____ _____ or think of it ourselves, we ought to remember that it is no vague thing but something that can touch our lives as closely as in (refer to examples used) .

ENDNOTES

1. In citing any *Britannica* since 1932 it is advisable to use the date of printing: "John Donne," *Encyclopaedia Britannica* (1971).

2. Adapted from an outline prepared for an informative speech in a beginning public speaking course at Herbert H. Lehman College, City University of New York. The author of the outline was Alma Lajara Franco. Used by permission. The classroom in which this speech was delivered overlooked Kingsbridge Road and was approximately one-half block from the park where Edgar Allan Poe's cottage is now located. It was two blocks from the Kingsbridge Armory and approximately six blocks from Fordham University.

3. This outline is based on one prepared by Joycelyn Clarke, Herbert H. Lehman College, City University of New York.

4. Used by permission of Ms. Wallingford.

CHAPTER 9

Among all other lessons this should first be learned, that wee never affect any straunge inkehorne termes, but to speake as is commonly received: neither seeking to be over fine, nor yet living overcarelesse, using our speeche as most men doe, and ordering our wittes as the fewest have done.—Thomas Wilson, *Arte of Rhetorique*[1]

Style

Where can you apply the principles of this chapter to everyday life?

1.	Wherever you are concerned with choosing words.
2.	Wherever you need to prepare written materials for oral presentation or prepare a speech for publication as an article.
3.	Wherever you need to edit prose for accuracy, clarity, economy, force, striking quality, or liveliness.
4.	Wherever it is necessary to adapt language for use with persons belonging to different age groups, at different levels of education, or at different levels of familiarity with English.
5.	Wherever it is necessary to emphasize or persuade by using special verbal forms, such as figures of speech.

When evaluating some one else's speech consider:

1.	Did the speech sound like talk, or did it have a *written sound?*
2.	How did the language clarify ideas? Where it failed to, what could be done?
3.	Was the language used suitable for the particular audience?
4.	To what extent did the phrasings and grammatical constructions lend imagery and activity to ideas?
5.	To what extent did word pictures help sustain interest and help listeners to understand and accept the central idea?

The work of public speech is not finished until ideas and feelings are couched *in the language of speech,* voiced, and given further meaning through bodily action. The ways we verbalize reveal our intellectual qualities perhaps more clearly than any other aspect of our communication because they tell the world whether we can discriminate among meanings, think clearly, and represent ideas precisely. That is true whether we write or speak, but the relatively unguarded expression of speech is taken by others as an especially sensitive mirror of our mental habits. This being so, all speakers and especially public speakers need to give conscious attention to improving their commands of language. That is what this chapter is about: the resources of language and how you can improve your verbal style.

Speech consists of *acoustic* language that stimulates listeners by standing for ideas and feelings. A fundamental problem in speaking, then, is to find and use language that is true to your actual meanings and yet within the capacities and experience of the particular people who listen. As a general guide Thomas Wilson's advice, quoted at the head of this chapter, is still sound. He was writing for English people at a time when they were just learning to use English for formal purposes, and his counsel was that speakers not be "over fine"—too obviously self-conscious—or "over careless"—too little conscious of language. "Using speech as most men do" but using it freshly "as fewest have done" states a goal in speaking that is as applicable in our day as it was when Wilson wrote in the sixteenth century.

The words we choose as symbols for our ideas, their capacities to stir meanings in listeners' minds matter. There is a great difference between saying, "A girl in a red dress hesitated at the head of the flight of stairs to peer over the railing," and saying, "A debutante in a scarlet gown paused at the top of the staircase to peer over the balustrade." Most of the words in these two sentences are synonyms—words having substantially the same meanings. But the sentences do not communicate the same images—of the scene or of the persons who spoke the words. We think Thomas Wilson would counsel a speaker to prefer the first sentence over the "finer" second version with its "inkhorn" term, *balustrade.*

Through such stylistic choices speakers control what their listeners perceive about meaning and about the speaker. If we are practical, then we must each be concerned with developing an efficient, telling style. It is simply common sense to give serious thought to what our verbal resources are and how each of us can take best advantage of them.

WHAT IS STYLE?

Oral style emerges from choosing and combining words as you compose and deliver speech. The qualities of your style will derive from the meanings of words, their grammatical construction, and their collective psychological impact. Hence we define *oral style* as *the personal manner of expression that gives impact and movement to ideas.* As soon as you have selected an idea or begun to arrange ideas for speech you will be creating and controlling the processes that determine the ultimate qualities of your verbal style in speaking.

Our purpose in this chapter is to discuss the resources you have whenever you make choices of these kinds, or more detailed and technical ones. We shall be using the term *style* in a limited way. That term has many applications. We think of life-styles, styles of dress, styles of airplane or auto design, as well as style in language and styles of delivery. But we shall deal here only with oral verbal style, reserving the topic of styles of delivery for our next chapter.

We want to emphasize, too, that we conceive of style neither as decoration nor as exhibition. Many think that verbal style is, as Lord Chesterfield said, "the dress of thoughts." They think of style as clothing or covering, as something you *put on* ideas or *do to* them. We reject this view as we reject the equally erroneous conception that the object of working on problems of verbal style is to produce something to be exhibited. When speakers try to dazzle their audiences with clever wordings, we think they mis-conceive the function of oral language in public speech. They miss the importance of directness and sincerity in human relations. We believe that when oral language is truly effective, meaning arises *from* and is one *with* thought. Rather than worrying about embellishment or exhibition, we contend that speakers should try to think clearly in the first place. We agree with Abba Eban, an exceptionally eloquent speaker:

> It's not a technique. I think it's really a function of intellect, like having a musical sense. It's a result of the shape of your mind and the gathering of resources by reading fine prose.[2]

This was Eban's answer to a questioner who asked whether he spoke the same way in each of the five languages he knows fluently. He insisted that "if you have any originality" the pursuit of good oral style is the same in all languages.

As we shall treat it in this chapter, style is *personal* management of words and their combinations so as to give impact and movement to ideas *spoken* about. Such management is "a function of the intellect" as Mr. Eban said. Some people seem to have a better "musical sense" of oral style than others, but we can all learn to make informed and sensible judgments in stylistic choices. And a fundamental distinction we have to make at the outset is the distinction between what makes language effective in writing and what makes it effective in *speaking*.

ORAL AND WRITTEN STYLE

Speaking is not writing. Both use words, sentences, and language in general. Writing often has oral elements. Still, to compose for the ear is not the same as composing for the eye.

James A. Winans once said, "A speech is not an essay on its hind legs." He meant that a good essay will not necessarily be effective orally. Some of the reasons have been well put by a prominent literary critic and expert on the teaching of writing:

The chief distinction between oral and written speech, when the two are considered from a functional point of view, is the absence, in writing, of a definite situational context. Oral speech normally takes place in an actual situation that provides abundant nonlinguistic clues to the speaker's intended meaning. Written speech, by contrast, must normally secure its meaning in some future time, in varied and unpredictable situations, and for the understanding of a varied and unpredictable audience. Admittedly, this functional distinction between speech and writing is a typical, not an absolute, one. Nonetheless, the important distinctive feature of written discourse and the chief difficulty of [written] composition is its isolation from any particular situational context.[3]

The limited amount of experimental research that exists argues that these functional, situational differences produce differences of degree rather than of kind between prose that is thought orally effective and prose that is thought effective in writing.[4] Available research and our personal observations in transcribing speeches into written symbols suggest the following hypotheses. In contrast to typical written prose, talk that is effective with listeners contains:

1. more personal pronouns
2. more variety in kinds of sentences
3. more variety in sentence lengths
4. more simple sentences
5. more sentence fragments
6. many more rhetorical questions
7. more repetition of words, phrases, and sentences
8. more monosyllabic words
9. more contractions
10. more interjections
11. more indigenous language
12. more connotative than denotative words
13. more euphony
14. more figurative language
15. more direct quotation
16. more familiar words

If you study this list of differences you should see two things: (1) the differences are differences of proportion rather than differences of form, and (2) the larger number of specific features in the list will tend to make oral style less formal and more closely fitted to particular people in specific rhetorical situations. Both points reflect precisely the situational differences stressed by Professor Hirsch. Aristotle recognized much the same differences when he said that:

> . . . each kind of rhetoric has its own appropriate style. The style of written prose is not that of controversial speaking. . . . A knowledge of both the written style and spoken style is required. . . . The written . . . style is more finished; the controversial is far better adapted to dramatic delivery. . . . On comparison, speeches of the literary

men sound thin in the actual contests; while those of the orators sound well but look crude when you hold them in your hands—and the reason is that their place is in a contest.[5]

To show you what the talk of an exceptionally effective speaker looks like when reduced to print, we quote a segment from Franklin D. Roosevelt's address, "The Philosophy of Social Justice Through Social Action." Using the best available records, L. LeRoy Cowperthwaite reconstructed this text of what Mr. Roosevelt actually said in Detroit. Notice how little the language resembles what we ordinarily call polished writing *for the eye.* Notice the broken sentence structures. Doubtless they were rendered smoothly meaningful by pauses and vocal inflections. Notice, too, the reinforcement gained by repetition of the words "crippled children"—reinforcement that writing for the eye might achieve in less obvious ways such as using italics. This is a carefully established sample of oral style. This is the way one of the most successful political speakers in history *talked*:

> Take another form of poverty in the old days. Not so long ago, you and I know, there were families in attics—in every part of the Nation—in country districts and in city districts—hundreds and thousands of crippled children who could get no adequate care, crippled children who were lost to the community and who were a burden on the community. And so we have, in these past twenty or thirty years, gradually provided means for restoring crippled children to useful citizenship; and it has all been a factor in going after and solving one of the causes of poverty and disease.[6]

Other differences between oral and written style will reflect a good speaker's constant effort to make meanings and relationships as clear as possible for listeners who cannot review as they might when reading. Transitional statements such as those we illustrated on pages 182–84 are apt to be frequent, whereas a writer might be content with single words such as *thus, therefore,* and *however.* If the speaker is astute, there will be few indefinite pronouns. *This* and *that* are ambiguous words for a listener because they always require the listener to remember some noun used earlier. It is often hard to recall that the "this" now heard actually means the "cathedral" heard ten seconds earlier. Effective oral stylists avoid such ambiguities wherever they can. In writing, but especially in speaking, you will be clearer and more forceful if you use verbs that suggest action and sensory experience and use them in the active voice. "The dog bit the man" conveys meaning more efficiently and more actively than "The man was bitten by the dog." In developing your own oral style you will find that if you think about making things easy and interesting for your listeners, you will naturally begin to make the adjustments we have just discussed.

As usual, there are no *rules* of good oral style. Whatever features of language fit the human relationships of your particular rhetorical situation will be appropriate, and the fact that it is a *specific* situation, not a general one, will lead you into such practices as we have just reviewed—provided you think about your listeners as you choose your words. The specificity of rhetorical situations for speech dictates that oral style be conversational, personal, and considerate of the thought processes of listeners.

DEVELOPING YOUR OWN STYLE

We have been implying that you can improve your speaking style. You already have your own particular manner of utterance—good or bad. Consider the other members of your speech class. You will notice that some of them have distinctive styles. One may help you see more visual images, let you see and feel the things talked about. Another may have a rough-hewn style—terser, plainer, or more homespun in wordings. Still others may be abstract, may habitually use colloquialisms, clichés, or slang, or may be exceedingly precise in explanations. Each one consciously or unconsciously endows his or her speech with particular hallmarks. Styles differ because each person has a different background, has formed individual habits, and thinks in individualistic ways.

A particular style is yours, too. You have a vocabulary at some stage of development and special habits of expression. Your background, prior education, and methods of writing have exerted their influences. Some of your habits of expression are good ones that need emphasis. Others are faults to be eradicated. Improvement comes from developing your strengths and removing your weaknesses. You start by surveying your present speech style and work from there. Developing an effective style is a slow process. You cannot expect fixed changes to emerge overnight, but you will be surprised at how you can gradually modify your habits by close attention to language and by experimenting with the kinds of resources you haven't fully used before.

What sort of program for long-range improvement should you follow? These steps will help.

1. *Become language-conscious.* Recognize that your *situation* determines what will be appropriate. There isn't one style for the purpose of informing and another for persuading. You need *all* of the resources of language for any purpose. So become sensitive to "good" and "bad" uses of words. Study your own and your colleagues' usages to see which are vigorously clear and which are apathetically abstract, which produce sharp images in your mind and which leave you with fuzzy images or none at all. And take an inventory of your own grammatical and other stylistic habits to discover where you seem to be most limited. Then set about eliminating your weaknesses, one or two at a time, cleaning out, say, excessive use of clichés and meaningless slang phrases first, then going on to something else. Follow Abba Eban's advice. Start to read material by expert writers to see what they do to avoid your kinds of faults. This will also make you sensitive to verbal constructions you have never used before.

2. *Increase your speaking vocabulary.* It is alleged that the average college student's day-to-day, working oral vocabulary is about 250 words. Is it any wonder that many students' speaking style lacks precision, color, and rhythmic variety? To improve your style try consciously to extend the number of words and phrasings at your command. You do not have to go out of your way to master unusual words and unique phrases; learn the meanings of the language you normally encounter but do not understand. You are after the most accurate and appropriate words.

Keep a dictionary handy and refer to it when you see or hear unfamiliar words. *Roget's Thesaurus* will also help, but look up the precise meanings of synonyms in the dictionary to fix their differences in your mind.

3. *Write.* This may seem strange advice after what we have said about differences between oral and written style, but if you practice writing *talk,* the act of writing will make you conscious of each word choice you make. A particularly helpful way to refine your language is to write out an important part of a forthcoming speech, then write it again without paying attention to your first version. Then compare the two versions noting where and why one is better than the other. Cicero said about this kind of practice, "Write with the ear." That's good advice, but write with your ear attuned to what will *sound* best *for the particular listeners* you are going to meet.

4. *Rewrite.* Experiment with parts of an extemporaneous speech by writing and rewriting them—not for the purpose of producing *a* way of saying an idea but for the purpose of discovering several good ways of saying it. The best speakers put their speeches through several drafts, even when not planning to speak from manuscript. Benjamin Disraeli, a great parliamentary debater, experimented with phrasings of key portions of his speeches, then rehearsed alone and before friendly critics, and rewrote again—to speak extemporaneously! Franklin Roosevelt, a master of the craft of manuscript speaking, put some of his speeches through as many as twelve drafts before he was satisfied. If you write and rewrite portions of speeches you can smooth out wordings, correct unclear constructions, tinker with phrasings, rearrange ideas and their linkages. All the while you will be expanding your verbal resources and, even when you speak extemporaneously or impromptu, these added "ways of saying" will be available in your mind.

5. *Study live and published speeches.* Listen to the speeches in your classroom to see what kinds of phrasings strike "true" and "false" notes for the class. Notice what it is that makes some speeches sound "learned" or "read." Listen to political and other speeches. The Cable Service Public Affairs Network (C-Span) broadcasts many speeches over certain local TV cable services. Regular features are the proceedings of the United States House of Representatives, important committee hearings of both the House and the Senate, and speeches by public figures to such audiences as the National Press Club in Washington, D.C. If this service is available to you, use it as a laboratory for studying the differences between effective and ineffective speakers. If you cannot hear these speeches, study presidential addresses when they occur on television, and the lecturers and other speakers who regularly appear on your campus. And, of course, anthologies of famous speeches are available in every library. Do not study the style of such speakers to copy them. Study their styles to find specific practices that you can naturally and easily fit into the kind of oral style that is particularly suited to you.

6. *Speak in public.* Take advantage of opportunities to refine your expression of ideas in both conversation and public address. Speak as often as possible. The more you speak, especially in the extemporaneous and impromptu modes, the

better you will become at finding ways to finish phrases and statements effectively no matter how you started them. The more experience you have with thinking on your feet and symbolizing your ideas as they develop in your mind, the more fluent and attractive your style will become.

LISTENERS' JUDGMENTS OF ORAL STYLE

What are the qualities that make anyone's manner of speaking effective? There are qualities of language that are especially important to listeners. There are at least seven: talk needs to seem *accurate, clear, appropriate* to the situation, *economical, forceful* where necessary, *striking* at climactic or emotional points, and generally *lively*. Whether they understand theories of language or not, listeners always expect these qualities of language that they perceive as competent. We shall therefore consider what is involved in achieving each of these qualities.

Accuracy

Whatever you say will have some degree of accuracy. You cannot use words without alleging something about what is or is not true, and so you will "get it right" or "get it wrong" by some margin or other. Whether you are accurate or not depends significantly on your ability to choose words that represent *to your listeners* substantially what you want them to understand. Here is the importance of our advice that you constantly try to enlarge your vocabulary. You need to understand the meanings of words very well to be perceived as expressing yourself accurately. If you use *infer* for *imply* or vice versa, no one can get your meaning precisely. Is it more accurate to say, "I *telephoned* my father" or "I *contacted* my father"? The first is more specific and therefore clearer and more accurate. So one way to make yourself more accurate in talk is to be as specific and as concrete as possible. Here we confront the reason for our earlier advice that you study the *differences* in the meanings of basically synonymous words. Take the trouble to find out the different meanings of *institution* and *corporation*, and you can be more accurate in talking about business affairs. Differentiate between *ghost* and *banshee*, and you can be more accurate when talking about the spirit world. In similar ways you can improve accuracy if you know the precise differences between *indulgence* and *clemency, coarseness* and *ribaldry, criminality* and *delinquency*, and other similar but differentiating terms.

The other major consideration when trying to be accurate in speaking is to know what meanings language will have *in your particular rhetorical situation*. For example, the formality of a situation may make an entirely intelligible statement "wrong." "I agree with George's idea" is a sensible and intelligible statement, but not in a situation where talk is governed by rules of parliamentary procedure. "I support the motion presented by George Green" is accurate in a parliamentary situation because all talk must be directed toward support or defeat of motions to be intelligible. A person who nods a friendly greeting to the auctioneer during an auction sale has just put in a bid for the article being sold; he has not expressed personal friendliness, as he might do by the same act on a public street. The "in" language of motorcycle buffs is unintelligible to "outsiders" but highly accurate and precise within the group.

Dictionary definitions, then, do not always guarantee accuracy in oral communication. Every rhetorical situation imposes its own definitions on words and combinations of words. To be accurate your language must be within the bounds of both general meanings *and* of situational meanings. If the two sets of meanings come into conflict, choose the one that will work in your specific rhetorical situation.

Clarity

Listeners ask for more than the precision we just discussed. At the beginning of his discussion of style in *The Rhetoric,* Aristotle said: "We may therefore . . . regard it as settled that a good style is, first of all, clear. The proof is that language which does not convey a clear meaning fails to perform the very function of language." He went on to say: "Clearness is secured through the use of name-words [nouns and adjectives] and, verbs that are current terms. . . ." [7] His judgment is still sound. Concreteness contributes to clarity. So do good transitions and simple, familiar sentence structures. So the more simply, concretely, and directly you say what you mean, the more likely you are to be clear.[8]

How much you can say and still be clear is a *situational* question. How much your listeners will know, or how little, and how eager they will be to learn from you are questions that must guide your answer. Also, whether they will understand your terms precisely and whether you have prepared them for the ways you put ideas together can influence how much you dare say and in what ways. Some years ago a commencement speaker, early in his speech, said:

> We place less and less emphasis on the joy of achievement—and more and more on the achievement of joy. . . . And when you grasp the full implications of our altering philosophy of work, you can no longer regard it with equanimity.

We are confident that his listeners had no notion of what he was talking about because he had not yet prepared them by clarifying what "achievements" and what "philosophy of work" he had in mind. His nice antithesis and his strong assertion of a danger were wasted because his audience was not yet ready to understand exactly what either referred to. To put this point another way, you may be entirely accurate but unclear. This is important to remember. Except among specialists and people who already agree with you, clarity requires that you interpret ideas precisely by filling in definitions of terms, analogies, contrasts, and the like.

Another danger must be watched for and avoided. *Mis*information can be communicated clearly. To explain the economics of supply and demand it has long been customary to explain that as demand rises prices first rise but higher prices will encourage greater supplies, which in turn, will depress prices by making supply exceed demand, and so on. This seems clear enough, but with the election of President

Reagan, a contrary, but still very clear, explanation came into vogue. It was called "supply-side economics." It posited that great supplies encourage great demand and short supplies produce diminished demands, so such phenomena as "stagflation" can occur when supplies are limited and depress demand. We are not economists. We do not pretend to know which explanation is "correct" as a description of economic forces. What we do know is that either position can be easily and clearly explained, though it seems clear, too, that one explanation must be misinformation.

Clarity in language and organization is a goal you should work for relative to your particular audience, but the ideas you deal with also will constrain you. Just as you cannot persuade every audience to accept every proposition you offer, some subjects are far more difficult to make clear than others. Compared to principles of nuclear fission, the principles of an internal combustion engine are easy to explain. Compared to making an argument for governmental regulation of radio and television stations, making an argument for governmental regulation of contraception and abortion is extraordinarily complex. Subject matter is not uniformly malleable. There is nothing you can do about that except talk as concretely as possible, use current terms wherever you can, apply even the most difficult concepts to your listeners' experiences and interests, define your terms clearly, and offer analogies and contrasts. Usually those resources are enough to make any discussable idea intelligible. Witness the methods of two of this century's most expert interpreters of technical information: Leonard Bernstein on music and Carl Sagan on astronomy. Study their methods if you would learn the routes to clarity.

Propriety

Stylistic propriety is very difficult to discuss, yet inappropriateness can destroy listeners' confidence in speakers. The difficulty in thinking about what is appropriate is that until you know the particular speaker, the particular subject, and the particular rhetorical situation, you cannot specify what *is* appropriate for that occasion. It is easier to say what the extremes of inappropriateness are. Writing about what is appropriate in public lecturing, Leonard Bernstein said:

> We don't ever want to talk down; but how *up* can we talk without losing contact? There is a happy medium somewhere between the music-appreciation racket and purely technical discussion; it is hard to find, but it can be found. It is with this certainty that it can be found that I have made so bold as to discuss music on television, on records, and in public lectures. Whenever I feel I have done it successfully, it is because I may have found the happy medium. And finding it is impossible without the conviction that the public is *not* a great beast, but an intelligent organism, more often than not longing for insight and knowledge.[9]

We think Bernstein here isolated the root of all propriety in speaking: *respect and friendliness toward the audience.*

It is your attitude toward your listeners that generates appropriate or inappropriate oral style. Perhaps we can see this by considering what we would all take as *inappropriate* style. What would you expect in the language of someone *pompous, condescending,* or *aloof*? A good deal would depend on the rhetorical situation, but among the qualities you would always expect are "big words" and perhaps too many of them, frequent references to self but few references to listeners and details of the situation, long sentences perhaps, formal or technical language rather than informal language with frequent clarifying analogies, and language that keeps the speaker and the subject in the foreground but never the listeners' immediate interests and comfort. Compare these two statements as illustrations of the inappropriate and the appropriate:

> My experience is that few undergraduates on the contemporary scene are equipped with the mental agility to conquer the intricacies of higher mathematics.
>
> The typical undergraduate is not well-enough trained to grasp immediately the principles of higher mathematics.

The first example is wordy and condescending toward undergraduates and implies their limitations are permanent; it uses relatively unfamiliar, high-sounding phrases (*contemporary scene, mental agility, intricacies*) where they are not really needed. The statement implies that the speaker's authority is final on this subject, with nothing to imply that the speaker is friendly toward anyone at all. The second example says what the first does but does not imply that the undergraduates are permanently limited or that their limitations are necessarily their fault. The message uses only common terms, but not imprecise ones, and it contains no pretentious phrases. The speaker's personal authority is not unnecessarily invoked. We suggest that the second kind of statement illustrates qualities of talk that are *always* appropriate: modest, simple, precise, concise, and considerate of the people talked about and the people talked to. That is about as far as anyone can go toward telling you when style has propriety for any situation. Respect your listeners; be friendly and helpful toward them, and your style can seldom be anything but appropriate. That is the way to Bernstein's "happy medium."

One other point deserves special mention. "The style again," said Aristotle, "should not be mean nor above the dignity of the subject, but appropriate." [10] To describe a commonplace operation, such as changing a tire, in flowery language would be ridiculous. To depict a sunset in the plainest vernacular is to rob the subject of meaning and emotional quality. To say "the sky was kind of red, sort of like a tomato or a radish" is as inappropriate as to say of a tire, "it was vulcanized rubber besmirched by dust and grime." What is at issue here is finding the combinations of words that suit the emotional responses most people have for whatever it is you are talking about. Changing a tire is an ordinary, uninspiring job, and it ought to be talked about in ordinary language. But a beautiful sunset is emotionally different for most people, and the words you choose ought to reflect your awareness of that special quality. Finally, when you deal with technical and abstract subjects about which people *feel* very little except perhaps some perplexity, your language will show due consideration for your listeners only if you build into your talk the kinds of activity, comparisons, contrasts, and novelty that enable listeners to feel as well as understand.

Economy

By economy in language we mean the right choice of words, in the right amount, and in the best order for instantaneous intelligibility.

In his *The Philosophy of Style* Herbert Spencer emphasized the importance of economizing the "mental energies" and "mental sensibilities" of auditors or readers. "To so present ideas that they may be apprehended with the least possible mental effort, is the desideratum towards which most of the rules ... point," he said.[11] He summarized his "principle of economy" thus:

> A reader or listener has at each moment but a limited amount of mental power available. To recognize and interpret the symbols presented to him requires part of his power; to arrange and combine the images suggested requires a further part; and only that part which remains can be used for realizing the thought conveyed. Hence, the more time and attention it takes to receive and understand each sentence, the less time and attention can be given to the contained idea; and the less vividly will that idea be conceived.[12]

Economy of attention is economy only if the idea is fully clear and understandable. At times, economy in style means not brevity or frugality but the necessary amplification. A further fact to consider is that speech needs to be more ample than writing. One reason is that listeners cannot review unless speakers provide the necessary words.

No one can tell you exactly how to judge in advance when you have thought out just enough to say about a point. But as you speak you have one major way of gauging what is needed. You can watch listeners closely, looking for facial and other evidences that they have or have not understood, have or have not accepted what you are saying. If you have prepared sufficient material and several different ways of stating things, you will find it possible to enlarge your discussions of ideas when you see signs of uncertainty and to cut out unneeded bits when you receive signs of acceptance. It is, in fact, a great advantage that in planning and rehearsing for extemporaneous speaking you can and probably will evolve several ways of saying most things. In final presentation, then, you can work from the briefest to the amplest expression of any point if feedback from listeners shows that *more* than a minimum of right words in best order is needed for intelligibility.

Force

Listeners like language that has drive, urgency, and action. Such language compels them to pay attention as it propels ideas forward. Economy, precision, and simple grammatical constructions produce force. Spencer supplies the link when he says, "... Other things equal, the force of all verbal forms and arrangements is great in proportion as the time and mental effort they demand from the recipient is small." [13] Modern research in linguistics and stylistics bears him out. The simplest, easiest, and so most forthright construction in English is the simple, subject–verb–object or modifier. This form you first experienced when you first read "I see the ball." Interfere with the sense between "I" and "see," and you will complicate understanding and also lose force: "I, to the best of my judgment, see the ball." The complexity of an idea or the character of your situation may make the more complicated kind of construction all but inevitable (for example, "The measurement, taken at 70 degrees Fahrenheit, is 60 millimeters"), but you should know that force and simplicity are sacrificed if you interfere with your listener's simplest thought movement from the subject to the predicate.

Some words are more forceful than others. It appears that it is not length or the origin of a word that makes it complex and unforceful. It is the number of "interior" meanings the word contains. Rudolph Flesch explains:

> Language gadgets... are of two kinds: words by themselves, like *against,* and parts of words (affixes), like *dis-.* The more harmful of the two for plain talk are the affixes, since the reader or hearer cannot understand what the gadget does to the sentence before he has disentangled it from the word it is attached to. Each affix burdens his mind with two jobs: first, he has to split up the word into its parts and, second, he has to rebuild the sentence from these parts. To do this does not even take a split second, of course; but it adds up.[14]

You need not avoid all complicating and force-diminishing affixed words, but whenever there is a choice you ought to prefer the simplest word that will be accurate. The student who said, "Your response is a variant of the teleological argument for the existence of God," was unnecessarily complex. He was, therefore, less forceful than he could have been. He could have said, "Your answer is like the argument that the world seems orderly, so a God must have organized it." He would have used more words, but they would have been simpler. His grammar would have been a bit more usual, and the gadgety word *teleological* would not steal force and clarity.

There is no clear empirical proof of it, but experience argues that listeners like active terms more than passive ones and pictorial words and phrases more than abstract ones. You can choose words that denote or suggest actions. You can also keep as much of your talk as possible in the active voice. Then both vocabulary and grammar will work toward successful communication. Any college student can approximate the precision, clarity, appropriateness, economy, and force that Leonard Bernstein attained in a televised broadcast. He was doing the difficult job of speaking about a musical composition:

> Whether you call this kind of weird piece "cool" or "crazy" or "futuristic," or "modernistic" or whatever, the fact is that it is bordering on serious concert music. The arrangement begins to be a *composition.* Take away the beat, and you might not even know it's jazz at all. It would be just a concert piece. And why is it jazz? Because it is played by jazz men, on jazz instruments, and because it has its roots in the soil of jazz and not of Bach.[15]

All the constituents of style we have so far discussed are present in this short passage from the speech of a brilliant expositor. Notice especially, however, that *no* subject is separated from its verb by intervening thought; of eighty-six words only about fifteen (depending on one's method of analyzing) are gadget terms; action words and descriptive words are scattered throughout; and the passive voice is never used. The English language offers you the same resources for creating straightforward, forceful style. What is required of you is forethought about simplicity and force and, of course, clear ideas to begin with.

Striking quality

The characteristic of style we choose to call *striking quality* gives speech heightened effect. Writers have called this characteristic "interestingness," "impressiveness," "vividness," or "beauty."

We reject "beauty" because speaking is a utilitarian art. Its primary function is never to be beautiful. A speech admired for the sole reason that it aroused the imagination as a poem would be suspect as rhetoric. A speech whose main virtue is that it is euphonious is also suspect. Beauty alone will not do in practical art. Moreover, the ugly can sometimes be useful; the revolting as well as the attractive can draw attention and have useful effect. "Striking quality" seems to us the better concept because it recognizes the many aspects of language that can seize and guide thought. The unknown writer called Longinus said in his "On the Sublime":

> ... The choice of proper and striking words wonderfully attracts and enthralls the hearer, and ... such a choice is the leading ambition of all orators and writers, since it is the direct agency which ensures the presence in writings, as upon the fairest statues, of the perfection of grandeur, beauty, mellowness, dignity, force, power, and any other high qualities there may be and breathes into dead things a kind of living voice.[16]

Longinus also pointed out, "... stately language is not to be used everywhere, since to invest petty affairs with great and high-sounding names would seem just like putting a full-sized tragic mask upon an infant boy." [17] Georges Louis Leclerc, Count de Buffon, echoed him: "Nothing is more inimical to this warmth [of style] than the desire to be everywhere striking." [18]

The quotations from Longinus and from Buffon suggest the delicacy of deciding how to express ideas verbally. From one side aspirations for accuracy, clarity, economy, and simplicity ought to tug at any speaker, but from another side the wish to make at least some ideas striking ought to pull. It is probably not too much to say that the history of John F. Kennedy's life will continue to be something a little special to Americans because he uttered the uniquely formal sentence, "Ask not what your country can do for you—ask what you can do for your country." The turn of phrase embedded a familiar idea within history and made it one specially associated with Mr. Kennedy. The college student who said, "The Inner City does this—it crushes and shatters thousands; it is our shame" struck a strong blow for serious consideration of urban decay. In telling of his summer's work in Harlem he wanted very much to shake up his fellow students on the subject. His striking phrasing helped to accomplish that. You may have similar needs from time to time.

Striking quality in language comes from giving poetic turns to words while keeping them prose, from painting word pictures that stir listeners' emotions, from combining words in unexpected and sometimes alliterative ways. In most circumstances a bit of uniqueness can serve almost any speaker's purposes. Aristotle's advice was that "... it is well to give the ordinary idiom an air of remoteness; the hearers are struck by what is out of the way, and like what strikes them." [19] But not everything is important enough to bear the honor of unique phrasing, as we said when discussing propriety. A fondness for being striking is all to the good as long as it does not produce exhibitionism. But effective speaking can also be accomplished without imbuing it with a striking quality. The passage just quoted from Bernstein illustrates that fact. Or is Bernstein's very simplicity striking?

Liveliness

Force, economy, and striking quality contribute to *liveliness* in oral communication. If the mission of rhetoric is to endow ideas with movement and if its goal is, as C. S. Baldwin said, "the energizing of knowledge and the humanizing of truth," [20] there is no more important stylistic quality oral discourse can have than liveliness.

Aristotle recognized the basic devices that generate liveliness when he said that listeners "... like words that set an event before their eyes; for they must see the thing occurring now, not hear of it as in the future." [21] The speaker, he said, must "aim at three points: Metaphor, Antithesis, Actuality." [22] He thereafter advised speakers to make their verbal pictures move—to make them motion pictures rather than still photographs, as modern photographers might put it. The goal is not still-life images but "objects ... invested with life," and thereby "an effect of activity." [23] The successful stylist is one who "... makes everything live and move; and movement is activity." [24]

In discussing "actuality" Aristotle says,

> We have said that liveliness is secured by the use of proportional metaphor and by putting things directly before the eyes of the audience. But we still have to explain what is meant by setting things "before the eyes," and how this is to be effected. What I mean is, using expressions that show things in a state of activity.[25]

Liveliness comes from animation, conflict, suspense, actuality (or realism), specificity, and proximity in what you say. It comes from using the present tense and the active voice. It comes from economy in wording, from simple rather than complex structuring, from vivid imagery, and from any other resource of language that sets moving images before the minds of listeners.

Relate events in a "you are there" rather than an "I was there" fashion. Take your audience with you as you relive the suspenseful moment when your boat capsized or your car crashed. Let the audience feel the tape breaking across your chest at the finish line of a race, the touch of your friend's hand at the moment of good-bye, the pull of your muscles as you lift a rock or kick a football. Make your images cumulate and build. Let your appeals to sight, touch, taste, hearing, and smell, to thermal and kinesthetic sensitivity, so combine that images in the mind are experienced. Combining images and constructing a *past* experience in the *present* tense might produce such a passage as: "I smell the pines. The morning air is crisp, and I hear the crunch of snow beneath me as I plod up the path. My tired muscles seem to cry out at every step.'' In this sequence, four kinds of sensory images combine to bring a whole experience to reality. These are ways to make use of those rhetorical features for which listeners are always ready, as we said in Chapter 3 (pages 64–66). Experiment with animation, actuality, and imagery and you will find that your speeches can attain realism and movement. What you say can run to its goal rather than limp to its conclusion.

Liveliness through metaphor, antithesis, realism, and progressive movement of ideas is possible with or without high excitement. That is fortunate, for some speech materials lend themselves better to lively discourse than others. Narratives are especially susceptible to animated treatments, and committee reports and speeches of inquiry often demand your diligent search for the means to liveliness.

To say that liveliness is the most important of all qualities of good oral style is no exaggeration; it is a forthright summary of all we have just said. Accuracy, clarity, propriety, economy, force, and striking quality are constituents of good style, but they are constituents of the ultimate virtue of speech that influences—liveliness.

THE RESOURCES OF LANGUAGE

Words are symbols; they stand for and suggest ideas. No word has exactly the same meaning for any two individuals. Words uttered are combinations of sounds that travel through air. We endow them with meaning. The meaning assigned depends on the human being who perceives the sounds. Background makes him or her interpret word symbols in particular and sometimes peculiar ways. Parental authority, environment, and learning combine to determine exactly what a word will mean to any one of us. Liveliness and the other qualities of style we have just discussed depend in part on your ability to forecast the denotative and connotative meanings your words will have in the rhetorical situation you will enter.

Connotations and denotations

The denotative meaning of a word is that which it names or identifies. Connotative meanings of words are those that people associate with the words and their denotative meanings. Some words denote much and connote relatively little. Connotations tend to have important emotive, subjective, personal qualities that go beyond merely logical, objective identifications. Such words as *mat, turn, digest, journal, shelf, dollar* are largely denotative; not many subjective associations attach to them, especially when the words are used in isolation. But words such as *mother, homecoming, democracy, black,* and *lover* are at least as significant for what they suggest as for what they name or identify. They arouse emotional responses and generate images in the mind.

Most words, of course, are both connotative and denotative because their objective meanings touch off personal reactions. The word *house* can in many cases be considered denotative, as in the sentence, "There are twenty houses in the 300 block of Elm Avenue." This same word in other contexts may call to mind a particular house or a particular experience with a house and thus becomes strongly connotative.

Because of variability of meanings, whenever you choose language for a speaking situation, you need to weigh carefully (1) whether these particular listeners understand the denotative meanings of the words you will use, and (2) just what additional connotations your particular audience in the particular situation attaches to those words. For example, at the University of Colorado an "academic term" means a fifteen-week semester, while at the University of Washington it means a ten-week "quarter." There are some terms that are indigenous and even peculiar to geographical areas. In one region of the country people buy sandwiches called *heroes*. In other areas they buy *submarines, grinders, hoagies, wedgies,* or *poor boys*. They are all buying the sort of sandwich that originated in the "Blondie" comic strip. The sandwich was first dubbed the *Dagwood,* a name taken from the character who first made such gastronomic creations. "The paper" will suggest a newspaper to a journalist but perhaps an academic dissertation to college professors and students. Your question, then, is, "What will the term denote and connote for *this audience?*"

Word choice   Word choice, then, is a matter of strategy as well as of sheer literacy. Mental pictures are altered and modified by changes in wording. To say, "I saw a *red* bicycle," prompts a different image from "I saw a *pink* bicycle," "I saw a *fuchsia* bicycle," "I saw a *vermilion* bicycle," ". . . a *Chinese red* bicycle," or ". . . a *Coca-Cola red* bicycle." The manufacturers of nail polish could extend the list of reds *ad infinitum.* Similarly, to say, "The child skipped *gaily* down the street," is different from saying the child skipped *merrily* or *joyously* or *boisterously,* or even *happily.* But a change of adjective or adverb is secondary to a change of noun or verb. Substitute *lad, youth, teenager,* or even *girl* or *boy* for *child* and the meaning changes markedly. Substitute *shuffled, skated,* or *strolled* for *skipped* and the mental picture is again modified drastically. To stir up an intended meaning, just any word will not do even though it conforms to all grammatical conventions.

At times the wrong choice of word, a *malapropism,* can make meaning ludicrous or spoil the mood created by a speaker, undoing several minutes' work. We think of the student who said that a speaker's body was "stagnant" when he meant "static," and of the student who spoke of "illiciting" rather than "eliciting" audience responses. We also think of the student speaker who, in describing a thief's actions during a robbery, coined a new word when he declared that the thief "slurked" around the corner. Whether the intended meaning was "slunk around" or "lurked at" or "sneaked around" was found out only by questioning the speaker. When he was questioned, something fundamental came out: the idea, the image, was not exactly clear in the speaker's own mind. His coined word was in fact a way of evading clear, denotative meaning. From these examples, we gain two basic guidelines for making meanings serve rather than hinder you. (1) Determine your own exact meaning. (2) Once you know your meaning, select from the accepted terms the one or ones that conform most closely to the meaning in your mind. But select those terms that are unlikely to connote anything incompatible with your immediate rhetorical purpose within the situation you plan to enter or have entered.

FIGURES OF SPEECH

Language and meanings shift, but certain ways of saying things seem always to work in fairly predictable ways. The Greeks seem first to have noticed and catalogued those especially influential forms of expression. Traditionally these have been called *figures of speech* or *rhetorical figures*. That simply means they are recurring *forms* of words that are used in all Western languages to secure attention and, often, to *argue* for a point of view.

The Belgian philosophical writers Chaim Perelman and L. Olbrechts-Tyteca have pointed out that, although these manners of expression have been known from antiquity, they have generally been thought of as "mere ornaments that made the style artificial and ornate." Their argumentative functions were, until the middle of this century, generally disregarded. Perelman and Olbrechts-Tyteca's definition of these figures is useful:

> In order that there may be a figure, the presence of two characteristics would seem essential: a discernible structure, independent of the content, in other words a form (which may, under the divisions recognized by modern logicians, be syntactic, semantic, or pragmatic), and a use that is different from the normal manner of expression and, consequently, attracts attention.[26]

Later these authors explain the argumentative work that such verbal forms can do:

> We consider a figure to be *argumentative,* if it brings about a change of perspective, and its use seems normal in relation to this new situation. If, on the other hand, the speech [utterance] does not bring about the adherence of the hearer to this argumentative form, the figure will be considered an embellishment, a figure of style. It can excite admiration, but this will be on the aesthetic plane or in recognition of the speaker's originality.[27]

Since these patterns of expression can either enliven speech or argue, or both, you ought to recognize them as resources and understand how they work. Students of rhetoric have counted nearly a hundred forms of this general type, but we think you have used or can use ten of them most profitably. These we will identify, describe, and illustrate, explaining also what each form can achieve for a speaker. Unfortunately a few of the forms have ancient names that are now obscure, but it is less important to remember the name than to see what the structure can do for you.

Simile is a *direct comparison* between things that are essentially dissimilar except in the particular qualities alluded to in the simile. This kind of comparison contains the words *like* or *as*. For example, Peter Marshall said, "There are voices hot, like scorching blasts from a furnace . . . and others cold as if they came from frozen hearts." [28] Or consider this example by Daniel O'Connell:

> The policy towards Ireland . . . was similar to that of the avaricious housewife who killed the goose who laid her golden eggs . . . and you will deserve the reputation for being the lineal descent of that goose if you be such ganders as not to declare . . . that no longer shall this system of plunder be permitted to continue.[29]

Metaphor is an implied comparison between two essentially dissimilar things. Words such as *like* or *as* are omitted. As you can see, the dictionary's distinction between simile and metaphor is wholly technical and of no practical consequence. We might be wise to go back to Aristotle's unpedantic position that the term *metaphor* is a sufficient word with which to talk about *any* stylistic comparison between essentially different things. Does it matter in the practical impact that *like* or *as* is missing from Richard Nixon's remark, "We have unlocked the doors that for a quarter of a century stood between the U.S. and the People's Republic of China"? [30] We think not.

From a practical standpoint the important thing about Marshall's, O'Connell's, and Nixon's verbal expressions is that each *made a claim and implied an argument* by means of the comparisons and contrasts used. Marshall implied that we should prefer hot voices to those from "frozen hearts"; O'Connell's goose analogy implied that tolerating English rule of Ireland was both wrong and, worse, stupid; and Nixon's locked-door comparison implied that his policy toward mainland China was a commendable undoing of an unfortunate policy of isolating one country from the other. Whether or not these speakers were conscious of it, all three made quick arguments through metaphoric comparisons. If Marshall did not wish to denigrate "cold" voices, he used the wrong verbal form. If O'Connell did not intend to magnify the injustice he talked about, he used the wrong verbal form. If Nixon did not mean to claim praise for his China policy, the "locked door" metaphor was the wrong one.

Metaphors (and similes) have serious effects, then. They can enhance, denigrate, or embellish. They are stylistic procedures we all use, and you will be wise to consider their probable impacts and use them often but in ways that will serve your purposes precisely. You will make metaphoric comparisons. We all do. They enliven speech and affect listeners' attitudes. They therefore need to be chosen purposefully and with a sharp eye to your listeners' tendencies and biases. Then they will work for you rather than against you. [31]

Rhetorical question is a query designed to produce an effect but not necessarily to evoke an overt answer unless an answer is verbalized by the speaker or, as in the example we shall give, some choral response can be called forth. Consider, for example, Ronald Reagan's acceptance speech:

> Can anyone look at the record of this Administration and say, "Well done"? [Audience cries, "No."] Can anyone compare the state of our economy when the Carter Administration took office with where we are today and say, "Keep up the good work"? ["No."] Can anyone look at our reduced standing in the world today and say, "Let's have four more years of this"? ["No."] [32]

Whether answered in the minds of the listeners, or by the speaker, or with shouts from the audience, as here, the question form achieves *reinforcement* of its answer. If the listener answers within, that listener's commitment to the answer is strengthened by being produced in personal terms. If a speaker answers his or her own question, the answer seems more pertinent because the question was verbalized. And if the audience shouts the answer as it did for Ronald Reagan, the apparent unanimity of the crowd creates the impression that the question was pertinent and no other answer is possible. There is, of course, a limit to when and how rhetorical questions can argue by emphasizing. It is unsafe to raise rhetorical questions unless you are sure your listeners *will* produce answers agreeable to your purposes and will share your implied view that the question was rightly posed and can be answered with certainty. Otherwise listeners' internal answers may refute you or their uncertainty may create more problems than they solve. Rhetorical questions are useful only where you are confident that you know how the listeners will answer.

Antithesis (an-'tith-ə-səs) is a parallel construction of words, phrases, or sentences that contains opposed or sharply contrasting ideas. Expressing the antithetical ideas in similar (parallel) language injects an additional claim that the matched ideas really are opposed or contrasting. In his 1960 Inaugural Address, John F. Kennedy said, "Let us never negotiate out of fear. But let us never fear to negotiate." [33] The paralleled wordings of the two parts of Kennedy's antithesis tend to argue that fearful negotiations and negotiating out of fear are genuinely opposed things we should never do. (Notice that in this construction Kennedy created an opportunity to *repeat* his key injunction, "let us never.") By emphasizing in this verbal manner the oppositions you want to talk about, you too can add touches of strength to your general claims that they are indeed opposed. By using parallel wordings in expressing things that are *alike* you can similarly emphasize through verbal form that they are indeed alike in the ways you say. This structure is usually called *balanced phrasing*.

Onomatopoeia (,än-ə-,mat-ə-'pē(y)ə) occurs when you choose a word in which sound suggests the meaning of the word. Notice the suggestive, descriptive function of "clattering" in this example of Robert Kennedy speaking: "The free Irishmen marching everywhere today to the tune of 'O'Donnell Abu' and 'The Wearing of the Green' are a dramatic contrast to the clattering of hobnail boots on darkened streets, the sound that marks the enslaved nations." [34] The symbol of enslavement, the "hobnailed boots," is surely made a bit more threatening because Kennedy chose to make them "clatter" rather than just "sound." He might have achieved a similar but slightly different effect if he had said, "the *thud* of hobnail boots." *Thud,* like *clatter,* is an onomatopoeic word. So are *ripple, crunch, slither,* and many other standard English words. All are available to you as means of adding realism and sometimes threat or promise to points you want to make.

Irony implies something different from and usually the opposite of what is stated. Here is an ironic passage from a university lecture:

> Mandatory retirement is the instant status of senility and incompetence we bestow on our aged, based on the elapsed time since their birth rather than on their ability or other relevant criteria. Poor, senile, old Maggie Kuhn has organized the 10,000 member activist group called the Gray Panthers, travels about 100,000 miles a year, gives about 200 lectures each year, writes numerous articles, and is a very effective Washington lobbyist for the elderly.[35]

There have been a few attempts to discover empirically what persuasive effects irony (and the related form, satire) has. The findings are by no means definitive, but they suggest that these forms of saying-other-than-what-you-mean do not *change* attitudes very much but may be excellent ways of reinforcing existing attitudes.[36] Professor Sipprelle was, of course, mixing "straight facts" with ironic statements contrary to his real meaning and with exaggerations ("status of senility and incompetence"). Maggie Kuhn's postretirement activities made it unmistakable that Sipprelle did *not* believe she was senile in any degree at all. There are two important cautions about introducing ironic statements: (1) the audience *must* know that they are ironically, not seriously, meant, and (2) to treat ironically something the listeners take seriously is likely to offend them. Ironic treatment of anything communicates scorn for whatever is made fun of (compulsory retirement in Sipprelle's case), and listeners must also be willing to scoff a bit at the subject.

Climax is developed in language by attending to the arrangement of words, phrases, and sentences in series according to increasing value or strength. For example, notice the mounting sweep of "pledges" called for by Senator Edward Kennedy at the Democratic National Convention on August 12, 1980:

> Let us pledge that we will never misuse unemployment, high interest rates, and human misery as false weapons against inflation [applause].
> Let us pledge that employment will be the first priority of our economic policy [applause].
> Let us pledge that there will be security for all those who are now at work. And let us pledge that there will be jobs for all who are out of work.[37]

There has been much discussion and experimentation seeking to determine exactly how climactic arrangement persuades. This problem, which exists in disposition, is duplicated in miniature when we consider climax as a stylistic device. The best conclusion seems to be that structuring language in this fashion *can* add persuasiveness, but that under some circumstances creating an anticlimactic structure in which the strongest thought comes first rather than last can yield at least an equal persuasive force. We cannot advise you beyond saying that to emulate Senator Kennedy when you feel it would be wise to build up to a telling point cannot possibly take away from the force of your key idea and may significantly strengthen it.

Repetition is one of the surest and simplest means of emphasizing. This is simply the process of reiterating words or phrases or sentences to call special attention to ideas. Evidence from experience and experiments indicates that repeating does give ideas new emphasis. We all use this procedure, though we don't always realize we are doing it. In the following example we think the English major who composed the statement knew quite well that he was striving for emphasis of an important point. Said Mr. Felipe V. Ponce, Jr.:

> There are other reasons why this movement should be understood. If you're interested in politics, nine million people are hard to ignore. If you're interested in social problems, nine million people are hard to ignore. If you're interested in business, a market of nine million people is hard to ignore.[38]

Notice that Mr. Ponce not only repeated the figure he wanted to establish in listeners' minds, but he repeated the entire verbal construction, "nine million people are hard to ignore." Repetition within such parallel verbal structures is believed to further enhance emphasis. Notice, too, that Mr. Ponce has probably gone about as far as is safe with this particular repetitive pattern. Experimentation shows that after something has been repeated three times, less and less emphasis is gained from subsequent repetitions.

Alliteration is repetition of sounds in words or in stressed syllables within words. Judiciously used, the repeated sounds can hold listeners' attention to an emerging idea and can sometimes render the idea easier to remember. The first of these functions is surely served in this question taken from a speech by Hubert Humphrey: "Shall we sit in complacency, lulled by creature comforts, until we are engulfed in chaos?" [39] Sometimes repetition combines repetition of idea with repetition of sounds. This has the further power to reinforce the idea, as in Lincoln's sentence, "As our case is new, so we must think anew and act anew." The sound, therefore the meaning, of *new* is thrice repeated and *newness* is made easier to remember.

Personification is the endowment of objects, animals, or ideas with human attributes. They can by this means be given qualities that seem attractive, unattractive, powerful, weak, and so on. Or motives may be assigned to things that ordinarily would not be seen as motivated. Consider Leonard Bernstein's statement, "For Gilbert and Sullivan, along with those other geniuses, Johann Strauss and Offenbach, had led the American public straight into the arms of operetta." [40] Bernstein makes "the American public" fall in love with—not just accept—operetta as a musical form, and by doing so he probably reports more accurately than if he had said the public "accepted" or "became interested in" operettas.

Personification offers an exceedingly valuable way of making persuasive statements about abstract or inanimate things and ideas. Congress may be seen as a giant enmeshed in procedural details. The personifying metaphor clearly argues that congressional inactivity has a particular kind of cause and that the human capabilities of Congress are more or less painfully constrained. The possibilities of thus activating, humanizing, and arguing on behalf of your ideas should always be thought about as you make final choices in preparing to speak.

Synecdoche (sə-'nek-də(,)kē) is the substitution of parts for wholes or of wholes for parts of things. For example, a newspaper editor addressing a press association said of the decline of the Roman Empire:

> There was, indeed, just cause for gloom when into the palaces of the Caesars went Nero and Caligula, and when the once-noble Praetorian Guard became a gang of assassins willing to sell the throne to the top bidder.[41]

Here "palaces of the Caesars" stands for the entire Roman government in presumably better days, Nero and Caligula stand for a series of often decadent rulers, and "the throne" stands for the entire government again. As Chaim Perelman and L. Olbrechts-Tyteca point out, what happens when a part is thus made to stand for the whole of something or vice versa is that attention is focused on a characteristic aspect of the whole (the decadence of later emperors and the corruption of government). If an entire class is named to represent what is characteristic of a part (for example, "Scottish frugality informed his every move"), attention is then focused on a particular aspect of the individual part—one Scot. In each case the figure of speech focuses attention on specifics or on the general and makes the subtle argument that whatever can be associated with the part belongs also to the whole or whatever is associated with the whole belongs to the individual part.[42]

The catalog of figures of speech could be continued, for there are other ways of bending language to the service of special or emphatic meanings. The figures we have identified are those you use for special purposes in your day-to-day speech. They are figures that are common in English usage but are too seldom focused on as *usages that can drive points home with the strength of complicated arguments.* They are not, however, the forms of speech we use all of the time. We seem to save them for special moments of meaningfulness; hence, each startles listeners mildly and so momentarily rivets attention and potentially makes a unique set of claims about ideas and things.

A skilled speaker needs to know these special ways in which he or she can achieve emphasis and direct minds persuasively if subtly. A speaker who does not know and understand at least the usages we have discussed simply does not know the affective possibilities his language system offers him. He is inept, resembling a landscape contractor who knows everything about his business except the conditions under which plants thrive or die. To refine your access to the resources of language, reflect on why these figures of speech work as they do. Look for them in speeches you hear and read, examining what they achieve or fail to achieve for those speakers. Learn, too, the distinctions between figures of speech that are functionally useful and those that distract. In preparing to speak, review at some stage how figures might help— or hinder—when emphasis, vividness, and subtle argument are needed. There is nothing unusual about using figures of speech to create effects in listeners; what differentiates expert speakers from casual ones is that the experts choose their figures and understand their workings and casual speakers only follow habits and fads without knowing why.

Style emerges from choices and combinations of language. Its psychological impact has been the subject of investigation in the preceding pages. It is not decoration but a facet of speech derived from reasonable and imaginative management of words.

Wording and thinking are inseparable processes wherever communication deserves its name; hence, style in speaking must always be viewed as one more means to winning a particular set of responses under particular circumstances that comprise the rhetorical situation you enter as speaker.

Oral style cannot be separated from the whole act of speaking, except for purposes of analysis and discussion. Style, good or indifferent or bad, is present in all speech and influences response. Its qualities color listeners' perceptions of the entire rhetorical situation. Nonetheless, there is no universal set of stylistic qualities appropriate to all speakers, even though they may speak in comparable situations. This is why we have contended that each of you as speakers must understand for yourselves the verbal resources from among which you need to make fitting, *personal* choices for *specific* rhetorical situations.

EXERCISES

Written

1.   Below are the first, second, and final versions of a statement from Lincoln's "Gettysburg Address." In a paragraph or two discuss what language problems Lincoln tried to eliminate as he worked on the speech and which of the successive changes he made yielded gains (or losses) in effective communication of the ideas. Be sure to say *why* each change was an improvement or a regression in stylistic effectiveness.

  •   *First draft:* We have come to dedicate a portion of it as a final resting place for those who died here, that the nation might live.

  •   *Second draft:* We have come to dedicate a portion of it as a final resting place for those who here gave their lives that that nation might live.

  •   *Third draft:* We have come to dedicate a portion of that field, as a final resting place for those who here gave their lives that that nation might live.

2.   Choose a speech from *Vital Speeches* or from an anthology of public addresses. Study it carefully. Write an essay in which you (a) identify the major stylistic devices the speaker used to support ideas; (b) point out particular word choices that give special clarity, propriety, and economy to the language; and (c) identify instances in which figures of speech function argumentatively or otherwise persuasively.

3.   Rewrite the following sentences for oral delivery:

  a.   Therefore, it is evident that before you can provide an elucidation of the operational functions of the system for the propagation and dissemination of information, you would be required to make a thorough investigation of the public relations branch of the corporation.

  b.   If one had one's preference, one would be likely to hold a preference for one's own photographic equipment with which to photograph one's own favorite subjects.

  c.   Easily seen is the fact that the playing field is surrounded by a large metal fence over which the ball often passes when a home run is made.

  d.   Even although I had been selected to represent my college, had planned my itinerary to the meeting, which incidentally was held sixty miles from the college itself, had packed my clothing for the journey, which I did the night before, had reserved my seat in the airplane, which was a jet and was flight 107, and had persuaded my close friend, whose name was Mark Smith, to convey me to the airport, I was still in fear that the weather would prevent my going to the convention at all.

  e.   "Like I said," she said, "Jane's cheeks looked as red as roses, however, I discovered that the effect was all due to the application by her of cosmetic in large quantity."

4. Rewrite the following paragraph in such a way as to give it the motion-picture quality discussed in the section of this chapter devoted to liveliness.

> My most embarrassing experience was when I was a boy. It was the result of my getting into a place I had no business being. I had crawled under our old back porch and had found some paint cans. I pried off the tops with a stick. Then I had put my hands into one can after another. First I put them into a can of green paint. Then I put them into a can of red paint, and then into a can of yellow. The color which resulted was an ugly brown. When I finally finished, my clean clothes had paint dribbled all over them. I was a mess. What was embarrassing though was that I couldn't get the paint off. After a licking by my mother, a bottle of turpentine was given to me, and I tried to get the paint off with that. I rubbed and rubbed with a cloth, but there was so much paint it just wouldn't come off. I was embarrassed for a whole week because it was summertime, and I looked as if I were wearing a pair of brown gloves. I guess I felt most foolish when my piano teacher came to give me my lesson and I had to explain why my hands were as they were. I also felt very foolish on Sunday. I was sure that everybody was looking at my hands when I was up there singing in the choir.

5. a. Identify the kinds of imagery used in the following passage taken from a speech by a college student on scenes depicted in early, silent movies.

> The quiet rural atmosphere had been effectively shattered. Chickens and feathers flew fast and furiously from both sides of the road. Cattle, only a moment before peacefully pastured, ran in aimless directions. Farmers' horses became frightened and reared into the air. A low-slung sports car, flashing and brilliant yellow in the afternoon sunlight, thundered through the rural village, a beautiful blonde movie queen at the wheel. An aroused policeman hauled the straw-haired beauty over to the side of the road, arrested her, and brought her before a justice of the peace who fined her five dollars. The indignant beauty thrust a 10 dollar bill into his hand and stalked out of the courtroom. "Just a minute," shouted the judge, "your change." "Keep it," she hurled back as she hopped into the auto, "I'm going out of here a hell of a lot faster than I came in." [43]

   b. Identify the figures of speech used in the above passage.
   c. List the kinds of imagery *not* used.
   d. Write a paragraph commenting upon strengths and weaknesses for speech in the rhetorical style of the passage.

Oral

1. Compose and deliver a two-minute persuasive talk in which you use (a) at least three figures of speech and (b) at least three kinds of imagery.
2. Using a speech you delivered during a prior session of your class and drawing on what you now know about style, rework the speech or a portion of it and deliver it again. Discuss the effects of your deliberate stylistic changes with your listeners.

3.   Some subjects are harder to talk about in words than others. For example, it is more difficult to find words to describe an abstract painting than it is to find words to describe an automobile. As an exercise in expanding your awareness of linguistic resources, prepare a short talk on one of the following subjects or a comparable subject:

a.   How abstract art tries to communicate.

b.   *Form* as communication.

c.   Red and yellow are warm colors.

d.   "Quick hands" are essential in a basketball player.

e.   Charisma is a quality public leaders need.

f.   Here's what to look for in (a statue, a piece of jewelry, tailoring in clothing, a top-quality first baseman, or other quality-oriented items of a similar sort).

g.   The reason this (car, book, movie, music group) was the best I've seen or heard is _____ .

ENDNOTES

1.   Thomas Wilson, *Arte of Rhetorique* (London, 1585), p. 162.

2.   Unsigned interview with then Israeli Foreign Minister Abba Eban, "in late June of 1967" and published under the title, "Speaker," *New Yorker* XLVI (November 14, 1970): 45–48. The passage quoted is on p. 46.

3.   E. D. Hirsch, Jr., *The Philosophy of Composition* (Chicago: University of Chicago Press, 1977), p. 21.

4.   See, for example, Gladys L. Borchers, "An Approach to the Problem of Oral Style," *Quarterly Journal of Speech* XXII (February 1936): 114–17; Gordon Thomas, "Effect of Oral Style on Intelligibility of Speech," *Speech Monographs* XXIII (March 1956): 46–54; Joseph A. De Vito, "Comprehension Factors in Oral and Written Discourse of Skilled Communicators," *Speech Monographs* XXXII (June 1965): 124–28; James W. Gibson, Charles R. Gruner, Robert J. Kibler, and Francis J. Kelly, "A Quantitative Examination of Differences and Similarities in Written and Spoken Messages," *Speech Monographs* XXXIII (November 1966): 444–51. The last study includes a valuable survey of contemporary studies of oral and written style. Hirsch, in the work cited in note 3, reviews a good deal of historical and linguistic research on differences between "oral speech" and "written speech."

5.   From *The Rhetoric of Aristotle,* translated and edited by Lane Cooper, p. 217, bk. III, chap. 12. © 1932, renewed 1960 by Lane Cooper. Reprinted by permission of Prentice-Hall, Inc., Englewood Cliffs, New Jersey.

6.   This text was edited by L. LeRoy Cowperthwaite using an official stenographic report, Roosevelt's own manuscript, and an audio recording. The text from which this excerpt comes appears in full in C. C. Arnold, D. Ehninger, and J. C. Gerber, eds., *Speaker's Resource Book* (Chicago: Scott, Foresman, 1966), 2nd ed., pp. 135–39.

7.   *The Rhetoric of Aristotle,* translated and edited by Lane Cooper, p. 185, bk. III, chap. 2. © 1932, renewed 1960 by Lane Cooper. Reprinted by permission of Prentice-Hall, Inc., Englewood Cliffs, New Jersey.

8.   You will find Rudolph Flesch's *The Art of Plain Talk* (New York: Harper & Brothers, 1946) exceedingly helpful and informative on this point and others. The work deals chiefly with writing, but the principles and methods discussed are valuable to speakers.

9.   Leonard Bernstein, *The Joy of Music* (New York: Simon and Schuster, 1959), pp. 16–17. Copyright © 1954, 1955, 1956, 1957, 1958, 1959, by Leonard Bernstein. Reprinted by permission of Simon and Schuster, Inc.

10. *The Rhetoric of Aristotle*, p. 185, bk. III, chap. 2.

11. Spencer, *The Philosophy of Style,* New York: D. Appleton, 1920, p. 11.

12. Ibid.

13. Spencer, *The Philosophy of Style,* p. 33.

14. Flesch, *The Art of Plain Talk,* p. 42.

15. From Leonard Bernstein's televised lecture "The World of Jazz," in *The Joy of Music.* © 1959. Used by permission of Simon and Schuster, New York. The text of this lecture is also available in Arnold, Ehninger, and Gerber, eds., *The Speaker's Resource Book,* pp. 67–76.

16. Longinus, "On the Sublime," trans. W. Rhys Roberts, in J. H. Smith and E. W. Parks, *The Great Critics,* 3rd ed. (New York: W. W. Norton, 1951), p. 95.

17. Ibid., pp. 95–96.

18. Georges Louis Leclerc, Count de Buffon, "Discours sur le Style," in Lane Cooper, ed., *The Art of the Writer: Essays, Excerpts, and Translations* (Ithaca, N.Y.: Cornell University Press, 1952), p. 151.

19. *The Rhetoric of Aristotle,* p. 185, bk. III, chap. 2.

20. C. S. Baldwin, *Ancient Rhetoric and Poetic* (Gloucester, Mass.: Peter Smith, 1959), p. 247.

21. *The Rhetoric of Aristotle,* translated and edited by Lane Cooper, pp. 207–8, bk. III, chap. 10. © 1932, renewed 1960 by Lane Cooper. Reprinted by permission of Prentice-Hall, Inc., Englewood Cliffs, New Jersey.

22. Ibid., p. 208, bk. III, chap. 10.

23. Ibid., p. 211, bk. III, chap. 11.

24. Ibid., p. 212, bk. III, chap. 11.

25. Ibid., p. 211, bk. III, chap. 11.

26. Chaim Perelman and L. Olbrechts-Tyteca, *The New Rhetoric: A Treatise on Argumentation,* trans. John Wilkinson and Purcell Weaver (Notre Dame: University of Notre Dame Press, 1969), p. 168.

27. Ibid., p. 169.

28. Peter Marshall, "Letters in the Sand," in Catherine Marshall, *A Man Called Peter* (New York: McGraw-Hill, 1951), p. 322.

29. Daniel O'Connell, "Speech at Tara." From text collated by William E. White in "Daniel O'Connell's Oratory on Repeal," unpublished dissertation, University of Wisconsin at Madison, 1954.

30. Richard Nixon, "Resignation Speech," nationally telecast from Washington, D.C. From text as published in *Time* Magazine, August 19, 1974, p. 14.

31. For valuable and thorough treatments of the rhetorical metaphor, see: Michael M. Osborn and Douglas Ehninger, "The Metaphor in Public Address," *Speech Monographs* XXIX (August 1962): 223–34; John Waite Bowers and Osborn, "Attitudinal Effects of Selected Types of Concluding Metaphors in Persuasive Speeches," *Speech Monographs* XXXIII (June 1966): 147–55; Osborn, "Archetypal Metaphor in Rhetoric: The Light-Dark Family," *Quarterly Journal of Speech* LIII (April 1967): 115–26; Osborn, "The Evolution of the Theory of Metaphor in Rhetoric," *Western Speech* XXXI (Spring 1967): 121–31.

32. Ronald Reagan, "Acceptance Address," Republican National Convention, Detroit, July 17, 1980. Text transcribed from national broadcast of the address.

33. John F. Kennedy, "Inaugural Address," in Wil A. Linkugel, R. R. Allen, and R. L. Jo-

hannesen, eds., *Contemporary American Speeches* 2nd ed. (Belmont, Calif.: Wadsworth Publishing, 1969), p. 300.

34.   Robert F. Kennedy, "Speech Delivered to the Friendly Sons of St. Patrick of Lackawanna County, Scranton, Pennsylvania," in Thomas A. Hopkins, ed., *Rights for Americans: The Speeches of Robert F. Kennedy* (Indianapolis: Bobbs-Merrill, 1964), p. 195.

35.   Carl Sipprelle, *Stereotypes and Alternative Life-Styles in Aging* (Vermillion, S.D.: College of Arts and Sciences, University of South Dakota, n.d.), p. 1. This speech was the twenty-eighth Annual Harrington Lecture at the University of South Dakota and was delivered on February 19, 1980.

36.   Two studies by Charles R. Gruner encourage these judgments. See "An Experimental Study of Satire as Persuasion," *Speech Monographs* XXXII (June 1965): 149–53, and "A Further Experimental Study of Satire as Persuasion," ibid., XXXIII (June 1966): 184–85. We are, of course, inferring that the effects of irony are probably comparable to the effects of its sustained form, satire.

37.   From the text as printed in the *New York Times*.

38.   The title of Mr. Ponce's speech was "La Causa." The speech was given in a course in Speech Composition at Indiana University in 1971. The text is found in Linkugel, Allen, and Johannesen, *Contemporary American Speeches*, pp. 66–70.

39.   Hubert H. Humphrey, "The Open Door," in Linkugel, Allen, and Johannesen, *Contemporary American Speeches*, p. 243.

40.   Leonard Bernstein, "American Musical Comedy," in H. Bruce Kendall and Charles J. Stewart, *On Speech and Speakers* (New York: Holt, Rinehart & Winston, 1968), p. 287.

41.   Jenkin Lloyd Jones, "Who Is Tampering with the Soul of America?" Mr. Jones, editor of the *Tulsa Tribune*, gave this address on more than one occasion. The text used here appeared in *Vital Speeches of the Day* XVIII (January 1, 1962): 180–83.

42.   For fuller discussion see Perelman and Olbrechts-Tyteca, *The New Rhetoric*, pp. 334–37.

43.   From the manuscript of a speech entitled "Seven Years of Silent Excitement," by Nelson T. Joyner, Jr.

CHAPTER 10

Delivery

Where can you apply the principles of this chapter in everyday life?

1. Wherever you communicate without using words.
2. Wherever you support what you say with movement, gesture, facial expression, or eye movements.
3. Wherever you communicate in a familiar or new physical setting.
4. Wherever you use your voice.
5. Wherever you read aloud.

When evaluating someone else's speech consider:

1. Was each idea realized as it was uttered?
2. Was there a "keen sense of communication"?
3. Was eye contact adequate?
4. Did the speaker's posture reinforce the verbal message?
5. Did the speaker move about meaningfully while speaking?
6. Did gestures reinforce verbal meanings? Why or why not?
7. Was the speaker easily heard and understood by all auditors?
8. Was voice used appropriately as far as rate, pitch, and quality were concerned?
9. Was the speaker fluent?

After surveying empirical research on delivery as an influence in communicative speaking, an author wrote:

> In summary: (1) visible action does not harm communication and perhaps helps; (2) certain deficiencies in the audible code, though listeners consider them unpleasant, do not affect comprehension. The conclusion to draw from the second point is not that speakers should cease striving for excellence, for clearly good delivery does no harm. The meaning rather is that in the whole complex of content, style, arrangement, and delivery no one presentational element, such as fluency or voice quality, is likely to affect the outcome significantly.[1]

There is still no clear evidence that any particular presentational behavior will surely affect your listeners' responses if that behavior is within those listeners' range of previous experiences. Nonetheless, problems of oral delivery have preoccupied speakers and theorists since the beginnings of Western thought about speech communication (see pages 327–32).

One is tempted to believe that this pervasive concern with aspects of delivery reflects inner needs and insecurities of speakers more than the pragmatic demands of rhetorical situations. The persistent search for "sure-fire rules" of delivery has produced none.

Because we believe the *way* you *think* about speaking is crucial to whether you speak well or ill, we want to preface discussion of *your* delivery with some comment on the chief ways delivery has been thought about in the last century and a half. Important cautions for all of us are embedded in that record.

Energetic attempts to create rule systems reflect speakers' desires to guard against uncertainties in speech. We do take risks when we speak. We know physical and vocal actions furnish cues by which other people judge our worth and self-control. So the question repeatedly raised is: can the risks of speaking be minimized by framing and following *rules* of delivery?

Four approaches have been used in attempts to achieve effective delivery: the *imitative* (which recommends copying the delivery skills of others); the *mechanical* (which recommends deriving and following rules based on empirical analysis of what people *do*); the *impulsive* (which throws caution to the winds, rejecting thought about delivery); and *think-the-thought* (which recommends concentrating on ideas, sometimes urging disregard of body and voice or sometimes urging particular ways of thinking about them).[2]

NONVERBAL COMMUNICATION

During the past twenty years there has been renewed interest in delivery, especially in bodily action as communication. Scholars and popular writers have turned their attention to *nonverbal communication* (also called *action communication, action lan-*

guage, and *body language*). Using the methods of science, they have tried to identify, classify, and explain the sources and effects of those aspects of human behavior that do not involve words. Exactly what "nonverbal communication" means and does not mean is not yet agreed on.[3] The major difficulty with this phrase is given by Abne Eisenberg and Ralph Smith:

> All communication except that which is coded in words is generally referred to as *nonverbal communication.* This rubric is in one way unsatisfactory. The term "nonverbal" aggregates different kinds of behavior which have in common only the quality of not being structured by a linguistic system. Like the term "nonhuman," which covers an infinity of life forms from protozoa to gorillas, nonverbal denotes that which is *not* included in the concept "verbal," but it tells us little about what *is* included.[4]

On the other hand, no entirely satisfactory substitute has been found for use when we want to refer to the behaviors that accompany words in oral communication.

These nonlinguistic aspects of our messages have some unique features, as contemporary scholars have pointed out. (1) At least when we are responding to them, nonverbal communicative functions seem continuous, whereas the sounds we hear seem to have beginnings and ends. Because of starts and stops anyone can choose *not* to talk verbally, but no one can choose not to communicate nonverbally. (2) Nonverbal communication is taken in through several senses simultaneously. You can feel, smell, see, and hear a nonverbal message and its source at one and the same moment. In contrast, verbal cues are taken in by fewer of the sense organs.[5] (3) Nonverbal cues yield less cognitive content than verbal ones because language can easily indicate objects and relationships. (4) Nonverbal cues are in many instances better suited for projections of emotional states.[6] (5) It may well be that we take in nonverbal cues and interpret them in ways quite different from those we use when taking in and interpreting verbal language.[7]

The specific aspects of nonverbal communication most studied today are paralanguage, proxemics, and kinesics. The study of *paralanguage* is concerned with voice set and nonverbal vocalizations. The influence of vocal properties such as resonance, rhythm, rate, and pitch and the effects of sounds such as *ums* and *ers* and silences between words fall within the purview of this class of nonverbal communication. *Proxemics,* a second broad category of nonverbal communication, deals with the spatial relationships that exist between a speaker's body and other people or objects in communicative settings. *Kinesics* or body movement has been viewed as a separate kind of communication by means of facial expression, head action, posture, walking, and gestures made by the arms and hands. Kinesics as defined by its originator, Ray Birdwhistell, is a system for classifying body language much as linguistic systems classify elements of language. Whether there is a "vocabulary" and a "grammar" of bodily action is at present seriously disputed.[8] However you interpret the processes, Birdwhistell's finding that the human face alone is capable of 250,000 different expressions [9] suggests the complexity of signals we give each other without words. Other striking findings by students of kinesics include Albert Mehrabian's claim that 55 percent of the impact of a face-to-face spoken message derives from facial expression and 38 percent from vocal features; however, these estimates seem to apply only where a listener sees the verbal and the nonverbal messages as inconsistent with one another. A generalization coming from experimentation with eye movement asserts that the closer people are to one another the less they make direct eye contact in communicating.[10]

Such findings underscore the *presence* of vast amounts of bodily and vocal activity accompanying verbal communication and the *possibility* that a great proportion of it has symbolic significance. However, as Knapp, Wiemann, and Daly point out, "researchers are increasingly realizing that matters of meaning in human communication need to consider the co-occurrences of verbal and nonverbal behavior."[11] We do not have much evidence concerning just how and when nonverbal and verbal behaviors communicate together or in conflict with one another. A psychiatrist and a psychologist wrote several years ago:

> We do not know (unambiguously) how we interpret body messages and we disagree (to some extent) about the end results of our interpretations. Was so-and-so being defensive, rejecting, or shy? Do vivid gestures indicate lively emotionality and spontaneity, or merely a hysterical and basically shallow search for theatrical effects? Do presentationally still waters run deep? Is it true that a person whose pelvis and lower extremities move awkwardly is emotionally out of touch with his lower body? ... Until the present, psychology and the social sciences have ... expanded the disagreements by elaborating various incompatible procedures for eliminating ambiguity. Something parallel to criticism ... in the arts is needed in the social sciences.[12]

Despite the impression created by popular books and articles, the situation has not improved as this book goes to press.

The recent investigations of nonverbal behaviors, apparently associated with communication, have for the most part failed to take *public* communication into consideration. What is chiefly implied for public speech is that recognition and adaptation to nonverbal feedback from audiences may be even more important and subtle than has been supposed. One pair of authors has said:

> The effective group member or public speaker constantly surveys his auditors to judge their reaction to him and his ideas. Even a group or audience that appears to be relatively passive sends many messages about their degree of involvement and acceptance of what is being said. Failure to look at the speaker, small nervous gestures, an overly relaxed posture, can all signal boredom.[13]

The other side of the coin is that your listeners will be "reading" *you* constantly. The evidence is becoming quite clear that, when a speaker says one thing but his or her nonverbal behaviors seem to convey an inconsistent message, listeners at first tend to be puzzled; if the inconsistency between the two messages is not promptly resolved, they are apt to reject the speaker and the verbal message.[14] We will be referring to the importance of feedback and consistency between verbal and nonverbal messages as we explore the general potentialities of delivery in the remainder of this chapter.

GENERAL PRINCIPLES OF DELIVERY

On the basis of common sense and the research we have just surveyed, the fundamental principle all speakers must respect in order to be effective is that *vocal and physical activity must be consistently supportive of one another if clear and acceptable meanings are to be communicated.* Translated into an overall guideline for all speakers, this principle says that *good delivery helps the listener concentrate on what is being said; it does not attract attention to itself.* There are no hard and fast rules by which consistency among bodily, vocal, and verbal activities is achieved and sustained, but several guidelines will, if followed, assist you toward that goal.

1. *Monitor your delivery to make it generate and show response to emotional and physical experiences of listeners.* Your delivery must communicate your goals to the listeners. It must also signal that you are receiving and adapting to signals from the listeners.

A fundamental task once invention, disposition, and language have been duly considered is to conceive of the sort of delivery that will *show* your full meanings to your audience. Just thinking about and discussing how speakers maintain lively contact with listeners and generate desirable emotional and physical experience can make your behavior more natural and conversational. A recent experiment showed that inexperienced speakers who had considered and discussed using feedback from listeners subsequently used dramatically fewer *ahs, ers,* and other vocal signs of unease than similar speakers who had given no special thought to capturing and responding to feedback cues from audiences.[15] In short, just knowing there *are* messages for you out there and determining to respond to them are likely to help you monitor your delivery and generate among listeners the kinds of emotional and physical experiences that will reinforce your message.

2. *Don't speak to perform or to exhibit yourself.* Concentrate on meanings. Make what you have to say plainly first in your concerns. Let manner be your *means.* The danger of inconsistency between verbal and physical messages rises whenever your actions suggest that your thoughts are on yourself more than on the ideas and feelings you are verbally communicating. Your mission should never be to show off your body, your grace, or your clothing.

3. *So keep your mind on the meaning of what you say as you speak.* To create or recreate ideas vividly at the moment they are being uttered means that you reactivate a subject and ideas to support it, that you regenerate the enthusiasm that led you to speak in the first place. This enthusiasm must last from the first moments of preparation through the last syllable of your speech. You must be in control of assimilated ideas so they are at your bidding. You must have become so intimately acquainted with them as you structured, worded, and orally rehearsed them that no matter what happens during the actual presentation of your speech, you will be master of your feelings and of your audience's responses. Professor Winans, who formulated this precept, said:

> ... There should be full and sharp realization of content. And this includes more than bare meaning; the implications and emotional content must also be realized.

The reference here is not merely to those striking emotions commonly recognized as such, but also to those attitudes and significances constantly present in lively discourse: the greater or less importance of this or that statement, the fact that this is an assertion and this a concession (with an implied "granted" or "to be sure"), this is a matter of course while this has an element of surprise, and so on through all possible changes.[16]

No matter how well you know your materials, you ought to give the impression of meeting the ideas for the first time. What was alive as you prepared and as you rehearsed must come to life again. The process of speaking must be one of creation, then re-creation for the sakes of listeners.

4. *Cultivate a keen sense of communication.* This guideline we also borrow from Professor Winans. Thinking of speaking in public as dialogue rather than soliloquy will help you achieve this sense. Talk *with* your audience, not *at* them. Try to feel in your speaker's position what you feel in talk with your friends over the dinner table, on the athletic field, or in bull sessions. We experience the sense of sharing minds daily. This is the sense you should try to recapture in public speaking. As Professor Winans said:

> We should make sure in our efforts to bring this communicative tone into our delivery that it springs from mental attitude; for it ... should [not] be assumed as a trick of delivery. The attempt to assume it is likely to result in an over familiar, confidential, or wheedling note which is most objectionable.[17]

5. *Be direct.* People are seldom evasive when they are in earnest. Look the audience in the eye. If you look at your audience, they will look back at you. Looking at a spot on the back wall will not produce directness. You will give the impression that you are in a trance. A dead-fish stare while you call up ideas and wordings will not do. Neither will darting your eyes from person to person or addressing one side of the audience to the exclusion of the other. In the first instance eye contact will be so fleeting that it will be no contact at all. In the second, a whole segment of the audience will think that you have ignored them.

Your eyes are decidedly expressive parts of your face. Haven't they been called "the windows of the soul"? More than other parts of your body, eyes and mouth reveal your emotions. So you should face front and direct your eyes to your listeners. Try looking at a segment of the audience or at one or two people in a particular area of the room as you develop an idea. When you have finished with that idea, and as you start the next one, direct your gaze to another part of the audience. As you move to subsequent ideas, refocus each time.

Directness is fundamentally a matter of direct eye contact. If you attain directness, that will also promote vocal directness.

6. *Punctuate and support your ideas with your body and your voice.* In speech making, facial expressions, gestures, pitch changes, variations in vocal rate and volume, pauses, shifts in posture, and walking take the place of the commas, italics, exclamation points, and question marks in written communication. Therefore, intelligibility and clarification often depend greatly on support and emphasis from your

physique. Learn to use *yourself* often and with control. Some special considerations in this connection are discussed in the next section, "Bodily Action."

7. *All aspects of your delivery should promote conversational quality.* If the ways you say things have the qualities we have referred to in discussing the six previous guidelines, your speech will tend to be much like your best conversation: meaningful, reflective of content, clearly intended for listeners, direct, and supported by natural physical and vocal behavior. But the larger your audience and the more formal your situation, the more your presentation will need to differ mechanically but *not in manner or intention* from everyday conversation. We noted differences between conversation and public speech in Chapter 1 (pages 7–8). Public speech contrasts with conversation in that we speak louder, are relatively uninterrupted, focus attention more sharply, are more systematically prepared, and have less opportunity to perceive auditors' responses in detail. But effective formal speaking still retains important characteristics of good conversation: directness, spontaneity, animation, and emphasis. It is, therefore, conversational in *quality* though not in *style*. Reproduced conversation does not satisfy. Public speech needs to sound like conversation enlarged —more dignified, more systematic, and more forceful than conversation under informal circumstances. Yet as far as is possible, a speech maker has to suggest to listeners that his or her *attitudes* toward them remain essentially those of one person conversing with others.

8. *Focus the attention of the audience on meaning.* Influence of some sort is any public speaker's goal. Manner must direct attention to the meaning of the moment. The task is not only to direct attention toward basic meaning; one must also act in ways that exclude irrelevant stimuli that might produce interfering noise. Manner of delivery can often displace distractions that come from other sources—a flapping window shade, a smell from a laboratory down the hall, your listeners' fatigue. If strong stimuli stem from your behavior, such interference can be overcome. Bodily movement and vocal variations are always available to you as means of specially focusing or refocusing listeners' attention. We will now discuss the specific physical resources open to you for this kind of control over attention.

BODILY ACTION

Your chief instruments of delivery in managing the attention of listeners are physical actions involving your face, limbs, and torso; your management of space within which you and your listeners relate to one another; and your voice. We shall consider physical action first.

Qualities of effective bodily action

The questions students ask about bodily action tend to be: how shall I walk? How shall I stand? How shall I move about? What shall I do with my hands? How can I show the right feelings in my face? Such questions are natural, but they are posed in the wrong way. They imply that some mechanical planning and execution of movement will achieve genuine communication. Possibly this is true for some actors some of the time, but even that possibility is debated by professional dramatic artists. Most people who speak in public are not actors whose bodies have been subjected to long and rigorous discipline. For those of us who are not, our bodily actions usually are reflections of our real private feelings and thoughts. We are not going to change that except by years of special training. So let us accept the fact that most of the time we behave as we feel and think. Then what is the best way of thinking about communicating bodily? It is to *think* communicatively and let your bodily action reflect that thinking. If your body does not respond conventionally, you will need to retrain it—but *not* while you are trying to make intellectual or emotional points with real audiences. We have provided some "retraining" exercises at the end of this chapter. They may help you strip away habits that inhibit you from responding physically to the communicative thoughts you have.

If inhibiting habits do not interfere, what should be the characteristics of your bodily action—your walking, standing, and general use of the space about you?

1. Your action should reveal that you are concentrating totally on your message and your listeners' involvement with it.
2. Your activity should contribute to your own comfort by being easy, unlabored, and unhampered.
3. All action should direct listeners' attention where your immediate purpose requires.
4. All of your actions should reinforce, illustrate, and enhance your immediate meanings.
5. Your actions should never contradict what your words are saying.
6. Your actions should be consistent with the conventions of nonverbal communication the audience is used to, should be in keeping with the relationships you are trying to generate, and should imply that you are seriously trying to resolve the exigences of your rhetorical situation.

The reason your communicative activity needs these qualities is that wherever these qualities are missing, your listeners will find inconsistency between what your words say and what your nonverbal actions say. Then you are in danger of invoking the *double bind* of interpersonal communication, which

> ... predicts that individuals will respond to inconsistent messages in one of the following ways: (1) they will attempt unsuccessfully to determine the literal meaning of the inconsistent message; (2) they will increase their level of concentration as they search diligently for what they believe to be overlooked clues that will clarify the meaning of the message; (3) they will withdraw from further involvement with the message sender.[18]

Gestures

The aspect of bodily action that troubles beginning speakers most is gesture. Gestures ought to conform to the six characteristics of effective bodily action we have just listed.

But because they seem to be of so much concern to speakers, we will make some special points about them.

Gestures are usually thought of as movements of hands and arms. They ought to grow out of your own feelings and meanings, but you should recognize that you

> ...can use gestures *descriptively* as well as *suggestively*. If you refer to a straight line, why not *draw* one in the air? If you refer to the blackboard, point to it—but do not stare at it; maintain contact with your audience. It may be more efficient to make an angle with two hands than to stop to draw the angle on the blackboard. Gestures are expressions of feeling and meaning, yes; but gestures can also be descriptive visual aids. To support your ideas fully, you should use gestures in this way as well as to suggest attitudes and feelings.[19]

To communicate effectively, gestures of any sort need to be *energetic, well coordinated, well timed, integrated with other bodily movement, normal for you,* and *appropriate to your meaning and feeling.* The inadequacy we see most often in student speakers is failure to gesture *fully.* Inner meaning causes a hand to be raised or a finger to be pointed at something or someone, but the movement is only partial so it does not really communicate its meaning. The hand only flutters or the finger only flinches. When inner meaning tells you to communicate with your body, *do it;* but do it *fully,* not indecisively.

It is also worth remembering consciously that the larger your audience, the broader your gestures will have to be to be easily seen and understood. Intimate situations allow subtle movements to be communicated, but large rooms and halls do not.

MANAGING SPACES AND FACILITIES

Whether you speak extemporaneously, read, or both, the physical features of your situation are resources and restraints. In the main, your command over your bodily action is your prime means of adjusting to spatial opportunities and restraints. Your relation to *things,* and your listeners' relations to them and to each other, are objects and forces to be commanded by your manner. Of course, in an open, spacious setting you will ordinarily have to move considerably more and use broader gestures than in a more confining space. But students of *proxemics,* the study of distances and their influences on communicators, draw attention to more subtle influences of space and distance on communicative effect.

You have probably passed up opportunities to look, before speaking, at what spaces and furnishings were available for your use in a room where you were to speak. But salespeople, lecturers, and office personnel often study systematically what positions, postures, and furnishings give them communicative advantages and which present disadvantages to be overcome by special adaptations of delivery.

Your adjustments to spatial conditions will be partly vocal, and we shall consider them next, but command of the spaces around you and your listeners is significantly a matter of regulating physical activity—yours and the listeners'. In these respects adjustments can *always* be made if a speaker is alert to them. If for example, there is no lectern or desk about which to center your speaking, what shall you do? Choose an imaginary "center" around which and from which to communicate. It is the *space* you use, not a furnishing, that determines from what spot you should speak. If there are no electrical sockets in the room or the only one is at the rear of the room, you must devise some way of presenting your message without using electrical equipment, get the audience to turn around, or engage an assistant to run your machinery. Where the furnishings are movable, perhaps you can arrange them or have them arranged in a new way so that you can better command the arranged space and your listeners will find it easier to attend to what you present. The central fact to remember is that *you* are the most versatile part of every setting in which you speak. *You* can move in any way you wish; *you* can gesture broadly or intimately; *you* can draw diagrams in the air; *you* can speak loudly or softly; and *you* can do just with words and gestures what you yearn to do with charts, easels, overhead projectors, or other ideal aids.

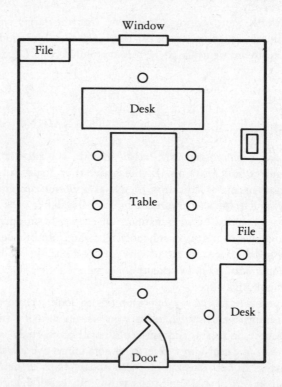

FIGURE 10–1 *Office arrangement*

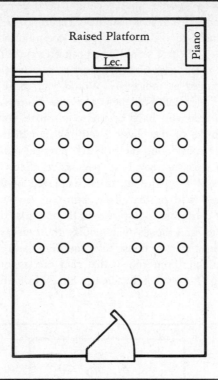

FIGURE 10–2 *Meeting room A*

There is really nothing complicated about this problem of commanding the spaces and spatial relationships of settings for speaking. Common sense solves most of the difficulties—not ideally perhaps, but adequately. To show you how true this is, we give you some problem situations in which we have spoken. In several of them we have watched students try to make speeches and conduct meetings. Use your common sense and your knowledge of the human relations of effective speaking to work out acceptable spatial movement problems presented by the rooms represented in Figures 10–1, 10–2, 10–3, and 10–4.

We invite you to consider: (a) What does the arrangement of the office space pictured in Figure 10–1 "announce" about the two faculty members occupying this space? (b) How would you want to rearrange this office if you and the other desk occupant wished to signal to others that you were of *equal* importance? (c) Where would you stand or sit to make a report in this room? If there were a blackboard on the otherwise blank wall of the room, would that make any difference in the speaking position you would choose for a report? Would you need to have any auditors shift their positions then? Where and why?

Ask further how a sensible speaker ought to direct his or her movements behind and around the lectern as it is placed in Figure 10–2. What would a speaker have to do by movement to maintain effective communication with the audience indicated in Figure 10–3? Where would you position yourself in Figure 10–4 if you were to preside over a meeting or make a report to ten people gathered in the room with the furniture arranged as indicated? Would you move any of the furniture? If you will make your judgments on these and like matters and discuss them with friends and colleagues, you will have begun to sensitize yourself to the uses (and abuses) speakers can make of the physical settings in which they talk.

Another benefit of considering carefully the physical settings in which you speak is that you will often discover they have persuasive effects. It is no accident that portraits of the leaders of the party are often displayed in the halls where national political conventions are held or that flags, bunting, emblems of brotherhoods or unions, of parties and patriotism, adorn the walls and platforms of meeting rooms. These create atmospheres and moods that modify the persuasiveness of what is said in such places. These inanimate symbols have meanings and stir up memories. They are there because it has long been known that they are important in reinforcing certain kinds of speaking. It was not by chance that Hitler often spoke in gigantic

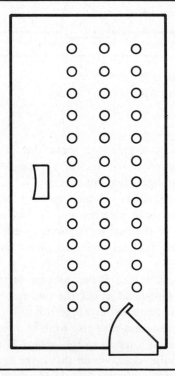

FIGURE 10–3 *Meeting room B*

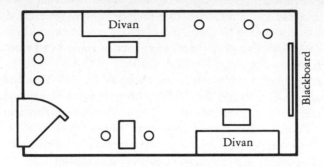

FIGURE 10–4   *Meeting room C*

stadiums at night with flags massed, torches flaming, and drums beating or that there were bugles blaring before his entrance into these carefully staged settings. Nor was it by chance that Mussolini always spoke from balconies, which he had built to order when none was available. Neither is it strange that speeches before mobs seem to get most effect if delivered from elevated places above the crowds or before symbolic façades. Words uttered in such settings have different meanings from the same words delivered in the sometimes sterile and cold settings of college lecture halls.

The place in which you deliver a speech, then, is first a space in which to move; second, it creates a part of the situation, especially if it contains visible symbols that will reinforce what you have to say or detract from it. Your task is to calculate ways to use or counteract the space and the symbols in the midst of which you try to attain your purposes.

VOICE

It is impossible to conceive of ordinary speech consisting of gestures alone. All public speech requires vocal ability.

Management of your voice, then, ought to be of concern to you. You must be able to use your voice flexibly. *Yet a sound course in public speaking cannot be a course in voice training.* Voice improvement is best achieved by individual work on poor habits or by a separate course of study. Poor vocal habits ought to be remedied by private exercise and practice. Public, group exercises consume valuable time that ought to be devoted to speech making.

Minimal vocal competence means you will (1) be heard, (2) be understood clearly, and (3) be free from annoying vocal habits and distortions. Most of us can fulfill these minimal requirements. Some fail to meet them because they have acquired poor habits in forming particular sounds—a *p* sounds like a *b, th* like a *d,* or an *l* like a *w*. Others' voices rasp, so the quality distracts. But most of us are endowed with adequate physical equipment for acceptable voice production. We make sounds that are usually heard and understood. We may be sloppy, yet every day we convert ideas into sounds that convey meaning. But everyone can do better. Even the Laurence Oliviers and Paul Newmans, after years of experience, continue to exercise their vocal mechanisms to improve intelligibility and quality.

Voice, like action, must be under the speaker's control. You must think about what you are saying. You should not "speak with your mind on your larynx," but you ought to pay attention to understandability and vocal flexibility. To attain clearness and variety a speaker needs to be generally acquainted with the process of producing meaningful sounds and with the variables of vocal expression: articulation, volume, rate, pitch, and quality. He or she cannot otherwise exercise control.

Voice production

Speech is an *overlaid function* of the speech organs because each of them has some other primary purpose such as breathing or swallowing. Inspiration takes place as air is taken into the lungs through the nose and/or mouth, passed through the pharynx (throat), the larynx (voice box, vocal folds, or Adam's apple), the trachea (windpipe), the bronchi, and the bronchial tubes. (See Figure 10–5.) As air fills the lungs, they expand; the chest walls within which they are contained move outward and upward to create the partial vacuum that causes this lung expansion. The muscles that control the actions of the ribs come into play in the expansion of the rib cage. During this action, the front wall of the abdomen also expands as the diaphragm—the muscular floor of the chest and the roof of the abdomen—moves downward, compressing the visceral organs. When the rib muscles and the diaphragm relax, the latter moving upward in a recoiling action, the size of the chest cavity is again reduced and the air forced out of the lungs and through the trachea. As this exhalation takes place, the air passes through the larynx, between the vocal folds that vibrate to produce sound as the air passes through the glottis (the opening between the vocal folds). The length and thickness of the vocal folds and their state of tension are responsible for the pitch of the voice produced.

The voiced and unvoiced sounds produced during exhalation are given character and quality as they are resonated from the surfaces of the pharynx, mouth, and nasal cavities. The sounds are reflected from these surfaces and reinforced by them. Finally, certain sounds are turned into consonants by the articulators: the tongue, the teeth, the lips, and the velum or soft palate, which controls the passage of air between the mouth and nose. These sounds combine to form words, and the cycle is complete. (See Figure 10–6.)

From this simplified description we see that the production of voice is a motor process involving breathing; a phonation process involving the vibration of the vocal folds; a resonation process involving the reinforcing surfaces of the mouth, throat, and nose; and an articulation process involving the formation and codification of specific sound symbols.

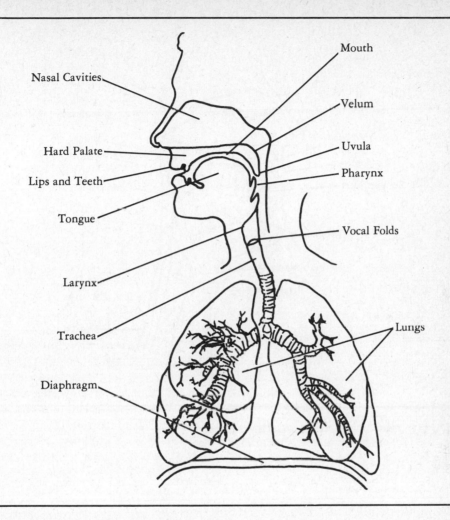

Nasal Cavities

Hard Palate

Lips and Teeth

Tongue

Larynx

Trachea

Diaphragm

Mouth

Velum

Uvula

Pharynx

Vocal Folds

Lungs

FIGURE 10–5   *Diagram of the vocal tract*

The cycle we have described repeats itself over and over as we speak, and what happens at the various stages in the cycle is responsible for the distinctive attributes of the voice. The physical adjustments and modifications that take place during speech and the general physical condition of the speaker are responsible for the individuality of each human voice. It has been argued that our voices are as distinctive as our fingerprints. Certainly we know we can readily identify one another by voice alone, that by the sound of the voice we know who is at the bottom of the stairs or around the corner.

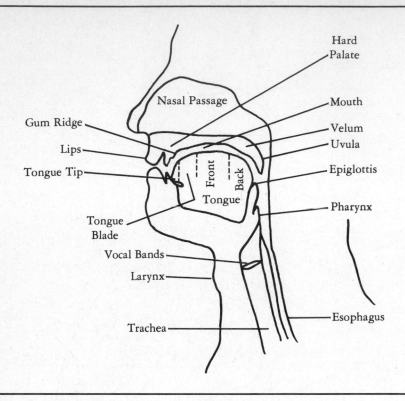

FIGURE 10–6   *Diagram of speech mechanism*

Articulation

What can you do with this knowledge? You can apply it in eliminating habits that interfere with your meanings. You do not have to slur words, drop off word endings, run sounds together. In private you can pay some attention to how you are using your articulators: your tongue, teeth, lips, and soft palate. Just attending to what is going on (but not in public!) will make you more precise.

You do not have to say "ath-a-lete" for *athlete,* "ex-scaped" for *escaped,* or "a-crost" for *across.* Here you have added sounds. Nor need you omit sounds by saying "reg-lar" for *regular,* or "nuff" for *enough.* You need not substitute one sound for another by saying "hyp-motism" for *hypnotism,* "car-toon" for *carton,* "ya" for *you,* or "fella" for *fellow.* These are all matters of choice. There are situations in which your choice matters little, of course, but there are other situations, including most situations for public speech, where the only safe, fully communicative choice is *pronunciation in accordance with the conventions of dictionaries, community leaders, and experts in the field in which a given word is commonly used.* Here is perhaps the most important point: no speaker loses influence by conforming to the best standards—provided he or she is businesslike, relaxed, unlabored, and unaffected.

Attributes of voice

Volume   Appropriate volume is the loudness that meets the needs of the audience and the physical setting. Without straining, an audience ought to hear every word a speaker says, no matter what the size of the place in which he or she speaks. When loud, strong utterance is required, a speaker ought to be able to produce it, but when the situation calls for soft or soothing utterance, a speaker must be equal to that necessity.

Beginning speakers are often unskilled in judging what vocal force is needed. Some speak in whispery, subdued voices that cannot be heard beyond the fifth row. They do this because they have not thought out how to command the space they share with listeners. Usually just concentrating on reaching the listener farthest away will lead such a speaker to speak loudly enough to be heard. Other beginners speak with too much volume. This unnerves the audience because, again, the sound fails to fit the actual space to be controlled. A little thought about how you are sounding to *both* the nearest and farthest listener is likely to correct this tendency toward too much volume. Another thing to be considered is that emphasis and intensity do not always require loud volume. You can emphasize or show intense feeling by speaking unusually softly. Usually it is *change* of loudness rather than *amount* that controls attention.

Adjusting to the requirements of rhetorical situations may require some practice if you err toward too much or too little loudness. Get comments on your loudness from your instructor or from colleagues; then practice in classroom drills or in private, producing different levels of loudness until you have become sensitive to the varying levels you can command. Once you know the range of your possibilities, the chances are that when you keep your mind on your meanings *and* on your relationship with listeners during public speaking, your volume will fit your intentions.

Rate   Effective speaking requires a rate of speaking that allows the audience to understand what you say without strain. Some beginners tend to race through speeches, slurring words and blurring important sounds. The audience cannot keep up or cannot understand key terms. If you exercise control, if you pace your utterances according to your *meaning,* your listeners will usually have little cause to complain. People who speak too rapidly usually do so because they do not take time to group words into clearly audible thought units. But if you take enough time to draw attention to the *units* of your thought, you will also be inclined to pause sufficiently so that the audience can keep up easily.

A speaker who talks too slowly is usually breaking ideas *within* thought units. Pauses tend to be stops during which the speaker collects past thoughts and grasps for the next word. These pauses are often filled with *uhs* and *ers* that interfere with the continuity of thought even more than silence does. Utterance that lags behind the listeners' abilities to comprehend can usually be corrected simply by preparing carefully so that you have plenty of language experience with each point to supply the necessary words automatically as you *think your meaning* for your listeners.

Attending closely to listeners' responses is another precaution against speaking too fast or too slowly. Watch for the signals of whether the listeners are or are not absorbing your message. If you see frowns or puzzled looks, slow down and modify what you are saying so that you can "come around again," restating the idea more carefully. If you see too much squirming, vacant staring, or bodily signs of indifference, speed up or slow down a little. This will introduce variety in pace and help to recapture attention. If you see nodding heads or agreeing smiles, you can take them as signals that say you are being understood. You can then conclude that either your pacing is about right or that the point just dealt with does not need further elaboration and you can move on.

What you are talking about frequently influences what an appropriate rate of speaking is. Saying an especially important point may call for elongating particular sounds (usually vowels) to give it emphasis. On the other hand, where excitement is being communicated, greater rapidity is in order. A blow-by-blow description of a boxing match would sound ludicrous if delivered slowly. To describe a quiet, calm canoe ride at a rapid rate using abrupt, staccato rhythms would not create the appropriate mood. Rate, then, ought to reflect the mood as well as allow listeners to comprehend easily.

If you speak to communicate meaning, mood, and responsiveness to listeners' signals, you are likely to speak at appropriately varied rates. It is when your mind is on something other than meaning, mood, and listeners that you speak too rapidly or too slowly.

Pitch   Listeners judge speakers to be indifferent or interested by "reading" the flexibility of pitch patterns. Monotony in pitch, volume, or rate can destroy meaning of even the best ideas.

Each of us has a pitch level that is natural and normal. Theodore Hanley and Wayne Thurman say, "Research findings for superior young adult male and female speakers are that their average (habitual) pitch levels are C_3 and $G\#_3$ respectively . . . or one octave and two musical notes, respectively, below middle C." [20] These authors and other authorities recommend that no one institute a program for relocating his or her habitual pitch without prior medical consultation. They further add:

> Pitch (frequency) is a function of balances among length, tension and mass in the vibration of a taut string, which your vocal cords resemble to a considerable degree. In your vocal mechanism these balances or adjustments have been arrived at over a span of many years. Your average level changed from infancy to childhood to young adulthood, where you now stand. In the absence of better information, we believe, it should be assumed that your physiological maturation has been as normal in the larynx as it has been in your upper arm, or ankle, or any other anatomical locus. If this is true, if you have normal cords that vibrate under normal tension, then the frequency at which they vibrate most often is the best, most effective, most efficient frequency, the optimum pitch level, the one at which you can produce

sounds longest, with least effort. Temporary movements away from that frequency are good, for obvious reasons. But an ill-considered shift of any magnitude away from that habitual level can result in vocal strain and other more serious effects. . . .[21]

Some speakers unintentionally adopt pitches too high or too low. This is especially true at the beginnings of speeches and at points where tenseness and nervousness impair ability to vary pitch levels. From any such artificial pitch it is difficult to inflect upward or downward for emphasis or meaning. Thus a speaker who does not take steps to reduce tensions such as those that were discussed in Chapter 2 will find himself or herself adopting pitch levels that do not allow reasonable expression of meaning.

Changes in pitch are effected by raising or lowering the key of the voice either gradually or abruptly between or within words. Gradual changes in pitch are referred to as *slides,* since we actually slide from one key to another. Abrupt changes are called *steps.* The ways in which we modify pitch often determine what we mean and the degree of emphasis we place on an idea. Through inflection it is possible to convey meaning opposed to the meanings of one's words. "Oh, no" inflected upward by means of a step may convey disbelief. "Oh, no" inflected downward by means of a slide may indicate indecision. "Oh no" inflected upward by means of a slide may indicate dismay or may mean "yes."

In ordinary conversation we do not think much about pitch inflections, stresses, or changes of key. We automatically make changes consonant with meanings. So you need to respond to material as you would under normal circumstances. Then your pitch patterns are likely to lend true meaning to what you are saying. But if your habitual pitch and stress patterns do not serve you well in impromptu and extemporaneous speaking, we suggest that you seek the help of a speech specialist who can competently analyze your speech patterns and devise a program of retraining. The public setting is not a suitable place to think about pitch and stress; there the task is to use the conventional patterns you have elsewhere learned to command.

If an audience perceives from inflection that you are not thinking about what you are saying or that you lack enthusiasm or are falsely enthusiastic or if they see that you are uncomfortable and therefore unable to move freely within your pitch range, you cannot expect them to respond fully and favorably.

Quality   Quality is produced by changes in the shapes and sizes of the resonators: pharynx, mouth, and nasal passages. It is common to say that an ineffective speaker's voice is nasal, denasal, guttural, breathy or aspirate. These terms are really attempts to say something about what is happening along the path of the breath stream that produces sound. To say a voice is *nasal* means that an unusual amount of the breath stream goes through the nose, strongly reinforced by resonance in the nasal passages. To speak of a voice as *denasal* means that there is little nasal resonance on the *m, n,* and *ng* sounds due to some closure of the nasal passages. You can hear this quality in almost anyone with a severe head cold.

Guttural voices are those that seem especially reinforced low in the back of the throat. Sometimes harshness is associated with this kind of speech production. In any case guttural quality or harshness is one of the qualities of voice that listeners repeatedly identify as unpleasant.

Breathy and *aspirate* describe voices produced by inadequate control over the breath stream. When more breath is released than is needed to vibrate the vocal folds efficiently, the result is a whispery sound, usually of inadequate volume. Often the reason for this is that the vocal folds are not firmly approximated; the air passing between them causes *some* vibration but also some sheer escape noise comparable to the sound of whispering.

The ways you tense the muscles of your vocal system and your general physical condition determine your vocal quality to a large extent. Tensed muscles are likely to produce harsh, guttural or strident qualities, which listeners in turn perceive as signs of tension. Too much relaxation is likely to produce breathy and nasal sounds. Listeners are apt to interpret breathiness as a sign of weakness or (especially in women) coyness or want of intelligence. Nasality or denasality tends to be interpreted as simply disagreeable.

What we have said about voice implies that speakers should strive for full, efficient, relatively relaxed use of their sound-producing and resonating apparatus. For those with full command of all muscles this usually means focusing on meaning and the importance of the people out there. One should not try to perform vocal or articulatory experiments during public communication; that is a time to reveal the precision of muscular and qualitative control that private experimentation and reflection have established as natural to you. You ought to experiment with your vocal and bodily resources to enlarge your communicative powers, but do so in private with a view to establishing the habits and versatility essential to evoking favorable, empathic responses from listeners.

EMPATHY

The ability to project ourselves into other people's personalities is important in any consideration of delivery. A concept concerning this sort of projection and involving both bodily action and voice is *empathy.*

The German word for empathy, *einfühlung,* provides a clue to distinctions we ought to make between sympathy and empathy. *Sympathy* is ordinarily thought of as a feeling *toward* or *for* another person or being. Empathy—*einfühlung*—is a "feeling in with." Our natural ability to take the role of another vicariously is the source of our empathic behaviors. Laurance Shaffer, B. Gillmer, and Max Schoen have said these ". . . empathic actions, postures or expressions are not deliberate mimicry, and the persons displaying them are usually unaware of what they are doing. As nonvoluntary acts therefore, they are explained in the same manner as suggestion." [22]

Many of you have had the experience of watching a speaker teeter at the edge of the platform so that his or her balance seemed precarious. You have heard speakers whose rates and bodily actions were so slow that you wanted to push them along. You may have listened to a speaker so gravelly-voiced that you came away feeling that you had a sore throat. At such moments we *empathize:* we feel we share in the other's condition. In speech situations we sometimes identify with speakers so strongly we ourselves make movements in imitation of them. The empathic relations in speech are not fundamentally unlike those that exist when you cry with the hero or heroine at the movies, lift your body as a high jumper clears the bar, or shift your body as you watch a tightrope walker.

People who listen to others *do* involuntarily "feel in with" those who talk to them. And, as we have said in many different ways in this book, listeners want to see evidence that a speaker is "feeling in with them." In an ideal rhetorical situation there is a two-way flow of empathic feelings. When you speak, you need to act and sound in such ways that the audience receives sensations (or suggestions) that draw them to "feel in with" your meanings. You also need to act so as to make clear that you "feel in with" their experience of listening to you. The listeners want to see signs you are inviting them to *participate* in meanings created *just for them,* as they are now, in the hearing. There is no such thing as *not* emanating cues concerning the degree of identification you feel with your listeners. In short, fully adaptive delivery is being sensitive to listeners' reactions, identifying with them, reacting to them, and guiding them toward identification with you.

Because we are turning to the problems of reading in public, we make the point in passing that empathic responses between speaker and listener are harder to achieve when speeches or parts of them are read from manuscripts or detailed notes. However, reading in public is sometimes necessary.

READING IN PUBLIC SITUATIONS

When to read

Almost anyone who functions in a community or other public role sooner or later has to read in public. The material may be your minutes of a meeting, your report for a committee, a special passage supporting the ideas of your otherwise extemporaneous speech, or an entire speech prepared in manuscript form because of some special demands of the occasion. At such times you become a public reader as well as a public speaker. Taking this role means that you take on the responsibilities of an interpreter—one who stands between an author and an audience. When presenting work from memory, a speaker similarly stands between the author he or she was and the speaker he or she is. Since the position of a reader is intermediate, the primary guidance for speaking derives from the material. The situation and its conventions force only minor modifications in behavior. The material to be read determines centrally *how* it needs to be read.

If we put aside private reasons such as personal convenience or uncertainty, there remain but two good reasons for reading to an audience: (1) to bring something new and unusual to the fore or (2) to give listeners meanings they would not get from reading the material by themselves either silently or orally.

Reading a speech or a portion of it involves stirring up meanings in those who listen. By uttering the sounds signified by black marks on a white page, you translate the marks into meaning. You must endow the printed words with the meanings their composer (you, if you happen to be the author) intended them to have. If you were the composer, you presumably know what the words mean; the problem is to revitalize your own ideas. If someone else composed what you choose to read, you must understand what that author meant before you can give the meaning to others. Whether you undertake to revitalize your own ideas, or to bring to life what another author meant, you have analytical work to do before you read.

Most people read badly because they are not aware of what is involved in getting and giving meaning. This is sufficient reason for discouraging beginners from reading their speeches. We cannot treat oral interpretation fully, but we can offer basic suggestions to public communicators who must sometimes read. Since a public speaker's reading is primarily for utilitarian rather than aesthetic purposes, the observations that follow focus on reading to convey practical meaning, leaving out of consideration the equally legitimate object of giving pleasure.

General principles

The following suggestions are arranged in the approximate order in which you are likely to confront problems.

Discover the author's purpose and method   To determine an author's purpose and method, sift the material for clues. Is the communication essentially utilitarian? Aesthetic? Or does the author's intent fall somewhere in between? At the utilitarian end of this imaginary continuum might stand a technical report or the minutes of a business meeting. At the aesthetic end you would expect to find love lyrics. Any author's purpose will lie somewhere along the line between these types. Consider the different communicative purposes that distinguish a news report, an editorial, a personal essay, a fictional narrative, a scene from a play, a ballad, or a sonnet.

Most authors have the same purposes you have: to inform, persuade, reinforce, inquire, or entertain. This gives you a clue as to what tone or mood to adopt in your general delivery. It also gives you a framework for further analysis of the material.

Discover the complete meaning   One of the chief causes of poor reading is failure to obtain complete meaning from the material. To discover the purpose is not enough. You should learn what the material says and what the author's attitude is. In so doing you may have to turn to other materials and read about the author or read critical essays written about the material.

Getting the full meaning entails knowing the meanings of all the words. You must know their meanings individually and in context. The associations and responses that words touch off are important. Make sure, then, that you are aware of the referents your author intends.

To achieve complete meaning you will sometimes have to study the setting for the material. The historical period depicted or to which the piece belongs may be as much a matter for concern as its objective meaning. You may have to answer for yourself questions such as: who is saying this? Why is he or she saying it? Who is the intended listener? Whether the words were spoken on the steps of the nation's Capitol during an inauguration or in the give-and-take of a legal debate will affect the manner in which you read them.

Knowing the author's mood—his or her attitude—is a related requirement. You, as the go-between, must reflect feelings in harmony with the author's, and for that reason, unless you are an experienced and accomplished reader, sight reading can be dangerous. The establishment of mood is especially important to effective presentation of materials with aesthetic purposes.

Sometimes paraphrasing a passage or writing a précis will aid you in assimilating its full meaning. You must undertake whatever research, peripheral reading, or review is needed to discover complete meaning. Only if you understand the whole can you understand how to read a work or any of its parts.

Discover the structure and unity of the selection   Every well-written composition—even a passage—has perceivable structure and unity. Some planned development of ideas dominates the work. If you can see what lines of thought or feeling contribute most to the structural pattern and the unity of the material, you have important hints about what to emphasize in reading. If you quote at length, you have need to examine the form the author has chosen as his or her medium of expression. Each literary form has distinctive structural patterns. For example, the most important facts or meanings are usually found near the start of a news story, but near the end of a dramatic scene. What is worth quoting, what is representative of the author's meaning, and what must be emphasized must be discovered. You can often tell what is worth quoting from a longer passage by attention to the structure and the unity of the work and its parts.

Cultivate a sensitivity to rhythm   Some of the subtlest shadings of meaning achieved through language are conveyed by changes in rhythm, changes in the beat or measure of sounds. This is especially true of poetry but it is also important in some prose. If you choose to quote Daniel Webster, Winston Churchill, John F. Kennedy, or Martin Luther King, you will seldom convey the full meaning of a passage if you do not express the rhythmic patterns so characteristic of these speakers' prose. Only by preserving rhythm, or by breaking it, can the meaning of some authors be conveyed. It is seldom necessary to do so with poetry. If you quote poetry you should be careful not to let meter dominate your utterance to such a degree that you destroy meaning. The extreme example of this fault is the small child's sing-song recitation of poetry. Your capacity to "hear" rhythmic meanings and to reproduce them will often determine what you should and should not try to quote.

Cultivate imaginative capacities   A further requisite for good reading is imagination. Watch for authors' unique achievements, their use of special patterns of expression, new relationships between ideas, and new word pictures. The more aesthetic the author's purpose, the more valuable imagination is in interpreting.

Imagination comes from experience and from temporarily divorcing yourself from reality. It comes, in part, from a capacity to dream. Let your mind range as you work over material to be read. Visualize possibilities. Create several versions of possible meaning in your mind; then choose the best one for your final interpretation. All of this is useful even if you are quoting yourself.

Cultivate the ability to group and pause   Grouping or phrasing is the art of breaking a text up into speech units. A word is a grammatical unit; the idea is the speech unit. According to W. M. Parrish:

> When we are creating thought as we go along, as in conversation, we generally make the grouping clear to our hearers, that is, make our ideas distinct. In reading from the printed page, our eyes must be trained to run quickly along the succession of words and organize them into proper groups before the voice attempts to utter them. If the voice fails to communicate this grouping to one's hearers, it fails to communicate meaning, for meaning lies in the grouping. And if we make a false grouping, we falsify or destroy meaning.[23]

In reading poetry the inexperienced tend to group mechanically, pausing at the end of each line, a practice to be avoided. You must learn to group by thought. Realistic grouping is no less necessary in quoting prose, although the problems are less complex.

You should be aware that there are two types of punctuation, oral and written. Oral punctuation makes meanings clear to an auditor by noticeable changes in voice or action, as written punctuation makes similar meanings clear to a reader. The two kinds of punctuation do not always coincide. There are many times when you will want to ignore the written punctuation altogether. Pausing at every comma, semicolon, or period does not always enhance meaning. It may confuse. When you read aloud you must determine in advance which written punctuation will assist you in grouping audible thought and which will not. Punctuation in oral reading, as in speaking, is achieved by changes in volume, rate, or pitch, and by gestures and other bodily movements that make groups of words stand out clearly and so convey units of meaning incisively.

A pause is a psychophysiological event. Proper pausing does more than any other one thing to make reading natural and realistic. There is never need to pause for breath alone since appropriate pauses for thought are plentiful enough to counter breathlessness. A pause is not mere silence. It is not a dead stop. In a true pause silence is pregnant with meaning. When the voice stops for a true pause, thought continues. The reader sees ahead and gains command of the next idea; the listener digests what has been said and becomes curious about what is to come. Pauses help both reader and listener to apprehend the relationships among the words and phrases. Professor Parrish explains why young readers do not pause. He says:

> First, they lack confidence. The excitement of reading before others causes a nervous acceleration of what is normally too rapid a rate of utterance. Under such circumstances, the cessation of vocal activity for a fraction of a second seems an ominous silence full of dreadful possibilities. The reader feels that his audience will begin to wonder whether he has not broken down. . . .

A second reason why young readers seldom pause is just that they do not *deliberate*. They skim. Their minds do not *dwell* upon the ideas to be communicated. As surely as the mind begins to dwell upon the ideas being expressed, there will be focusing on separate word-groups (How else *can* one think?), and these word-groups will generally be separated from each other by pauses.[24]

We add, parenthetically, that Parrish's observations are true of speakers as well as of readers.

Cultivate ability to subordinate ideas   You must realize in reading, as in speaking, that ideas are not all of the same value. Some ideas are subordinate to others. They support and amplify. In your analysis of material to be quoted you must look for these relationships. Then you must try to *convey* these relationships of degree by voice, gesture, and movement. Emphasize the most important ideas and deemphasize the less important ones. If you read every word in the same way with the same rate, pitch, and volume, you will be boring.

Cultivate ability to maintain visual directness   Preserving visual directness is a greater problem when reading to an audience than when speaking to it. Speakers who bury their noses in books or who gaze at papers on the lectern destroy the liveliness that ought to prevail during public speech or reading. As Ben Henneke says:

> The reader has a special eye problem. He must look at his manuscript and still maintain eye contact with his audience. His best answer is a compromise. His eyes should follow the manuscript until he is certain of what he is going to say. Then he may look at his audience until he has completed saying that phrase or group of phrases.[25]

Preserving visual contact with an audience and an intimate speaker-audience relationship during reading is a skill attained only through practice. To take in a group of words and then lift your eyes to focus on the audience as these words are uttered requires that you remember what the eye first took in long enough to deliver it meaningfully and without interruption. The process demands a high degree of physical coordination with memory. Visual directness—or its absence—usually reveals whether the reader has thoroughly or haphazardly prepared to read.

Cultivate the "illusion of the first time"   Flexibility and variety are essential for all good speaking or reading. In extemporaneous speaking one responds afresh to ideas, sifted though never fixed by preparation, but in reading from the printed page it is fixed content and form that must be recaptured. The oral reader's material is inevitably static. The material is precisely that thing to which he or she responded again and again during preparation. Thus, the illusion of fresh experience with content is much harder to convey when reading than when speaking.

It is not limitations of vocal and bodily equipment that constrain most speakers who read; it is an inability to recapture whole meanings and to respond with full powers of intellect and imagination while under the stresses of public communication. There is no easy remedy. As is true with other arts, so it is here: given understanding of how to study material and of the resources of delivery, then practice, evaluation, and more practice produce the controlled and lively responses that superior reading requires. The "illusion of the first time," to which audiences enthusiastically respond, is largely the result of experience and painstaking practice. For the speaker who reads only brief passages in the midst of extemporaneous speaking there is this encouraging fact: careful analysis, modest experiments with the resources of delivery, plus less than formidable amounts of practice can produce meaningful readings of utilitarian prose and uncomplicated kinds of poetry.

In this chapter we have examined delivery as a means to an end rather than as an end in itself. It seems sensible to approach personal presentation of speeches by first recognizing that constructively communicative behavior arises as controlled but free response to thought and feeling fully experienced. If physical and vocal behaviors are means rather than ends in speaking, a general standard for good delivery is easily found: *good delivery helps the listener concentrate on what is said; it does not attract attention to itself.*

There are, as we have tried to show, general principles of bodily and vocal action that encourage free and full use of the human body in reinforcing thought and feeling. There are also specific behaviors to be learned if listeners are to empathize favorably with speakers' messages. In essence, however, it is a speaker's attitude toward his or her ideas, self, and audience that govern the functional value of the delivery. We have offered suggestions concerning constructive use of body and voice and on reading for public speaking. But our belief is that it is from knowing and reflecting on the possibilities of communicative action, and from private drill to achieve conventional and variable habits, that effective delivery ultimately emerges in informal or formal public speech.

EXERCISES

Written

1.   Write a description of the bodily action used by one of the following:
     a.   a professor during a lecture
     b.   a classmate delivering a speech
     c.   your roommate as he or she goes about daily activities
2.   Write an analysis of your voice after listening to a recording of it. Comment especially on volume, rate, pitch, and quality.
3.   Listen to a live speech delivered in person or over television. Write a description of the speaker's delivery with these questions in mind: What did the

speaker do to support ideas visually and vocally? What did the speaker do with his or her body and voice that detracted from what was being said?

4. Observe one of your classmates as he or she delivers a speech and during an informal conversation. Write a comparative account of his or her use of body and voice in these two situations. Note the similarities and differences in vocal and visual elements.

Oral

1. Make a short speech during which you read aloud from at least three literary forms: news account, scientific report, fictional prose, sonnet, ballad, essay, or dramatic scene.

2. Prepare and deliver a speech three to six minutes long in which you explain some procedure requiring much action: how to do a dance, how to perform artificial respiration, how to handle a fencing foil, how to execute wrestling holds, how to direct calisthenics, or some similar subject. (Note: if you feel unduly nervous about speaking to a group, you will find this exercise or something of its kind particularly helpful in reducing your tensions.)

3. If bodily movement is not your style in communication, try this exercise. Below are a series of common events that need at least *some* nonverbal communication regardless of what you say about them. Put the items in some narrative or make an explanation that will allow you to use each idea; then give a brief talk in which you convey the meanings physically as well as verbally.

   a. A man was outdoors and, for some reason, *he studied the sky.*

   b. A *small* cloud intrigued him. It seemed about this size (choose a size) and it was *shaped* like this (choose the shape and communicate it verbally and nonverbally).

   c. For some reason his thoughts drifted to air travel (perhaps he hears a plane), and he looked toward the horizon *somewhat to his left.*

   d. He had a thought of *great importance* (to you, to your audience, or both). Perhaps it was about pollution, how small the world is (or whatever you choose).

   e. You would like *to offer us* your own interpretation of this thought.

   The italicized ideas are spots at which some kind of movement, if only of eyes, will be essential if you are to observe the speaking conventions of our culture.

4. Explain the layout of a supermarket. Tell your listeners, in your own words, that as one enters past the shopping carts into the main display area, the fresh produce will be on one side, the frozen foods will be on the other, the meat department in a far corner, and so on. Without being dramatic, try at least to *suggest* by some kind of action and vocal variety the spatial pattern of such a store. (Note: if you need practice in broader physical movement, try this exercise using a large space and *demonstrate* the spatial positions; or use a blackboard drawing if you need experience in using visual aids.)

5. If using your hands in communication seems unusual or awkward, try this ex-

ercise. Give a two-minute talk on "Some Geometric Figures We Couldn't Do Without." You might try describing rectangles of different sizes, an octagon, various shapes of triangles, or others. If you refuse to use a blackboard or other externally derived visual aid, you will discover (a) that you have to describe with hands, arms, and other movements, and (b) that these are quite natural and easy things to do.

6. Assign each of the following sentences to three or four members of your class. Ask each person to say or read his or her sentence with an emphasis different from that used by the preceding person, changing the meaning of the sentence each time it is read. Following the readings, discuss the differences in volume, pitch, and rate employed to achieve the differences.

    a. Whom do you suppose I saw in class today?
    b. Oh yes I'd love to go.
    c. You aren't really sure of that are you?
    d. I've never seen such food.
    e. There are always a lot of men at the movies on Saturday night.
    f. It was the most spectacular yet peculiar race you ever saw.
    g. There was the book just where I'd left it rain soaked and falling apart.
    h. No I simply can't believe that that is so.
    i. Whoever heard of a person doing such a thing?
    j. Oh my dear what have you done?

ENDNOTES

1. Wayne N. Thompson, *Quantitative Research in Public Address and Communication* (New York: Random House, 1967), p. 92.
2. These approaches may be investigated by consulting S. S. Curry, *The Province of Expression* (Boston: The Expression Co., 1927), pp. 301–25; Richard Whately, *Elements of Rhetoric*, ed. Douglas Ehninger (Carbondale, Ill.: Southern Illinois University Press, 1963), especially pp. 346–53; Frederick W. Haberman, "John Thelwall: His Life, His School, and His Theory of Elocution," *Quarterly Journal of Speech* XXXIII (October 1947): 294; Joshua Steele, *Prosodia Rationalis: Or an Essay Towards Establishing the Melody and Measure of Speech, to Be Expressed and Prepetuated by Peculiar Symbols* (London, 1779); and Gilbert Austin, *Chironomia or a Treatise on Rhetorical Delivery* (London, 1806).
3. Six different ways of defining *nonverbal communication* are identified by Peter A. Andersen, John P. Garrison, and Janis F. Andersen in "Implications of a Neurophysiological Approach for the Study of a Nonverbal Communication," *Human Communication Research,* VI (Fall 1979): 74–88.
4. Abne M. Eisenberg and Ralph R. Smith, Jr., *Nonverbal Communication* (Indianapolis: Bobbs-Merrill, 1971), p. 20.
5. Jurgen Ruesch, "Nonverbal Language," in Robert Cathcart and Larry Samovar, eds., *Small Group Communication* (Dubuque: William C. Brown, 1970), pp. 260–63.
6. Eisenberg and Smith, *Nonverbal Communication*, p. 22.

7.   Andersen, Garrison, and Andersen, "Implications of a Neurophysiological Approach," pp. 74–82.

8.   Andersen, Garrison, and Andersen, "Implications of a Neurophysiological Approach," p. 85. See also Mark L. Knapp, John M. Wiemann, and John A. Daly, "Nonverbal Communication: Issues and Appraisal," *Human Communication Research* IV (Spring 1978): 272.

9.   Ray L. Birdwhistell, *Kinesics and Context* (Philadelphia: University of Pennsylvania Press, 1970), p. 8.

10. Albert Mehrabian, *Nonverbal Communication* (Chicago: Aldine-Atherton, 1972), p. 182.

11. Knapp, Wiemann, and Daly, "Nonverbal Communication," p. 275.

12. John Spiegel and Pavel Machotka, *Messages of the Body* (New York: The Free Press, 1974), p. 345.

13. Eisenberg and Smith, *Nonverbal Communication,* p. 64.

14. Dale G. Leathers, "The Impact of Multichannel Message Inconsistency on Verbal and Nonverbal Decoding Behavior," *Speech Monographs* XLVI (June 1979): 88–100.

15. Steven C. Rhodes and Kenneth D. Frandsen, "Some Effects of Instruction in Feedback Utilization on the Fluency of College Students' Speech," *Speech Monographs* XLII (March 1975): 83–89.

16. From *Speechmaking,* by James A. Winans. Copyright, 1938, D. Appleton-Century Company, Inc., p. 25.

17. Ibid., p. 28.

18. Quoted from Dale Leathers, "The Impact of Multichannel Message Inconsistency," pp. 99–100. The *double-bind* concept originated with Paul Watzlawick, Janet H. Beavin, and Don D. Jackson, *Pragmatics of Human Communication* (New York: W. W. Norton, 1967), pp. 217–18.

19. For a useful discussion of the roles of gesturing in interpersonal communication, some of which also occur in public speech, see Paul Ekman and Wallace Friesen, "The Repertoire of Nonverbal Behavior: Categories, Origins, Usage, and Coding," *Semiotica* I (1969): 49–98.

20. Theodore D. Hanley and Wayne L. Thurman, *Developing Vocal Skills,* 2nd ed. (New York: Holt, Rinehart and Winston, 1970), p. 184.

21. Ibid., p. 185.

22. Laurance F. Shaffer, B. Von Haller Gillmer, and Max Schoen, *Psychology* (New York: Harper & Brothers, 1940), p. 195.

23. Wayland Maxfield Parrish, *Reading Aloud,* 4th ed. (New York: The Ronald Press Co., 1966), p. 21. Copyright © 1966 The Ronald Press Company. Used by permission of the publisher.

24. Parrish, *Reading Aloud,* p. 36.

25. Ben Graf Henneke, *Reading Aloud Effectively* (New York: Holt, Rinehart, and Winston, 1954), p. 143.

CHAPTER 11

Judging public speech

Where can you apply the principles of this chapter in everyday life?

1. Wherever you need to evaluate what you see and hear.
2. Wherever you need to support critical judgments on any subject.
3. Whenever you see and hear a live speech in the classroom.
4. Whenever you see and hear a live speech outside the classroom, for example: in church, at a club meeting, during a committee meeting, during a political or sports rally, or during a sightseeing trip.
5. Whenever you see and hear a formal speech, an interview, or a talk show on television.
6. Wherever you read the text of a speech or report on a speech.

When evaluating someone else's speech consider:

1. What you ought to look for in what you see and hear.
2. Whether you have located the right criteria on which to base your judgment.
3. Whether you need to teach as well as evaluate.
4. Whether your specific judgments are clear and well defined.
5. Who will use your critical judgments, and how.

Criticism is the way we tell ourselves what is going on and the way we learn to practice an art with greater insight. A liberally educated person ought to be able to explain what happens when speech occurs and be able to reason about the strength of the rhetorical effort. Such a person ought to be able to describe the speech and to explain why and how it contributed to the lives of those involved with it. But just as with criticism of fiction, poetry, painting, or architecture, criticism of public speech requires knowledge of the possibilities of the art and a capacity to analyze the specimens of the art that the critic examines. As Robert S. Cathcart has said, "Usually we know whether we like a speech, but being able to judge that speech as effective or influential is quite a different matter."[1] In reference to oral expression or any other artistic expression, *judging* the qualities of the expression in a reasonable, intelligible way is the function of criticism. Cicero described the practical usefulness of criticism when he said that the "expert and the plain man" see things alike, but the expert or critic can give reasons for his or her judgment.[2] For *giving reasons* a person needs to know what was and was not possible in creation of the thing to be judged; it is that knowledge that makes the person an "expert."

The broad aims of liberal education are to equip students to be critics—to think about several areas sensibly in a variety of ways, to be able to see alternatives, and so to increase the ability to judge with a significant degree of expertise. The final result of studying public speaking as a liberal art ought to be the same—qualification to judge public speech with expertise. There are some who believe students are too inexperienced to function as critics. We hope your study and practice makes you sufficiently experienced in this art and its possibilities. From reading this book you have derived some basic facts and theories about human oral communication, about the allowances and restraints of rhetorical situations, about rhetorical invention and disposition, and about uses of language and self in public presentation. With this knowledge we believe you are equipped to "judge speech effective or influential" and to do so like Cicero's "expert"—with intelligible reasons. And any citizen needs some degree of this expertise. What Dean Everett Lee Hunt said half a century ago still applies:

> . . . We might be better satisfied with the returns from the money and energy spent on rhetorical training if we cared more about producing educated and critical audiences. . . . Critical and analytical study of rhetoric and oratory should not be limited to those who expect to become professional speakers or writers, or to those who expect to teach it; it should be offered to all students who desire to understand the significance of rhetoric in modern life.[3]

Perhaps the most practical reason of all for exercising your critical faculties on public speech is that the colleagues who study speech with you *need* your reasoned judgments, and you need theirs. By openly registering your responses to your peers and giving clarifying and informed reasons, you can aid in others' improvement; in the same way they can help you to improve. Further, the more you examine speaking, your own and others', the more you teach yourself about the art. Pragmatically, then, reasoning about what was and could have been done in speaking, judging the strength and influence of what was done, and explaining those judgments intelligibly will be learning experiences for *you,* as well as critical aids to your colleagues. Let us become more specific about the nature of criticism of speaking.

THE NATURE OF SPEECH CRITICISM

Criticism of any kind is judgment and/or appreciation. Evaluation and criticism imply analysis and comparison and commendation or censure. Assessments that evaluate are criticism. Mere descriptions, reviews, commentaries, and surveys are not. Unless they also discriminate and evaluate, they merely report data.

Criticism is essentially a comparative activity. Whenever we make judgments or register appreciation, we discriminate with some standards of quality in mind. We try to be more objective than subjective, and we then become consciously aware of the standards by which we weigh what we observe. As we apply those standards, our judgments place what we judge somewhere along a continuum of excellence. The speech we appraise is always measured by some standards and found to correspond to them in some degree. Either it corresponds closely to our standards, or it does not. Such is the nature of our critical judgments—of speech or anything else. Whether our judgments are useful to anyone else depends on our capacity to communicate both our standards and our judgments. This is the kind of communicated, objective criticism that is necessary if classmates are to profit. It is also the kind of criticism that makes criticism of speech—or anything else—informative to general listeners or readers.

Speech as a critical object

A focus on some object is the beginning of any type of criticism. The object may be tangible or intangible. It may be material or a combination of materials, an action or an ideal. In aesthetic criticism the object of criticism may be a specific painting, such as Picasso's "The Lovers"; a pattern of sounds, such as Beethoven's Fifth Symphony interpreted by a great orchestra; or physical action performed by dancers, such as the *pas de deux* from *The Firebird.* Objects for literary criticism are novels, short stories, poems, or essays, usually in the tangible form of printed words on a page. Whatever the kind of criticism, there is some object that exists to be appreciated and/or evaluated and perhaps to be praised or condemned.

A critic who assesses live speaking, speaking as it is delivered, deals with a distinctive critical object. What he or she examines, appreciates, and judges consists of a combination of sounds and actions symbolizing ideas, existing in time, air, and sight. This object is in constant flight. It is not static, not arrested. It is unlike many other critical objects. It is not a statue placed on a pedestal and viewed from all sides. It is not a musical score nor a play script to be consulted again and again. It is not a painting that can be gazed at for hours. In more cases than not the life of a live speech will end with its last sounds—except as memory of it lingers in the minds of people who heard it.

Live speech cannot be taken in fully with either the eye or the ear alone. Ideally it must be seen and heard—all in the moments of its creation. Like dance, it will not freeze for examination, and yet its verbal nature makes it seem analogous to the more stable objects of literary criticism. But speech is different; the contrasts go further. It is true that a critic viewing a painting takes in first one part, then another; and the critic of music hears sounds in sequence, in time, but a critic of live speeches faces a more exacting assignment. He or she must see *and* hear sequences that have never before occurred in just that way. Nor will they ever occur again. Usually this critic will not even have a drama critic's advantage of consulting a script before or after seeing and hearing the object, although this is possible with very formal and with recorded speeches.

As a critic of live speaking, a speech critic deals with a critical object that exists once and only once. Normally there will be no public preview, and there may even be no subsequent record. And the components of a speech situation constantly shift. Two speeches by the same speaker may be on identical subjects and in identical words, but exact duplication is impossible. At least delivery is bound to be a bit different.

Take another set of cases. In public interviews the interviewee cannot foresee what he or she must next talk about until the interviewer's question. Furthermore, in these and similar situations the bits of talk that may be regarded as small speeches occur in settings that are flexible and in constant flux. Such minispeeches can never be exactly reproduced in any future place or time. Despite all of this, anyone who wants to understand and evaluate public speech must try to note and account for the on-going adjustments speakers are or should be making.

To complicate matters further, a speech critic cannot always be present when the speech he or she needs to evaluate takes place. For example, the critic may want to get a detailed understanding of an oral utterance only after he or she finds it was of some importance to society or that it exerted some particular influence. The critic may not know a press conference was news until it is over. In such circumstances a critic is unable to experience the *real* speech; yet it may still be worthwhile to ask what happened when the speaking took place and how well the speaker or speakers lived up to their possibilities.

The most advantageous situation for criticism of past talk rarely exists. Our would-be critic with luck might obtain a videotape or sound motion picture that made all possible observations of visible and audible elements. A tape or film of this sort would come closest to reproducing the real speech, but it could not reproduce the entire rhetorical situation because it would fail to reveal some three-dimensional aspects. Neither could it fully explain the needs and expectations of the people who were part of the situation. A videotape or film is simply not as reliable as on-the-spot observation for assessing factors such as environment, history, and audience reactions. When films are available, they often contain only portions of major speeches. Ideally, a critic would make his or her own film and record useful situational information.

A second kind of critical speech object is some form of electrical transcription. This will not give you the visual aspects of the speech, but it does allow some evaluation of vocal performance, of listeners' responses, and affords a precise check on what was actually said. The last item is important since most printed texts of speeches are inaccurate in some respects. If a critic can tape speeches and discussions while he or she makes other kinds of observations, the best use of tapes is possible. They can be used to check on accuracy—of general impressions and textual detail. Somewhat less thorough checking is possible when you obtain recordings from commercial sources or from reporters other than yourself.

Very often a critic who was not present when a speech was delivered will have to be content with some written record. This record can sometimes be supplemented with other written accounts that help in reconstructing the rhetorical situation and audience reaction. Possibly there will be others' criticisms or reviews that can be useful. It may even be that the literatures of historical, literary, and social scientific research can be useful in filling out understanding of what went on during the living event. But with all these aids a critic dependent on written records has the least satisfactory critical object of those we have discussed. The primary virtue of a written record of a speech event is that it can be pored over, analyzed, outlined, and otherwise studied intensively. This is a reason, we suspect, that a good many rhetorical critics use the texts of speeches much as they would use editorials, books, and other linguistic artifacts—as data for historical, sociological, and psychological study. Reconstruction of the living situation is simply very difficult, but it is not impossible, as many rhetorical critics have demonstrated.

The critical objects for critics of spoken discourse, then, are four: the object may be (1) the live, pulsating, reacted-to utterance of the moment; (2) a videotape or film; (3) an electrical sound transcription; or (4) a text. If any of these kinds of records is to be used as a basis for constructing a description of the actual rhetorical event and afterward for evaluation of the merits of the communication, *the context of the message must be known*.

Assuming you want to determine how meritorious a speech was *as a speech*, the basic purpose of all rhetorical speaking must be taken into account. Of this kind of inquiry Herbert A. Wichelns wrote:

> . . . We find that its point of view is patently single. It is not concerned with permanence, nor yet with beauty [as may be the case in the judgment of literature]. It is concerned with effect. It regards a speech as a communication to a specific audience, and holds its business to be the analysis and appreciation of the orator's methods of imparting his ideas to his hearers.[4]

Wichelns was thinking mainly of criticism as a scholarly activity involving the analysis of speech texts, but what he says also applies to audiences and critics who hear and see speaking in classrooms or outside and to those who read or hear records of speaking. His elaboration of rhetorical criticism bears quotation because he concisely identifies the basic questions all speech critics need to raise if their concern is to understand speech at work, alive.

> Rhetorical criticism is necessarily analytical. The scheme of a rhetorical study includes the element of the speaker's personality as a conditioning factor; it includes also the public character of the man—not what he was, but what he was thought

to be. It requires a description of the speaker's audience, and of the leading ideas with which he plied his hearers—his topics, the motives to which he appealed, the nature of the proofs he offered. These will reveal his own judgment of human nature in his audiences, and also his judgment on the questions which he discussed. Attention must be paid, too, to the relation of the surviving texts to what was actually uttered: in case the nature of the changes is known, there may be occasion to consider adaptation to two audiences—that which heard and that which read. Nor can rhetorical criticism omit the speaker's mode of arrangement and his mode of expression, nor his habit of preparation and his manner of delivery from the platform; though the last two are perhaps less significant. "Style"—in the sense which corresponds to diction and sentence movement—must receive attention, but only as one among various means that secure for the speaker ready access to the minds of his auditors. Finally, the effect of the discourse on its immediate hearers is not to be ignored, neither in the testimony of witnesses, nor in the record of events. And throughout such a study one must conceive of the public man as influencing the men of his own times by the power of his discourse.[5]

Speech criticism that aims at evaluation of a speech in its living setting must involve sensitivity to all the aspects of the rhetorical situation in which speaking has occurred, to the artistic qualities of the speech as an object of criticism, and to the use your findings may have for yourself and others. Such criticism, as Loren D. Reid expressed it,

> ... is not simply a discussion of the speaker's ideas, ... not simply a narrative of the circumstances under which a speech is delivered, ... not simply a classification or tabulation of rhetorical devices, ... [and] not primarily an excursion into other fields of learning.[6]

As we have tried to show, speech criticism that takes rhetorical, live speaking as its critical object may involve some study of all the topics Professor Reid identifies; the critic needs to know these *in order to apply standards of oral rhetoric and in order to draw evaluative comparisons between the actual speech and the standards applied.*

Critical points of view

Three different philosophical positions have informed most criticism of public speech. They have generated three differing but not necessarily contrary vantage points from which to view speakers and speaking. These points of view can be labeled *pragmatic, ethical,* and *artistic.*

The *pragmatic* view of speaking focuses especially on effect. The central question raised is: Did the speech get the intended result? The matter of central concern when speech is looked at from the *ethical* point of view is goodness or constructiveness. Here the all-embracing question is: Did the speech reveal the truth? The *artistic* viewpoint focuses inquiry on the question: Did the speaker wisely and ably use available methods in fashioning discourse? Another way the artistic question can be phrased is: How fully did the speaker employ the resources that the entire body of rhetorical literature shows were available? We shall not argue the relative merits of these three critical viewpoints. We contend that in early courses in speech and rhetoric, the artistic point of view is most constructive for you to take. By adopting it, at least for the time being, we believe you will enjoy certain advantages.

What we have called an artistic perspective on public speech will cause you to (1) identify the particular methods and possibilities that were open to any speaker in his or her rhetorical situation; (2) identify the methods the speaker *did* use and consider how far those exhausted the possibilities; (3) consider whether the rhetorical methods used were used in the best ways the resources of rhetorical art allow; and (4) give an explained judgment concerning the *fullness of achievement* within the constraints of the rhetorical situation. If in working from this viewpoint you can find out the actual, immediate results of the speaking, that knowledge can constitute a realistic check on or confirmation of your theoretical, artistic estimates. They will not alone explain a speaker's art or lack of it; but if you conclude that the speaker met all appropriate artistic standards but the audience did not respond favorably, you will be further, constructively encouraged to explore the situation for factors that can explain the discrepancy between your expert judgment and the "plain man's" unfavorable judgment. When the speaking raises ethical issues or reflects a speaker's ethical choices, taking an artistic perspective on the matter will enable you to explain how and why these choices succeeded or failed to succeed in the particular rhetorical situation you examine.

We think that adopting an artistic point of view on ordinary speeches does not prevent you from weighing what the results signify or what "truths" were promoted and how, but at the same time this viewpoint draws your critical attention to how the speaker *handled* whatever he or she took responsibility for inventing, developing, and adapting to a particular situation. This is essentially the viewpoint used by the students whose critique appears in Appendix B, although they drifted sometimes toward an unqualified amount of pragmatic judgment. Their critical inquiry revealed to a mature speaker some artistic strengths he did not know he had, and they put their fingers on the moral tone of his address. They might have gone farther. They might have shown Dr. Upcraft and their classroom colleagues where improvement was possible. This is only to say that they might have pressed their artistic analysis farther.

APPLYING CRITICAL STANDARDS

We have said that all criticism begins with description. To make any informed judgment of speaking requires that you first get an accurate, fair description of precisely what the speaker or speakers did.[7] Your description need not always be detailed or intricate. This is especially true in your speech class where you will be functioning as a critic much of the time.

In your classroom, where the goal of criticism is to teach, it is essential that you know what each speaker is trying to accomplish. Data about this can come from the nature of the assignment or from what the speaker can tell you beforehand. In any case, if your criticism is to teach, you must know the speaker's intended purpose so you can compare what he or she did to achieve it with what might have been done for that purpose. Knowing the purposes of classroom speeches also tells you that what is important in one critique might not be of equal importance in another.

If you were employed by a utility company to evaluate how effectively the corporation's public relations officer was presenting the company's case for increased industrial electrical service rates as he or she went about addressing chambers of commerce, you would be expected to apply all the standards of rhetorical effectiveness in any critical report you gave. But this is not true in classroom and other training situations. There, critical emphases need to be shifted as those being criticized undertake different rhetorical tasks.

Shifting emphasis in speech criticism

Especially when you evaluate speaking in a classroom you need to suit your criticism to each speaker's learning task. Then it is important to choose what you will emphasize in each critique. On one occasion the organization of the speech may be at the top of your list of the aspects of the speech to be commented on. On another occasion structure will be far down the list. When, for example, you have been concentrating on style in classroom study, such matters as striking images and precision in choice of words are apt to take priority as you observe and evaluate.

Even outside the classroom you will need to emphasize one aspect of speaking over another in developing sound critiques. Such a change of emphasis may come about because *you* decide that ideas and arguments will be more important in a given situation than style. It is obvious that the students who evaluated Dr. Upcraft's speech decided this. For them, matters of style and structure seem to have been rather low on their hierarchy of rhetorical features to be analyzed. They believed the audience was initially hostile to Dr. Upcraft because he was a representative of the university's administration. They may have been right in their decision to concentrate on ideas and arguments for the most part, but their critique would have been stronger had they told their listeners *why* they gave organization and style so little attention.

Our basic point here is that not every aspect of speaking is equally important in every rhetorical situation. Thus a critic's rankings of criteria shift according to the aims of the speaker, his or her subject matter, and the demands of the situation. You must decide on your critical hierarchy each time you criticize speech. As you listen or read, you must separate the important from the unimportant qualities of discourse. If you do not, you may end up by concentrating on trivial matters to the neglect of items that deserve more attention.

Consideration of ideas and their reasoned structure is often neglected. You can assist your colleagues in classroom speaking by considering with special care what you and the other listeners are *required* to believe if you are to agree with what the speaker is saying. Here Professor Toulmin's concept of argument can help. Toulmin maintains the logical persuasiveness of an advocate depends especially on whether his or her listeners can and will accept the **data** and the **warrants** offered in support of conclusions (see pages 117–21). You can assist your colleagues greatly if you will consider why you *do* or *do not* accept the **data** and **warrants** on which their **claims** rest. Obviously, speaking cannot be persuasive unless those who hear it accept the **data** on which **claims** depend. Unless "How do you get there?" (from information, or **data,** to conclusion, or **claim**) is answered satisfactorily for the listeners, a speaker cannot hope to convince them. So if you disagree with a colleague's **claims,** it will be very useful for you to explain whether it is the **data** you doubt or the **warrants** you question. In other words, "*Why* do I believe?" and "*Why* do I doubt?" are questions you need to answer for a colleague if you arc to explain your own critical reactions to his or her persuasion.

You will need to guard against developing fixations, especially about delivery. For some, voice or bodily action always occupies first place when they listen to the speech of others. These seem easiest to comment on. In your critiques of classmates a danger sign is present if you always say, "Jim doesn't make any gestures," or "Joanna has too many breaks in fluency," or "George rattled thc kcys and change in his pocket —most distracting!" All you have said may be true, but you must focus on the total speech or its most important aspects for this situation, unless some special agreement within your class has determined that delivery is your only concern.

Making standards clear

Once you decide which matters are most important in criticizing a specific bit of public talk, you will become concerned with more specific judgments. Usually you will start with the broader aspects of the communication and work to the details. In assessing a unit of speech giving information, for example, you will want first to ask yourself questions about the communication as a unit. Did it have an identifiable central idea? Did it have a recognizable introduction, body, and conclusion? What was the quality of its total impact?

You will want on many occasions to ask special questions about speeches or units of speech that constitute communication calculated to give information. You might ask, "Does the audience understand the subject better now that they have heard what was said?" To answer why they do or do not, you may pose questions relating directly to expository techniques: Was there justification in the subject matter and in the audience's interest for the way this speaker used exposition, description, and narration at various points? Did this speech or unit of talk meet the special demands for good expository speaking by being accurate, comprehensive, and interesting? Were visual aids used or needed to clarify points, or were they used for their own sake?

From these kinds of questions you may turn to specific details that may or may not be exclusively applicable to informative speaking. Here you will ask questions such as, "Did the story of the male student who knitted his own socks and ate light bulbs illustrate originality or peculiarity?" "Were reliable statistics used to show the relationship between monetary support and the quality of higher education? Were they truly representative?" "Were appropriate gestures used to support the idea that sailing is a vigorous sport? Were they well coordinated? Definite enough?" "Isn't the word pronounced *grim*-ace, not gri-*mace?*" These and like questions of detail complete your movement: evaluating the speech or unit of communication first as a whole, then as a particular kind of speech, and finally as a communicative effort consisting of detailed strengths and weaknesses.

Criticism sheets used to assess classroom speaking will sometimes assist you in deciding which questions to ask and which questions are most important. The criticism sheet we have designed for use with formal speeches is shown in Figure 11–1. It provides for both structured and unstructured comment. Aspects of speech making that need constant attention, no matter what the kind of speech, are arranged along the left side of the paper with spaces in which quick reactions can be entered while the speech is being delivered. The right half of the sheet provides space for personal notations and for revised, final reactions to the speech. The box in the lower right-hand corner encourages the user to recommend areas for improvement so that the criticism will fulfill the constructive obligations of any critic's task.

We want to emphasize two things about this criticism sheet. First, there is no need to expect that every question on the sheet ought to be answered every time you evaluate a speech. As we have said, especially in a classroom the *pertinent* questions shift from speech to speech. If style has not yet been discussed in class, why bother the speaker about "Language" unless there was something especially strong or weak to which attention must be drawn immediately? Secondly, the sheet is not a checklist of most important qualities of speech. It is simply a quick-answer sheet on which are listed items that experienced teachers have to comment on repeatedly in speech classes. If you use this or any comparable form for speech criticism, use the checking system to dispose quickly of matters that need no special work and to call attention to items that you criticize specifically and constructively in full-sentence form. And with this or any other criticism sheet, remember what we have said about the importance of shifting your critical standards to suit speakers' different purposes and different situations. You, not a prepared criticism sheet, must decide what critical response is relevant and helpful in each rhetorical situation.

CRITICISM IN THE CLASSROOM

A good classroom critic, like a good speaker, considers the effects his or her observations will have on the audience. The critic expresses judgments that cast the most light for the largest audience. In public he or she minimizes personal preferences and deals minimally with problems of concern only to a particular speaker. This critic is both student and teacher. Instead of using class time to comment on one speaker's peculiar vocal habit, he or she dwells on problems and strengths important to all speakers, concentrates on whatever can be useful to all and to himself or herself as a student of an art. All faults and strengths are fair game for criticism if treated constructively. In the classroom, as elsewhere, matters having general application deserve public comment; basically personal matters are best criticized in private conferences or in tactful notes.

Your education as a speech critic begins in the classroom. To make the most of it and to give others greatest benefit from your judgments, we suggest you approach classroom criticism in the following ways.

NAME: _____ SPEECH NO: _____

SUBJECT: _____ DATE: _____

Subject and purpose

  Subject worthwhile? _____

  Purpose delimited? _____

Content and organization

  Introduction

    Get attention? _____

    Needed information given? _____

    Purpose made clear? _____

  Development

    Organization—soundly planned? _____

      —easily followed? _____

      —transitions effective? _____

      —internal summaries appropriate? _____

    Supporting material—clear? _____

      —enough of it? _____

      —interesting? _____

      —convincing? _____

      —visual aids effective? _____

  Conclusion

    Provide a note of finality? _____

    Whole speech in focus? _____

Delivery

  Mental Alertness

    Realize each idea as uttered? _____

    Keen sense of communication? _____

  Body

    Eye contact adequate? _____

    Posture acceptable? _____

    Movement meaningful? _____

    Gestures effective? _____

  Voice

    Distinct? _____

    Vocal variety adequate? _____

      Rate? _____ *Pitch?* _____ *Volume?* _____

    Fluency adequate? _____

Language

  Have good oral qualities? _____

  Convey ideas clearly? _____

  Grammar correct? _____

  Pronunciation correct? _____

  Increase interest and impact? _____

Overall evaluation

  Adapted to situation? _____

  Purpose fulfilled? _____

  Make good personal impression? _____

  Interesting? _____

Symbols:

  X—No

  √—Yes

Grades:

  Papers:

  Speech:

  For the round:

  Consult Instructor?

  _____

  _____

NEXT TIME work especially for:

FIGURE 11–1   *Criticism sheet*

1. *Ready yourself for your critical task by preparing to concentrate on what you will see and hear.* Focus, visually and aurally, on the speaking that is going on. You must listen intently (see Chapter 2, pages 22–25). Try to rid yourself of distractions from without and within. Exclude all bids for attention except those by the speaker.

2. *Locate your critical criteria consciously.* Decide what you are listening for, what aspects of speech deserve your special consideration because of their importance in *this* speaking situation. In other words, decide which achievements in speaking rank highest in importance at *this* time, for *this* speaker, in *this* situation. By attending to the facets of speech making you are currently studying in class, you will give your criticism purpose.

Do not try to observe every aspect of the speech at once. Define the scope of your analysis. Register your reactions accordingly. Scattering your attention over many items will be of little service to the speaker and will impede the development of your own critical faculties. A speaker is not helped by superficial comments about a dozen things. He or she will be able to solve only a few artistic problems at a time. Aim to substantiate and develop a few major, situationally appropriate critical judgments.

3. *Adopt a constructive attitude.* As you try to detect the choices the speaker has made, consider the alternatives. As you note merits and flaws, ask, What else might have been done in this situation given the speaker's purpose? What specific, constructive suggestions can I offer for this speaker's improvement? Negative comment, without substantiating evidence and affirmative suggestions, will be of little help. To say, "Your speech was poorly organized," or even "Your economic argument was unsound," does not get to the heart of the matter. It does not get to the "why" of the trouble. It does not offer an analysis on which someone else can build. "You didn't look at your audience," "Your sentences were clumsy," or "You committed several grammatical errors" may be accurate descriptions of speech, but unless they are accompanied by suggestions for correction, they are of no help. Such comments are critical, but they do not teach. It is probably a good rule not to point out negative features if you cannot suggest remedies.

Starting critical remarks with positive things, with strong points, and proceeding to the less praiseworthy works well. Such an approach is simply good audience adaptation. The speaker will listen to what you say, will know you are not picking him or her apart for malicious reasons, and will be likely to remember to do again those things done well and to remedy those done poorly. It has been said, "Only those who have the heart to help have a right to criticize."

4. *Measure the speech against the criteria you are applying.* Measure what the speaker did against criteria that relate specifically to ideas, proofs, arrangement, style, and delivery. But keep the rhetorical situation uppermost in your mind as you make your educated guesses on the effectiveness, apparent intentions, and skill of what the speaker is doing.

As you listen, jot down reminders of your descriptive observations and of the criteria you are applying; then note your judgments along with the most pertinent examples and illustrations. A few notes will do. Do not become a stenographer. You and your colleagues are members of an audience, although you are also critics. You should remember that no speaker can be at his or her best when trying to address a roomful of bowed heads. Remember, too, that no critic functions effectively without giving himself or herself the opportunity to take in the visual as well as the aural elements of spoken communication.

Your job is to judge the speaking, not the person. Of course, there is never speech without a speaker, but your business is to assess that speaker's *communicated* personality as a force in the speech. Consider how the speaker's *ethos* contributes to the speech, not what contributes to your like or dislike for him or her as a person.

5. *Make a judgment.* This admonition may sound superfluous, but we make it because we have found it is needed. In too many cases you will be tempted merely to describe what you see and hear. Description is a first step in fruitful criticism, but it is not your main business as a critic. Your ultimate function is to deliver a decision —a judgment—based on the relationship between what you perceive and what you know. To be an effective critic you must avoid straddling the fence. Decide whether the aspect of speech you are considering is effective or ineffective, adequate or inadequate, skillfully or unskillfully handled, successful or unsuccessful, and why.

6. *Be as specific as possible in formulating your judgments.* Document your criticism with descriptive evidence. Refer directly to the speech, to specific arguments, illustrations, and wordings. Provide examples to back up both favorable and unfavorable evaluations. If you are criticizing style, strive to identify moments during which style was effective and other moments when it was less so. Refer to specific sentence structures, phrasings, and images. This will be constructively useful to all who hear your criticism. Find segments of the speech illustrating strengths and weaknesses in clarity, liveliness, force, and the like. The more precise you can be about exactly what was done and exactly why it was effective or ineffective, the more worthy of attention your observations will be.

7. *Register your judgment.* When you present your critical assessments orally or in writing, articulate your convictions. Silence during an oral criticism period following a speech or submitting doodlings on a scrap of paper will contribute nothing to the speaker or to your own development as an intelligent, informed critic. Do not feel that you must couch your judgments in rhetorical jargon. Do feel that you must be tactful in wording and frank in your remarks. Clear, direct, precise expression of your position, the data on which it rests, and your suggestions are required.

We have emphasized that public speaking does not always take place on the platform, nor is it always a matter of a speaker making a speech that functions apart from all other talk. Public interviews draw forth units of talk. Debates occur in business meetings and at conference tables. The students who presented a critique of Dr. Upcraft's speech made a series of interrelated speeches that together formed a total communication that might be called a public speech. Rap sessions involve public speeches. To understand such talks you may need to conceptualize them as *units of speeches* (the several contributions to one side of an ongoing debate, or the individual speeches of the presentation in Appendix B). Or perhaps you can conceptualize several separated units as comprising a *whole speech* (an interviewee's total presentation of himself or herself or the total critique of Upcraft's speech). If you view interrupted speech in these ways, you will often find that this kind of speaking is entirely amenable to such critical evaluation as we have discussed.

How well someone communicates according to his or her purpose in an interview or as a contributor to a general purpose shared with other speakers has as much importance as how well that person does in platform speaking. To see public speech as the assumption of responsibility for maintaining communicative relations on behalf of some purpose allows you to evaluate such informal speaking. We suggest below some ways you can approach minimally formalized speech in the same critical spirit you would apply to formal speech.

The kind of shared presentation that is represented by the students' critique in Appendix B occurs very commonly. These kinds of presentation need to be looked at with two general questions in mind: (1) How fully did the entire group of speakers succeed in communicating a single unified message to the audience? (2) How well did each individual speaker communicate a clear message that supported or contributed to the impact of the group's total message? Approaching the material in Appendix B in these ways you could apply all of the critical procedures we have discussed.

Almost any press conference creates situations in which the interviewee can (and often should) make responses up to several minutes in length. Those responses can also be understood and evaluated if you think of them as short, often one-point speeches occasioned by a rhetorical situation. However impromptu, such speeches affect listeners essentially as other public speeches do. You can approach such units of response in interviews, discussions, or public meetings as speech inviting criticism of the same sort as we are considering in this chapter.

EVALUATING LIVE SPEECHES OUTSIDE THE CLASSROOM

If your assignment were to criticize a live speech outside the classroom, how might you proceed? Suppose you were asked to appraise a sermon delivered at your church or synagogue next week or to make an evaluation of a speech by a local political candidate currently campaigning. What steps ought you to take?

1. If the speaker or someone else can furnish you with a text in advance of the speech, get it. It may show you some changes between plan and execution. If a transcription of any kind will be available after the speech, be sure to get it. Even if not exactly accurate, it will be a useful record of how someone understood the event.

2. Assuming you can attend the speech, you will be in the immediate setting and can make your own notes about the situation, the characteristics of the speaker's delivery, and the apparent impact of the speech on the audience.

3. You ought to gather whatever information you can about the situation, including the background news of the day and the philosophical, religious, and political ideas that might influence the relationship between speaker and audience. Since you will be a part of the situation, little research should be necessary here; unless you are a "complete outsider," you should be aware of the forces influencing the other people attending.

4. You will need to inform yourself about the speaker if you do not already know

his or her reputation, place in society, and values. In some instances you will be so familiar with the speaker that you can bypass this step in critical research.

5. Listen to the speech and if possible tape record it so you can devote yourself *during* the delivery of the speech to noting special, nonaural qualities of the speech and response to it.

Having taken these steps, you should be ready to think critically about the live speech you observed. From here on you can proceed essentially as you would in classroom criticism except that (1) you probably will have no "teaching" assignment and so need not be quite as specific about what the speaker should work on for "next time," and (2) you will need to be much more precise in the descriptive phase of your critical comment because whoever reads or hears it will not have shared the experience with you.

EVALUATING TEXTS OF SPEECHES

You may be assigned or choose to critique a speech that now exists only in print. How should you proceed in those circumstances? The undertaking is more complex than criticizing a live speech because your critical object will be a printed *record*, not a speech as it was in the moments when it originated. Perhaps the record appears in an anthology of speech texts or appeared in the *New York Times*. You have a *remnant* of what was once live, oral discourse. You will have to treat it rather as an archeologist would treat some pieces of a Greek vase. From the shards the archeologist tries to reconstruct an image of how the *whole* must have been. That does not make the work unsound, but it does mean that a number of essentially historical judgments have to be made before the archeologist—or you—can frame an overall image or description of the object finally to be evaluated. It is arriving at a satisfactory *description* of the speaking events that is special when you work from printed texts only.

Some things you simply cannot know in full when you deal with printed texts of speeches. Delivery cannot be described fully, if at all. On this topic you usually have to depend on accounts furnished by others who heard and saw what happened. Even the record of the words said may be imperfect, for sometimes texts are those issued *before* the actual speech. And, of course, you will usually have no or only a little firsthand knowledge of the rhetorical situation. In consequence, there are a number of steps you must take before you can begin the critical analysis on which we focused when we considered criticism of live speeches.

1. *Determine the authenticity of your text.* Determining how far you can trust the *record* before you is not always easy. (See written exercise 4 at the end of this chapter.) If possible, you ought to match your text against others, unless there is clear evidence that the record you have was directly transcribed from the live presentation or an audio recording. Even then there may be minor errors. It may also be useful to know whether the speech was actually composed and delivered by the speaker personally. Ghost writers are nothing new! They have been employed since the fourth century B.C. at the very least. And there are cases where we have texts of "speeches"

that were prepared but never actually given, or for some reason were delivered by someone other than the apparent author. In any case, you ought to find out if possible to what extent your text was prepared *for* the speaker and to what extent it was prepared *by* the speaker.

2. *Inform yourself about the immediate rhetorical situation.* We have fully discussed why this kind of knowledge is essential to understanding the appropriateness of any speech. You must know when and where the speech took place, to whom it was directed, and what expectations and exigences needed to be adapted to. Getting this kind of knowledge is essentially historical research. You should try to find out who was present and who saw and heard the speech. If possible, it is desirable to interview some who witnessed the communication. When you have completed such steps you will want to turn to any other accounts that deal specifically with the communication and the circumstances that probably influenced the speaker's subject matter, composition, and delivery.

3. *Inform yourself about the milieu.* If the speech occurred some time in the fairly distant past, you may need to get to know the historic events that recently preceded it, the ideas that were in the air, and the day-to-day concerns of the people. No one can understand Lincoln's "Second Inaugural Address" without understanding how the Civil War was going at the time and what visions some Northerners had of reconstructing the South. No one can understand President Ronald Reagan's February 18, 1981, "Economic Message" to the nation without knowledge of what Reagan's platform had been when he ran for the presidency in 1980. To understand such background material is essential if you are to specify, as finally you must, what the exigences of the rhetorical situation were as the speaker entered the situation.

Exploring the immediate situation and the milieu is simply building up information with which to *describe* the event in a clear, full way so that ultimately you can apply your critical standards to the speech *as it was.*

4. *Inform yourself about the speaker.* Here the task is the same as step 4 in evaluating a live speech. You need to find out the speaker's reputation, personal background, values, and the like. If the speech occurred in a period other than your own, you may need to study autobiographical and biographical materials, diaries, memoirs, photographs, letters, and any other sorts of documents that will help you understand this speaker as a "public person." You may even be able to find out about his or her speech training, methods of oral composition (for example, Franklin Roosevelt's extensive revisions for all important speeches), and habits of thought (such as Ronald Reagan's firm conservatism). All such information helps you envision how the speaker was *seen by others* on entering the immediate rhetorical situation.

5. *Read the criticism written by others.* The amount of published criticism of oral utterance is usually not great, and you will sometimes find it difficult to locate. But often there are at least some news articles, essays, headnotes, and journal articles containing criticism of speakers of the past and present. Often the newspapers published the day after a speech will give some appraisal of what was said and of the speaker's performance. The appraisals may be judicious or superficial, but you are not reading the criticism of others so you can imitate them. Your purpose is to sift through all the judgments you can find and arrive at your own point of view.

Criticizing oral communication when only a record is available is more difficult than criticizing an utterance you can personally witness, but it is not at all impossible or unsatisfying. The ideal situation is, of course, that of the students who criticized Dr. Upcraft's speech. They attended the meeting, made their own audio recording, and then made their own written text. But another group from the same speech class evaluated a famous legal plea from the eighteenth century with equal profit and satisfaction. By following the pattern of textual and historical-sociological research we have been describing, this group was able to produce a very well-informed judgment of why and how Lord Thomas Erskine was able to sway a jury in a British courtroom in 1794. What is more, they could then explain to themselves and their classmates why that speech was still in print in the twentieth century. The object of background research is simply to produce a description—a re-creation of the rhetorical situation and the speech that occurred within it. And the object of producing such a description is to allow yourself to make a judgment on this question: What were the exigences (the needs and possibilities) in this situation as the speaker addressed it? In a classroom you know the answer to that question because you are part of the situation. When observing a live speech outside the classroom, you are present to learn the answer at first hand. It is when you are limited to the data of a speech text that the answer depends on what you can learn through historical and sometimes literary, philosophical, and sociological research.

Criticism is judgment and/or appreciation based on informed description examined in the light of criteria. Criticism is comparative. No matter what art is investigated, criticism calls into play knowledge of the art's resources, the function of the art in the given case, and the essential features of the object being examined. When the critical object is public speech, it is necessary to understand what is possible in speaking, what are the allowances of the situation, and what are the characteristics of the speaking that is done.

The purposes that dominate in creation of most public utterances are utilitarian. Practical influence tends to control wise choices more than do considerations of permanence or beauty. In our chapter openings we have provided the kinds of specific questions you can ask about the practical achievements of any speaker. To judge rhetorical discourse by its effects alone is to forget that not all situations allow immediate success, measured by agreement, votes, or conversion. To judge by abstract ethical or moral standards alone is to forget that the same ethical standards do not apply across all rhetorical situations. We have therefore argued for speech criticism based on artistic standards, testing the degrees to which speakers exhaust the resources of their art in meeting the exigences of the rhetorical situations they enter.

In the classroom or out of it, criticism of speech requires method and wisdom. It requires (1) concentration on speech, not peripheral matters, as the critical object, (2) conscious identification of both data and criteria relevant to understanding rhetorical events in full, (3) comparison of observed performance with criteria that define the ideal, (4) formulation of judgments that are specific, cogent, and constructive, and (5) supported, documented expression of the criticism itself.

Although public speech occurs in many forms other than formal speech making, the methods of criticism as we have described them prove applicable to a vast amount of public discourse beyond individual speeches of traditional sorts. It is possible and satisfying to apply the methods of speech criticism to either immediately perceived or historical speaking. Few intellectual enterprises are more liberally educative.

EXERCISES

Written

1. Identify in advance some speech that is going to be delivered in your community. The speech should be one you can both see and hear. Prepare to criticize this speech by writing in systematic fashion all available, pertinent information concerning the speaker and his or her presumed purpose, the audience, the occasion, and the apparent exigences of the situation he or she will enter. Attend the speech. Make both descriptive and evaluative notes during the speech, using a set of criteria you have decided to make the basis of your criticism (the criteria being those you settle on after preliminary analysis of the situation and its rhetorical potentialities, if any). Finally, develop and write a balanced evaluation of the speech as given.

2. Select a famous speech from a past era. Obtain the best record of the speech available. Collect background material on the period, including data on prevailing cultural values, living habits, and beliefs. Establish what the public's image of the speaker was as he or she entered the speaking situation. Once you have acquired an understanding of the total situation and of the entire speech, choose one of the following topics and write an analysis and criticism of:
    a.   the speaker's rational justifications
    b.   the speaker's use of amplifying materials such as examples, narration, statistics, and definitions
    c.   the structure of the speech as it relates to the subject matter, the audience, and the occasion
    d.   the speaker's style in relation to his or her purpose and the situation
    e.   the authenticity and usefulness of the record of the speech you used.

3. Select some piece of recorded rhetoric that most people would not think open to the methods of speech criticism; for example, the lyrics of a song, a poem, a newspaper editorial, the copy in an advertisement, a dramatic scene that contains a fairly large segment of uninterrupted discourse, or the copy of a flyer or pamphlet handed to you on the street.
    a.   Using the pattern for criticism discussed in this chapter, write a criticism of your critical object.
    b.   Write several paragraphs explaining how you had to modify your pattern of criticism (if you did) to do justice to your critical object.

4. Read Professor Robert W. Smith's "The 'Second' Inaugural Address of Lyndon Baines Johnson: A Definitive Text," *Speech Monographs* XXXIV (March 1967): 102–8. Then do the following:

    a. Prepare a definitive text of any public speech. Defend its definitiveness either orally or in writing.

    b. Write an essay (or make a speech) evaluating the reliability of some speech that exists exclusively in printed form.

5. Write on (or give a speech on) the rhetorical effectiveness of one of the committee of critics whose report is in Appendix B.

Oral

1. Listen closely to a classroom speech assigned to you for evaluation. Keep in mind the requirements contained in the speaker's assignment and avowed purpose. Make written notes as appropriate, and note your judgments on selected aspects of the speech. During the oral criticism period reserved for the speech assigned to you, give a one- to two-minute extemporaneous speech evaluating and advising the speaker.

2. Prepare and deliver a speech in which you discuss one of the following:

    a. The considerations essential in appraising a speaker's *invention, disposition, style, delivery, or memoria* (choose one).

    b. The differences between the procedures for criticizing a live speech and those for criticizing the printed text of a speech.

    c. The distinctions between the critical object in speech criticism and the critical object in criticism of some other art.

    d. How you would arrive at a particular set of criteria to be used in judging a particular speech. (You specify the kind of speech to be considered.)

    e. The critical criteria you would apply in evaluating the rhetoric of a critical presentation such as that in Appendix B.

    f. Aspects of artistic achievement you believe the panel in Appendix B overlooked in evaluating Dr. Upcraft's speech.

3. With four or five of your classmates form a problem-solving committee and take as your problem question, "To what extent did X fulfill the situational requirements when speaking on the occasion of ————————?" (This is the kind of question used by the committee whose presentation appears in Appendix B.) As a committee, carry out the kind of critical investigation described in this chapter and form a *group* evaluation of the speaking you have studied. When you have completed your criticism, prepare a presentation for your class in which you enable your audience to reconstruct the speech in its situation and in which you explain the reasons for your collective critical judgment. Note that there are ways you can reconstruct the speech for your listeners other than letting your audience hear or read the entire speech: presenting only important excerpts, summarizing, presenting through dialogue the overall description on which you based your criticism, and so on.

ENDNOTES

1. Robert S. Cathcart, *Post Communication: Critical Analysis and Evaluation* (Indianapolis: Bobbs-Merrill, 1966), p. 1.

2. Cicero, *De Oratore,* trans. E. W. Sutton and H. Rackham (Cambridge, Mass.: Harvard University Press, 1942), vol. II, pp. 157, 159, bk. III, chap. 51.

3. "From Rhetoric Deliver Us," editorial, *Quarterly Journal of Speech* XIV (April 1928): 266–67.

4. Herbert A. Wichelns, "The Literary Criticism of Oratory," in *Studies in Rhetoric and Public Speaking in Honor of James Albert Winans* (New York: Century, 1925), p. 209. Reprinted in Donald C. Bryant, ed., *The Rhetorical Idiom* (Ithaca: Cornell University Press, 1958), pp. 1–42. This essay may also be found in William A. Linsley, *Speech Criticism* (Dubuque, Ia.: Wm. C. Brown, 1968), pp. 7–38, and in other anthologies of essays on rhetorical criticism.

5. Ibid., pp. 212–13 or p. 35.

6. Loren D. Reid, "The Perils of Rhetorical Criticism," *Quarterly Journal of Speech* XXX (December 1944): 416–22.

7. To achieve an adequate description, the students whose critique appears in Appendix B went together to the meeting at which Dr. Upcraft spoke. They all took notes on the situation and the speaking. They made a tape recording of the speech and of some speaking before and after the speech. Working as a problem-solving group, they then drew up their collective description of the event to describe its details. They also made a written transcript of Dr. Upcraft's speech with this goal in mind. All of these steps were taken to create a description from which interpretation and evaluation could then be developed.

APPENDIX A

The question "What makes speech effective?" has been pondered since the days of the ancient Greeks. Plato (c. 429–347 B.C.) and Aristotle (384–322 B.C.) discussed the nature of man speaking. Famous Romans such as Cicero (106–43 B.C.), a great orator, and Quintilian (c. A.D. 35–100), a great teacher, reorganized and refined what they found in Greek writings on public communication. St. Augustine (A.D. 354–430) and medieval scholars added to and adapted their inherited bodies of rhetorical theory as they attempted to help men of their times function effectively in new kinds of speech situations. Especially in America and Europe, scholars have continued to search for new insights and fuller understanding to solve the problems of spoken discourse.

It is our purpose in this section to tell you about important thinkers and explain how some of their theories of rhetoric and speech communication have developed. We hope that knowledge of the origins of what is thought today will help you to think about the problems you face as a human being with powers of speech.

As a first step we shall identify some important writings that serious scholars of rhetoric and speech have used in arriving at theories of their own. Then we set forth the five major problems all communicators face. These problems were first conceptualized by Greeks and Romans sometime before the Christian era, but as creators' problems they remain with all of us. They are the problems of: *invention* (discovering communicable ideas and their logical aspects); *disposition* (organizing or structuring ideas); *style* (finding the right language); *delivery* (deciding how to present a message); and *memoria* (command of an entire speech, once planned and composed, a problem our term *memory* inadequately represents). We shall stress ideas about these problems that have attained special importance in Western thought. Our general objective is to show that most questions you will raise as you seek to improve yourself as a speaker are questions others have raised and tried to answer ever since Westerners have taken the powers of speech seriously.

LANDMARKS OF RHETORIC

Landmark works on speech and rhetoric in ancient Greece have been of towering influence to the present day. Especially important were Plato's two dialogues, *Gorgias*

Rhetorical theory: A heritage

(c. 387 B.C.) and *Phaedrus* (c. 380 B.C.), and Aristotle's *Art of Rhetoric* (c. 330 B.C.). During the period of the Roman Republic the most influential writings published were *Rhetorica ad Herennium* (c. 82 B.C.), formerly attributed to Cicero,[1] and Cicero's *De Oratore* (55 B.C.). Quintilian's *Institutio Oratoria* (A.D. 93) and Longinus's *On the Sublime*[2] belong to the period of the Roman Empire.

St. Augustine's *De Doctrina Christiana* (c. 426) is a work on Christian preaching and stands as the greatest rhetorical study produced during the late Empire–medieval period. Bacon's *The Advancement of Learning* (1605) and its Latin revision, *De augmentis scientiarum* (1623), contain the most profound thought touching human communication to emerge during the Renaissance.

Fénelon's *Dialogues on Eloquence* was published in France in 1717 and was influential in France and England in the eighteenth century. This and other works of major importance in the eighteenth and nineteenth centuries can be divided into three groups.

The originators of the elocutionary movement in England had vast influence in England and America. Representative writers in this group include: Thomas Sheridan, *A Course of Lectures on Elocution* (1756); Joshua Steele, *Prosodia Rationalis* (1775); and Gilbert Austin, *Chironomia* (1806).

In a rival tradition other writers sought to integrate classical theory and the newly emerging science of human nature. They include British writers such as George Campbell, *The Philosophy of Rhetoric* (1776), and Richard Whately, *Elements of Rhetoric* (1828). Hugh Blair's *Lectures on Rhetoric and Belles Lettres* (1783) stands as the chief example of a third tradition reflecting classical influences filtered through writers such as Fénelon and "Longinus." Blair also reflects a wish to intertwine the arts of rhetoric and poetic.

In the twentieth century several works have had especially wide influences on thought about speech communication. They are James A. Winans, *Public Speaking* (1915); Charles H. Woolbert, *Fundamentals of Speech* (1920); I. A. Richards, *The Philosophy of Rhetoric* (1936); Kenneth Burke, *A Grammar of Motives* (1945) and *A Rhetoric of Motives* (1950); Stephen E. Toulmin, *The Uses of Argument* (1958); and Chaim Perelman and L. Olbrechts-Tyteca, *The New Rhetoric* (1969), originally published as *La nouvelle rhetorique: Traité de l'argumentation* (1958). These and other works will be briefly discussed on later pages when we sketch the development of Western thought about the five major constellations of problems in speech making. We provide at the end of this appendix a bibliography of the most easily obtainable, reliable editions of the works mentioned in the foregoing paragraphs.

RHETORICAL INVENTION

That whoever communicates rhetorically must make decisions about *what* to say is a truism that was recognized at the very beginning of Western thought about speaking. Sometime between Aristotle's day and the appearance of early Latin rhetorics, theorists' and teachers' ideas on speakers' problems of discovery came to be grouped under the general heading of *inventio*. Thus the so-called canon of *invention* came into being. The term is actually no more than a topical heading for whatever a rhetorical theorist has to say concerning problems of generating and adapting communicable ideas and whatever other forces can be directly controlled in evoking responses to speech.

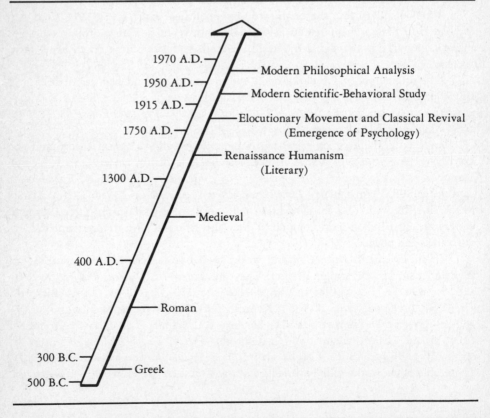

FIGURE A–1 *Diagram showing major periods in the development of rhetorical theory*

Aristotle was the first to see that a speaker invents more than just ideas. He argued that there are three major kinds of force or proof by which a speaker gains his or her ends. These are the intellectual content of the communication, which the Greeks called *logos*[3]—the *content;* the emotional forces in the rhetorical situation, which the Greeks called *pathos;* and the forces emanating from the speaker's apparent nature, which the Greeks called *ethos.* Across 2500 years this analysis of persuasive forces has never been successfully challenged, although what is involved in the *logos, pathos,* and *ethos* of communications has been understood and misunderstood in a variety of ways. We review leading attitudes people have had about how to create and manage these forces, hoping you will gain a better understanding of these power sources in spoken communication.

Logos: *the content*

The earliest attempts we know of to answer the question "How do I discover what to say?" came from two Sicilians of the fifth century B.C., Corax and Tisias. They were counselors to citizens who had to plead their own cases in court. According to Corax and Tisias, the main thing to prove in court was that what you advocated was *probably* more true than your opponent's contention.[4] Allegedly these teachings on probability were carried to Athens and promulgated there.

Other views having to do with rhetorical invention included those of Gorgias of Leontini (c. 483–376 B.C.), a leading sophist.[5] He held that nothing can truly be known to exist; if anything does truly exist humans cannot know it, and even if someone could know what exists, that person could not communicate that knowledge to others. Invention for Gorgias, then, became exploration of the alternate ways of using language to display the "splendors" of humans' varied perceptions of the world.

Other sophists (teachers) also wrestled with the problem of how people should think and talk about the uncertain. Protagoras of Abdera (c. 480–410 B.C.) maintained that even the existence of the gods was uncertain, that truth was relative, and that man is the measure of all things. Accordingly he taught that there are two sides to every question and that both ought to be argued. He had his pupils give speeches of praise and dispraise on human qualities such as friendship, patriotism, and cupidity because he thought the many standard themes or "commonplaces" that would then emerge were suggestive of ways to develop thoughts approving or disapproving qualities.

A very different tack was taken in the teaching of Prodicus of Ceos (c. 450 B.C.), another sophist. He taught that to face death courageously was a virtue, and he spoke in praise of the ideals of labor, hardihood, and simplicity. Clearly what and how to think were for Prodicus ethical questions as well as scientific ones. Much the same was true of Plato's view. He deplored the sophists' teachings. In *Phaedrus* (see opening quotation to Chapter 3) he asserted that a true rhetorician must know the subject completely and also know human psychology well enough to fit his or her own thought to the particular "soul" the rhetorician addressed. Plato seems to have felt that only a true philosopher could know enough to speak the truth. The inventional problems of philosophers and orators, as speakers, thus become identical. In solution, Plato recommended the intellectual processes of defining the subject thought or spoken of and then analyzing all the details of the subject implied in its definition.

Aristotle, in dissatisfaction, stated his counterposition concisely:

> All teaching and learning that involves the use of reason proceeds from pre-existent knowledge. This is evident if we consider all the different branches of learning, because both the mathematical sciences and every other art are acquired in this way. Similarly too with logical arguments, whether syllogistic or inductive; both effect instruction by means of facts already recognized, the former making assumptions as though granted by an intelligent audience, and the latter proving the universal from the self-evident nature of the particular. The means by which rhetorical arguments carry conviction are just the same; for they use either examples, which are a kind of induction, or enthymemes, which are a kind of syllogism.[6]

This statement and its amplification in places such as Aristotle's *Rhetoric, Topics, Politics, Ethics,* and *Sophistical Refutations* constitute the Western world's most comprehensive conception of human inventional processes. Particularly important is that Aristotle's analysis recognizes the distinction between thinking and discovering in *scientific logic* (by rigorous induction and deduction) and in *rhetorical communication* (by psychologically oriented induction through *examples,* and by psychologically oriented deductions through *enthymemes*). By calling rhetorical reasoning "example" and "enthymeme" Aristotle was indicating that what an audience knows and wants and can make use of must be the chief content in all rhetorical situations. In scientific discovery and reasoning absolute self-evidence, formal logical rigor, and judgments of the best thinkers govern intellectual processes—but the knowledge and wants of audiences have no place in such thinking. Aristotle's great contribution to understanding rhetorical invention, then, was to emphasize that although its processes *resemble* those of scientific investigation, these rhetorical processes are different from the scientific because *the audience to be addressed must always guide* the speaker's search for ideas and his or her creation of chains of reasoning.[7] The differences between logical and rhetorical invention have occupied the theorists and philosophers of rhetoric ever since.

In their love of refining and classifying earlier theory, Romans gave special attention to two questions pertaining to invention: "How does one amplify ideas and themes already discovered?" and "How does one discover which available data ought to be used in pleading a legal case?" Cicero made the contributions of most significance. He reexplored the *topoi* or topics the Greeks had referred to as places to look when searching for thoughts useful in developing a theme. In his *De Inventione* (confined to legal speaking) and *De Oratore* (his most inclusive book), he showed how lawyers and legislators ought to work their minds in preparing for speaking. He posed four inventional questions about an issue of fact: "Is it?" (Are there any facts?); "What is it?" (What are the facts?); "What is its quality?" (What does it mean?); and "Is this the forum in which to discuss it?" It would not be unfair to say that these four analytical questions were the most significant contribution the Romans made concerning the theory of rhetorical invention.

In the Roman era an unfortunate confusion of Aristotle's distinction between logical and rhetorical invention also occurred. In the centuries of the Roman Empire *all* thinking became increasingly looked on as *rhetorical* thinking. The probable judgments of an *audience* came to control and constrain virtually every kind of thought. Science, philosophy, and literature naturally deteriorated as what the audience-is-*used-to* confined even private reflections.

During the Middle Ages and the Renaissance the confusion of rhetoric with logic, inherited from the Romans, persisted. Until the time of Francis Bacon (1561–1626) leading writers treated logic as the method that would work in a debate or disputation. With the distinction between thinking to investigate and thinking to communicate lost, there was no need for a theory of *rhetorical* invention, so rhetoric became the art of dressing logical arguments with ornaments of style and, perhaps, delivery.

There was, however, one powerful idea about the content of communication expressed by St. Augustine in the fifth century A.D. It was influential well into the sixteenth century. This was the thought that a Christian speaker's inventional problems were chiefly problems of *interpreting* sacred works. Once he had abandoned paganism for Christianity, Augustine's original mind discerned that his old rhetorical rules for amplifying a theme and analyzing a legal question were irrelevant to his new mission of expounding the Scriptures. Thus was born a new and specialized art of rhetoric called *homiletics*—literally, the art of preaching. The notion that the rhetorician's main task is to *interpret* the authority, then organize and make persuasive the interpretations, was uniquely appropriate to religious speaking. But when applied to other communication, the scheme encouraged people of the Middle Ages and the Renaissance to believe that rhetorical invention—if there was any at all—consisted merely of choosing an authority, defending the choice, and interpreting it.

In the sixteenth century two views of rhetorical invention came into open competition. The classical view that inventing for communication was a special process was espoused in England, first by Leonard Cox in *The Arte or Crafte of Rhetoryke* (1530). This was the first book on rhetoric in English, as far as we know. Thomas Wilson's *Arte of Rhetorique* (1553), a book that passed through eight editions, insisted still more strongly on the classical view of rhetorical invention. Cox and Wilson contended that rhetoricians must search the world of popular ideas for the content of their rhetoric. But in France a counter and ultimately more popular view was offered by Petrus Ramus (1515–72). He was determined to eliminate the confusion of logic and rhetoric inherited from the Middle Ages. Thinking had two aspects, Ramus thought: discovering through reason (invention) and evaluating one's findings (judgment). He denied that the same process could exist in two "arts," assigned "invention and judgment" to logic, and thus reinforced the medieval notion that the function of rhetoric is simply to dress the products of scientific thought. Since he made no distinction between *stating* something and *discovering* something, Ramus's concept of logic was naive to the point that it was incapable of generating scientific discovery, nor was there any place in his vision for restudying the known to discover that which was adaptable to an audience. But for a century his was the dominant theory of intellectual activity taught in the schools of Western Europe, in England, and to a lesser extent in the American colonies.

A man of far greater perception than Ramus was Francis Bacon, whose primary interest was in restoring creativity to scientific thought. Threaded through *The Advancement of Learning* and *De augmentis scientiarum* were many new terms and details of an essentially Aristotelian conception of communication and rhetorical invention. Bacon deplored the exclusive stress on style and delivery in the rhetoric of his day and reexplained the distinction between investigating to discover what is true and investigating what is already known to discover what to communicate to a prospective audience.[8] Bacon defined rhetoric as applying reason to the imagination for the better moving of the will. Finding out what to do to achieve this end, he thought, required inspecting existing knowledge for its psychological appropriateness for a specific audience. For this process he recommended use of *topoi*—topics not different in kind from Aristotle's *topoi*. Additionally he analyzed kinds of fallacies and predispositions found in popular thinking. His famous Idols of the Tribe, Cave, Marketplace, and Theatre are identifications of the kinds of fallibility humans are heir to.

Bacon's reaction against medieval logic and Ramistic rhetoric grew out of his desire to reorder all human knowledge and prepare the way for true scientific investigation. A generation later in France, and then in England, a different reaction developed in opposition to the authoritarian interpretation of rediscovered classical works by Renaissance scholars. A young priest, François Fénelon (1651–1715), for example, undertook to apply the then-popular doctrine "follow nature" to the art of preaching.[9] Drawing especially on St. Augustine, Plato, Longinus, and frequently on thoughts found in *The Art of Poetry,* written by his contemporary Nicholas Boileau-Despréaux, Fénelon emphasized the social character of rhetoric and the necessity of adapting even scriptural meanings to the differing intelligences and motivations of audiences. He stressed "instruction" and "making men better" as the proper ends of speaking. He insisted that a right understanding of religious and moral truth, coupled with an awareness of audiences' differences and a determination to be both "natural" and "tasteful," would lead a preacher to discover what to say and how to say it. True knowledge was, of course, lodged in religious sources; rhetorical invention involved intuitively and psychologically adapting that truth to specific congregations. Howell says that Fénelon's was "the earliest statement we have of what may be said to have become the dominant modern attitude toward rhetoric." [10] The statement seems fair, for "follow nature and adapt to your audience" does sum up what most modern rhetorics have advised.

From Bacon's time the naturalist-literary-religious trend in rhetorical theory paralleled attempts at scientific theory building. In his *Philosophy of Rhetoric* George Campbell (1719–96) clearly drew on the writings of Francis Bacon and the eighteenth-century philosopher-psychologist David Hume. Campbell saw analysis of evidence as the persistent problem in finding truth and estimating probabilities. But once data are obtained, he thought, the object of rhetorical communication becomes to find means of arousing passions that will make listeners *want* to accept the speaker's claims. The explanation was unorthodox in its time but not basically inconsistent with much modern psychological thinking. Under this explanation rhetorical invention becomes much as Aristotle proposed: the discovery in the *known* of that which can by rhetorical methods be made desirable to hearers.

Hugh Blair (1718–1800), on the other hand, said almost nothing about the processes of rhetorical invention in his *Lectures on Rhetoric and Belles Lettres*. With Fénelon he believed that art or method could not help. Following nature, following standards of good taste, and thinking about "the viscera of the cause" were his only answers to how to handle content.

Richard Whately (1787–1863) extended some of George Campbell's thoughts and contracted others. Whately wrote only of argumentation in his *Elements of Rhetoric*. Other possible functions of rhetoric such as explaining, impressing, and blaming go undiscussed. Discovering the best *strategies* for supporting a proposition, given a specific audience and situation, was the main aim in Whately's view of invention. Thus he omitted much that might have been said, but he did add several especially useful observations. He pointed out, as Aristotle had not, that arguments from example have persuasive force different from arguments by analogy. He was also first to notice that a defender of the status quo usually is assigned a lighter "burden of proof" by listeners and hence has a lighter inventional obligation than an arguer who contends for change in what *is*.

With Whately we come to the end of the list of older theorists who tried to cope with how rhetorical communicators invent what they communicate. From the 1820s to the mid-1900s writers have variously said, "Follow nature," or "Dress what 'logic' gives you," or "Think," or "Read what others have said." It has been assumed that rhetorical theory has nothing to tell a communicator until he or she has by some unfathomable means acquired all that he or she would say; then it can advise the communicator on how to arrange, style, and deliver the content he or she has discovered and thought about.

A line of thought in philosophy began to break in on this complacent view of rhetorical invention in the mid-1900s. A few philosophers in America and abroad pointed forcibly to the fact that formal or scientific logic does not and cannot explain how thought is communicated by people such as lawyers, judges, or even philosophers. The real, not the assumed, *logos* became the object of intensive philosophical speculation. For explanations of how *logos* actually works, some philosophers like Richard McKeon, Stephen Toulmin, Chaim Perelman, L. Olbrechts-Tyteca, Henry Johnstone, Jr., and others turned back to the classical explanation: the *logos* or content in a communication is the product of (1) some degree of logical investigation into what is or seems to be true, (2) a combination of that information with what is already popularly known, and (3) a further adjustment of the content to suit the knowledge and desires of whatever audience the communicator has in mind. This view has come to seem philosophically defensible. Some empirical evidence justifies it. It allows advisers on rhetoric to give speakers and writers more help than is given by telling them to "follow nature" or "dress your logic." It is the view we have taken in this book.

We believe that *logos,* or content of speech, has most force if it is drawn from the significant knowledge of the world and so adapted as to be meaningful to the particular audience addressed.

Pathos: *the emotive force*

From earliest recorded time in Western culture it has been recognized that the emotive force of things said has power. Homer dwelt on leaders' powers to sway others by appealing to their feelings. Thucydides attributed a part of Pericles' ability to lead Athens to the fact that he evoked necessary feelings according to his will. But when the Greeks began to think analytically about communication and its effects, many of them became uneasy concerning the right uses of emotion. As with so many things, the conclusions drawn by Plato and Aristotle proved representative of kinds of judgment later preserved in Western thought.

Plato granted that a complete rhetorician must understand the nature of human feeling. The reason was that "men of a special sort under the influence of speeches of a particular kind are readily persuaded to take action of a definite sort because of the qualitative correlation that obtains between speech and soul." [11] But Plato was unwilling to grant that everyone should have and exercise this kind of affective power. Accordingly, in his *Republic* he conceived an ideal system in which only philosopher-kings would have full power and only they would decide who should influence the masses intellectually and emotionally and by what means.

Aristotle was uneasy too; but as usual he was pragmatic. In his view all people act because they have desires that reflect the emotional aspects of their natures. All but the most technical communications will thus be responded to emotionally as well as intellectually. Aristotle wished it were otherwise—that humans were truly rational beings—but he was convinced that human nature encompassed more than intellect. Somewhat sadly, perhaps, he concluded that *pathos* was bound to be a persuasive force in all rhetoric and that speakers must understand the different kinds of human emotions, what causes them, toward whom they are likely to be directed, and how to arouse them and allay them. This knowledge was an integral part of a speaker's necessary equipment, Aristotle thought, and he devoted most of Book II of his *Rhetoric* to a discussion of these topics. The section is a veritable social psychology of Athenian audiences.

The Romans were no less sensitive to the inevitability of emotional power in communication, but their responses to that fact differed from those of the Greeks. In *Rhetorica ad Herennium,* for example, the author undertakes to tell his pupils exact ways to put emotional qualities into their speaking. Among other things, he tells them how to sound indignant, accusing, and calm. He cautions against being emotional in introductions but calls for emotionality in conclusions. Many Roman teachers of ·rhetoric followed this lead, treating emotion as something to be *put into* the content of a speech or its delivery. They treated the emotive power of speech as something a speaker added or subtracted in composing and delivering his or her ideas. The

Greek idea that feelings occur not in language but in people, and are to be regulated by speech, was drastically narrowed.

Even Cicero and Quintilian failed to see the full difference between advising speakers how to *put in* emotional appeals and advising them how to *understand* the emotions of audiences and *adjust* to that reality as purpose required. However, Cicero, as a statesman, had a further concern with the acknowledged emotional power of content, style, and delivery, and Quintilian followed Cicero's lead. To Cicero it was important that emotions displayed and emotions aroused be properly Roman, with due gravity, dignity, and decorum always maintained. Both attitudes toward emotional force in communication, as revealed in Cicero's writings and the *Rhetorica ad Herennium,* had the severe limitation of emphasizing study of the speaker's emotionality and minimizing study of the emotional readinesses of listeners. Ultimately, in the later days of the Roman Empire, it became difficult to distinguish speakers from actors, so strong was concern with how emotions could be portrayed.

St. Augustine, once converted to Christianity, had to rethink the implications of emotions' roles in speaking and in the responses of listeners. His conclusion was perhaps simplistic, but it was more functional than the conventional Roman views. One must give information (Christian teaching) *pleasingly,* he said, else it would not be attended to. Once understanding was achieved, the speaker must arouse strong feelings or there would be no change in the listeners' actual behavior. It was aroused emotion that caused the will to change. Augustine's analysis was more lasting than any previous thinker's. Its main weakness was that it saw teaching, pleasing, and moving emotively as separated functions, but it restored to Western thinking the conception that emotions are present or absent in people, not in messages per se.

Logic, grammar, and disputation preoccupied the attention of most commentators in the Middle Ages. Men like Ramus tended to ignore audiences, and men like Bacon were suspicious of the feeling states of human beings. It was therefore not until Fénelon that another major rhetorician gave serious attention to the role of emotion in the proofs of rhetorical speech. This was natural, for he depended heavily on the writings of St. Augustine and was caught up in the thought of literary figures eager to free themselves from the tyranny of neoclassical rules of communication. As we have already suggested, Fénelon saw the preacher's function as providing first the "bread" of reasoning to generate understanding and then the "spice"—"everything capable of arousing your [the listener's] sentiments, of making you love demonstrated truth. This is what is called persuasion." [12] Fénelon clung to Augustine's conception that emotion was not involved in understanding but was a different force that moved people to accede to the content of messages. The philosopher, he said, acts only to convince, but the orator must go beyond, using every resource capable of arousing sentiments. Only so will the orator secure willful adherence to the demonstrated truth.

Here, the Western world's ideas on the role of emotion in rhetorical response stood for more than a century. In the eighteenth century, the scientific spirit in England led David Hume and then George Campbell to reexamine these dimensions of communication. Campbell came to a conclusion that would have troubled Plato, Aristotle, Augustine, and Fénelon:

If the orator would prove successful, it is necessary that he engage in his service all these different powers of the mind, the imagination, the memory, and the passions. These are not the supplanters of reason, or even rivals in her sway; they are her handmaids, by whose ministry she is enabled to usher truth into the heart and procure it there a favourable reception. As handmaids they are liable to be seduced by sophistry in the garb of reason, and sometimes are made ignorantly to lend their aid in the introduction of falsehood. But their service is not on this account to be dispensed with; there is even a necessity of employing it, founded on our nature. . . . Nor are those mental powers, of which eloquence so much avails herself . . . perfectly indifferent to good and evil, and only beneficial as they are rightly employed. On the contrary, they are by nature . . . more friendly to truth than to falsehood, and more easily retained in the cause of virtue, than in that of vice.[13]

The modern, psychological age appears to have arrived prematurely in Campbell's analysis of the inseparable, inevitable, emotional, and logical forces that rhetorical communication expresses and governs. He saw reason and feeling as "handmaids" existing outside the message, in the audience. He saw the complex response capabilities of humans as challenges to speakers' intelligent, purposeful art. Aristotle might have agreed sadly; Augustine and Fénelon would have found the "handmaid" concept hard to understand; but with Campbell the interrelatedness of the thinking-feeling forces of communication were at last recognized.

The "handmaid" notion remained difficult for those who could not see humans as unitary beings. Although he was Hume's personal friend, Hugh Blair never recognized the new psychology's challenge to the old reason-emotion dichotomy, and Whately avoided the issue in a way that was generally followed for the next century. Using different terms, he readopted St. Augustine's formula. Part I of his *Elements of Rhetoric* was labeled, "Of the Address to the Understanding, with a View to Produce Conviction (Including Instruction)." Part II reasserted (without reference to them) Augustine's and Fénelon's conceptions of instructing and moving as two separate steps in communication. Whately entitled his second section, "Of the Address to the Will, or Persuasion." It was here that he treated "address to the feelings generally" and "of the favourable or unfavourable disposition of the hearers or readers toward the speaker or writer, and his opponent."

In nineteenth- and twentieth-century books on speaking and writing the conviction-persuasion dichotomy persisted almost without challenge until Charles Henry Woolbert (1877–1929) attacked it in a series of essays published in the *Quarterly Journal of Speech,* beginning in 1917.[14] Although many would quarrel with Woolbert's purely behavioristic premises, few psychologically sophisticated persons today would dispute his basic contention against the rhetorical tradition that conceived the emotive power of speech as separable from its intellectual power. Wrote Woolbert:

. . . The error of the conviction-persuasion, emotion-intellect, thought-action duality is found in the fact that we discuss this issue not in terms of what the responder actually does, but in terms of what the observer perceives him doing. . . . *It is a difference, not between acting and thinking, but between one kind of action that happens also to be perceivable movement* [emotional response] *and another kind of action in which the movement is invisible and unperceivable* [intellectual response].[15]

In the same essay Woolbert concluded:

> The whole theory of argumentation, conviction, persuasion, the rhetoric of public address, must be rewritten to fit the facts of mind as accepted today; which will be tantamount to restating them in terms of stimulus-response, object-subject, and environment-attitude.[16]

Speech scholars continue to investigate the functioning of emotive power in human communication. They have arrived at no final explanation. But it seems psychologically clear that: (1) the emotional power of a communication is not in the communication or its delivery but in the readiness of listeners to respond both feelingly and reasoningly to particular features of *logos* and to the credibility of the messenger; (2) speech can modulate but it cannot create feelings that are not at least latent in listeners; (3) people do not feel *or* reason, they reason because they feel and feel because they think they have reason for it; (4) human experience in response to speech or any other stimulus is *unitary*—there is always some blend of what the world has come to call, probably mistakenly, "reason and feeling."

In our earlier discussions of invention, disposition, style, delivery, and speech criticism, we have tried to hold to this modern understanding that the emotive power of speech is not devoid of reasonableness nor reasons devoid of appeal to human desire.

Ethos: *credibility of the source*

What creates or diminishes the credibility of a speaker and how perceptions of credibility prove or disprove in the minds of listeners fascinated the Greeks and Romans and has received more attention than any other single aspect of rhetoric in the twentieth century. These questions seem first to have been raised in connection with the teaching and speaking of the Greek sophists. To some, the sophists seemed less credible because they took money for teaching and speaking. Some of them insisted rhetoric was an amoral art, and this made all they said seem less believable to their critics. If we can rely on Plato's and Aristotle's probably unfair pictures of him, Gorgias of Leontini claimed not to care what means he used as long as he achieved his rhetorical ends. In his *Gorgias* Plato condemns both Gorgias and the entire art of rhetoric as dishonest, deploring rhetoric as a mere art of flattery.

Aristotle explored the sources of credibility in rhetoric more deeply than any other of the ancients. He conceptualized all speakers as communicating an *ethos*—a complicated quality of believability or unbelievability comprised of their *seeming* intelligence, personal integrity, and good will toward their listeners. Interestingly, modern empirical researchers have identified "expertness" and "trustworthiness" as clear constituents of any communicator's "credibility." Aristotle's idea that good motives are searched for by listeners has not been confirmed to date, nor is it certain that "dynamism," a quality some experimenters suggest is an aspect of credibility, is responded to by hearers.

We are left to believe, therefore, that there is such a persuasive force as *cred-*

ibility or *ethos* in all speaking, that this force either reinforces or undermines a speaker's content, and that intelligence-expertness and integrity-trustworthiness are qualities listeners constantly measure in their minds as they determine whether to accept what they hear.

Cicero's conception of the force of *ethos* in speaking was naturally that of an orator, not that of an analyst such as Aristotle. "What *ought* a speaker to *be* as well as seem?" was the question that interested him. His answer was deeply colored by his love of the Roman Republic and his personal philosophy concerning the duties of people to each other and to the state. Perhaps the clearest statement of what he thought could produce a *proper* identification between speaker and listener is in his philosophical essay, *On Duties:*

> . . . Of all the ties that cement us together, there is none stronger or more admirable than that which unites in genuine intimacy good men of like tastes and character; for if we behold even in another that goodness to which I refer so frequently, we are attracted by it and seek the friendship of him who seems to us to possess it. And though every virtue attracts us and makes us love those in whom it appears to us to dwell, yet justice and charitableness exert the most powerful attraction of all. Besides, nothing draws men more closely and affectionately together than the mutual appeal of good character; for when both have the same interests and inclinations, it follows . . . that each loves the other as himself, and . . . many have become one.[17]

It is clear that possessing substantially the virtues Aristotle isolated, plus "like tastes and character," was the source of *ethos* in Cicero's view.

Quintilian also attempted to establish the "oughts" of credibility; however, his method was not descriptive, as was Cicero's, but definitional. In the twelfth book of his *Institutes* Quintilian makes his argument on behalf of Cato's definition: an orator is "a good man, skilled in speaking." The argument is circular and ends with Quintilian contending no more than that if he cannot call a speaker "good" he will deny him the name "orator." Quintilian's difficulty exemplifies how easily one can confuse answers to two quite different questions about a speaker: Do *I* endorse this person? Is this person credible *to those he or she addresses?* Like a good many commentators before and after his time, Quintilian gave his answer to the first question and then treated that answer as though it were a statement about the *actual* credibility or *ethos* of the speaker in a specific rhetorical situation. Aristotle's and Cicero's insistence that it is *seeming* qualities that affect response in rhetorical and personal relationships furnishes the classical era's clearest analysis of how the force of *ethos* works in actual speaking.

In *On the Sublime* "Longinus" sought the *source* of that credibility that critics said was present in great oratorical works. Ultimately, the author thought, there must be evidence of "nobility of soul" or "largeness of conception." Boldness in thinking and feeling, and enthusiasm, seemed to him also discernible in works admired over generations. The uniqueness of "Longinus"'s observations lies in the fact that his is the first great effort to infer critically, from works themselves, what human qualities contributed to their popularity.

St. Augustine was, of course, concerned chiefly with the credibility of preachers. Their humbleness before God, their love of others, and their knowledge of sacred works were the qualities he most wanted speakers to reveal. He insisted that *display* of art was likely to invite either distrust or ignorant applause from listeners. Either effect would demolish the true function of preaching: teaching and reminding listeners of the truths that were within them. On the whole St. Augustine's view of *ethos* as a force was like Cicero's, with Christian virtues and duties substituted for virtues Cicero associated with the Roman Republic. For St. Augustine as for Cicero, if the speaker possessed virtue, it would show through and become a part of the proof; if the speaker lacked virtue, this too would show and operate in listeners' minds against even good content.

Fénelon's was the next major discussion of *ethos*. On the whole Fénelon's *Dialogues* restated St. Augustine's position, applying that view to seventeenth-century French preaching. But, perhaps reflecting literary theory of the time, Fénelon also contended that things cannot be truly beautiful unless they are true, and he made this idea the basis for severe criticism of showy French preachers who sought to be impressive not for their truth and devotion but for their artistry. Their choices showed shallowness and self-centeredness, Fénelon insisted, and these qualities must detract even from truths they might utter.

Bacon gave little direct attention to the role of *ethos*. Campbell, Blair, and Whately were all Christian preachers who tended to presuppose the moral integrity of the rhetoricians for whom they wrote. Campbell, ahead of his time as usual, also thought a speaker's reference groups, as we would now put it, significantly modified this *ethos*. Blair followed Cicero and Quintilian and treated the subject unoriginally. He reflected the times in which he lived by emphasizing the importance of good taste and acquaintance with all the liberal arts as qualities speakers must show to influence the educated. Blair followed Augustine in insisting that preachers, in particular, must be known to live impeccable lives, else their reputations would undercut their religious messages.

In most respects Whately, too, treated *ethos* traditionally, but he made the important point that having a reputation for eloquence can damage a persuader's *ethos*. Such speakers are apt to be suspected of trying to succeed by art rather than by substance. Whately made Cicero's and Blair's comments on "good taste" more practical by pointing out that tastes vary among audiences. If speakers are to enhance their *ethos*, they must adjust marks of taste to specific audiences, said Whately.

As we have hinted, the functioning of *ethos*, or credibility, has been a major topic of interest in the twentieth century. Rhetoricians, advertisers, image makers, journalists, and social psychologists have discussed, studied, and speculated about this force. The literature is too large to summarize here,[18] but on the whole Aristotle's analysis has been confirmed. Practical speakers may operate confidently on his counsels: that *ethos*—listeners' impressions of the speaker himself—is a powerful force in determining the effects of any rhetorical message; that it is important for speakers to *improve on* their reputations for intelligence and trustworthiness *during* speaking; and that they need to give evidence of good motives toward listeners or of identification with them.

DISPOSITION

Ideas about structuring oral presentations seem to have appeared in the very earliest writings on rhetoric. A lost work attributed to Corax and Tisias apparently taught that a speech ought to have at least three parts: a proem or introduction to win the favor of listening judges, a narration or proof of one's case, and an epilogue or conclusion. In his *Phaedrus* Plato also argued that discourse ought to have three parts, comparable, he said, to the parts of the human body. Introduction, body, and conclusion are to a composition as head, torso, and feet are to a human being.

Aristotle took issue with the older three-part concept. He opened the final section of Book III of his *Rhetoric* by saying that earlier speculations on the divisions of speeches were absurd. A speech has only two *essential* parts, he said: one in which you state your point or case and one in which you prove it. In certain kinds of speaking there would be room to narrate a relevant set of circumstances, but these adjustments of the essentials were seen as *special* responses to special speech situations. They were not always needed in effective, satisfying communications.

Some of what Aristotle had to say about rhetorical structure was specifically related to the *types* of speeches commonly composed in his day: the epideictic (or ceremonial), the deliberative (or legislative), and the forensic (or speech for the court). He also gave scattered bits of advice concerning ways claims to *ethos* and variations in style might be necessary to fulfill the functions of divisions of speeches.

Cicero, Quintilian, and the authors of most Roman school manuals discussed the organization of speeches (especially legal speeches) with great enthusiasm. They detected six divisions in normal speeches: introduction, statement of facts or the narration, division or preview of proofs to be offered, proof, refutation, and conclusion. As is plain from this list, it was in what we would call the *body* of a speech that the Romans thought they found additional, special functions regularly carried out. The list reflects their special concern with legal speaking. There are, of course, facts of a case to be given or events and conditions to be described as a normal part of presenting the case. Arguments to be developed are often previewed as the pleader asserts what he or she will and will not try to prove. Once the arguments have been supported, it is also common in courts to refute and try to remove obstacles before concluding. Roman theory about organization was, then, largely a theory for forensic speaking. Thinking was highly formalistic in contrast to Aristotle's functionalism, but in most later periods the formal, Roman views about building speeches overshadowed the Greek in Western thought.

Between Roman times and the Renaissance there were few fresh thoughts about rhetorical organization. When the humanists of the Renaissance rediscovered their ancient heritage, they tended to collapse rhetoric, poetry, and history into a single art of eloquence. Style was seen as the interesting common property of all verbal art and adaptive structural differences received little attention in theory and criticism.[19]

Fénelon understandably rejected the rigid, artificial rules of organization inherited from Rome and medieval homiletics. In his *Dialogues* he contends that the organic unity of a communication is destroyed by imposing complicated divisions on subject matter. Fénelon's arguments resembled those of some modern teachers who also feel that speech ought to follow natural forms allegedly inherent in subjects. Fénelon made milder claims for another idea sometimes contended for today: that the order in which ideas reach the threshold of a creator's consciousness is a natural order for presentation. A problem with both views is that if carried to their logical conclusions they justify purely expressive, stream-of-consciousness communication lacking adaptations to the requirements of specific rhetorical situations.

If we except psychological writers like Bacon and George Campbell, it is fair to say that from Fénelon's time to the twentieth century most commentators on rhetoric have taken refuge either in rigid classical (Roman) rules or in the doctrine of natural order we have mentioned in referring to Fénelon. Twentieth-century experiments to discover the effects of formal structures on listeners have produced conflicting results and yielded little reliable advice. One contemporary, empirical scholar accurately says: "Indeed, the original question asked . . . [Should the most important point be presented first or last?] is still unsolved." [20]

We suggest that at least two misunderstandings contribute to the confusion and contradictions in past and present thought about disposition of ideas in oral communication. First, the full subtlety of the best ancient thinking about disposition has been missed by many. As Russell H. Wagner pointed out years ago:

> The service which will be rendered by a return to "disposition" in rendering *dispositio* and in referring to its classical doctrines, will be nugatory indeed, if we do not restore the full meaning behind the term. . . . It is concerned with the principles of disposing (in the sense of using) the materials invented for a speech, in the best possible manner, for the purpose of effecting the end intended by the speaker in any given situation. The discussion of disposition usually begins by describing the typical form of the speech—the parts or divisions—or it may be altogether organized under those conventional heads. But always, in the best writers, the principle of adaptation to need is uppermost, and the distinction between conventional organization and functional use of material is insistently made. It is this meaning—the functional selection and use of materials for a particular purpose which must supplant "arrangement" and which, as "disposition," may well be added to our rhetorical terminology in English.[21]

Experience makes it plain, as you will find, that how you manage or dispose or marshal what you say is a problem you cannot solve apart from *what* you choose to say—the products of your rhetorical invention. As we have shown in Chapter 7, there is the further fact that ideas are not maneuverable entirely at your will. To some extent they will impose their own constraints on your organizational choices. This is a fact to which the natural-order theorists responded rightly if too exclusively. Second, the experience and expectations of listeners determine to some degree how communicated ideas must be structured. One will err at least sometimes if one tries to structure every communication in the same way—strictly according to rule. Introductions, bodies, and conclusions are normally necessary, but not invariably, as Aristotle was first to point out. Certain units do appear in the bodies of legal speeches, but not all audiences are like courtroom audiences. So there is no reason to suppose that statement–division–proof–refutation is a universally desirable sequence of ideas for the body of a talk. Sometimes what hearers receive *first* will impress them most, but in other circumstances and on other subjects what they hear *last* will be best remembered. Efforts to make rules about the parts of a speech or the importance of first and last positions are based on the assumption that what is being said, who is listening, and where the speech is happening have no influence on how we are to dispose ideas for presentation. As you have seen in Chapters 7 and 8, our advice is that you adopt a middle position between the natural-order and the rule-seeking theorists, organizing your communications with an eye to standard organizational strategies that work *most* of the time but are not rules, while remaining artistically alert to the *special* organizational demands that subject matter, a specific audience, and a specific rhetorical situation impose on you.

STYLE

Referring to what we call *style,* a Roman or medieval writer or speaker would have said *elocutio.* Yet *we* associate derivatives from *elocutio* (eloquent, elocution, etc.) with aspects of delivery. This semantic shift needs explanation before we discuss theories of style and then theories of delivery.

Our word *style* derives from Old French, which in turn derived its term from the Latin *stilus,* the name of the instrument used in writing. Between 1650 and 1750 the word *style* replaced the Latin word *elocutio* as the name for problems associated with language and its use in composition. As *elocutio* and its derivatives ceased to mean style, the Latin word *pronuntiatio* and its derivatives came into use to designate the peculiarly oral aspects of using language; hence the modern term *pronunciation.* To students of oral rhetoric the shifts are of some significance because they reflect the modern tendency to associate style with the written word and to emphasize the delivery aspects of the spoken word. We have shown in this book that there is place for more serious thought about *oral* style than is often given.

Among the early sophists, Protagoras of Abdera observed and classified grammatical parts of speech, verb tenses, and moods, founding the concepts of grammar. Gorgias of Leontini is often called the founder of the *art* of prose because he experimented with ways of giving beauty to prose. Prodicus of Ceos was a kind of early semanticist, exploring meanings and the workings of synonyms. Isocrates (436–338 B.C.) rejected Gorgias's excesses, seeking to conceal his verbal art while creating speech that was at once striking but unified. These and others among the early Greeks may be said to have *founded* the study of language as a resource open to conscious use in communication. Even among them, the perennial issues about choice of language arose: What is *correct?* What is *beautiful?* What *works?* As we will see, it is about the relative importance of these three questions and their answers that theorists of rhetorical style have chiefly differed.

Plato was a brilliant, inventive writer; yet he makes Socrates say in the *Phaedrus* that *correct* diction is the leading standard to be applied to style and that writing is of *doubtful* value because it produces forgetfulness. Plato's art rather than his theory has exerted influence on the development of style in the West.

Predictably, Aristotle was more direct. He began Book III of his *Rhetoric* by asserting that however important argument might be, *how* things are said must be seriously weighed. Clarity and liveliness were the two qualities of speech Aristotle insisted on most strongly, provided appropriateness to the situation was observed. Metaphors, similes, antitheses, realism, and varied rhythms were the speaker's major resources for achieving clarity and liveliness, he thought. Aristotle's answers to what speakers ought to seek through style were decidedly pragmatic. *"What works?"* and *"Why?"* were the questions he chose to try to answer.

As they had in exploring the structural patterns, the Romans who studied rhetorical style seemed more interested in identifying possible maneuvers than in finding out what those maneuvers did and why. Probably the trend had been set by post-Aristotelian Greeks; at any rate, the oldest existing Latin treatise on rhetoric defined and illustrated more than sixty figures of speech. Having finished his lengthy list of verbal forms exemplified, the unknown author concluded:

> I have here carefully collected all the principles of embellishing style. If, Herennius, you exercise yourself diligently in these, your speaking will possess impressiveness, distinction, and charm. As a result you will speak like a true orator, and the product of your invention will not be bare and inelegant, nor will it be expressed in commonplace language.[22]

Knowing and inserting known and approved verbal devices would produce the impressive, distinctive, and charming speaker!

Cicero, the orator, was likewise fascinated by the options offered by known, approved forms of verbal manipulation. He discussed at length the characteristics and uses of "plain," "middle," and "grand" style. His emphatic belief that there were clearly distinguishable *levels* of style was derived from rhetoricians before him, but he seems to have been oblivious of the fact that *plain, middle,* and *grand* express impressions *people* have of language, not *data about* that language. The goals to which he urged speakers to aspire were correctness (presumably as *he* defined it), clearness (presumably an absolute quality), appropriateness (to the speech of a "proper" Roman citizen), and ornateness (achieved by full use of verbal resources).

The great Roman teacher of rhetoric Quintilian was most concerned with the question, What is *correct?* "Style," he said, "has three kinds of excellence, correctness, lucidity and elegance. . . . Its faults are likewise three-fold, namely the opposites of these excellences." [23] Much of Quintilian's advice on style is scattered through his work, but he concentrates on the subject in Books VII and IX. On balance, he is an apostle of formal correctness, although he does not wholly disregard the pragmatic question, "What works and how?" Where he deals with the latter question, however, his eye is almost exclusively on the courtroom.

"Longinus" is a perplexing Roman figure. Whenever he may have written and whoever he was, no extant ancient work on rhetoric draws on his thoughts concerning the relation of language to effect in communication. Parts of his book are lost—several important bits of thought development are missing—but some of his observations read like direct challenges to the traditional formalism of Roman doctrine on style. For example:

> What, then, is this puerility? Clearly, a pedant's thoughts, which begin in learned trifling and end in frigidity. Men slip into this kind of error because, while they

aim at the uncommon and elaborate and most of all at the attractive, they drift unawares into the tawdry and affected.[24]

But "Longinus" 's complaints of classical formalism appear to have influenced no one until the French literary critic Boileau rediscovered and translated his work in 1674!

As far as the record shows, then, the classical interest in how language works in practical communication moved from exploration by the sophists through a period of practical experimentation and theorizing, of which Isocrates and Aristotle were part, into a long period in which artifice was increasingly admired. "What is beautiful?" became the primary question. "What is correct?" meant much the same thing.

This view of rhetorical style predominated for centuries. Through the Middle Ages and the Renaissance rhetorical and poetic styles were badly confused. As late as the sixteenth century beauty was lauded as an end of rhetorical style. In about 1510 the Englishman John Lydgate published his *Court of Sapyence,* in which he asserted that the chief purpose of rhetorical language was to give pleasure to the ear. Stephen Hawes had in 1506 written a work with a similar theme: *The Pastime of Pleasure.* Hawes's book contained an allegorical treatment of the liberal arts in which rhetoric was called the "honied speech" of poets.

Fénelon had nothing to say in his *Dialogues* about the figures of speech that had made up so much of the centuries' lore on style. Instead, he offered a newly popular perception of what spoken or written words can do for people: words can *portray.* "Prose has its paintings, albeit more moderated [than poetry]. Without them one cannot heat the imagination of a listener or arouse his passions," Fénelon wrote.[25] A theory was emerging that language achieves its effects through visual qualities and should therefore be concrete to stimulate the passions of hearers and readers, and Fénelon was one of the first to reflect the development.[26]

George Campbell and Hugh Blair both drew on the conception that a major power of language is portrayal, but Campbell's development of the idea was the more interesting. Lloyd F. Bitzer says of Campbell that, "Vivacity, or the lively idea, is without doubt the key concept of Campbell's theory of rhetoric—the concept which fixes the character of his theory." [27] Aristotle's idea that liveliness is essential to effective style became the cornerstone of Campbell's theory of communication, now based on the new science of human nature and the view that the main function of language is to generate experience as near as possible to experiencing through the senses. Vivacity together with *perspicuity* (clarity) and nationally reputable grammar and vocabulary were, in Campbell's view, primary forces in effecting rhetoric's ends of enlightening, increasing understanding, pleasing the imagination, moving the passions, and influencing the will. Expressing indebtedness to Bacon and to David Hume, Campbell brought functionalism back to the theory of how and why language serves the purposes of rhetoric. But Campbell did not hold the field.

Blair's cast was, of course, literary, and he dealt with style at length. Fifteen of his forty-seven lectures were devoted to discussion of the subject and, if we count the four lectures on taste and the four on language, just under half of his famous *Lectures* was devoted directly or indirectly to style. His touchstones for excellence in choice of language were "taste" and "beauty." His definition of style had wide influence in England and America.

> [Style] is the peculiar manner in which a man expresses his conceptions, by means of language.... Style has always some reference to an author's manner of thinking. It is a picture of the ideas which rise in his mind, and of the manner in which they arise there.... Style is nothing else, than that sort of expression which our thoughts most readily assume.[28]

Blair's pronouncements did not yield much insight into *how* language works, but his widely circulated lectures spread the concepts that beauty, good taste, and correctness were the ideal avenues to effective portrayal through words.

Richard Whately's nineteenth-century treatment of style in his *Elements of Rhetoric* was, according to one of his editors, "a dreary rehearsal of time-worn advice about the selection and arrangement of words." [29] It is true there was nothing very new in what Whately had to say about oral style, for he undertook to blend Campbell's and Blair's observations. In doing so, he tended to blunt Campbell's pragmatic view by appending Blair's and others' traditional injunctions that speakers should seek elegance or beauty in utterance.

Whately's mixture of formalism and pragmatism forecast most of what would be said in the nineteenth century about style. A few, but not many, additional thoughts emerged to affect us today. Samuel Taylor Coleridge emphasized in his essay "On Style" (1818) that major stylistic qualities are not translatable from language to language. Alexander Bain's *Manual of English Composition and Rhetoric* (1866, rev. ed. 1872) expanded Blair's laws of the sentence and put into formal circulation what we now hear of as "laws of the paragraph." On the whole American teaching of composition, oral and written, followed Bain's insistence that the study of rhetoric (meaning *style*) is the study of managing the words and the structures of language and has little or nothing to do with content or oral presentation per se. Nineteenth-century rhetorics in England and America were mainly rhetorics of style, chiefly written style detached from content. They were what Douglas Ehninger has called *managerial rhetorics,* and by the late 1800s virtually all of Aristotle's, Bacon's, and Campbell's pragmatic inquiries about language had been lost.

In reaction perhaps, twentieth-century treatments of literary and rhetorical style have often returned to the pragmatic question, "What *works* and *how?*" How words work psychologically and how we arrive at their meanings have been the main focuses of I. A. Richards's studies.[30] Richards's theory was that all language is metaphorically symbolic and that to understand language we must differentiate the emotive and referential functions of words. This constitutes a theory of semantic analysis that had much influence in literary and rhetorical studies from the 1930s through the 1950s. Word-by-word analysis of literary works and audience-centered criticism reflect the indebtedness to Richards of the literary group promoting the "New Criticism." So, too, does some of the emphasis on metaphor and image now found in a good deal of speech criticism.

Kenneth Burke's studies of rhetorical style have had influence on rhetorical theory and literary criticism. His *Philosophy of Literary Form, A Grammar of Motives,* and *A Rhetoric of Motives* have been especially influential. "Identification" is Burke's key concept. He sees use of language as a search for interpersonal identification—a search motivated by the divisiveness that seems part of the human condition. People use language as a public and collective instrument for reducing their separateness. Burke thus provides a fresh interpretation of the rhetorical function of language. He emphasizes the importance and value of the human power to symbolize and sees study of rhetoric as the method of studying symbolic behavior aimed at "petitioning" on behalf of one human's action toward another within a given "scene" or situation.

Two other theorist-critics who suggest expansions of critical methods by starting from traditional premises about the nature of rhetorical style are Wayne C. Booth and Ross W. Winterowd. In *The Rhetoric of Fiction* (1961) Booth suggested that even in fiction authors *address* their readers to control attention and belief in rhetorical ways, and he analyzed the rhetorical strategies they use for these purposes. Winterowd's *Rhetoric: A Synthesis* (1968) and other of his writings draw on the thoughts of Kenneth Burke and on those of grammarians who have developed the theory of *generative grammar.* From these, from classical sources, and from the findings of psycholinguistics, Winterowd hopes to evolve better principles of both composition and criticism.

Special concern for objectivity and the social significance of meanings motivated Alfred Korzybski to write his *Science and Sanity,* published in 1933, and to found a branch of study called General Semantics. His work, aimed at minimizing subjectivity in human communication, was the basis for a popular version of the theories of General Semantics, S. I. Hayakawa's *Language in Action* (1941), later revised as *Language in Thought and Action.* Levels of abstraction are illustrated by General Semanticists with an abstraction ladder representing the levels of meaning beyond the denotative. General Semanticists make the special point that people develop problems when they react to words as though the words *were* the things they name. That our language maps of the world are *not* the territories of the world is a central lesson taught by this group of students of style.

A still different way of looking at rhetorical style has come from a group of philosophers interested in the branch of philosophy called *theory of argument.* Especially important to practical rhetoricians is *The New Rhetoric* by Chaim Perelman and L. Olbrechts-Tyteca. Working from both classical and modern theories of language, these authors demonstrate that in rhetoric words and word forms *argue* as surely as do traditional argumentative forms such as inductions, deductions, analogies, and arguments from cause. Reflections of this line of thought will be found in our treatment of figures of speech in Chapter 9, pages 242–47.

Thought about the role of language in rhetoric, including oral rhetoric, has completed something of a circle. "What works and how?" was the question most interesting to some Greek sophists and to Aristotle, and it is the question increasingly asked today in Western Europe, England, and the United States. The nineteenth century's oratory of beauty and impressiveness is little heard, and the standards that bred it seem little valued. The practical student of practical speaking can, we think, congratulate himself that this is an age in which study of the pragmatic uses of languages is in vogue. Doing business, not observing forms for their own sakes, is the thrust in the modern speech classroom—as it was in Aristotle's and Isocrates' schools!

DELIVERY

We have seen how Western thinking about disposition and style vacillated between practical considerations and the search for formal rules, doctrines of correctness, and principles of aesthetic beauty. The same vacillation characterized thought about presentation of public speech. During many periods our ancestors seem even to have thought about delivery more than was good for practical communication.

We do not know just when students of speech began to analyze the manners of delivery they thought effective, but it must have been very early. From the time of Theophrastus (c. 370–285 B.C.) we have evidence of writers' analyses of vocal and gestural patterns. In *De Oratore* Cicero repeats a story that goes back at least to *Theophrastus,*[31] that Demosthenes was once asked what was most important in speaking. He replied, "Delivery." When asked what was next in importance, he answered the same, and to the question of what came third, he repeated, "Delivery." This story, like the legend telling how Demosthenes improved his articulation by speaking with pebbles in his mouth, indicates that practitioners at least were preoccupied with delivery from the earliest part of the classical period. It was not so with the earliest theorists we know of.

Plato did not mention delivery specifically, although he did say practice would add to a speaker's natural capacities. Aristotle discussed the subject almost grudgingly in a brief passage at the beginning of Book III of his *Rhetoric*. There he said delivery must be attended to as "something we are bound to do." He granted that it was not enough to know what to say; one must know *how* to say it. But he said these things reluctantly, apparently feeling that such matters fell in the province of actors and were therefore vulgar—at least for a theorist to discuss. Similarly, a book by an unknown author, written probably in the generation after Aristotle's, omitted mention of problems of oral presentation. The work's Latin title is *Rhetorica ad Alexandrum.*

Although concepts about presenting speeches were slighted by the Greek theorists we know, the subject received detailed attention at Rome. The unknown author of *Rhetorica ad Herennium* showed that he had some fairly detailed works to draw on when he classified and described vocal qualities under three headings: volume, stability, and flexibility. He endorsed what he called *conversational tone* and identified four variations of it: the dignified, the explicative, the narrative, and the facetious. He then discussed how these tones should be used in the various parts of speech. He gave little attention to gestures and facial expressions beyond mentioning their importance, and he concluded by confessing he was not sure it was possible to explain delivery in writing. His confession may be a hint that delivery was still the concern of more practitioners and pedagogues than theorists.

Cicero wrote of delivery as a practitioner, naturally enough, although in what he had to say he offered some interesting speculations on the relative importance of various aspects of presentation. His most significant observations appear in *De Oratore,* some being confirmed in his later book, *Orator,* a discussion of the "perfect" speaker. Cicero seems to have accepted the emphasis on delivery reflected in the story of Demosthenes to which we have referred. In Cicero's view, dignity and grace were so important in speaking that those with highest mental capacity would lose esteem without these qualities and speakers of only moderate intellect but great skill in delivery would surpass their intellectual betters. He went beyond the author of *Rhetorica ad Herennium* by discussing both vocal and gestural activity, and he followed the earlier author in stressing that qualities of delivery express speakers' emotions and must, therefore, be precisely suited to thoughts being uttered. Words, Cicero said, can move only those who share your language, but all mankind—illiterates and even barbarians—can see and understand physical behavior.

Aristotle's notion that rhetorical presentation and the presentations of actors are alike did not satisfy Cicero. He insisted that gestural patterns in public speaking were markedly different from the patterns appropriate to acting. Accordingly he paused over the uses of gestures of the hands and arms, stamping one's foot, and, especially, the emotional expressiveness of the eyes. He thought that of all the facial features, the eyes best expressed a speaker's emotion.

Quintilian's *Institutio* contained a good many descriptions of vocal and gestural behaviors without differing much from what the author of *Rhetorica ad Herennium* and Cicero had said. But Quintilian did make two points of special importance. He insisted that the ideal speech—in court or elsewhere—was one that had been fully written beforehand, and he revealed that at least some Roman teachers thought speaking and singing required the same kinds of vocal resources and management. Not so, said Quintilian, pointing out that speakers need "strong and enduring" voices, not "soft and sweet" ones and that singers must strive for perfection in pitch although speakers need not worry about that problem. In general, Quintilian's third chapter of Book XI of the *Institutio* shows that he and presumably other Romans had studied the speech-production system of humans with considerable care and were at least beginning analyses of the human voice not unlike those that reemerged as delivery began to receive scientific attention in the eighteenth century.

On the whole the Romans *described* vocal and gestural behavior and then tried to *prescribe* specific behaviors for specific emotions, parts of speeches, and rhetorical situations. The special interest in *style,* which marked the resurgence of literary interest during the Middle Ages and the Renaissance, discouraged thought about oral delivery. Insofar as the subject was important, the issue was: How shall one read aloud? That question was, of course, quite different from the one the Romans had, at least at first, tried to ask: How shall one speak to be understood as thought and feeling demand?

Fénelon gave much more attention to aspects of delivery than others of the Renaissance. In his *Dialogues* he seemed to be trying to fill out, for delivery, Augustine's themes of devotional directness and pastoral adaptation. These St. Augustine had developed at length relative to style, but he had said little about the preacher's delivery. Fénelon addressed the issues directly, condemning the rigid, artificial rules he found too much followed by his contemporaries. The goal in delivery ought to be artlessness rather than mechanical control, said Fénelon. In the spirit of St. Augustine and of emerging literary theories, Fénelon urged all speakers to put their reliance on cultivated, earnest feeling toward listeners; right feeling would naturally yield appropriate, reinforcing, vocal and gestural behaviors.

In contrast with Fénelon's doctrines of naturalness there grew up less than a century later a new-old body of theory called *elocution*. Its concepts were the antitheses of Fénelon's. To a degree the new concepts were scientific extensions of the Romans' ambition to *describe,* then *prescribe;* but there was also new driving force in this movement. Frederick W. Haberman writes:

> Elocution was an offshoot of rhetorical study. It was an exhaustive and systematic analysis of delivery. The elocutionary movement, which began about 1750, was a response to the demands of the age. This widespread and intense study of delivery was an answer to the eighteenth-century denunciations of oratorical frigidity, to the pressure for professional and educational training in speech, to the new consciousness of the need for standardization of spoken language, to the desire of the people to obtain facility in speaking a language of which they were becoming proud, and to demands of those who dealt with democratic movements. The elocutionary movement, however, was more than a simple renaissance of a particular canon of rhetoric. It was, rather, a new ordering of an old subject.
>
> This new ordering resulted from the application of the tenets of science and of rationalism to the physiological phenomena of spoken discourse. The new study of delivery was affected by the impact of science and of rationalism in precisely the same way that the study of history, of economics, of politics, of poetry, and of prose style was affected.[32]

Three kinds of textbooks came out of the elocutionary movement: thorough, often research-based, works treating voice, rhythm, and gesture; elementary rule books; and collections of useful and elegant extracts for practice. The elocutionists developed systems for observing voice, gesture, and language and means of recording these observations. In these efforts their work resembled that of modern-day students of nonverbal behavior.

As Haberman indicates, the elocutionists worked from scientific-rationalistic premises. They presupposed that man is ruled by natural laws. Nature is a compelling force. It has immutable laws in the physical universe and immutable codes in the social universe. These laws and codes are systematic and can be disregarded only at one's peril. These theorists thought speech and all worldly matters were capable of scientific systematization. So they embarked on their mission to reduce speaking to system.

The outpouring of elocutionary books and magazines during the last half of the eighteenth and throughout the nineteenth centuries was much too vast to review here, but Haberman has identified four founders of the movement, and a note on each will suggest the directions of research and exposition that characterized this movement.[33] Thomas Sheridan (1719–88) published *Lectures on Elocution* in 1756. In it he examined the individual sounds of speech and the gestural behaviors associated with familiar emotions. Among other things, he was seeking a scientific phonetics with which to describe pronunciation and a kind of grammar of gesture by which to teach appropriate and natural physical action. Joshua Steele (1700–91) devised a system of musical notations by which to describe the management of the voice. His *Prosodia*

Rationalis treated patterns of melody, rhythm, and pitch in speech and music. John Walker (1732–1807) was an actor turned elocutionist. He invented a system by which to describe the natural interrelations between vocal inflections and grammatical forms. His chief publication was *Elements of Elocution* (1781). James Burgh (1714–75) expressed the article of faith Cicero had expressed that gave the elocutionists much of their driving energy. In *The Art of Speaking* (1761) Burgh said "nature had given every emotion of mind its proper expression." The task for the elocutionists, as for some Romans, seemed to be to catalog those nonverbal, emotional expressions, the better to *teach* them "naturally"! One such was Gilbert Austin, another leading figure in the movement. His *Chironomia* (1806) exerted great influence on the theory of gesture by analyzing bodily action in four systems of notation and producing descriptions for charting over fifty foot movements, over a hundred arm positions, and thousands of hand positions.

The elocutionary movement, with its research impulse, its enthusiasm for detailed description, and its determination to *prescribe* natural behavior in speaking and acting, dominated English and American thought about speech delivery until the beginning of the twentieth century. In their desire to apply the laws of nature to man's speaking behavior, the elocutionists often produced artificial rules and systems more complex than any Roman had had the tools to produce, but in a number of cases their research became the foundation for modern sciences such as phonetics, vocal acoustics, and some branches of linguistics. Indeed, a good deal of current research on nonverbal behavior covers ground on which the elocutionists were pioneers.

The classical revivalists who wrote on communication during the period in which elocution burgeoned insisted on a different way of thinking about speech behavior. Both Hugh Blair and Richard Whately differed from the elocutionists, but they also differed from one another, and the viewpoint of each has its knowing and unknowing followers today.

Blair's conception of delivery and the aspects he considered important are discussed chiefly in Lecture XXXIII of his *Lectures on Rhetoric and Belles Lettres*. The lecture is titled "Pronunciation, or Delivery." Blair saw delivery as vocal and gestural behavior that operates within natural languages understood by all. Words, he said, are arbitrary symbols of ideas and therefore are not universally understood. The natural symbolizations of voice and gesture are not so confined in meaning.

There are hints that Blair thought what he called "pitches of voice" were naturally and uniquely associated with specific kinds of speaking. Also, other remarks scattered through his lectures indicate that he thought different styles of delivery were peculiarly suited to different kinds of speech. In most other respects Blair's comments on delivery were traditional, but his advice to speakers contained subtle, internal contradictions one can also see in discussions of speech making today.

Like most writers, Blair urged speakers to let delivery reflect their actual feelings. "Follow nature," he says in effect. On the other hand, he suggested that the secret of effective delivery is thinking one's thought clearly while uttering it. Further, he counseled study of proper models and practice, "for many persons are naturally ungraceful." But then, "Whatever is native, even though accompanied with several defects, yet is likely to please; because it shows us a man; because it has the appearance of coming from the heart." [34] Blair seems not to have considered these pieces of advice incompatible, and in this he resembled many moderns who advise speakers to "be natural" but then criticize those speakers' grace and taste.

Richard Whately was more vigorous in reaction against the elocutionists, but he did not, as some have believed, counsel "following nature" in impulsive, undisciplined ways. What he said of naturalness echoed Blair but was more clearly thought out. Whately was strongly critical of all mechanical guides to effective presentation, but it is evident that he did not advocate impulsive response to feelings. He did say:

> The practical rule to be adopted, in conformity with the principles here maintained, is, not only to pay no studied attention to the Voice, but studiously to *withdraw* the thoughts from it, and to dwell as intently as possible on the Sense; trusting to nature to suggest spontaneously the proper emphases and tones.[35]

At an earlier point Whately had inserted this qualification:

> When however I protest against all artificial systems of Elocution, and all *direct* attention to Delivery, *at the time,* it must not be supposed that a *general* inattention to that point is recommended; or that the most perfect Elocution is to be attained by never thinking at all on the subject; though it may safely be affirmed that even this negative plan would succeed far better than a studied modulation.[36]

It is clear that Whately was recommending that speakers occupy their minds with ideas rather than prescribed behaviors, and in this he was injecting a new thought into Western lore on how people can best express what they mean, vocally and physically. The notion was radical and it required modification, but in the mind of the American James A. Winans, Whately's thought evolved into a balanced, cogent view of what is required mentally for the most natural delivery possible in public speech.

Winans's (1872–1956) influence on contemporary theories about practical delivery has been immeasurable since 1915. Contending that Whately's "think-the-thought" doctrine could as easily produce soliloquy as direct, effective, public speech, Winans altered the formula by adding to it. He wrote:

> ... Your delivery will have the desired conversational quality when you retain upon the platform these elements of the mental state of live conversation:
> 1.   Full realization of the content of your words as you utter them, and
> 2.   A lively sense of communication.[37]

Winans's first point was Whately's; his second the corrective. Winans was convinced that effective delivery depends on awareness of one's thought *and* a strong wish to convey the thought to someone else.

Refining another familiar notion—that effective delivery is somehow related to the conversational—Winans also argued for a distinction between *conversational quality* and *conversational style*. Public speech ought to have the *quality* of conversation, Winans insisted, but if it *imitated* the style of ordinary, informal conversation it would belie the publicness of the speaker's situation.

To us, at least, Winans seems to have resolved the paradox of centuries: speakers have to *mean* what they say, both vocally and physically; yet they speak with special responsibilities in public settings, and these responsibilities are *not* natural for them. Greek rhetorical theory, as we know it, virtually ignored the problem. Romans and elocutionists counseled *learning* proper behaviors of nature. Fénelon and others trusted nature and feelings completely, but candor forced the eclectic Blair to admit that some who want to speak are naturally clumsy until they *learn* otherwise. Whately saw the *thought* as the generator of meaningful behavior, but it remained for Winans to emphasize the importance of being *dually* aware—of thought and of the communicative relationship with others. Our treatment of delivery in Chapter 10 is developed from the Whately-Winans principles.

MEMORIA

Memoria has been called the "lost canon" of rhetoric, presumably meaning that no one pays attention to it any more. The term *memoria* refers to that body of theory and advice that concerns managing and controlling utterance, according to plan, when speaking occurs.[38] The English term *memory* connotes considerably less than the full range of rhetorical problems that confront a speaker who has prepared a speech and now must present it. More than memorizing or recall of a plan is involved. It is for this reason we are using the Latin term, there being no sound equivalent in English.

Speakers face problems involving *memoria* from the outset of speech preparation. They must choose subjects they will be *able to command;* they must set purposes they *will still understand* when they are speaking; they must build structures and frame outlines and notes they, themselves, *will be able to follow;* they must choose language natural enough to them so they *will be able to command it under pressure;* they must make plans for delivery they *will be able to execute;* and, of course, they must keep their wits and all their plans about them as they speak. Much more than memory is involved, but this has not always been recognized in Western thought about *memoria.*

For much of the classical era *memoria* meant little more than memory of one's speech. The earliest writers seem to have felt that the best service they could render speakers was to pass on instructions on memory systems. Thus the story of Simonides of Ceos is repeated in several books on rhetoric. Simonides was a poet. After reading a long, lyric poem at a banquet, he was called from the hall. Moments later the roof fell in, killing the remaining guests and disfiguring them beyond recognition. But Simonides was able to match the bodies and the names by mentally picturing the former seating arrangement. His alleged success dramatized for others the usefulness of associating ideas with spaces. One could then call up the spatial image and, by association, remember the ideas "put there."

The Simonides story came from Greece, but the Greek theorists we know of did not deal with those problems the Romans called the problems of *memoria.* The first extended treatment of the subject now known appears in the *Rhetorica ad Herennium.* There *memoria* is called "the guardian of all the parts of rhetoric," but the author seems not to have had a conception of a speech as a *plan* of internally grouped ideas. The story of Simonides is told to illustrate how an *artificial* memory system can help the *natural* memory. In short, this early Roman author seems to have been mainly interested in supplying his pupils with mnemonic devices for jogging their memories, whether the task was to recall words, related ideas, or situations.[39]

Cicero treated *memoria* briefly in *De Oratore,* and he emphasized the point that it is possible to store proofs in the mind in *interrelated ways* so they can be recalled as pertinent to specific lines of argument useful in building legal cases and legislative arguments. For him, the problem was to file away data and ideas in ways that would allow a speaker to recall and use those ideas *adaptively.* The problems of *memoria* were more complex for Cicero than the mere problem of memorizing, although he also gave advice on memorizing.

Quintilian's was the most extensive treatment of *memoria* among the existing ancient writings, but he generally followed Cicero's topics of discussion. Quintilian seems to have seen new dimensions of the subject, however, for he touched on at least two new points. He observed—and was the first known writer to do so clearly— that paying attention to the (logical?) principles of rhetorical division and composition can be of great value to a speaker trying to command his or her speech in anticipation of delivering it. "If our composition be what it should, the artistic sequence will serve to guide the memory." [40] Here the connection between a speaker's *planning* and his *capacity to command* the whole discourse seems recognized. A second new consideration recognized by Quintilian was that the psychological problems of commanding ideas and language during extemporaneous speaking are different from those faced when a speaker memorizes and delivers a *set* speech. Once more, Quintilian seems to have been the ancient writer who saw most clearly that Simonides' mnemonic devices could not answer all of an active speaker's problems of self-command.

Except as treated in tracts on preaching, which stressed *division* (preview) as helpful to determining and remembering systems of arrangement, little was said in rhetorical treatises on rhetoric written during the Middle Ages. True, Alcuin (c. 735–804) did advise the emperor Charlemagne that a speaker who expected memory to function effectively ought to avoid drunkenness.[41] In the main, however, it was not until the appearance of Thomas Wilson's *Arte of Rhetorique* that *memoria* was again discussed even at the level of Roman sophistication. Since succeeding rhetorics tended to deal with both speaking and writing, the special problems of speakers' *memoria* received limited attention until the twentieth century.[42]

It is in textbooks on speaking published in the twentieth century that speakers' *memoria* problems have been faced with greater penetration than Quintilian's. James Winans's and Charles Woolbert's early textbooks explained the contributions of the new discipline of psychology to solving speakers' problems of command during speaking. Borrowing from pragmatic psychology, Winans pointed to the importance of outlines as mental guides and assurances that speeches would be presented with their planned, "due proportion, emphasis, unity, and coherence." Said Winans, outlines serve as visual images of the soundness and the "logic" of interconnections among ideas; once seen, these interconnections allow speakers to sense their observations as *wholes,* not as series of points. Woolbert was devoted to a different psychology, behaviorism, so he stressed a different aspect of the theory of *memoria.* Let speakers *condition* themselves properly, was his major counsel. Accordingly, he urged that speakers (and readers) first formulate the perspective of their material, then concentrate on details, doing both *orally*—so as to involve their sense of hearing in the acquisition of material—and performing all these functions in imagined or real circumstances as nearly approximating the actual circumstances of speaking as possible.

The psychologies on which Winans and Woolbert depended are partially outmoded today, but as each advance is made in understanding how human beings *learn,* advances can be made in solving the perennial problems of *memoria* that *public* speakers face. How we can best command the whole of our plans during the moments of speaking and adjusting to rhetorical situations is still not fully known; there is much mystery still.[43] But one idea held by both ancients and moderns seems especially valuable: commanding a *visual* plan of ideas and their interconnections—in outline or other form—establishes content and plan in the mind but with sufficient flexibility to allow the adaptive restructuring that public speech so often demands.

We have been concerned with command of material and action throughout this book—with mental and physical command. As we have treated invention, disposition, style, and delivery and the special problems of audience adaptation, we also have treated ways of solving the problems of command through consciousness of what one is doing in preparation and through bringing plans into visual, practiced form, the better to assure true *memoria* in the moments of speaking.

The matter of commanding the entire speech means that you must prepare carefully, both on paper and in oral rehearsal, to be wholly familiar with your material. What you intend to say must be at your beck and call to the degree that (1) you can return to your train of thought should there be some unforeseen interruption; (2) you can recover from a lapse of memory involving the omission of material you intended to include; (3) you can answer questions your audience may have when you have finished speaking; and (4) you can conceal your thoroughness of preparation by appearing to summon your thoughts freshly at the moment you utter them.

The degree of a speaker's command is revealed most in the moments of delivery. Evidences that the speaker is not in complete control include: slips of tongue, mispronunciations, forgetting ideas and connections, breaks in fluency (the "ers" and "uhs" we hear), awkward silences, poor transitions or none at all, and staring into space while trying to recapture his or her thoughts. (See pp. 35–36, 259–61).

These are the reasons we have been concerned with command of material and action.

In the history of Western thought about oral rhetoric only disposition and *memoria* of the five great constellations of communicative problems have missed their hour in the limelight. Neither has ever dominated thought about public speech; invention, style, and delivery have so dominated, not without unfortunate results for balanced, forceful speaking.

The ancient Greeks laid a foundation for the art of public speech, importantly stressing the necessity of transforming thoughts into *communicable* thoughts. Romans refined and amplified, ultimately stultifying the art by excessive formalization in the period of the Roman Empire. St. Augustine christianized the Roman lore, but for preaching only. His achievement could not prevent later confusion of rhetoric with poetic or the ultimate absorption of rhetoric into logic. When the residual rhetoric was style, there were some who clung to the classical tradition in which invention was the key process in speech communication—an emphasis ultimately restored in the twentieth century despite the tempting distractions of naturalism and elocution. To the new classical revival, modern psychological and philosophical investigation has added and continues to add to the ways speakers can learn to meet those invariably present problems of speaking: deciding what to say, how to give it form, what language to use, how to present it, and how to keep plans under command.

If there is a practical lesson to be learned from this historical review, it seems to be that to neglect *any* or to overvalue *one* or *two* of these sets of problems has proved mistaken wherever it has occurred, across more than 2500 years. But when men and women have thought as hard as they knew how about *all* of these problems, they have produced thought and historic significance and public speech of great practical and artistic merit.

BIBLIOGRAPHY OF LANDMARK WORKS IN RHETORIC [44]

Plato. *Gorgias.* Translated by W. R. Lamb. Cambridge, Mass.: Harvard University Press, 1925*

————. *Phaedrus.* Translated by H. N. Fowler. Cambridge, Mass.: Harvard University Press, 1914.*

Aristotle. *The Rhetoric of Aristotle.* Translated and edited by Lane Cooper. Englewood Cliffs, N.J.: Prentice-Hall, 1960.

Rhetorica ad Herennium. Translated by Harry Caplan. Cambridge, Mass.: Harvard University Press, 1954.ˣ

Cicero. *De Oratore.* Translated by E. W. Sutton and H. Rackham. 2 vols. Cambridge, Mass.: Harvard University Press, 1942.*

Quintilian. *The Institutio Oratoria of Quintilian.* Translated by H. E. Butler. Cambridge, Mass.: Harvard University Press, 1953.*

Longinus. "On the Sublime." Translated by W. Rhys Roberts. In J. H. Smith and E. W. Parks, *The Great Critics,* 3rd edition. New York: W. W. Norton, 1977.

Saint Augustine. *On Christian Doctrine.* Translated by D. W. Robertson, Jr. Indianapolis: Bobbs-Merrill, 1958.

Bacon, Francis. See Wallace, Karl R., *Francis Bacon on Communication and Rhetoric.* Chapel Hill: University of North Carolina Press, 1943. (This is a masterful synthesis of Bacon's ideas on rhetoric as found in the works mentioned in this appendix.)

Fénelon. *Dialogues on Eloquence.* Translated by Wilbur S. Howell. Princeton, N.J.: Princeton University Press, 1951.

Sheridan, Thomas. *A Course of Lectures on Elocution.* London, 1756.

Steele, Joshua. *Prosodia Rationalis.* London, 1779.

Austin, Gilbert. *Chironomia or a Treatise on Rhetorical Delivery.* Edited by Mary Margaret Robb and Lester Thonssen. Carbondale: Southern Illinois University Press, 1966.

Campbell, George. *The Philosophy of Rhetoric.* Edited by Lloyd F. Bitzer. Carbondale: Southern Illinois University Press, 1963.

Blair, Hugh. *Lectures on Rhetoric and Belles Lettres.* Edited by Harold F. Harding. Carbondale: Southern Illinois University Press, 1965.

Whately, Richard. *Elements of Rhetoric*. Edited by Douglas Ehninger. Carbondale: Southern Illinois University Press, 1963.

Winans, James A. *Public Speaking*. New York: Century Company, 1917.

Woolbert, Charles H. *The Fundamentals of Speech: A Behavioristic Study of the Underlying Principles of Speaking and Reading*. New York: Harper & Brothers, 1920.

Richards, I. A. *The Philosophy of Rhetoric*. New York: Oxford University Press, 1965.

Burke, Kenneth. *A Grammar of Motives* and *A Rhetoric of Motives*. Berkeley: University of California Press, 1969.

Toulmin, Stephen E. *The Uses of Argument*. New York: Cambridge University Press, 1958.

Perelman, Chaim, and Olbrechts-Tyteca, L. *The New Rhetoric: A Treatise on Argument*. Translated by John Wilkinson and Purcell Weaver. Notre Dame, Ind.: University of Notre Dame Press, 1969.

EXERCISES

Written

1. Write a book review (1500–2000 words) treating the whole or a part of one of the works on rhetorical theory mentioned in this appendix.

2. Write an essay comparing the treatments of one of the rhetorical canons (invention, disposition, style, delivery, or *memoria*) in two of the books cited in this appendix. For example, compare Aristotle's theory of oral style with Blair's, or Cicero's theory of delivery with Whately's.

3. Explore some contemporary psychological research on communicative credibility and write a report comparing those findings with Aristotle's speculations (or Cicero's or Quintilian's).

Oral

1. Prepare and deliver a two- to three-minute speech introducing a person whose name is mentioned in this chapter. Assume that the person is about to deliver a lecture to your class on an aspect of rhetorical theory.

2. After reading in one of the works mentioned in this appendix, make a short report on some aspect of theory that you feel is applicable to speech making today.

3. With four or five classmates, engage in a discussion on the question, "What is it to be 'natural' in speaking publicly?" When your group has come to a conclusion or to unresolvable disagreement, report the results to your class.

ENDNOTES

1. It is now generally agreed that the work is by an unknown author. Its earlier attribution to Cicero added immeasurably to the book's reputation. For an authoritative discussion see Harry Caplan's Introduction to *Rhetorica ad Herennium* (Cambridge, Mass.: Harvard University Press, 1954), pp. vii ff.

2. The author and date of this work are uncertain. Authorities place its date at either the first or third century A.D. and remain in doubt about the real author. See G. M. A. Grube's Translator's Introduction to *Longinus on Great Writing* (*On the Sublime*) (New York: Liberal Arts Press, 1957), pp. vii–xxi.

3. All classical scholars agree that there is no single English word that expresses the meaning of this very general Greek term. Quite mistakenly, many twentieth-century rhetoricians have equated *logos* with *logic*, but this is far too narrow an understanding of the Greek idea. " 'Discourse' and 'reason' are one and the same thing—in Greek they are designated by one and the same word, *logos*," says John Herman Randall, Jr., in his *Aristotle* (New York: Columbia University Press, 1960), p. 6.

4. Just what the relationship was between these two men and what they did teach is uncertain, but whatever the facts may have been, later rhetoricians traced their discipline back to Corax and Tisias and to these teachings. See George Kennedy, *The Art of Persuasion in Greece* (Princeton: Princeton University Press, 1963), pp. 58–61.

5. The sophists were professional traveling teachers in fields such as general culture, politics, and rhetoric. Although many of them were teachers of excellence, some were so practical in their aims that they emphasized ingeniousness and speciousness more than soundness of argument. Some were early scientists and mathematicians, and others preceded Plato and Aristotle in explorations of the nature of perception and logic. Sophists also evolved the basic concepts of grammar as a result of the special interest many of them had in the nature of language. See pp. 322–23.

6. Aristotle, *Posterior Analytics*, trans. Hugh Tredennick (Cambridge, Mass.: Harvard University Press, 1960), p. 25.

7. Further details of Aristotle's contributions to the theory of rhetorical invention are discussed and applied in Chapter 5. For an especially penetrating discussion of Aristotle's *Rhetoric* in relation to other intellectual arts see Robert Price, "Some Antistrophes to the *Rhetoric*," *Philosophy and Rhetoric* I (Summer 1968): 145–64.

8. Bacon's scattered observations on communication have been organized and synthesized by Karl R. Wallace in his *Francis Bacon on Communication and Rhetoric* (Chapel Hill: University of North Carolina Press, 1943). Some important extensions beyond Wallace's interpretations appear in M. Cogan, "Rhetoric and Action in Francis Bacon," *Philosophy and Rhetoric* XIV (Fall, 1981): 212–33.

9. His *Dialogues on Eloquence* were written while he was a young man but were not published until 1717, after his death.

10. Wilbur Samuel Howell, Introduction to Fénelon, *Dialogues on Eloquence*, trans. W. S. Howell (Princeton: Princeton University Press, 1951), p. 46.

11. Plato, *Phaedrus*, trans. W. C. Helmbold and W. G. Rabinowitz (New York: Liberal Arts Press, 1956), p. 63.

12. *Dialogues*, trans. W. S. Howell, "Second Dialogue," p. 89.

13. George Campbell, *The Philosophy of Rhetoric*, ed. Lloyd F. Bitzer (Carbondale, Ill.: Southern Illinois University Press, 1963), p. 72, bk. I, chap. 7.

14. From premises of behavioristic psychology Woolbert attacked the notion that respondents to communication experience reasoned and emotive responses as separable processes. His essays included, "Conviction and Persuasion: Some Considerations of Theory," *Quarterly*

Journal of Speech III (July 1917): 249–64; "The Place of Logic in a System of Persuasion," ibid., IV (January 1918): 19–39; "Persuasion: Principles and Methods," ibid., V (January 1919): 12–25; "Persuasion: Principles and Methods," ibid., V (March 1919): 101–19; "Persuasion: Principles and Methods," ibid., V (May 1919): 212–38. (The journal referred to was published under varying titles but is indexed under the title given here.)

15. "Conviction and Persuasion: Some Considerations of Theory," ibid., III (July 1917): 258. Italics in the original.

16. Ibid., p. 264.

17. Cicero, *On Duties,* trans. Hubert M. Poteat, in *Brutus, On the Nature of the Gods, On Divination, On Duties* (Chicago: University of Chicago Press, 1950), p. 485.

18. The 1975 cumulative index to speech journals lists 105 published papers on the subject not including the many studies reported in journals of other academic fields. See Chapter 5, pp. 124–31 for further discussion of basic findings and their implications.

19. For a full treatment of these developments see Jerrold E. Seigel, *Rhetoric and Philosophy in Renaissance Humanism* (Princeton, N.J.: Princeton University Press, 1968), especially pp. 260–62.

20. Ernest C. Thompson, "Some Effects of Message Structure on Listeners' Comprehension," *Speech Monographs* XXXIV (March 1967): 50.

21. Russell H. Wagner, "The Meaning of *Dispositio,*" in *Studies in Speech and Drama in Honor of Alexander M. Drummond* (Ithaca, N.Y.: Cornell University Press, 1944), pp. 292–93.

22. *Rhetorica ad Herennium,* trans. Caplan, p. 409, bk. IV, sec. 69.

23. *Institutio Oratoria,* ed. and trans. H. E. Butler (Cambridge, Mass.: Harvard University Press, 1920), I, 79, bk. I, sec. 1.

24. Longinus, "On the Sublime," trans. W. Rhys Roberts, in J. H. Smith and E. W. Parks, *The Great Critics* (New York: W. W. Norton, 1951), pp. 67–68.

25. *Dialogues on Eloquence,* trans. Howell, p. 93 (Second Dialogue).

26. Gerard A. Hauser discusses these seventeenth- and eighteenth-century developments in his "Empiricism, Description, and the New Rhetoric," *Philosophy and Rhetoric* V (Winter 1972): 24–44.

27. Editor's Introduction to Campbell, *The Philosophy of Rhetoric,* p. xxv.

28. Hugh Blair, *Lectures on Rhetoric and Belles Lettres,* ed. Harold F. Harding (Carbondale: Southern Illinois University Press, 1965), I, 183–84.

29. Editor's Introduction to Richard Whately, *Elements of Rhetoric,* ed. Douglas Ehninger (Carbondale: Southern Illinois University Press, 1963), p. xxi.

30. For example, I. A. Richards, *The Meaning of Meaning,* written with C. K. Ogden (1923), and his *The Philosophy of Rhetoric* (1936).

31. Kennedy, *The Art of Persuasion in Greece,* p. 283.

32. Frederick W. Haberman, "John Thelwall: His Life, His School, and His Theory of Elocution," *Quarterly Journal of Speech* XXXIII (October 1947): 294.

33. Frederick W. Haberman, "The Elocutionary Movement in England, 1750–1850," unpublished Ph.D. thesis (Cornell University, Ithaca, N.Y., 1947).

34. Hugh Blair, "Pronunciation, or Delivery," Lecture XXXIII, in *Lectures on Rhetoric and Belles Lettres,* ed. H. F. Harding, II, pp. 223, 224.

35. Richard Whately, *Elements of Rhetoric,* ed. Douglas Ehninger, p. 352.

36. Ibid., pp. 346–47.

37. James A. Winans, *Public Speaking* (New York: The Century Co., 1917), p. 31.

38. For a thorough discussion of memoria emphasizing its role among the ancients, see Harry Caplan, *Of Eloquence: Studies in Ancient and Mediaeval Rhetoric* (Ithaca, N.Y.: Cornell University Press, 1970), Essay IX, "Memoria: Treasure-House of Eloquence," pp. 196–246. Another excellent and penetrating treatise on the subject is Frances Yates, *The Art of Memory* (Chicago: University of Chicago Press, 1966). Professor Yates traces theories of *memoria* and memory systems from the beginning to 1900.

39. Today people still use mnemonic systems such as those found in Harry Lorayne and Jerry

Lucas, *The Memory Book* (New York: Stern and Day, 1974); Donald A. Laird and Eleanor C. Laird, *Techniques for Efficient Remembering* (New York: McGraw-Hill, 1960); David M. Roth, *Roth Memory Course* (Cleveland, Ohio: Ralston Publishing, 1959); and Bruno Furst, *How to Remember* (New York: Greenburg, 1944).

40.   Quintilian, *Institutio Oratoria,* trans. Butler, IV, p. 235, bk. IV, sec. 39.

41.   Wilbur S. Howell, *The Rhetoric of Alcuin and Charlemagne* (Princeton, N.J.: Princeton University Press, 1941), pp. 137, 139.

42.   A more detailed discussion of *memoria* as treated in works we are passing over is Wayne E. Hoogestraat's "Memory: The Lost Canon?" *Quarterly Journal of Speech* XLVI (April 1960): 141–47.

43.   See, for example, Will Bradbury, "The Mystery of Memory," *Life,* November 12, 1971, pp. 66–76, and Mark R. Rosenzweig, "Biologists Try to Learn Exactly How We Learn," *New York Times,* January 12, 1970, p. 72C.

44.   We have listed here the most reliable and, where contemporary editions are available, most readily obtainable editions. The works are listed in chronological order. Works identified by * are in the Loeb Classical Library series.

What follows is the text of a classroom presentation of a critique developed by a group of students enrolled in a first course in effective speaking. The course stressed processes of group problem solving as well as problems in public speaking. The first assignment or problem to be solved by each of several groups of students was this: "To what extent, if at all, did _____ fulfill the exigences or requirements of the rhetorical situation he or she faced?" Each group of students chose some example of public speech, studied the situation and the speech for approximately two and one-half weeks, outlined the group's critical conclusions about the rhetoric involved, and organized and presented its findings to the entire class.

The group whose presentation is printed here chose to attend a mass meeting of students, presided over by a student panel, which assembled to consider and, probably, to protest a new university policy regulating the consumption of alcohol on university premises. Having tape recorded a considerable portion of the meeting, the group of speech students decided to focus their criticism on a talk given at the mass meeting by Dr. M. Lee Upcraft, director of residential life at the University Park campus of The Pennsylvania State University.

While developing their criticism, the students studied and discussed the contents of Chapters 1, 5, portions of Chapter 9, and Chapter 11 of *Public Speaking as a Liberal Art*. Since the group presentation was the student's first formal speaking in this class, they had also read and discussed portions of Chapter 2.

On the evening before the presentation printed here, one of the students in the group telephoned Dr. Upcraft to tell him of the presentation and to invite him to attend the class if he found it convenient. He attended. Neither the instructor nor most of the speakers realized until moments before the presentation that Dr. Upcraft would be present to hear and respond to the critique.

The presentation illustrates what is commonly called a *panel* or *symposium* format, in which several speakers participate in presentation of a public message. It also exemplifies the everyday fact that problem-solving groups are very often responsible for presenting their informal findings to audiences.

Joe: We're going to analyze for you a speech by Dr. Lee Upcraft, and the reason we picked the Upcraft speech was that it's a contemporary speech, a relevant speech

Speech criticism:
A case study

to all the people that were involved, and it was something that the rest of you students in the class could relate to.

First I want to give you a little more background on the overall problem that the speech was concerned with. Are you all familiar with the incident this summer, in which a student consumed too much alcohol and nearly died? [Indications that the audience knew of the incident.] OK. The result of this incident and what followed was much student unrest. There were massive demonstrations planned, and everyone was hating the university and hating Dr. Upcraft for the change in the policy [concerning the presence and consumption of alcohol in university housing].

So this was the reason a meeting was called, so that all the people that were concerned could testify at this hearing—give their opinions. And all the information could be brought out, so that a decision could be reached [by the Student Government Panel].

Now, the goals of our project are to show (1) how Dr. Upcraft made clear to the students the position that the university was in, and (2) how he defused the meeting and redirected the students' anger away from the university and the Office of Residential Life onto the State of Pennsylvania.

Now, the way we have our presentation set up is, first, you all have mimeographed sheets of that speech. Second, we're going to play the tape of the speech so that you can get a little bit of the atmosphere and know how the speech was presented. Afterwards we're going to analyze the speech section by section, as we have it set up on the mimeographed sheets.

Now we'll play the speech; after that Kathy will be first, and she will analyze the introduction of the speech. OK, now we'll play the speech. [Copies of the following text were distributed to those in the room.]

DR. M. LEE UPCRAFT: TO A MASS MEETING OF STUDENTS
[1] I appreciate the opportunity to make a few remarks about this. I think it's important to talk a little bit about the context under which this policy was developed. For those of you who weren't around in 1972, before 1972, there were no alcoholic beverages permitted on campus, anyplace. In '72, the committee that was

revising the discipline system suggested that, as a part of the code of conduct, students who were twenty-one would be allowed to drink in their individual residence hall rooms. As a result of that committee's recommendations, the president and the board accepted Article J of the current code of conduct, which, to paraphrase it, says something like: use and possession of alcohol are prohibited on campus, except in individual residence hall rooms.

[2] I think, for a while, the consumption of alcohol was contained in individual resident hall rooms; so it didn't present a problem for us. But I think over the last four years, the consumption of alcohol in the residence halls has increased. It's increased not only in terms of individual consumption in rooms, but it's also increased in the number of larger gatherings where people who were of age, and who were not of age, were consuming alcohol in the residence halls.

[3] I think the Collegian *is probably quite correct, in a sense, that the university probably did adopt a policy of what they called "benign neglect." That is, unless the alcohol consumption created a problem for us in terms of a disturbance or some control problem, unless it was directly brought to our attention, we were ignoring it.*

[4] Then the infamous incident this summer in which a student nearly lost his life as a result of overconsuming alcohol. And I think that probably brought to my attention, and to the attention of the university, the potential dangers and the potential liabilities involved in continuing to tolerate underage drinking in the residence halls.

[5] I think the reason why we have gone in the direction we have is that, historically, the university has and does assume the responsibility for enforcing the university rules and regulations. Once you accept that responsibility, then, if you're negligent in the performance of that responsibility, I think you can be held legally liable. Our attorneys tell us that that is a definite possibility; and if we directly observe it, we have to do something about it. If we don't do something about it, then we can be held accountable in the courts.

[6] I'm not going to comment on the specific incident of this summer, or the action that was taken as a result of it, because it is a personal matter. But let's suppose there was a student at some hypothetical university, at some hypothetical time, who did consume too much alcohol, and nearly died, or something serious happened to him. If one of our staff members directly observed the alcohol going into that room, and if one of our staff knew that there were underaged people in the room or were planning to be there, and if the staff member directly observed people drinking and did nothing about it, then if something happened at that party which resulted in physical or psychological damage to someone, it's fairly clear that the university could be held liable and could be held responsible.

[7] As the director of residential life, I am not going to put my staff in a position where, through "benign neglect," they're going to get themselves into legal trouble, and in some way be held accountable for something that some student does that's dumb.

[8] I think, probably, if there is any one reason why we decided to pursue this policy, it was precisely that—that we could no longer continue to skate on thin ice; we could no longer continue to put the university, and my position, and the position of the RA's [resident assistants] in such jeopardy.

[9] I think as a state institution, we have assumed the responsibility of enforcing state laws. And so long as that responsibility stays with the institution, I

don't see how we can back away from doing something about underage drinking in the residence halls, when we observe it, and when we know about it.

[10] *I think it's a very difficult position that I'm in. It's a very difficult position the RA is in, and a very difficult position the university is in. I think—my own personal opinion is that the state drinking age should be lowered to eighteen and the privilege should be extended to include all of the people of Pennsylvania. When they're eighteen they can own a bar, but they can't drink in it. That doesn't make much sense to me. I'm surprised that it hasn't been constitutionally challenged. I'm not on a moral crusade. I grew up in New York. I went to school in New York. I was able to drink when I was eighteen, and I don't think the problems of alcohol and alcohol abuse among students in New York is any greater or any less than they have with students in Pennsylvania.*

[11] *As far as courses of action are concerned, I think there are several things that I hope the panel will look at. First of all, probably Article J of the code of conduct ought to be reconsidered. From a very practical standpoint, this article, if strictly interpreted, and strictly enforced, would mean that no one could drink in the residence hall rooms. Because it would be illegal to transport alcohol from the source of supply to the room. It's also not consistent with practice in that the Nittany Lion Inn has a liquor license. The Faculty Club would like to get one, and the Kern graduate building, under certain circumstances, allows alcohol to be served. But I think, at a basic level, we have to look at Article J and at least bring it into line with current practice. I think a second issue that the people here tonight ought to consider and the panel ought to consider in its recommendations, is whether or not the university should continue* in loco parentis, *that is, continue to act on behalf of the state in enforcing underage drinking laws in the residence halls. I personally think that issue ought to be thought through very carefully. Apparently what happens is, if your RA catches you drinking, he writes a referral. If you're twenty-one, and caught drinking in the wrong place, chances are you'll get a warning letter from the Office of Public Standards, with no disciplinary action, merely a warning letter. If underage drinking is involved, and it's proven that that was the case, chances are you'll get a disciplinary warning. That's the lowest of the disciplinary actions taken. It's on your transcript for the length of the time of the action, and it's removed from your transcript—your permanent transcript—once that's over. The advantages of this system are that, in no way does your university record—rather, there is no criminal record kept.*

[12] *If the university absolves itself of its responsibility for liquor enforcement, then the alternative, if a student wanted to do something about somebody, underage, drinking, would be to call the police. In that instance you would involve civil authorities, you would involve the possibility of establishing in your record a fact which might influence such things as getting into law school, graduate school, and medical school, and so forth. So I think when you're considering whether or not the university should absolve itself of that responsibility, what you are in effect doing is transferring the consequences for the student from the university to society. Frankly, society is much more strict, and keeps records around a lot longer than the university does. But I think that's a legitimate question to raise and talk about.*

[13] *I think probably the other thing I'd like to comment on, which I spoke to you of briefly before, is the fact that I think it's probably going to be very difficult to deal with this situation unless the state of Pennsylvania does something about its drinking age. As an administrator, I don't like to say that to a student, "OK if*

you don't like what's going on here, write to your congressman." I think in some ways that's a put-off. On the other hand, I do in this instance feel that part of the problem is the fact that the state has an unrealistic drinking age, and I think steps should be taken to encourage the legislature to lower the drinking age, or to challenge the constitutionality of that law. These are some things you should give consideration to.

[14] I don't particularly like the position I'm in, but I don't feel as if I have any other choice. And I think until something changes in regard to the circumstances I am presented with, I really don't feel as though any other stance can be taken by the university at this point.

[15] I'd like to say something else about strategy, particularly if you're concerned about lowering the drinking age. A lot of outraged students, and I think justifiably outraged students, have suggested some sort of massive action, some demonstration of that outrage. I think you have to very carefully consider what the impact of that is going to be. There are people in the legislature who, for one reason or another, think that eighteen-year-olds shouldn't drink. Whether they think you're too immature to handle it, or whether they think that traffic accident fatalities will increase, or whatever. But I don't think that the prospect of 2,000 roaring drunk students in the quad of East Halls is going to convince the legislature of your maturity. I furthermore don't think it's going to convince the university to change its policy. I think the most constructive forms of action are the three things I've suggested: consider Article J, consider whether or not the university should continue its enforcement stance for this location, and consider taking some constructive steps to lower the drinking age. As I said in the Collegian, *if any of those things change, I'll be the first one to stand in some public place in the university, and personally burn this policy.*

[16] I will be here for the rest of the evening. I want to listen carefully to what the students have to say, and I'd be glad to respond to any questions of the panel.

Kathy: A thing any speaker has to do in introducing what he has to say is get and keep the audience's attention. And he has to somehow let the audience know what he is talking about. Dr. Upcraft did this by presenting the history of the policy. He brought the audience up to date about how the policy came to be and how the situation had worsened. He points out, in fact, that although the university didn't corral anyone, it was the rule that students under twenty-one were not to drink.

It's important to notice that he implies that students over twenty-one *were* allowed to drink, so long as no disturbances resulted. In other words the university was giving a privilege to students. One student took advantage of that privilege, and in so doing he forced the university to change and adopt the new system.

Dr. Upcraft argues that as long as Article J is there to be enforced, the university is going to have to more stringently enforce it and the state laws.

Dr. Upcraft redirects the students' hostility from the university to the state by saying that the university was allowing the students to enjoy themselves until one student, as you'll recall, forced the university to completely change its policy in order to enforce the laws of the state, or face a stiff lawsuit, or be held otherwise accountable in the courts.

Now, Ron will show you more about this redirection of attitudes.

Ron: I have two points to make about how Dr. Upcraft redirected the hostility of the students in his audience, and the university Student Government in general.

The first point is that he used special examples to sway the hostility of the students to the state. Without such examples, it would be hard to change a hostile person's opinion. Just as, if as I talk to you, I *tell* you to change opinion, that says nothing. I need to use examples, too. Now here is my example of Dr. Upcraft's use of examples. It will show you what I mean. It's on your first page, fifth paragraph. Dr. Upcraft says, "I think the reason why.... [Reads the entire paragraph.]

Now here, Upcraft has used a good example, because he doesn't try to snow his audience, but he tells them what can happen in the state courts. This shows they are *forced* to be responsible.

The second point I would like to make is in reference to a sentence in which Dr. Upcraft says it is the state laws which make the university adopt the antidrinking policy. Therefore it is the state, and not the university, at which the students should be hostile. This sentence is on the second page, paragraph 9. Here Upcraft says, "I think as a state institution, we have assumed the responsibility of enforcing state laws." In other words, as long as the university stands as a part of the bureaucracy, it must enforce the laws of the bureaucracy. Just so long as, he says, the university is a part of that system, "responsibility stays with the institution." So, the university must do what it does because it is a state institution.

We believe these examples of the university's position work not so much to admit that the university *chooses* to enforce its policy as to assert that it is the state laws that *compel* the university to be responsible, not just to students. We think this is another way Dr. Upcraft diverts students' irritation. You can almost hear them say, "If it wasn't for those blankety-blank state laws, and if the university wasn't a blankety-blank state institution, there'd be no problem with the university at all." Dr. Upcraft might have said this himself and gotten applause, but, of course, this wasn't possible for *him,* in this rhetorical situation, without repercussions.

Now Patti, and a little later Greg, will point out how Dr. Upcraft uses himself as a proof in this speech.

Patti: Dr. Upcraft also tried to persuade the students to see *his* side of the issue. This happens, for example, on the second page of the text at paragraph 10. There, he asks the audience to consider the difficulty of the position he is in. Immediately he gives his own personal opinion that the drinking age ought to be lowered, and with this he identifies with the audience's probable views. By these processes he establishes his own status as a persuader, apart from the state and its rules. This is another turning point at which he switches blame from the university, *and himself,* to the state; he absolves himself and the university of blame by this process.

Another example of how he develops his own image as a source of proof appears in this same paragraph 10. Here Dr. Upcraft is saying the university is in a very difficult position because of the law. And he criticizes the law, first with irony: an eighteen year old can own a bar but can't drink in it. He gets some humor here, but he makes a point and makes himself believable. Then he goes on to a personal testimony: "I grew up in New York, I went to school in New York. . . ." [reads entire sentence]. We think he not only uses himself as an experienced authority here but that he probably made students think additional things like, "And I can drive at eighteen and be drafted at eighteen," and so on.

From this he goes on to use his built-up authority with the audience to propose revision of Article J and other steps. We think he's in a position to do this, now, just because he has established himself as a person not responsible for what he had to do, and as one whose opinions are very much like the students'. You'll also notice that in paragraph 11 he is shifting the responsibility for future action. In other words, the university personnel can't do anything except what they are doing until *someone else* changes the rules.

Now, Greg is going to continue with this analysis.

Greg: You'll notice that Upcraft points out that the penalties imposed by the university are a lot less severe than those that would be imposed by civil authorities. This is especially true with regard to records of any infraction. As Upcraft pointed out in his speech, your academic record won't carry anything that will stand against you if you're trying to get into med school or law school or something like that. University records of infractions are expunged when the time of a penalty is over.

Now, you'll have to admit that it's doubtful that Dr. Upcraft convinced his audience that the university acts out of the bigness of its heart in protecting students against a police record. But he has made progress toward his goal, which seems to be to make the state, rather than the university, the villain here. And he gives some reasons for hanging on to Article J. In paragraph 12 he's arguing that for the university itself to accept responsibility is really a good thing. This puts Dr. Upcraft, the university, and the students—even on this drinking policy—all on the same side, against state policies regarding drinking and enforcement on a campus.

It's in paragraph 13 that Dr. Upcraft really throws the blame on Harrisburg for the whole situation. He calls the Pennsylvania state law on the drinking age unrealistic, and he continues with recommendations for positive action by the students. He encourages students to try to convince the legislature to change the law, and even to challenge the constitutionality of the law.

Now, probably, none of these solutions is really practical. It's unlikely that students could make them work. However, just the fact that he gives them supports the belief that Dr. Upcraft is really on the students' side and that he and the university have been forced into this situation by an unrealistic and possibly unconstitutional law about the drinking age. Dr. Upcraft again establishes himself as a support for his own position because he declares his support for students' efforts to get these changes.

Now, Stephanie will show you how Dr. Upcraft closed his speech.

Stephanie: The conclusion of this speech fulfills the important functions of any conclusion. It shows that Dr. Upcraft was there to help the students find some action that would do some good. He repeats that he doesn't like the position he's in, but that until outside policies change he'll continue to be in this awkward position. But instead of just saying, "This is your problem. You take care of it," he goes on to offer three cautions about what the students can do and how to do it. This again shows that he's not against the students. It's very important that he doesn't condone any outrageous behavior by the students—like a demonstration at East Halls. Here, he gets at the students' reason and practical sense. He makes the students see how much of a drawback it would be to their real goals. Then he turns to a new strategy and, in what I think is a key point in the speech, he repeats a pledge he made earlier in the *Collegian*: "If any of those things [policies] change, I'll be the first one to stand in some public place in the university and personally burn this policy." Thus, at the end, he clarifies one last time that he is for and not against the general principle for which the students came together at this meeting. He implies, as he has throughout, that he's also willing to work *with* the students.

He ends by saying he's going to stay with the students, *here*. He will listen, and he implies he will do so sympathetically. And he'll respond to any questions. All in all, the speech ends on precisely the right note to put aside anger at him or at the university. The last part of the speech adds up to saying, "If you help me, I'll help you. So, let's work together on *our* problem."

Now, Joe is going to sum up our analysis of Dr. Upcraft's address to the students and officers of the university Student Government. Joe.

Joe: I'd like to conclude our presentation by giving you a brief summation of what actually happened as a result of this rhetorical effort.

In regard to Dr. Upcraft's goal, which was to, we believe, redirect the students' anger away from Penn State onto the state of Pennsylvania, the committee that heard him sent out a report on the alcohol policy. The main points of this report were to reconsider Article J, as Dr. Upcraft advised, and, second, to initiate a statewide lobby and letter-writing campaign in order to lower the state drinking age to eighteen, which Dr. Upcraft also mentioned.

As far as the students were concerned, there was no mass action resulting from this meeting, so our group has concluded that the speech was very effective in actual fact. We think he attained his goals by means of the rhetorical processes we have outlined in our report today.

That's our presentation, and we'll be glad to answer any questions. As an added factor on this particular occasion, Dr. Upcraft is sitting in the back of the room, so we can also get his opinions on our opinions about his speech.

Dr. Upcraft: I wish the people who attended the hearing that night had been as open minded as these six panelists were. It wasn't an entirely open-minded audience; let's put it that way. I went into that situation mainly to state my position and do the things you've suggested. My main goal was to get students to understand why we did what we did. I wasn't, I think, in a persuasive mood quite so much as you tend to suggest. When you use words like *strategy* and so forth, I want to say that I knew the audience and I wasn't foolish enough to think I was going to *persuade* very many people one way or the other. For that reason I tried to focus my attention on the members of the panel that was to lead discussion that night, because I knew they were reasonable students. I was there more to persuade the panel [at the meeting] than to testify before all the audience of students. The whole audience, I felt, was pretty much a lost cause.

I think you're right. I was trying to redirect students' concern to the liquor laws of the state and away from Penn State. I was trying to get them to *understand* why we did what we did, rather than trying to persuade them that what we did was *right*.

I wish I had your optimism about how successful my speech was. I don't think the issue is quite as dead as, perhaps, you think it is.

I gave a completely extemporaneous speech. I was not operating from any notes. I just did a lot of thinking about what I wanted to say, before I went there. It's a strange feeling to hear yourself again, and to read yourself in print. I also want to say to the class that I didn't know anything about this whole business until last night when Joe called to invite me here. I appreciate that.

Now, the only criticism I would have of your critique of my speech is that I think you're giving me too much credit. At least, I didn't set about, consciously, to accomplish all the things that you said I did. I was just hoping to get out of there alive.

SPECIAL INDEX FOR THE
STUDY OF TYPES OF SPEECHES

This index is designed as an aid to students and teachers who want to structure the study or preparation of speeches around purposes for which speeches are made. The general section of the index identifies treatments of topics pertinent to all or to several purposes. Subsequent sections indicate the portions of this book that relate directly or have special relevance to a specific type of speech.

INDEX